BIBLICAL POETICS BEFORE HUMANISM AND REFORMATION

Biblical Poetics Before Humanism and Reformation is a study of the interpretation of the Bible in the late Middle Ages. Scholastic theologians developed a distinct attitude toward textual meaning in the thirteenth and fourteenth centuries which departed significantly from earlier trends. Their attitude tended to erode the distinction, emphasized by the scholars of St. Victor in the twelfth century, between literal and spiritual senses of scripture. Christopher Ocker argues that interpreters developed a biblical poetics very similar to that cultivated and promoted by Protestants in the sixteenth century, which was reinforced by the adaptation of humanist rhetoric to Bible reading after Lorenzo Valla. The book is a comparative study, drawing from a variety of unpublished commentaries as well as more familiar works by Nicholas of Lyra, John Wyclif, Jean Gerson, Denys the Carthusian, Wendelin Steinbach, Desiderius Erasmus, Philip Melanchthon, and John Calvin.

CHRISTOPHER OCKER is Associate Professor of History at the San Francisco Theological Seminary and the Graduate Theological Union at Berkeley. He is also Co-Director of the Center for the Study of Religion and Culture at Berkeley. He is the author of *Johannes Klenkok: A Friar's Life* (1993) and has published in a number of journals including the *Journal of Ecclesiastical History*, the *Harvard Theological Review*, and the *Scottish Journal of Theology*.

Frontispiece: Antonella da Messina, *Saint Jerome in His Study*. 46 × 36.5 cm. London, National Gallery, inv. 1418. Biblical translation and interpretation, according to medieval biographers, were Jerome's principal accomplishments as a monk at Bethlehem. Antonello portrays Jerome's study as an enclosure within a large room of his monastery, bathed in a heavenly light, with conspicuous references to paradise in the foreground (peacock, potted plant, and bowl of water). If this is a disguised portrait, as some believe, a living human being is inserted into the scene, with its allusions to Eden, the incarnation (pyxes on the shelves), the penitential life (the contrast of worldly play in the left background window and pure nature in the right window), and the flight of redeemed souls from the world to heaven (birds alighting the window, above). Jerome's studious self becomes emblematic of reading from the point of view of a divine light. Reading recovers paradise.

BIBLICAL POETICS BEFORE HUMANISM AND REFORMATION

CHRISTOPHER OCKER

PUBLISHED BY THE PRESS SYNDICATE OF THE UNIVERSITY OF CAMBRIDGE
The Pitt Building, Trumpington Street, Cambridge, United Kingdom

CAMBRIDGE UNIVERSITY PRESS
The Edinburgh Building, Cambridge CB2 2RU, UK
40 West 20th Street, New York, NY 10011-4211, USA
477 Williamstown Road, Port Melbourne, VIC 3207, Australia
Ruiz de Alarcón 13, 28014 Madrid, Spain
Dock House, The Waterfront, Cape Town 8001, South Africa

http://www.cambridge.org

© Christopher Ocker 2002

This book is in copyright. Subject to statutory exception
and to the provisions of relevant collective licensing agreements,
no reproduction of any part may take place without
the written permission of Cambridge University Press.

First published 2002

Printed in the United Kingdom at the University Press, Cambridge

Typeface Baskerville Monotype 11/12.5 pt.   *System* LaTeX 2_ε [TB]

A catalogue record for this book is available from the British Library.

Library of Congress Cataloguing in Publication data
Ocker, Christopher.
Biblical poetics before humanism and reformation / by Christopher Ocker.
p.   cm.
Includes bibliographical references and index.
ISBN 0 521 81046 9
1. Bible – Criticism, interpretation, etc. – History – Middle Ages, 600–1500.   I. Title.
BS500 .O25   2002
220.6′09′02 – dc21   2001037757

ISBN 0 521 81046 9 hardback

for Varda

... τὸ τῶν ποιητῶν μυθῶδες οὐκ ἀφιλόσοφον εἶναι. Hoc est, secretum uel fabulamentum Poetarum non est sine Philosophia.
Plutarch, *De audiendis poetarum*, according to Heinrich Bullinger's *Ratio studiorum* (Zürich, 1527)

Contents

Preface		*page* xi
Abbreviations and sigla		xvi
	Introduction	1
1	Medieval exegesis	8
	1. Books and commentaries	8
	2. Ways to understand	15
2	Signification	31
	1. Signification and allegory	31
	2. Theology	48
3	Rhetoric	72
	1. Rhetoric	73
	2. The difference between literal and spiritual	75
	3. The biblical image	78
	4. Figurative exegesis	93
	5. Biblical rhetoric	107
4	Divine speech	112
	1. Simplicity	112
	2. Causality	123
	3. Double-literal and parabolic meaning	142
	4. Inspiration	149
	5. Logic	161
	6. History	179
5	Reformation	184
	1. Dialectic	185
	2. Rhetoric	192
	3. Divine speech	199

Conclusion	214
Appendix: Selections from commentaries	220
Bibliography	239
Index	263

Preface

This book began, as some books do, with a question. How is it that late medieval commentators had trouble maintaining the distinction between literal and spiritual meanings? I began to document the confusion of literal and spiritual, and then I sought the grounds for it in two areas of intellectual life: scholastic views of signification and religious notions of knowledge.

The method I pursue is comparative. The medieval development of commentary literature and of the sources and methods of exegesis, with the possible exception of Nicholas of Lyra's *Postilla*, was complete by the year 1300. It therefore seemed to me more useful to identify hermeneutical commonplaces, study them in a variety of commentaries, and look for shared convictions and attitudes about the text and the ways it conveys meaning. I examined a diverse sample and supplemented this with a detailed study of Johannes Klenkok's commentary on the Acts of the Apostles, a good text from the third quarter of the fourteenth century to which Beryl Smalley called attention. The commonplaces seemed to cluster around three main topics, although not without repetition: semantics, rhetoric, and theology. I then compared the treatment of these topics to interpretation in the Reformation, about which we have learned so much in recent years.

Only a small part of my research on Klenkok's commentary on Acts appears in this book. I intend to publish a detailed monograph on that commentary in the near future. While this book provides a broad, comparative look at late medieval interpretation, that monograph will provide an overview of a single commentary and a thorough examination of its sources and techniques, around the same main topics treated here – signification, rhetoric, and theology. This book does not pretend to provide a comprehensive introduction to any single commentator or to trace traditions of the interpretation of particular passages. It uses comparative evidence to determine general hermeneutical presuppositions and the ideas that commonly expressed them. A chronologically systematic or even genetic method, tracing techniques, interpretations, and ideas from teacher to student, is impossible. Very few late medieval scholars commented on the entire Bible, nor did any significant number of them comment on one book of the Bible over against the others, which means that there is no constant biblical reference point that we can exploit. It would be extremely difficult to find commentaries on particular books of the Bible by scholars with some definite relationship to each other. Finally, very few late medieval scholars discussed biblical hermeneutics in an elaborate or self-conscious way, forcing us to rely on the rare treatise (two figure in my study: Hermann of Schildesche's handbook on the senses of the Bible and Heinrich of Langenstein's commentary on Jerome's prologue to the Bible) and to seek theory in the practice of interpretation. Either we study single commentators exhaustively, or we study a variety of commentaries by equally various authors comparatively. The latter is the approach of this book. Other books, I freely admit, do more than I have, and this work will at best supplement them, to what extent the reader will judge: Minnis and Scott's *Medieval Literary Theory and Criticism* exploits a fairly coherent body of prologue literature from the twelfth to the early fourteenth centuries, and G. R. Evans's *The Language and Logic of the Bible* examines the full breadth of ideas relevant to late medieval views of the Bible and its interpretation.

Because I relied heavily on unpublished texts, which is hardly avoidable in the study of late medieval exegesis, this book is part argument, part workshop. Especially in chapters 3 and 4, I take soundings from a variety of commentaries and also translate and expound long excerpts from a few texts that illustrate verbal techniques and key theological ideas. Again, I am not pretending to offer a history of the development of techniques or ideas. More than anything else, those chapters try to document broad hermeneutical trends in a variety of commentaries, and they contextualize interpretation within scholastic approaches to argument and problem solving. As the specialists know, late medieval intellectuals prided themselves on the originality of their views and arguments, but the Bible was a book that was supposed to transcend scholars' idiosyncracies. It provided a kind of universal "metanarrative," and that is what I am trying to reach through diverse evidence. This makes for a less conventional book, but perhaps a more useful one, in that it steers from diverse individuals toward the general and exposes the reader to more interpreters and, through liberal translations, to styles of presentation and manners of argument.

I have a chronological bias toward the fourteenth century. Scholasticism was an international culture, rendered so by the mobility of scholars, especially in the thirteenth and fourteenth centuries, and by the extensive system of schools outside universities in the mendicant orders. The movement of scholars decreased somewhat in the fifteenth century, with the proliferation of regional universities, as Paris itself became a regional school. By then the culture of late medieval exegesis was entrenched, as fifteenth-century sources suggest, awaiting the discovery of humanism by theologians. The fourteenth century is the period when that culture became entrenched.

I did not want to write a polemical book, although one could. My subject is what many scholars, at least since Wilhelm Dilthey's famous essay, published in 1900, "Die Entstehung der Hermeneutik," have ignored and still ignore as a regressive interlude between classical and Renaissance hermeneutics. Others see it as the ragged aftermath of the exegetical successes of the twelfth and thirteenth centuries. It seems to me that these impressions arise from too narrow a focus on the methods of classical rhetoric, which are eclipsed by logic in the late Middle Ages, and too narrow consideration of twelfth-century theology, which was transformed by Aristotelian metaphysics in the early thirteenth century. If one focuses on the study of classical rhetoric and twelfth-century theology, late medieval scholasticism will look shabby. I hope to show that late medieval theologians took a distinct approach to the text of the Bible that, in its own way, led naturally to the adaptations of classical rhetoric to Bible study in the sixteenth century. There was no degenerate interlude, insofar as hermeneutics is concerned. I hope, too, that this study will expand the chronology so interestingly treated by Kathy Eden, Olivier Millet, and Peter Harrison (see their works in the bibliography).

Commentaries are layered texts, containing quotation of original sources – the passage commented upon as well as other sources – with explanations. In excerpts from commentaries, I have italicized words of the Bible passage being commented upon, but have put all other quotations in quotation marks, as in this excerpt from Nicholas Gorran's commentary on Exodus 3.2:

And the Lord appeared to him in a flame, which was done, as Andrew [of St. Victor] says, lest they make a statue of him. A *flame* is in constant motion, and thus one cannot make an image of it. Because God might be depicted in an image, God has to be under certain terms of *fire*, which was done on account of his greatest active power, so that thus he might show himself to be above the Egyptians, just as fire is above all the elements. Deuteronomy 4 [verse 24], "Our God is a consuming fire."

It will help the reader to have an English Bible at hand when reading the excerpts of commentaries in chapters 2, 3, and 4, but unless noted otherwise, I translate a commentator's quotations of scripture rather than translating directly from the Vulgate or copying any modern Bible translation. The sigla used are noted along with the Abbreviations. In Latin quotations that appear in the footnotes, textual notes are placed in brackets immediately after the relevant word or phrase, except in some long quotations, where the notes are placed at the end of the passage following the usual conventions of textual editing. For additional comments on the Latin editing, see the beginning of the Appendix.

Since most texts used in this study originated as lectures in schools, their language is sometimes rough and inexact, and, had they been written as literature, they would deserve the humanistic reproach heaped upon scholastic commentaries since the days of Lorenzo Valla. I strove for clarity, but I also tried to preserve the oral, often erratic tone of commentary idiom.

I am grateful to the following libraries for allowing me to use their manuscript collections or providing microfilms and photocopies: Augustinus-Institut, Würzburg; Baden-Württembergische Landesbibliothek, Stuttgart; Bayerische Staatsbibliothek, Eichstätt; Bayerische Staatsbibliothek, Munich; Beinecke Library, Yale University; Biblioteca Nacional de Catalunya, Barcelona; Biblioteca de la Universitat de Barcelona; Bodleian Library, Oxford; Herzog-August Bibliothek, Wolfenbüttel; Österreichische Nationalbibliothek, Vienna; Speer Library, Princeton Theological Seminary; Stadtsbibliothek, Mainz; Trinity College, Cambridge; Universitätsbibliothek, Basel; Universitätsbibliothek, Frankfurt am Main; Universitätsbibliothek, Würzburg; Wissenschaftliche Allgemeinbibliothek, Erfurt. An earlier version of chapter 1 appeared in the *Scottish Journal of Theology*. I'm grateful for permission to adopt it here.

Much of the research for this project was begun while I was a fellow of the Institut für Europäische Geschichte in Mainz some years ago. I owed the privilege to the late Peter Manns, who received me as a fellow, and I am grateful to Rolf Decot, Markus Wriedt, Rainer Vinke, and Gustav Benrath for their interest and advice, which by now they have forgotten, but I have not. I am grateful to the San Francisco Theological Seminary for its ongoing support. The library of the Graduate Theological

Union at Berkeley, its director, Bonnie Hardwick, and its librarians in San Anselmo, Michael Peterson and Allan Schreiber, have hastened the completion of my work by stretching the limits of a sane lending policy.

Karlfried Froehlich introduced me to the study of late medieval exegesis, as the focal point of scholastic labor that it was, but also, more than I am able to demonstrate, as the locus of extremely diverse cultural transactions, where fundamental and broadly shared attitudes toward nature, history, life, and their representation are expressed. Whatever may be found good in this study is imperfect testimony to his enthusiasm for this subject and his teaching. I am also grateful to those others who have corrected me, especially Richard Muller, Don Compier, Herman Waetjen, Robert Coote, and three anonymous readers. They read the manuscript whole or in part and offered advice that was meticulous and entirely compelling. They will recognize how in many places their influence has been decisive. Among those to whom I owe a more general debt, I should mention Thomas A. Brady, William Bouwsma, Randolf Starn, Otto Gerhard Oexle, and Reindert Falkenburg. Philip Krey and Lesley Smith were kind enough to let me see a prepublication copy of their important collection of essays on Nicholas of Lyra. Lorna Shoemaker, Ph.D. candidate in history at the Graduate Theological Union, helped with the initial collation of Hermann of Schildesche's *Compend*. Chris Seeman, Ph.D. candidate in the Joint Degree Program in Near Eastern Religions of the Graduate Theological Union and the University of California, helped check the Latin transcriptions and translations. My special thanks to Dr Rosemary Williams at Cambridge University Press, who is more than a copy editor and has saved me very many embarrassments in both Latin and English. Michelle Walker helped assemble the bibliography. For every mistake that remains, I alone am responsible.

Abbreviations and sigla

add	*addit / addunt*
al man	*alia manu*
corr	*corrigit / corrigunt*
del	*delet / delent*
leg	*lege*
marg	*marginalium*
om	*omittit / omittunt*
rep	*repetit / unt*
supersc	*superscripto / is*
trans	*transponit*

CHLMP	*The Cambridge History of Later Medieval Philosophy*
CHRP	*The Cambridge History of Renaissance Philosophy*
CCl	Corpus Christianorum, Series Latina
CCM	Corpus Christianorum, Continuatio Mediaevalis
CICan	Corpus Iuris Canonicis
CICiv	Corpus Iuris Civilis
CSEL	Corpus Scriptorum Ecclesiasticorum Latinorum
DThC	*Dictionnaire de théologie catholique*
Glossa cum Lyra	*Biblia sacra cum glossis, interlineari et ordinaria, Nicolai Lyrani postilla et moralitatibus, Burgensis additionibus et Thoringi replicis* (Lyon, 1545)
LthK	*Lexikon für Theologie und Kirche*
PG	*Patrologia Graeca*
PL	*Patrologia Latina*
RB	Friedrich Stegmüller, *Repertorium Biblicum*
RS	Johannes Baptist Schneyer, *Repertorium der lateinischen Sermones des Mittelalters*
ST	Thomas Aquinas, *Summa Theologica*
TRE	*Theologische Realenzyklopädie*

Introduction

Theology is wisdom, said Bonaventure. Theology is science, countered Thomas Aquinas, drawing the lines of a fundamental debate in medieval schools.[1] Bonaventure hoped to preserve divine truth from unfettered rationalism, but in the late Middle Ages, it was Aquinas' *scientia* that appealed to most theologians. The term "science" sufficed. It preserved the spiritual benefits of Bonaventure's *sapientia*. It still allowed theologians to debate the power of the mind, the relation of a rational conclusion to faith, and the need for extraordinary revelations from God, such as occurred when God became flesh. But whether theology was wisdom or science, all scholastic theologians agreed that theology arose from the literature of the Bible.

They were also agreed that theology is not poetry. It could have been. Cicero and Varro, remembering the Platonic exegesis of Homer and adapting Aristotle's distinction between philosophy and fable, accepted poets as theologians of myths – teachers, by way of *fabulae*, of metaphysics.[2] There are three kinds of theology, said Varro: poetic, natural, and civil. Sure, poets "tell lies," writing absurd things in their fables, but such poetic theology could be controlled by the traditions of the state, by civil theology. Far more reliable than both was natural theology, which was metaphysics – straightforward, rational, and true. Poetry was good if you could find natural theology in it. As Plutarch warned, care must be taken not to enjoy the "gravy" of fabulous stories too much while

---

[1] Marie-Dominique Chenu, *La théologie comme science au xiiie siècle*, 3rd enlarged edition (Paris: J. Vrin, 1969), pp. 53–92. Albert Lang, *Die theologische Prinzipienlehre der mittelalterlichen Scholastik* (Frieburg im Briesgau, 1964), *passim*. See also A. J. Minnis and A. B. Scott (eds.), *Medieval Literary Theory and Criticism, c. 1100–1375* (Oxford: Clarendon, 1988), pp. 200–3.

[2] Varro, *Antiquities*, iv.27. Augustine, *On the City of God*, v.6. Lactantius, *De ira Dei*, xi.8. Ernst Robert Curtius, *European Literature and the Latin Middle Ages*, trans. W. R. Trask (Princeton University Press, 1953), pp. 203–27. For early Greek and Jewish allegory, see Jon Whitman "Present Perspectives," *Interpretation and Allegory. Antiquity to the Modern Period*, ed. Jon Whitman, (Leiden: E. J. Brill, 2000), pp. 33–70, here 34–40 and the literature cited there.

I

neglecting the nutritious element in what you read. Poetry is like the delicious Polypus fish, whose head is a delicacy that will give you bad dreams. It upsets as much as nourishes, for poets mingle their truth with lies. Even so, "the fables of the poets are not without philosophy," if one only knows how to read them.[3]

Medieval theologians knew the tradition of poetic theology and rejected it. Lactantius and Augustine recorded Varro's three-fold division, even while ridiculing pagan writers for thinking they could squeeze ultimate truth from fables: superstitions make for bad theology, they said.[4] Isidore of Seville copied out the division in his *Etymologies*. So too did the encyclopedists Rabanus Maurus and Vincent of Beauvais. But scholastic theologians followed Augustine and eventually adapted Aristotle. Aristotle thought poets were no better than theologians – they lie.[5] It was a stinging rebuke. So the theologians put their writing and teaching in Varro's philosophical middle category. They set their work beside the philosophers and pretty much banished the poets from their discussions. They insisted they were not poets.

The poetic theologian was rescued from neglect and hostility only in the fourteenth century. He was promoted by the early Paduan humanist Albertino Musato and, more famously, by Dante and Petrarch.[6] How did theologians respond? They resisted the humanists' overtures. Even the classicizing friars of early fourteenth-century England, made famous by Beryl Smalley, tried to avoid the remarriage of Christian and pagan learning, while they insinuated it. They used classical sources as they used natural philosophy, to expand their moral tropes. But in the end, "their modest little diversions were subsidiary to the real business of academic life," and that was ruled by philosophy.[7] When Dante attributed

---

[3] Plutarch, "How a Young Man Ought to Hear Poems," *Plutarch's Complete Works*, 6 vols. (New York: Wheeler Publishing Company, 1909), 6:648–95, and quoted by Heinrich Bullinger (as in the epigram to this book), *Ratio studiorum* (Zürich: Johann Wolf, 1594), f. 10v.

[4] Curtius, *European Literature*, pp. 203–27; see Lactantius and Augustine references in note 2, above.

[5] Aristotle, *Metaphysics*, 983 a 3, 983 b 29, *The Works of Aristotle*, trans. W. D. Ross, 12 vols. (Oxford: Clarendon, 1908–52), 8:983 a 3, 8:983 b 29.

[6] Curtius, *European Literature*, pp. 203–27, who overstates the acceptance of poetic theology among medieval intellectuals. For Petrarch, Carol E. Quillen, "Plundering the Egyptians: Petrarch and Augustine's *De doctrina christiana*," *Reading and Wisdom. The* De doctrina Christiana *of Augustine in the Middle Ages*, ed. E. D. English (University of Notre Dame, 1995), pp. 153–71. For Musato, Ronald G. Witt, *'In the Footsteps of the Ancients.' The Origins of Humanism from Lovato to Bruni* (Leiden: E. J. Brill, 2000), pp. 156–61. For the novelty of Petrarch's Christian humanism among early humanists, ibid., p. 497.

[7] Beryl Smalley, *English Friars and Antiquity in the Early Fourteenth Century* (Oxford: Blackwell, 1960), p. 301.

philosophy to his poems, he distanced himself from the theologians of his day.

How could the theologians take their position, when their most sacred and authoritative book is full of legend and myth? The question had confronted Christians in antiquity, as soon as learned people joined their ranks, so the scholastics had an old tradition on which to draw. Medieval theologians learned their definition of Christian literature from Jerome and Augustine, who taught that the primal writing of their religion, the Bible, is utterly distinct from the myths of the poets. Its stories are not fictions but a form of speech invested with a peculiar power that helps accomplish God's redeeming purposes in the world. The "obscure" speech of the Bible, they said, reveals mysteries to those who believe and hides them from the unworthy.

This was the substance of what we might call a classical Christian point of view. Biblical language is mystical. We may also call this a textual attitude. The text is not myth but mysteriously conveys spiritual truth. Ironically enough, to defend it, Christians of late antiquity adapted the allegorical methods of the philosophical readers of pagan verse. They borrowed from Platonists of the second and third centuries the distinction between the few who know how to read with insight, spiritually, and the many who take pleasure in silly stories, literally. They believed in the privileged knowledge of the few who were initiated by education, baptism, or both. Later, this textual attitude belonged to the educated of Europe, when the culture of learning was predominantly aristocratic and monastic, from the ninth to the twelfth centuries – before and while the schools of Paris formed a university.[8] This attitude was esoteric; it belonged to godlike men.[9] It belonged only to spiritually heroic individuals who through a rigorous discipline achieved divine knowledge. Bible commentators and poets, for example Bernard Silvestris and Alan of Lille, required the esoteric view of texts. It was a prerequisite of their view of education as internal formation. The search for metaphysical secrets in the text finally received its most concise justification in the theory of allegory taught by theologians of the monastery of St. Victor at Paris in the twelfth century, who asserted the habits and desires of monastic reading in the face of the new rationalism of the schools.[10] In the twelfth century, the search for privileged knowledge would only survive when and where it was reconciled to a thorough study of the letter.

---

[8] C. Stephen Jaeger, *The Envy of Angels: Cathedral Schools and Social Ideals in Medieval Europe, 950–1200* (Princeton University Press, 1994).
[9] Ibid., p. 280.   [10] Ibid., p. 278. See also pp. 15–16, 34–7 below.

It is, perhaps, the twelfth-century study of the letter and its thirteenth-century outcomes that have most impressed English-speaking scholars today.[11] Continental scholars, especially Friedrich Ohly and his students, emphasized instead the medieval preoccupation with both the textuality of the literal sense (the philology and history of documents) and the metaphysics of the spiritual sense (the internal meaning).[12] For my purpose, which is to understand late medieval exegesis, it is important to focus on two convictions belonging to the esoteric view of texts, one about the object of knowledge and the other about the knower.[13] With respect to the object of knowledge, a reader does not really know a text but the natural world standing behind it. With respect to the knower, the one who knows the inner truth of the natural world has a natural affinity with that truth: his or her nature approaches it. Poetry is for pleasure, taught Aristotle, whose *Metaphysics* ranks it among the pleasurable arts. As such, it posed a problem to the reader of sacred literature, who could not enjoy the text like the reader of poetry. The reader had, as Augustine suggested, a religious investment in reading.[14] Only God could be enjoyed, who was the truth depicted by nature and to whose purposes the monastic reader aspired. The text was to be a vital *instrument* of the reader's ambitions. One's ambition had to go beyond the text toward God. Theology was not poetry because true knowledge was ultimately not textual.

Scholastic theologians – the late medieval critics of poetry in theology and theology in poetry – accepted these arguments. They accepted them and fell under the spell of a new philosophy and logic, inspired by the rediscovery of Aristotle. With philosophy and logic, they laid the groundwork for an entirely different textual attitude. That is the subject of this book.

The new textual attitude of late medieval interpreters of the Bible was not esoteric. It was in a sense rhetorical and poetic. They anticipated what Benoît Girardin, Susi Hausamann, Charles Trinkaus, William Bouwsma, Manfred Hoffmann, Quirinus Breen, and most recently Olivier Millet have uncovered in Christian humanism and the

---

[11] See the comments of Alastair Minnis and Robert Lerner: Minnis, "Fifteenth-Century Versions of Thomistic Literalism," *Neue Richtungen in der hoch- und spätmittelalterlichen Bibelexegese*, ed. R. E. Lerner (Munich: Oldenbourg, 1996), pp. 178–9; Lerner, "Afterword," ibid., pp. 181–8. Consider also Henri de Lubac, *Exégèse médiévale. Les quatre sens de l'Ecriture*, 2 parts (Paris: Aubier, 1959–1964), 2/2:263–367 and Marie-Dominique Chenu, "Lecture de la Bible et philosophie," *Mélanges offerts à Etienne Gilson* (Paris: J. Vrin, 1959), pp. 161–71.

[12] See works by Ohly, Christel Meier, and Heinz Meyer and Rudolf Suntrup in the bibliography.

[13] This is discussed further in chapter 2, below.

[14] Margaret Gibson, "The *De doctrina christiana* in the School of St. Victor," English (ed.), *Reading and Wisdom. The* De doctrina christiana *of Augustine in the Middle Ages*, pp. 41–7.

early Protestant movement: the adaptation of classical rhetoric to biblical exegesis, which allowed them to read the Bible as they read poetry.[15] But scarcely any rhetoric was studied or taught in late medieval scholasticism. Its absence is evidence of the ongoing contest over "the disciplinary status and cultural privilege of rhetoric," to which Rita Copeland has called our attention.[16] Copeland and others have noted that grammar absorbed the functions of rhetoric in the twelfth century, becoming the field that provided intellectuals with theories of reading, understanding, and translating literature.[17] I am considering the subsequent history of the contest in scholasticism, where logic infiltrated the teaching of grammar after the middle of the thirteenth century, with the rising popularity of "speculative grammar."[18] In the universities, rhetoric as a discipline was then lost. Soon after came the rise of terminist logic. Both provided new tools for the analysis of texts. Just as grammar supplanted rhetoric in the twelfth century, so logic took the place of rhetoric in the thirteenth and fourteenth centuries.

For a long time, it has been suspected that late medieval logic carried out, to some extent, the functions of rhetoric in intellectual life. Nikolaus Häring and William Courtenay have pointed out that speculative grammar and terminist logic were really exegetical methods, but Courtenay noted a curious fact: the methods were not applied in biblical commentaries.[19] This is perplexing. With the decline of rhetorical study in the thirteenth century, logic alone provided theologians with a theoretical approach to language and its relation to thought. How could logic not affect biblical exegesis? I will argue that it did so indirectly by helping scholars form basic attitudes toward language as the site of meaning, and these attitudes were at odds with the best rationale for spiritual exegesis. This was, for theologians, a first step toward the equalization of Bible and poetry, even though it happened in the predominantly logical culture of late medieval scholasticism.

Late medieval scholars held two convictions about the text of the Bible. These contrast sharply with twelfth-century sensibilities. First,

---

[15] See their works listed in the bibliography.
[16] Rita Copeland, *Rhetoric, Hermeneutics, and Translation in the Middle Ages* (Cambridge University Press, 1991), p. 2.
[17] See especially Suzanne Reynolds, *Medieval Reading: Grammar, Rhetoric and the Classical Text* (Cambridge University Press, 1996).
[18] This is discussed in chapter 2.
[19] William J. Courtenay, *Schools and Scholars in Fourteenth-Century England* (Priceton University Press, 1987), p. 261; Nikolaus Häring, "Commentary and Hermeneutics," *Renaissance and Renewal in the Twelfth Century* (Cambridge, Mass.: Harvard University Press, 1982), p. 195. See also pp. 69–70, below.

whatever a reader learns of the world in a text may be known in its literal sense. It is not necessary to go beyond the letter. And secondly, insight depends not on the affinity of the nature of the knower with the nature of internal truth; rather, insight occurs in a kind of inter-subjectivity, a communion of readers and writers. The text itself, in its literal sense, becomes a meeting place – in the words of the sixteenth-century Augsburg reformer Wolfgang Musculus, a garden of pleasure. I don't doubt that these convictions owe a great deal to the advances in literal interpretation that began in the twelfth century and that are so well known to students of the medieval Bible. It is not my intent to document the late medieval history of those methods. Instead, I am interested in a new kind of biblical textuality, a textuality that emerged in the late Middle Ages, and in the ways it may have played a role in the Reformation.

My argument adapts an insight of two scholars. In his study of the interpretation of the Song of Songs in the high and late Middle Ages, Denys Turner emphasized Thomas Aquinas' biblical semantics as an innovative basis for the literary analysis of biblical texts.[20] Although my nomenclature differs from his, my point will be the same, except for this: I think Aquinas was more representative of late medieval interpretation than Turner does. In the context of Song of Songs commentaries, Turner found that Aquinas' literary explanation of metaphor, taken up again by Nicholas of Lyra in his interpretation of the Song of Songs as an historical allegory (which Turner calls typology), was unique and unrepresentative.[21] I intend to show in this book that a linguistic framework for literary explanation of biblical imagery is present in many late medieval commentaries, including the commentaries of Denys the Carthusian (who represents, in Turner's study, resistance to Thomas' hermeneutic). Furthermore, I intend to show that it weakened the distinction between literal and spiritual meanings, precisely as Turner found it so weakened in Denys the Carthusian's exegesis of the Song of Songs. The second scholar, Yves Delègue, has also drawn attention to the importance of Aquinas' theory of biblical signification.[22] Like Turner, Delègue points out its importance in the work of Nicholas of Lyra.[23] By

---

[20] Denys Turner, *Eros and Allegory: Medieval Exegesis of the Song of Songs*: (Kalamazoo Cistercian Publications, 1995).
[21] "Typology" can be a confusing term, so I avoid it. See p. 18, below.
[22] See pp. 38–40, below.
[23] Lyra was a well-established theologian when he composed his *Postilla litteralis*, a literal exposition of the entire Bible, between 1322 or early 1323 and 1331. Parts of it began circulating before the *Postilla's* completion. He later prepared a resume of the *Postilla* under the title *On the Difference of Our Translation from the Hebrew Letter of the Old Testament*, or *The Book of Differences*, and produced a moral

drawing on a larger number of commentaries, I will show that Turner and Delègue have uncovered the theoretical basis for the common view of the text in the late Middle Ages – a new textual attitude. Aquinas is often credited with solving the problem of the relation of literal and spiritual senses by strictly separating them.[24] I will argue that he made it extremely difficult to distinguish spiritual from literal, and interpreters were glad for it.

I begin with a survey of the history of exegetical literature and an introduction to medieval hermeneutics (chapter 1). I make my case in chapters 2, 3, and 4. My argument progresses from theories of biblical signification (chapter 2) to the problems of figurative language (chapter 3) to the religious conceptualization of biblical literature (chapter 4). I try to show that changing notions of biblical signification, experiments in rhetorical analysis, and a concept of divine speech reveal a new textual attitude that unites biblical narrative and philosophical and theological subject matter. The significance of this new textual attitude is obvious not only in comparison with the principles enunciated at the school of St. Victor in the twelfth century, but also in comparison with interpretation in the Reformation (chapter 5). Scholars like Susan Schreiner and David Steinmetz have observed the similarities to and dependencies of Reformation scholars on medieval exegetical traditions.[25] This book suggests a reason for it: a fundamental continuity between late medieval and Reformation conceptions of the Bible as a text, forming one aspect of early modern Protestant religiosity and its well-known biblicism.

exposition of the entire Bible, the *Postilla moralis*, among other things. Charles-Victor Langlois, "Nicolas de Lyre, Frère Mineur," *Histoire Littéraire de la France* 36 (1924): 372–74. Franz Pelster, "Quodlibeta und Quaestiones des Nikolaus von Lyra O.F.M. († 1349)," *Mélanges de Ghellinck* (Gembloux, 1951), pp. 951–73. See also C. L. Patton, "Nicholas of Lyra," *Historical Handbook of Major Biblical Interpreters*, ed. Mckim, pp. 116–22.

[24] Beryl Smalley, *The Study of the Bible in the Middle Ages* (Notre Dame: University of Notre Dame Press, 1964), p. 300. A. J. Minnis, *Medieval Theory of Authorship*, 2nd edition (Philadelphia: University of Pennsylvania Press, 1988), p. 91.

[25] See, for example, Susan E. Schreiner, *Where Shall Wisdom Be Found? Calvin's Exegesis of Job from Medieval and Modern Perspectives* (Chicago: University of Chicago Press, 1994) and the bibliographical essay by Richard Muller, "Biblical Interpretation in the Era of the Reformation: The view from the Middle Ages," *Biblical Interpretation in the Era of the Reformation*, ed. R. A. Muller and J. L. Thompson (Grand Rapids: Eerdmans, 1996), pp. 3–22.

CHAPTER 1

Medieval exegesis

Bible commentary was a genre of scholastic literature. It represents a significant part of the work of theologians in schools. This chapter surveys medieval commentary literature, introduces the basic principles of medieval interpretation, and notes the difficulty late medieval scholars had in maintaining a basic hermeneutical conviction, namely the separation of literal and spiritual meanings.

1. BOOKS AND COMMENTARIES

Whereas ancient Jewish scripture, written on leather or papyrus, was usually bound in scrolls, Christians, beginning in the second century, abandoned scrolls for another structure, the codex, a book of leaves of papyrus, then parchment and later, beginning in the fourteenth century in Europe, paper, folded into sections and sewn together between two boards.[1] By the end of the fourth century in western Christianity, sixty-six books with an additional eight of less certain authenticity ("apocrypha") were accepted as scripture, yet the border distinguishing these books from other kinds of sacred literature was neither frozen nor fluid, but somewhere in between, and this can be seen in the codices themselves.[2] Jerome's Bible translation, the Vulgate, which became the only translation recognized in the medieval west, was usually copied with "prologues" – brief texts that served to introduce the sections and books of scripture.[3] Jerome authored the prologue to the entire Bible,

---

[1] Medieval Hebrew Bibles were also usually bound in codices. Emanuel Tov, *Textual Criticism of the Hebrew Bible* (Minneapolis: Fortress, 1992), pp. 201–7. Kurt Aland and Barbara Aland, *The Text of the New Testament* (Leiden: Brill, 1987), pp. 75–7.
[2] The same sixty-six books of modern Bibles, the seven apocryphal books, and an additional letter of Paul to the Laodiceans included in a number of Vulgate manuscripts. Bruce M. Metzger, *The Canon of the New Testament* (Oxford: Clarendon, 1987), pp. 229–47.
[3] In fact, some Latin prologues circulated before Jerome and were carried over into fourteen of the twenty earliest manuscripts of the Vulgate. Maurice Schild, *Abendländische Bibelvorreden bis zur Lutherbibel* (Gütersloh: Gerd Mohn, 1970), pp. 71–2.

the prologue to the Pentateuch, and various others wholly or in part, but the rest were drawn from a surprising variety of sources. They even include material composed by heretics, like the Pelagian prologue to the Pauline Epistles that circulated with most Vulgate manuscripts, or the Monarchian material hidden beneath a first sentence taken from a letter of Jerome in the prologue to the Catholic Epistles, the Book of Acts, and the Apocalypse (the last section of the medieval New Testament).[4] Medieval scholars knew that these texts were not scripture, even if they did not know the unorthodox origins of some of them, and they took this material critically. But the physical form of the Bibles they used nevertheless displays well the intimate connection of scripture and interpretation in their minds. For the Bible itself was a library of documents that gave the record of salvation from the past to the future, and reflection upon the same was expected to be taken up into its world of thought. Even the monastic library, according to Hugh of Saint Victor, ought to be organized according to biblical categories: the Old Testament section should include pseudepigrapha – together with law, prophets, and hagiography – and the New Testament section should include "decrees" and the writings of the "fathers and doctors of the church."[5]

The codices included non-canonical prologues. In addition, those Bibles designed for study often combined scripture and exegesis by adding glosses to the page.[6] Bible glosses were brief explanatory notes added between the lines (interlinear glosses) and longer explanations mostly culled from patristic literature and placed in the margins (marginal glosses, a technique also found in Jewish commentaries on the Talmud).[7] The earliest biblical glosses known in the west were probably

---

[4] Ibid., pp. 69–102. See also the comments of Karlfried Froehlich in the introduction to the *Biblia Latina cum Glossa Ordinaria: Facsimile Reprint of the Editio Princeps, Adolph Rusch of Strassburg 1480/81*, 4 vols. (Turnhout: Brepols, 1992), 1:xv.

[5] "Decrees" refers to the authoritative pronouncements of popes, bishops, councils, and church fathers in the canon law. *Didascalicon*, iv.2 "De ordine et numero librorum." Pierre Petitmengin, "La Bible à travers les inventaires de bibliothèques médiévales," *Le Moyen Age et la Bible*, p. 42.

[6] This was true only of those copies designed for study, which did not comprise the largest number of biblical manuscripts. Other forms and uses: divided for liturgical reading in the mass, in the form of epistolaries or evangelaries, as codices used for the daily readings in a monastery's refectory, less frequently in vernacular translation for private use. Ibid., p. 35 (which does not mention the last use).

[7] Guy Lobrichon, "Une nouveauté: les gloses de la Bible," *Le Moyen Age et la Bible*, ed. P. Riché and G. Lobrichon (Paris: Beauchesne, 1984), p. 98. Commentaries on the Talmud were first written in Mesopatamia (the Abbasid Caliphate) in the ninth century, and in North Africa, Iberia, Italy, France, and Germany from about the beginning of the eleventh century. Meyer Waxman, *A History of Jewish Literature*, 4 vols. (New York: Thomas Yoseloff, 1960), 1:250–80. Rabbinical commentaries on the Bible, a literary genre that followed a long tradition of oral commentary and halakic interpretation of scripture, were written from the tenth century in Mesopotamia and

written in Northumbria and Ireland by the turn of the eighth to ninth centuries,[8] but the technique did not catch on until the third quarter of the eleventh century, in the monastic and cathedral schools that spawned the beginnings of scholasticism in the north of France.[9] This form of commentary was first applied to single books that were interpreted by a school's master. Glosses gradually assumed a more uniform design, while striving (especially under the influence of Anselm of Laon [d. 1117]) to encompass patristic exegetical opinion for the whole Bible. By the middle of the twelfth century glossed Bibles began to circulate in France, England, and Germany, apparently from a center of production at Paris, whose famous schools attracted book-buying students and teachers from throughout Christendom. Around 1220 the first complete glossed Bibles were produced, and about the same time what was by then a more or less standard text came to be called the *Glossa ordinaria*, the Ordinary Gloss to scripture, its status promoted, if not at first achieved, in connection with the theology faculty of the new university of Paris.[10] Some of these standard glosses compiled material from many authors (glosses to the Psalter, Song of Songs, Pauline Epistles, and Apocalypse). Others drew predominantly from a single source (Bede in Ezra to Nehemiah, Mark, Acts, and the Catholic Epistles; Rabanus Maurus in the Pentateuch and the Books of Maccabees).[11] In addition, these Bibles with commentary were

---

the eleventh century in the west. Aryeh Graboïs, "L'exégèse rabbinique," *Le Moyen Age et la Bible*, pp. 234–5.

[8] An early example, a copy of the visions of Ezechiel with interlinear and marginal glosses, was produced by an Irish monk who came to the monastery of Saint Gall, suggesting that the idea if not the text followed the movement of Northumbrian and Irish monks to the continent in the late eighth and early ninth centuries. Lobrichon, "Les gloses," pp. 98–9.

[9] The beginning of European theological literature independent of biblical commentary occurred at about the same time, and this apparent departure from exegesis into the systematic analysis of doctrine has often been emphasized. Artur Michael Landgraf, *Einführung in die Geschichte der theologischen Literatur der Frühscholastik* (Regensburg: Gregorius-Verlag, 1948), pp. 39–47. J. de Ghellinck, *Le mouvement théologique du xiie siècle* (Bruges: Editions de Tempel, 1948). But the fact that the biblical gloss developed alongside the new literature has often been overlooked. Jean Châtillon, "La Bible dans les écoles du xiie siècle," *Le Moyen Age et la Bible*, pp. 163–97. For the early history of the *Glossa ordinaria*, consider Christopher De Hamel, *Glossed Books of the Bible and the Origins of the Paris Booktrade* (Woodbridge, Suffolk: D. S. Brewer, 1984); Lobrichon, "Les gloses," pp. 99–110 (the most up-to-date general account); Smalley, *Study of the Bible*, pp. 46–52; Mark A. Zier, "The Manuscript Tradition of the Glossa Ordinaria for Daniel, and Hints at a Method for a Critical Edition," *Scriptorium* 47 (1993): 3–25, esp. 3–5 for a brief summary of scholarship.

[10] Lobrichon, "Les gloses," pp. 101, 103, 112–14. Margaret T. Gibson, "The Glossed Bible," *Biblia Latina cum glossa ordinaria: Facsimile Reprint of the Editio Princeps, Adolph Rusch of Strassburg 1480/81*, ed. Karlfried Froehlich and Margaret T. Gibson (Brepols: Turnhout, 1992), pp. vii–xi. The *Glossa ordinaria* was, according to Margaret Gibson, consolidated between 1110 and 1120 possibly at Laon or Auxerre, but the history of the Gloss from that time until c. 1140/50 is "shrouded in an uncertain and deceitful mist." Ibid., p. xi.

[11] Ibid., p. ix.

uniformly organized in the nine volumes described in the sixth century by Cassiodorus, an arrangement of the biblical text also followed in Romanesque display Bibles and texts for common use: Genesis to Ruth, six books of Kings, the four major and the twelve minor prophets, the Psalter, Wisdom literature, lives from Job to Nehemiah, the four Gospels, Pauline and other Epistles, Acts and the Apocalypse.[12]

The Ordinary Gloss exercised tremendous influence within scholastic exegesis, even though its reproduction in western Europe seems to have been on the wane by 1300.[13] There were other forms of exegetical literature. These were discursive commentaries, proliferating in twelfth-century monastic schools and bearing various names often attached to the texts by copyists rather than authors (authors, as monks, preferred anonymity and did not put titles and ascriptions to their work): "commentary," "exposition," "explanation," "reading" (*lectura*), *postilla* (more on this below), "questions," "little notes" (*notule*), "annotations," or "distinctions on" such and such a book.[14] These diverse names point to the fact that the literature of interpretation, like the methods of reading, was expanding. While glosses multiplied in the twelfth century, scholars also collected topical opinions in books of "Sentences" (the school of Laon again played an important role), and they explored contradicting authorities and problems of interpretation in books of "questions."[15] Some of these were taken from the exegesis of masters like Anselm of Laon. Other works, like the commentary on the Psalms by Bruno the Carthusian, founder of the Carthusian Order (d. 1101), integrated the treatment of questions into exegetical work, while the commentary on the Epistles of Paul attributed to him also posed questions, and tried to get the apostle to answer by evoking arguments "proved" by Paul, proofs discovered by considering the circumstances, subject matter, and intention of the author.[16] In connection with the school of Saint Victor in the

---

[12] Cassiodorus, *Institutiones* I.xi.3, ed. R. A. B. Mynors (Oxford University Press, 1937), p. 36. Gibson, "The Glossed Bible," p. vii.

[13] Lobrichon believes that the production of the Gloss was tardy in Central Europe, following upon the late introduction of universities there. "Les gloses," p. 101 n. 18. Peter Lombard's citations of it in his *Four Books of Sentences*, the basis of theological lectures in universities up to the sixteenth century, and its use by Peter Comestor, chancellor of the university of Paris in the third quarter of the twelfth century (who composed the gloss on the four Gospels and a widely used compendium of biblical history, the *Historia scholastica*), "canonized" the Ordinary Gloss. Ibid., p. 110.

[14] Häring, "Commentary and Hermeneutics," pp. 173–5.

[15] Landgraf, *Einführung*, pp. 35–39, 40–2; De Ghellinck, *Mouvement*, pp. 133–48; Karlfried Froehlich, "Christian Interpretation of the Old Testament in the High Middle Ages," *Hebrew Bible/Old Testament. The History of Its Interpretation*, ed. Magne Saebo, 3 vols. (Göttingen: Vandenhoeck und Ruprecht, 2000), 1/2: 496–558, here 509.

[16] Châtillon, "Les écoles," pp. 172–5.

second and third quarters of the twelfth century, a variety of works on theology and on the Old Testament clarified the distinctions between "historical" and "spiritual" meanings, according to principles adapted from Augustine's *On Christian Doctrine* and explained in the *Didascalicon* of Hugh of Saint Victor (d. 1141, more on this below): principles that could serve either literal exegesis (at the hands of Andrew of Saint Victor, d. 1175) or the spiritual senses (at the hands of Richard of Saint Victor, d. 1173). The clarity achieved at Saint Victor allowed Peter Comestor, a master at Paris and chancellor of the school of Notre Dame, to succumb to the pleas of his friends and compile, by the year 1175, the knowledge scattered throughout the Bible and its glosses within a coherent and continuous narrative. The result came to be known as the *Historia scholastica*, the first comprehensive and – unlike the glosses – fairly coherent treatment of the Bible in Europe and one of the most widely used exegetical works of the later Middle Ages.[17] But this compellingly sensible form of exegetical writing did not immediately provoke imitators. Rather, it took its place beside the Ordinary Gloss.

A consistent and coherent kind of literature employed widely by professional interpreters (that is, theologians) did not arise until the second quarter of the thirteenth century. That kind of commentary was developed at the Dominican school at the university of Paris under the leadership of a master there, Hugh of Saint-Cher, and it was given the inexplicable name "postilla."[18] The thirteenth-century postilla was a running commentary, ordinarily composed at a school, especially the schools of the mendicant orders in the thirteenth century. Originally, it was supposed to complement the Ordinary Gloss, which compiled patristic opinions, by adding interpretations from the principal exegetes of the twelfth and early thirteenth centuries. Although this new form of exegetical literature came to dominate biblical interpretation, it never did so exclusively. Thirteenth-century postillators could use questions to evade undesirable implications in the Ordinary Gloss.[19] Scholars could

---

[17] Smalley, *Study*, p. 179; Châtillon, "Les écoles," p. 195; James H. Morey, "Peter Comestor, Biblical Paraphrase, and the Medieval Popular Bible," *Speculum* 68 (1993): 10; Froehlich, "Christian Interpretation," pp. 506–7.

[18] The name consists of two words, "post illa(m)", "after that", or "after those things". No one knows to what "that" refers. Mark Zier's guess is the best I know. He suggests it derives from a reference to the Ordinary Gloss, "post illam glossam", which had received its final shape shortly before Hugh of St. Cher's postilla was compiled. Zier, "Glossa Ordinaria," p. 15. See also Smalley, *Study*, pp. 270, 272; For the development of exegetical tools at the Dominican school at Paris, see M. Michèle Mulchahey, "*First the Bow is Bent in Study.*" *Dominican Education before 1350* (Toronto: Pontifical Institute of Mediaeval Studies, 1998), pp. 485–526.

[19] Buc, *L'ambiguïté du livre*, p. 150.

still compose questions on a book of the Bible as late the 1360s, as a master at the university of Oxford did.[20] And by the middle of the fourteenth century the name "postilla" was used in Central Europe, at least, not only for running commentaries but also for sermon collections.[21] The classic postilla, if you will, is represented in some of the greatest achievements of scholastic interpretation: the commentaries of Bonaventure and Aquinas in the middle of the thirteenth century and of the Dominican Nicholas Gorran in the fourth quarter of that century; the *Postilla* of the Franciscan Nicholas of Lyra in the second quarter of the fourteenth century; the commentaries of John Wyclif in the third and fourth quarters of that century, and the commentaries of Denys van Leeuwen (also known as Dionysius the Carthusian) in the second and third quarters of the fifteenth century. One early fourteenth-century interpreter, the Franciscan Pierre Auriol, made a handy *Compendium* to rival the old *Historia scholastica*.[22] But the form of these achievements was not exclusive. In addition to the erratic appearance of questions on a book of the Bible, already mentioned, some interpreters (like the city school teacher Johann Müntzinger in the second quarter of the fourteenth century, and the Augustinian Hermit Martin Luther in his Psalms lectures of 1513 to 1515) continued to gloss Bibles.[23] Luther's use of gloss commentary

---

[20] Johannes Klenkok, *Questiones super totam materiam canonice Johannis*, Oxford, Bodleian, Hamilton Ms. 33, ff. 247ra–258va. C. Ocker, *Johannes Klenkok: A Friar's Life, c. 1310 to 1374*, volume 83/5 of the *Transactions of the American Philosophical Society* (Philadelphia: American Philosophical Society, 1933), p. 33.

[21] A widely distributed example was a sermon collection of the pre-Hussite reformer, Konrad Waldhauser, known as the *Postilla Pragensis*. Johannes Baptist Schneyer, *Repertorium der lateinischen Sermones des Mittelalters*, 9 vols. (Münster: Aschendorff, 1969–80), nos. 72ff.

[22] The common spelling of Aureol's name may not be strictly correct (the most likely alternative being "Auriol"). See A. Teetaert, "Pierre Auriol," *DThC*, 12/2:1810. Cf. also N. Valois, "Pierre Auriol, Frère mineur," *Histoire littéraire de la France* 33 (1906): 479–527, who is followed by Katherine H. Tachau, "The Preparation of a Critical Edition of Pierre Auriol's Sentences Lectures," *Editori de Quaracchi 100 anni dopo, bilancio e prospettive*, ed. A. Cacciotti and B. Faes de Mottoni (Rome: Edizioni Antonianum, 1997), pp. 205–26, here p. 205 n. 1.

[23] Basel, Universitätsbibliothek, A V 28, ff. 146r–226v, f. 146r bottom margin: "Cartus[iensium] Bas[iliensium]," which is the ownership mark of the Carthusians of Basel. The incipit gives the title: "Iste liber intytulatur liber leccionum epistolarum sancti, que lecciones leguntur in diuino officio." The explicit names the author: "Et sic per Dei materiam explicunt epistole Pauli collecte per reuerendum magistrum Johann Munczinger Deo gracias." Müntzinger also wrote a Middle High German exposition of the Lord's Prayer which I have examined in Würzburg, Universitätsbibliothek, M.ch.f. 109, ff. 316r–328r. This commentary also contains numerous and diverse questions, each introduced, "Hie mag man ein frag thun," which sound like hypothetical questions posed by a teacher to his students; they would, then, reflect what a teacher anticipated of their concerns. See also Albert Lang, "Johann Müntzinger, ein Schwäbischer Theologe und Schulmeister am Ende des 14. Jahrhunderts," *Aus der Geisteswelt des Mittelalters*, ed. A. Lang, 3 vols. (Münster: Aschendorf, 1935), 2: 1200–30. Luther's early lectures on the Psalms have been translated into English. Martin Luther, *First Lectures on the Psalms*, 2 vols., edited by Hilton C. Oswald, vols. 10, 11 of *Luther's Works* (St. Louis: Concordia, 1974).

in these lectures hardly demonstrates his "modernity."[24] Others, like Meister Eckhart, wrote commentaries with a strong mystical and theological bent that defy easy classification. Still others, like the Dominican Robert Holcot and the Augustinian Hermit Heinrich of Friemar, wrote commentaries with a pronounced moral and homiletical bias. Even at its later stage of development, the medieval commentary remained a book with loose ends, a living if sometimes evasive genre.

The requirements of universities encouraged the production of exegetical literature. Both the Bible and Peter Lombard's *Four Books of Sentences* were standard texts of theology there, and the university's curriculum, at times in a less regular form, also trickled into the widely distributed schools of the mendicant orders. Scholastic interpreters drew from twelfth-century accomplishments: the *Glossa ordinaria* and the *Historia scholastica*. They also devised new tools of study, beginning with an edition of the Bible itself, which Stephen Langton, apparently adapting earlier attempts, divided into chapters shortly before 1203, a task completed by another scholar, Thomas Gallus, who divided the chapters into paragraphs. This became the standard edition of the Bible at Paris, and from there it moved to all universities.[25] At the Parisian Dominican cloister of Saint Jacques, friars made an alphabetical concordance of Latin terms that covered the Old and New Testaments (the new chapter divisions providing an efficient means of referencing), probably between 1230 and 1235. It was succeeded by a deluxe bookstore edition put together by the year 1275, which enjoyed wide distribution.[26] Interpreters also used concordances to canon law as a source of authoritative opinions to apply in their exegesis, and two concordances composed in the fourteenth century harmonized canon law and scripture, one by the abbot Jean of Nivelles, and another by the Bolognese law professor Johannes Calderinus.[27]

The Ordinary Gloss, the *Historia scholastica*, *Postillae*, and concordances, together with a Bible divided into chapters, became the chief tools of

---

[24] Cf. Gerald L. Bruns, *Hermeneutics Ancient and Modern* (New Haven: Yale, 1992), pp. 139–40.
[25] Langton was also the first to try to write commentaries on the entire Bible in imitation of Peter Comestor's *Historia scholastica*. Jacques Verger, "L'exégèse de l'Université," *Le Moyen Age et la Bible*, pp. 199–232, here 202. The division of chapters into verses did not occur until the sixteenth century. Froehlich, "Christian Interpretation," p. 508.
[26] A second alphabetical concordance was compiled at Saint Jacques before this final, influential edition, but it exercised little influence. Mary A. Rouse and Richard H. Rouse, "La concordance verbale des Écritures," *Le Moyen Age et la Bible*, pp. 115–22.
[27] Ocker, "The Fusion of Exegesis and Papal Ideology in Fourteenth-Century Theology," *Biblical Hermeneutics in Historical Perspective*, ed. M. Burrows and P. Rorem (Grand Rapids: Eerdmans, 1991), pp. 131–51, here pp. 137–43.

scholastic exegesis. Interpretation also occurred in other media, like sermons, art, devotional literature, and derivatively even in saints' legends, which quote and infer scripture, especially the narratives of the passion of Christ, by alluding to older stories and well-known images. But the most developed and self-conscious technology of exposition was scholastic exegesis, which navigated the realms of authoritative ideas within the Bible and outside of it. What did that methodology produce?

2. WAYS TO UNDERSTAND

In the twelfth century, scholars who began to collect questions and "sentences" were introducing a separation of logically disciplined theology from exegesis.[28] Some early scholastic theologians seemed to use the difference between exegesis and reflection as an excuse to abandon the traditional sources of religious knowledge in favor of a self-indulgent rationalism,[29] but the most influential theorists of biblical interpretation argued that exegesis and reflection are complementary, not adversarial, and consistent with the nature of language and with the composition of the universe. The Victorines were the great theorists of this complementary difference, and it was best expressed in a brief sentence by one of them: "not only words, but things also are representational."[30] This theory of signification explained, they believed, how the Bible, a literary product, was like all literature and at the same time better than all literature. There are two kinds of secular literature, said Hugh of St. Victor: the seven liberal arts, which contain philosophy, and writings dependent upon the arts, which are not philosophical – tragedies, comedies, satires, heroic verse and lyric, iambics, didactic poems, fables, histories,

---

[28] De Ghellinck described the growing distinction between divine speech and reflection upon it by tracing the changing meaning of "sacra pagina." It referred to the Bible, including glosses on the Bible, but in the thirteenth century it came to mean theological literature independent of scripture. De Ghellinck, " 'Pagina' et 'sacra pagina.' Histoire d'un mot et transformation de l'object primitivement désigné," *Etudes d'histoire littéraire et doctrinale de la scolastique médiévale offertes à Auguste Pelzer* (Louvain: Université de Louvain, 1947)", pp. 23–59. See also Smalley, *Study of the Bible*, p. 271, and Paul De Vooght, *Les sources de la doctrine chrétienne* (Bruges: Descleé De Brouwer, 1954), pp. 27–8.

[29] Margaret Gibson, "The *De doctrina christiana* in the School of St. Victor," *Reading and Wisdom. The De doctrina christiana in the Middle Ages*, ed. E. D. English (Notre Dame: University of Notre Dame Press, 1995), pp. 41, 45.

[30] "non solum voces, sed et res significativae sunt." Richard of St. Victor, *Exceptiones* ii.3, "De scripturae divinae triplici modo tractandi," *PL* 177:205. Essential reading on this subject is the essay by Friedrich Ohly, "Vom geistigen Sinn des Wortes im Mittelalter," *Schriften zur mittelalterlichen Bedeutungsforschung* (Darmstadt: Wissenschaftliche Buchgesellschaft, 1977), pp. 1–31, and E. Ann Matter, *The Voice of My Beloved. The Song of Songs in Western Medieval Christianity* (Philadelphia: University of Pennsylvania Press, 1990), pp. 49–85.

and prose. In secular literature, words mediate knowledge of the subject matter of a piece of writing, but in the non-philosophical variety, it is often done obscurely under various images.[31] Like non-philosophical secular literature, the Bible also relies on much figurative language. But scriptural figures work differently. Scripture contains the "far more excellent" significance of things,[32] or as Richard of St. Victor noted, "in divine literature not only do meanings signify things, those things signify other things. Whence it is clear how greatly useful knowledge of the [liberal] arts is for understanding the divine scriptures."[33] What in secular literature was obscure became in the Bible profound.

Building upon Augustine's account of the role of philosophy in biblical education and adapting his semantic theory (I will return to this in the next chapter), they argued that not only does scripture tell stories, but the minute elements of a story, its "things," *res* (rocks, trees, virtually any objects, but also the events that put "things" in the sequence of a narrative) in turn function as signs that indicate meanings that may seem, to a reader lacking insight, to have nothing to do with the biblical passage. Hugh of St. Victor named six "circumstances" under which "things" bear meaning, an adaptation of the doctrine of circumstances in medieval grammar: physical objects as such and their properties; persons who signify mysteries in their deeds and experiences; numbers in their various arrangements and computations (he names nine); places; times (such as seasons); and events.[34] Those meanings were believed to be closer to spiritual truth. They were called the spiritual senses or allegory.

The possibility of allegorical meaning was attributed to a layered quality of the meaningfulness of texts. Words tell a story, as for example the text in the Song of Songs, where the bride says, "the king has led me into his wine cellar, he has planned love for me" (Song of Songs 2.4).[35] The sentence literally says, as the Ordinary Gloss explained, that the bride of the story is very excited to enter the king's "wine cellar," which the Gloss takes as a metaphor for her awareness of her glory and her feeling

---

[31] *Didascalicon* iii.4, trans. J. Taylor, *The Didascalicon of Hugh of St. Victor* (New York: Columbia University Press, 1961), pp. 87–8.
[32] Ibid., v.3, pp. 121–2.
[33] "In libris autem ethnicorum voces tantum mediantibus intellectibus res significant. In divina pagina non solum intellectus et res significant, sed ipsae res alias res significant. Unde claret scientiam artium ad cognitionem divinarum scripturarum valde esse utilem." Richard of St. Victor, *Speculum ecclesiae*, PL 177:375.
[34] Hugh of St. Victor, *De scripturis et scriptoribus sacris praenotatiunculae*, xiv–xvi, PL 175:20–24. For "circumstances" and grammar, see pp. 73–4, below.
[35] *Glossa ordinaria in Canticum Canticorum*, ii.4, ed. Mary Dove, CCM 170:146–47 (my translation differs slightly from Dove's): "introduxit me rex in cellam uinarium ordinauit in me caritatem."

of exaltation as bride of the king, a metaphor still within the parameters of literal meaning. The objects and event of the sentence involve certain abstract things – in this case, the graciousness of the king who romances the bride and the bride's thrilled feeling. The Ordinary Gloss points to these abstractions with a paraphrase of the bride's words: "As soon as my throat tastes the sweetness of [the king's] grace [in taking me as his bride and lover], I feel myself recreated in spirit and carried away from love of earthly things into the realms above, as if, led into the wine cellar, I am refreshed with the smell of new wine and with drinking." The Gloss is still talking about the feeling she gets from the king's love, and it assumes that her love for him arises only from the thrill of his love, and not from the promise of sharing his kingly wealth. These observations should allure the reader. The metaphorical abstraction – the bride's elation at the king's graciousness, his wanting to give her his love – are so good, so compelling, that they must mean something more than earthly love, and accordingly the Gloss points to further abstractions, which are spiritual: "Allegorically, by 'wine' is signified the grace of the Holy Spirit. The wine cellar is the church, in whose unity the Holy Spirit is customarily given and received, so much so that God has built for himself a house, the church, gathered together from the whole world, which he has consecrated with the gifts of his Spirit."[36] The Gloss then explains the bride's feeling of love in this allegorical context of the church, describing it as the pure love that God arranges for people in good order (love of God, parents, sons, and servants), emphasizing, as Jesus insisted (Matthew 22.37, 39), the love of God above all else.[37] In addition, the references to the gifts of the Holy Spirit allude to the sacramental means by which grace is given. These allegories, prompted by words of the sentence, thus linked this amorous text with the main institution of religious life, the church, and its sacramental routines. But it also invested those things with other abstractions identified in the literal text, things not limited to individual words like "love" and "wine cellar," namely the emotions of love poetry – the elation, if not arousal, of receiving the love of a great man. Here, the Gloss did not need to restate what is already obvious to its medieval readers, that Christ loves his bride the church like this king. It linked the bride's response to the groom with a perfectly balanced universe of truth and love, divine and spiritual, and the associations, linking the earthly

---

[36] Ibid., pp. 146–9.
[37] This move illustrates well a definition of allegory given by Gerald Bruns, "[making sense allegorically] means integrating a text (and its meanings) into a radically new cultural environment": *Hermeneutics Ancient and Modern*, p. 83.

and the heavenly, established the beauty of the text for the monks and nuns who excelled at this kind of reading. To disclose links between the particular experience of love in this sentence and a divine universe was, as Judson Allen once said, "their ... poetic privilege." Karlfried Froehlich has aptly called this style of spiritual reading, upon other evidence, "affective interpretation."[38]

Interpreters found the same layered quality of abstractions in physical objects (for example, gemstones) and images (for example, an image of the dove of Psalm 68.13, as described and painted with silver, gold, and other colors by Hugo of Fouilloy, prior of Saint-Laurent near Amiens in the middle of the twelfth century).[39] The physical qualities of gemstones, such as they were understood, and abstractions associated with silver, gold, colors, and the characteristics and habits of animals (for example, doves), could prompt spiritual meanings.[40] Numbers could serve as the basis of allegory.[41] So too could events, as the example from the Song of Songs indicates:[42] it was not merely the text's words, the referents of single nouns, or the qualities of particular objects that prompted allegory. In the example from the Song of Songs, the *res*, the thing indicated by the text, was really the bride's response to the king's affection, portrayed in the event of her being led into the wine cellar. The poetic force of the allegory rests as much upon the scene, which portrays the reciprocal affections of lovers, as it does upon the transference of meaning in single names like "wine cellar." Events, or I should say entire scenes, that put individual allegorical elements (like the object "wine cellar") in order were as integral to allegorical reading as particular things in the text. In other words, there was no distinction between allegory and typology, and in fact typology – whereby Old Testament narratives serve as types of New Testament events – was the basis of allegory.[43]

---

[38] Judson Boyce Allen, *The Ethical Poetic of the Later Middle Ages* (Toronto: University of Toronto Press, 1982), p. 70; Froehlich, "Christian Interpretation," p. 498.

[39] Ohly, "Mittelalterliche Bedeutungsforschung," pp. 48–86 and plate 2.

[40] See the important study by Christel Meier, *Gemma spiritalis: Methode und Gebrauch der Edelsteinallegorese vom frühen Christentum bis ins 18. Jahrhundert* (Munich: Wilhelm Fink, 1977).

[41] See the exhaustive study by Heinz Meyer, *Die Zahlenallegorese im Mittelalter: Methode und Gebrauch* (Munich: Wilhelm Fink, 1975).

[42] For problems with *gesta* allegory, consider Ohly's introduction to *Schriften zum mittelalterlichen Bedeutungsforschung*, p. xix.

[43] Henri de Lubac distinguished between typological analogies of Old and New Testament events on the one hand and a richer, more personal spiritual comprehension implied by "allegory." De Lubac, *Exégèse médiévale*, 1/1:352–53. It is a weak distinction in that typology so defined nevertheless has as much to do with the soul as allegory. See D. W. Robertson, *Essays in Medieval Culture*, pp. 220–1. Others may see typology as a transference of meaning based on events and allegory as one based on objects. It is better to view allegory as something to do with imagistic narratives and one's response to entire scenes, contexts, and stories, and not as the deciphering

Belief in creation buttressed the theory of allegory, and allegory, in its twelfth-century formulation, likewise indicated a pervasive monastic attitude toward nature. Creation was a divine work, and the qualities of created things, their "properties," betrayed the character of their maker. "All nature bespeaks God. All nature teaches human beings. All nature imparts reason, and there is nothing barren in the universe."[44] The visible world was the necessary starting point for knowledge of God, and in the same way so too was sacred literature. What distinguished the Bible from other literature was not magical language but accurate representation of the real connection between visible and invisible reality, between a microscopic perspective on particular objects and a macroscopic, abstract perspective on the universe. Therefore, it was necessary to start with the most tangible things – the books, their histories and their manner of speaking – and to move gradually and self-consciously, girded with the liberal arts, from sign to thing to divine matters.

The progressive movement from biblical texts to abstract philosophical knowledge began with literal, historical meaning. Scholars who played a key role in the consolidation of gloss technique – Lanfranc, abbot of Bec (d. 1089), Berengar of Tours (d. 1088), Drogo of Paris (late eleventh century), and Bruno the Carthusian (d. 1101) – promoted the use of the non-mathematical core of the medieval liberal arts, the trivium

---

of words and objects, as I just tried to point out. See also Rosemond Tuve, *Allegorical Imagery* (Princeton University Press, 1966). In any case, as is often pointed out, the term "typology" was not used in medieval Europe, allegory being the preferred if sometimes ambiguous name, be it rhetorical or metaphysical and mystical. Patristic and medieval writers saw a distinction of convenience and not substance between what Augustine called *allegoria in factis*, events in the Old Testament that prefigure events in the New (typology), and what he called *allegoria in verbis* (allegory). Jean Pépin, *Dante et la tradition de l'allégorie* (Paris: J. Vrin, 1970), pp. 45–50 and *passim*. Turner, *Eros and Allegory*, pp. 102–4, 197–8, argues that allegory "is a literary device, a narrative metaphor, interpreted by reading off events in the narrative as metaphors for other events whose relation with one another is similar to the relation of the events in the allegorical narrative.... Typology, on the other hand, is not a literary, but a theological doctrine – or rather is based upon one, namely upon the theology of history according to which earlier events do not merely *match* later events in formal outline, but are prophetic anticipations of them." This seems to me an unnecessary distinction. Allegory, in this definition, is more restricted than the Victorine definition, which embraced the "reading off" of "events in the narrative" as revealing metaphysical facts, such that allegory was not really a literary device; it was more than literary. The evidence of this book will suggest that Turner is correct, however, to identify the literary qualities of allegory, as we find them in Thomas Aquinas, as factors that blur the requirement of spiritual explanation. The concept of prophecy in Turner's definition of typology in fact also exercised an important function in literal reading, as will become apparent in chapter 4. For additional perspectives on typology, see Whitman, "Present perspectives," *Interpretation and Allegory*, p. 42 and the literature cited there.

[44] Hugh of St. Victor, *Didascalicon*, vi.5, *PL* 176:805. For the relation of this hermeneutical conviction to medieval natural philosophy, consider Peter Harrison, *The Bible, Protestantism, and the Rise of Natural Science* (Cambridge University Press, 1998), pp. 34–63.

(grammar, rhetoric, and dialectic), in literal exegesis. The adaptation of the trivium to exegesis was especially evident in the work of the school of Laon at the turn of the eleventh to twelfth centuries and in the work of its most important teacher, Anselm of Laon (d. 1117).[45] The Victorines built on those foundations and demonstrated that this kind of literal exegesis was a prerequisite to spiritual knowledge. The result was a new sophistication in literal exegesis, represented in Andrew of St. Victor's Hebrew scholarship and in his recourse to rabbinical commentary for historical information.[46] His accomplishment was not superseded until nearly two hundred years later by the Old Testament sections of Nicholas of Lyra's postilla. Upon the establishment of universities, the faculties of theology required students to come with a Master of Arts degree, with the exception of members of religious orders (they were granted advanced standing for work done in monastic schools). The prerequisite reflects the ongoing, Augustinian conviction that the liberal arts support Bible study, and it reflects a scholastic goal: the reconciliation of textual, especially biblical, authority with rational analysis.[47]

The difference between literal and spiritual senses seemed clear. The fourfold division of meanings laid out by Cassian in the early fifth century now was taken to describe the standard alternatives. It was expressed in a rhyme first observed in a Dominican textbook of the late thirteenth century and repeated at the beginning of Nicholas of Lyra's postilla,

> Littera gesta docet
> quid credas allegoria
> quid agas tropologia
> quo tendas anagogia.
>
> The letter teaches events
> allegory what you should believe
> tropology what you should do
> anagogy where you should aim.

---

[45] Lobrichon, "Les gloses," p. 105.
[46] Smalley, *Study of the Bible*, pp. 112–95.
[47] For the liberal arts and Bible study, Evans, *The Language and Logic of the Bible*, 2 vols. (Cambridge University Press, 1984–5), 1:31–6. For authority, Martin Grabmann, *Geschichte der scholastischen Methode*, 2 vols. (Freiburg im Breisgau: Herder, 1909–11), 1:33–7 and *passim*, and most importantly, Hermann Schüssler, *Der Primat der Heiligen Schrift als theologisches und kanonistisches Problem in Spätmittelalter* (Wiesbaden: Franz Steiner, 1977), pp. 294–97; Albert Lang, *Die Wege der Glaubensbegründung bei den Scholastikern des 14. Jahrhunderts* (Münster: Aschendorf, 1930); idem, *Die theologische Prinzipienlehre*. Landgraf, *Einführung*; De Ghellinck, "'Pagina' et 'sacra pagina'"; idem, *Le mouvement théologique du douzième siècle* (Paris: Desclée-De Brouwer, 1948). De Ghellinck emphasized, more than Landgraf, the role of Aristotelian dialectic and methods developed in the study of law to effect the transition from the contemplative reading of sacred literature to scholastic theology.

The typical example is Jerusalem, which comes straight from Cassian.[48] According to history, Jerusalem is a city of the Jews. According to allegory, it is the church. According to tropology it is the human soul. According to anagogy, it is the heavenly city of God. This sounds like a cliché because it was, and like most clichés it exaggerated the obvious: that biblical texts and nouns yielded historical meanings more remote from the reader or the reader's world and other meanings that touched on a present religious life – the church, the moral condition of the soul, the future. The fourfold sense indicated a process of abstraction and the possibility of lithe movement, seldom if ever a procedure for chopping Bible passages into quarters.

But theologians had difficulty assuming that the literal sense of the Bible was indeed remote from contemporary readers, and they expressed this in three well-known ways, which will be explored in detail in the remainder of this book. First in the early twelfth century in the Psalms commentary of Gilbert of Poitiers, some scholars began to insist that literal meaning held priority in theological argument. In the thirteenth century, some, Thomas Aquinas being the most important, constructed their discipline as a unique human science of divine things, and in this science the literal sense of scripture was to exercise a definitive role.[49] Secondly, they continued to grant spiritual senses broad validity. Scholars who accepted the priority of the literal sense in theological argument did not always restrict themselves to literal meanings when they argued; moreover, the elaborate use of the spritual senses in preaching suggests that people generally took allegory as persuasive interpretation.[50] Thirdly, they discovered literal explanations of non-literal speech. In some books of the Bible the language seemed literally spiritual. Bonaventure and Thomas Aquinas recognized a multiple literal sense and a "parabolic" meaning of texts.[51] According to Nicholas of Lyra, some Psalms refer to

---

[48] Froehlich, "Christian Interpretation," p. 512; Cassian, *Collationes*, xiv.8. *Conférences*, ed. E. Pichery, 3 vols., Sources Chrétiennes, vols. 42, 54, 64 (Paris: Editions du Cerf, 1955–9), 2:190–1.

[49] Froehlich, "Christian Interpretation," p. 502; Lang, *Theologische Prinzipienlehre*; Chenu, *Théologie comme science*.

[50] Beryl Smalley, "Use of the "Spiritual" Sense of Scripture in Persuasion and Argument by Scholars in the Middle Ages," *Recherches de Théologie Ancienne et Médiévale* 52 (1985): 44–63. Eberhard Winkler, *Exegetische Methoden bei Meister Eckhart* (Tübingen: J. C. B. Mohr, 1965), pp. 65–69. Thomas Aquinas appears to have consistently avoided the use of spiritual senses in argumentation, but without denying the religious value of non-literal meaning. Marc Aillet, *Lire la Bible avec S. Thomas. Le passage de la littera à la res dans la Somme théologique* (Fribourg: Editions Universitaires, 1993), pp. 241–51.

[51] De Lubac, *L'Exégèse médiévale*, 2/2:283. Winkler, *Exegetische Methoden*, pp. 7–8, notes that Aquinas saw the "sensus parabolicus" as a kind of literal meaning, whereas Bonaventure, following Peter Lombard, could also contrast parabolic meaning with the historical sense.

Christ according to their historical meaning, not according to allegory, as the classical fourfold division of senses would imply. Late medieval interpreters like Lyra, Paul of Burgos, Matthew Döring, and Jean Gerson argued that prophets wrote both with a view to their own circumstances and with the intention of predicting the coming of Christ – a double literal sense in the prophets.[52] How could the difference of literal and spiritual senses be absolute?

We will see other evidence of the fading distinction between the literal and the spiritual in the late Middle Ages in chapter three. It marks an important change of attitude toward the text. In late antiquity, Christians, following the precedent of the allegorical interpretation of Homer and Hesiod by Greek philosophers from centuries before and the precedent of Philo of Alexandria's allegorical interpretation of the Septuagint, used allegory to evade the apparent absurdity or obscenity of some biblical passages. The point was repeated by the Victorines: "the Divine Page, in its literal sense, contains many things which seem both to be opposed to each other and, sometimes, to impart something which smacks of the absurd or the impossible. But the spiritual meaning admits no opposition; in it, many things can be different from one another, but none can be opposed."[53] The problem was, to theologians, a psychological one: some things in the Bible could excite the soul the wrong way, but the spiritual meaning of scripture could only do the soul good. By the late Middle Ages this use of spiritual interpretation as a kind of interpretation of last resort had lost some of its force. The distinction between truth spoken obscurely in absurd stories and truth spoken plainly could be historicized in terms of the obscurity of the Old Testament and the transparency of the New, as it was pointedly stated by Jacques Fournier, for example, in the early fourteenth century.[54] If so, the problem was not really psychological at all; the frame was not the soul but the linear frame

---

[52] W. Werbeck, *Jacobus Perez von Valencia. Untersuchungen zu seinem Psalmenkommentar* (Tübingen: J. C. B. Mohr, 1959), pp. 120–1, 130. For Lyra, see Mark Zier, "Nicholas of Lyra on the Book of Daniel," *Nicholas of Lyra: The Senses of Scripture*, ed. P. D. W. Krey and L. Smith (Leiden: Brill, 2000), pp. 173–93.

[53] Hugh of St. Victor, *Didascalicon* vi.4, trans. J. Taylor, p. 140.

[54] Jacques Fournier, *Postilla super Mattheum*, Barcelona, Biblioteca Nacional de Catalunya, Ms. 550, f. 12ra (I follow the orthography of the manuscript): "In veteri enim testamento multe erant hystorie que ad devotionem animum non excitabant, ymo magis quandoque ad lasciuiam, sicut patet in multis hystorijs, quandoque etiam ad crudelitatem, sicut etiam patet in multis locis. Hystoria autem noui testamenti omnis excitat homines, si diligenter attendant, ad devotionem, et maxime domini facta pro nobis, ac etiam promissa." For the commentary, see Anneliese Maier, "Der Kommentar Benedikts XII. zum Matthaeus-Evangelium," *Archivum Pontificum Historicum* 6 (1968): 398–405.

of history. In addition, there was in the late Middle Ages a different sense of the text as such, as one can see in an observation made by Denys van Leeuwen in the mid fifteenth century. He criticizes theologians who say that "the literal meaning is that which is first signified by the literal words" while claiming that there are places in scripture, "especially the prophets," impossible to interpret literally. He offers an alternative directly opposed to the Victorine theory of biblical signification, built on the idea of authorial intention. The literal sense is the meaning first intended by the author, therefore "every passage of holy scripture has a literal meaning, which is not always what is first signified by the literal words, but is often what is designated through the thing that is signified by the literal words."[55] What the Victorines called spiritual meaning, Denys called literal. Even Nicholas of Lyra, Denys alleged, was too allegorical when occasionally appealing to a sense "rather mystical and spiritual than literal," for example, in his exegesis of Jacob's deathbed speech to his son. Against Lyra, Denys said Jacob "speaks metaphorically... namely through similes of corporeal things. In such language, the literal sense is not what is immediately signified through terms, but what is signified through those things, according to their properties and the similarities to that which is principally designated." He rehearses examples: a lion is David, "or rather Christ"; a vine "literally designates the synagogue, Christ, and even the church."[56]

Interpreters began to recognize that what, in the twelfth century, was described as a quality of thought *beyond* speech in fact was a quality *of* speech.[57] This reflects their uncertainty about the difference between what Denys Turner has called "semantically literal speech" and spiritually allegorical speech, a topic to which I will return in chapter 2.[58] Late

[55] Dionysius Carthusiensis, *Ennaratio in Job*, art. 13, *Opera omnia*, 42 vols. (Montreuil: Typus Cartusiae S. M. de Pratis, 1896–1935), 4:362–3. Consider also *Opera* 14/2:725. I would not agree that Denys' exegesis "runs together with an hermeneutical and theological deracination" or that it exemplifies "a marked hardening of the lines in the practical employment of the doctrine of the four senses," a conclusion based exclusively on Denys' *Songs* commentary (see Turner, *Eros and Allegory*, pp. 159–74, 411–48, esp. 168–69, 171). It seems to me that Denys van Leeuwen does not conceive his exegesis of the Song of Songs as an allegory distinct from the historical sense because "Solomon, before his downfall and filled with the Holy Spirit, resplendent with the spirit of prophecy, knew in his spirit the mysteries of Christ," and he then enumerates precisely those things that pertain to allegorical, tropological, and anagogical senses: they are expressions of the literal sense. Ibid., pp. 414–15.
[56] *Enarratio in Genesim*, art. 100, *Opera* 1:444.
[57] For rhetorical allegory in the eleventh and twelfth centuries, Hennig Brinkmann, *Mittelalterliche Hermeneutik* (Tübingen: Max Niemeyer, 1980), pp. 214–26, and especially Reynolds, *Medieval Reading*, pp. 110–49. See also Winkler, *Exegetische Methoden*, pp. 85–9.
[58] Turner, *Eros to Allegory*, pp. 93–4.

medieval interpreters still talked about progressively abstract knowledge and literal meaning as analogous to knowledge of the natural world, assuming a metaphysical context of reading, in which minds rose to God. For example, the Carmelite John Baconthorpe described cognition according to the "fourfold sense" of natural knowledge. The first is literal, in which one procedes from ideas in one's mind to ideas of nature itself, much the way one moves from the letter of the Bible to a thing indicated by it. This begins an abstract movement that can go in three directions: to God (spiritual knowledge), to the forms of natural things (figurative knowledge), or to human society (moral knowledge).[59] The Franciscan Pierre Auriol encouraged his reader to ascend from the corporeal to the spiritual: to take "the brisk flight of meditation," "like birds," by seeking profound meaning in the sacred letter, by going from term to meaning, from meaning to matter, from matter to reason, and from reason to the truth. Truth is derived from the "literal understanding, the superficial meaning, the plain discourse of the narrative."[60] But a gradual, rhetorical turn in the way scholars understood literal meaning reduced the difference between literal and spiritual interpretations: it looked like a fine distinction, but it was not quite so relevant any more.[61] For their convictions about ascending knowledge could rest upon a literal understanding of figurative speech.

Why? Whereas in the twelfth century interpreters might assign some books of the Bible to one or another field (Genesis relates to physics, the letters of Paul to ethics, and the Psalms to logic, noted Honorius Augustodunensis), in the late Middle Ages intellectuals took a more uniform approach, systematically relating the main themes of the Old and New Testaments to one subject.[62] The subject of the Bible is the essence

---

[59] Johannes Bacon, *Questiones in quatuor libros Sententiarum et Quodlibetales*, 2 vols. (Cremona: Marcus Antonius Balpierus, 1618), 2:225, 226.

[60] Petrus Aureolus, *Compendium litteralis sensus totius divinae scripturae*, Biblioteca de la Universida de Barcelona, Ms. 121, ff. 2vb–3ra: "Ascendamus primo cum volatu perspicue meditationis, ut aves, quia scriptum est quod in lege is meditabitur die ac nocte [qui] uult in ea proficere. In sacris quidem litteris profunda est intelligencia requirenda, ubi per uocem ad intellectum, per intellectum ad rem, per rem ad rationem, per rationem peruenitur ad ueritatem." Consider also Albert the Great, Henry of Ghent, and Jacob Perez of Valencia: de Lubac, *L'Exegèse*, p. 308; Werbeck, *Jacobus Perez von Valencia*, p. 103.

[61] Consider also Jean Gerson's criticism of the "sensus logicalis" and his insistence that the Bible bears its own logic. Karlfried Froehlich, "'Always to Keep to the Literal Sense Means to Kill One's Soul': The State of Biblical Hermeneutics at the Beginning of the Fifteenth Century," *Literary Uses of Typology from the Late Middle Ages to the Present*, ed. E. Miner (Princeton University Press, 1977), pp. 20–48, here 42–3.

[62] *PL* 172:270. Häring, "Commentary and Hermeneutics," p. 187 and n. 140. The themes of the Old and New Testament were discussed in terms of the "division" of the Bible into parts.

of God effecting through Christ the work of human restauration, said Alexander of Hales.⁶³ It is theology, Bonaventure explained: a book that illumined the now unreadable book of creation, whose teachings have been obscured by sin.⁶⁴ It is theological narrative in simple form, said Nicholas Gorran.⁶⁵ According to Lyra, the subject is God – or Christ, according to Johann Michael, Ugolino of Orvieto, and Jan Hus.⁶⁶ Jacques Fournier agreed, but noted that in the Gospels the subject is more specifically defined as Christ, divine and human.⁶⁷ These amoeba-like ideas could encompass, maybe enclose, the variety of biblical genres, encouraging readers to think of the text as a uniform body of literature, "the book

---

⁶³ Michael Seybold, *Die Offenbarung. Von der Schrift bis zum Ausgang der Scholastik*, vol. 1, fascicle 1a of *Handbuch der Dogmengeschichte* (Freiburg: Herder, 1971), pp. 120–1.

⁶⁴ Bonaventura, 1 *Sent.*, Prol. q. 1, *Opera omnia*, 10 vols. (Quaracchi: Collegium S. Bonaventure, 1882–1902), 1:7. Seybold, *Offenbarung*, pp. 121–8. This form of argument was later adapted by John Calvin, *Institutio Christianae religionis*, I.vi.1, ed. P. Barth and W. Niesel, *Opera selecta* 3:60–4. There was a strong Franciscan tradition identifying the subject of theology as Christ. Petrus Aureolus, 1 *Sent.*, Proe. v, pp. 302ff. Ockham, 1 *Sent.* Prol. q. ix, Guillelmus de Ockham, *Scriptum in librum primum Sententiarum ordinatio*, ed. Gedeon Gál, vol. 1 of *Opera theologica* (St. Bonaventura, NY: Franciscan Institute, 1967), pp. 226–76 (and for John Duns Scotus, ibid., p. 227 n. 1).

⁶⁵ Nicholas de Gorran, *Postilla super Genesim*, Würzburg, Universitätsbibliothek, M.p.th. f. 151, f. 11rb: "in canone sacre scripture, id est in novo et veteri testamentis, traditur theologia per modum simplicis narrationis ueritatis simpliciter assentientis. In libro sentenciarum traditur per modum scrutationis ueritatis inquirentis et defendentis compendiose."

⁶⁶ *Glossa cum Lyra*, 1:3r. See also Schwendinger, "Vaticiniis," pp. 163–6, Minnis, "Intention," p. 20, and M. Fischer, "Des Nicholaus von Lyra Postillae perpetuae in vetus et novum testamentum in ihrem eigenthumlichen Unterschied von der gleichzeitigen Schriftauslegung," *Jahrbücher für Protestantische Theologie* 15/3 (1889): 452. For Johann Michael *Lectura super Bibliam*, Munich, Bayerische Staatsbibliothek, Clm 9411 (= *RB* 9:215–18 nos. 4783, 4785.1, 4786, 4787, 4789–98), f. 7r. For the Augustinian friar Ugolino of Orvieto, who wrote in the second or third quarter of the fourteenth century either as a master at Paris or as a lector in Italy, see Willigis Eckermann, "Zwei neuentdeckte theologische Principien Hugolins von Orvieto," *Schwerpunkte und Wirkungen des Sentenzenkommentars Hugolins von Orvieto O.E.S.A.* (Würzburg: Augustinus-Verlag, 1990), pp. 43–83, here 49–65. There is no indication when either of the two inaugural lectures were delivered. See also Adolar Zumkeller, "Leben und Werke Hugolins von Orvieto," ibid., pp. 3–42. Jan Hus equated Christ, the word of God, and the Bible: 1 *Sent.*, incepcio, 1; *Super IV. Sententiarum*, pp. 14–15. John Wyclif treated the poverty and humility of Christ as the subject of the Bible (expressly stated in his Psalms commentary, but according to Benrath, typical of all his exegesis): Gustav Adolf Benrath, "Traditionsbewußtsein, Schriftverständnis und Schriftprinzip bei Wyclif," *Antiqui und Moderni*, ed. A. Zimmermann (Berlin: Walter de Gruyter, 1974), pp. 359–82, here 367–9. Consider also Wyclif's "scopos" of the poverty and humility of Christ (ibid). Consider also Alexander of Hales (Seybold, *Offenbarung*, pp. 120–1); Bonaventure, 1 *Sent.*, Prol. quaestio 1, *Opera omnia*, 1:7; Petrus Aureoli, *Scriptum super primum Sententiarum*, ed. E. M. Buytaert (St. Bonaventure, NY: The Franciscan Institute, 1952–6), pp. 302–3.

⁶⁷ Jacques Fournier, *Postilla*, f. 10ra: "Sicut enim in factione rerum naturalium, materia uel subiectum dicitur fundamentum factionis earum, ut patet i. Metaphysice, ita etiam illud de quo tractant scientie dicitur scientiarum fundamentum, materia autem et subiectum totius scripture, licet sit Deus, tamen in euangelijs principaliter tractatur de Christo uero Deo et homine et eius dictis et factis et de reductione hominum ad ipsum. Unde et in principio libri unum ex quattuor dicitur materia euangelii sunt scientie trinitatis misterium, Christus secundum diuinam et humanam naturam dictam et factam eius maiorum que facta et dicta ad ipsum."

containing sacred scripture, which although divided into many partial books, comprises one book, which is called by the general name 'Bible,' and is named 'the book of life,'" said Nicholas of Lyra.[68] The intention was, after all, to give Jewish scripture an unambivalently Christian meaning and to clarify the distinction between sacred and profane writing, as we have seen.[69] By the middle of the thirteenth century, scholars also intended to show that theology was a coherent body of knowledge to some degree consistent with Aristotle's definition of science in the *Posterior Analytics*, so they argued that the *principia*, "principles," upon which this science is built are, to one extent or another, taken from scripture.[70] There can be no doubt that the Bible was universally accepted as the foremost religious authority in late medieval scholasticism, all the way down to the dawn of the Reformation.[71] For this reason Bible study remained commonplace throughout the late Middle Ages. It had a fixed place in the theology curriculum from the beginnings of universities through the Reformation.[72]

Hugh of St. Victor encouraged the idea that the Bible is a uniform body of literature. He noted that the Bible is divided harmoniously in two, the Old and New Testaments. Each of these is subdivided in three.

---

[68] Nicholas of Lyra, first prologue to the Bible, *Postilla super totam Bibliam*, f. 1ra, commenting on Jerome's letter to Paulinus and its contrast between scripture and the books of Plato and Demosthenes, which are about the present life and can be called books of death: "Sed liber continens sacram scripturam, que licet in multis libris partialibus diuidatur sub uno tamen libro continetur, qui nomine generali biblia dicitur liber vite proprie nominatur."

[69] See p. 15, above.

[70] Chenu, *La théologie comme science au treizième siècle*, pp. 37–52; eadem, *La théologie au douzième siècle* (Paris: Vrin, 1957), pp. 196–209.

[71] Schüssler demonstrated this conclusively in *Der Primat der heiligen Schrift*. See also Evans, *Language and Logic*, 1:73; Paul de Vooght, *Les sources de la doctrine chrétienne d'après les théologiens du quatorzième siècle et du début du quinzième siècle* (Bruges: Desclée de Brouwer, 1954); George Tavard, *Holy Writ or Holy Church: The Crisis of the Protestant Reformation* (New York: Harper and Brothers, 1959); Heiko Augustinus Oberman, *The Harvest of Medieval Theology. Gabriel Biel and Late Medieval Nominalism* (Cambridge, Mass.: Harvard University Press, 1963), pp. 361–422. For the relation of literal interpretation to emerging scientific attitudes toward nature in early modern Europe, see Harrison, *The Bible, Protestantism, and the Rise of Natural Science*. For Lyra, see Krey and Smith, eds., *Nicholas of Lyra: The Senses of Scripture*. For Wyclif and the Lollards: Smalley, *English Friars and Antiquity in the Early Fourteenth Century*; William J. Courtenay, "The Bible in the Fourteenth Century: Some Observations," *Church History* 54 (1985): 176–87; Margaret Gibson, "The Study of the Bible in the Middle Ages," *Journal of Ecclesiastical History* 39 (1988): 230–2. See also Froehlich, Feld, Turner, and Smalley in the bibliography.

[72] Jacques Verger, "Patterns," and Monika Asztalos "The Faculty of Theology," in *Universities in the Middle Ages*, ed. H. De Ridder-Symoens, vol. 1 of *A History of the University in Europe* (Cambridge University Press, 1992), pp. 35–74, 409–41; Pierre Glorieux, "L'enseignement au Moyen Age. Techniques et méthodes en usage à la Faculté de Théologie de Paris au xiiie siècle," *Archives d'Histoire Doctrinale et Littéraire du Moyen Age* 43 (1968): 65–189; Courtenay, *Schools and Scholars*, pp. 41–8.

The Old Testament contains law, prophets, and hagiographers, and the New Testament contains Gospels, apostles, and fathers of the church, whose "works are so limitless that they cannot be numbered."[73] Within each Testament, the parts progress from past to present, from doctrine to practice, beginning with the core teachings of law and Gospel, which through books about their dissemination (prophets and apostles) culminate in books about living (hagiographers and fathers).[74]

At the core of this view of the Bible's organization lies a conviction that biblical literature and its history are arranged to facilitate spiritual progress. The Bible is organized to be effective, just as the New Testament, it was believed, builds upon and improves the Old. Even when the parts of the Bible were put in a linear, historical frame, as by Bonaventure, it is important to remember this underlying interest in human progress.[75] The point was made at length by the late thirteenth-century Dominican Nicholas Gorran, who pointed out how the subdivisions of biblical parts reflect the symmetrical structure of the two main parts, the Old and New Testaments.[76] Each subdivision and its subcategories present figures of Christ in ways unique to each particular genre.[77] Prophecy, with the law and the Psalms one of three principal parts of the Old Testament, is divided into that which concerns the head of the church, that is, Christ, and that which concerns Christ's mystical body, the church itself, and he cites textual examples of each.[78] The New Testament presents the same content without figures, in two categories: knowledge about Christ himself (the Gospels) or about Christ's body, the church (the rest of the New Testament).[79] The latter receives a further subdivision into books dealing with its origin (Acts), its consummation (the Apocalypse), and its progress (the letters), which last group is also divided into books that address particular groups: Latin (Romans), Greek (the Corinthian letters), and Jewish (Hebrews) converts or common subordinate clergy (1 Corinthians to 2 Thessalonians); and prelates (1 Timothy to Hebrews).[80] The concept of the Bible's organization around the two Testaments seems to have remained prevalent in the late Middle Ages. In the fourteenth century,

---

73 Hugh of St. Victor, *Didascalicon*, iv.2, trans. J. Taylor, pp. 103–4.
74 Ibid.
75 For Bonaventure, Seybold, *Offenbarung*, p. 124. Consider also Albert the Great's division of the Bible into three kinds of law: law given (Pentateuch, wisdom literature, prophets, and Psalms), law received (historical books of the Old Testament), and law fulfilled (New Testament). Froehlich, "Christian Interpretation," 536.
76 From Nicholas Gorran's commentary on the preface to the Bible, which appears at the beginning of his *Postilla* on Genesis, f. 9vb.
77 Ibid., ff. 9vb–10rb.   78 Ibid., f. 10rb.   79 Ibid., f. 10rb–10va.   80 Ibid., f. 10va.

John Baconthorpe and Nicholas of Lyra used the distinction of Old and New Testaments to describe the organization of a single book of the Bible, the Gospel according to Matthew.[81] Nicolau Eimeric broke up the Gospels into particular aspects of Christ's identity and life: Matthew treated his humanity; John, his divinity; Luke, his passion; and Mark, his resurrection.[82] The Gospels record Christ's history and doctrines, said Heinrich of Langenstein.[83] In the early fifteenth century, Denys the Carthusian, who attributed the three-fold division of the Bible to Jerome and his Jewish source, offered little more than a paraphrase of Hugh of St. Victor.[84] Pierre Auriol may have been the only scholar to challenge – or at least to challenge in a book as influential as his *Compendium* – the basic three-fold division of the two Testaments with a more strictly literary division of the Bible into eight parts distinguished by "the eight methods of teaching that it assumes" ("scriptura divina potest dividi in octo partes principales, secundum octo modos docendi quos assumit").[85] In his view, the literature is distinguished not by its theological content *per se*, but by distinct modes of writing: 1. political and legal, 2. chronical and historical, 3. "hymnic" and quasi-poetical, 4. prophetic and homiletical, 5. dialectical and disputational, 6. monastic or ethical and consultative, 7. testimonial and affirmative, 8. epistolary and conditional.[86] By making this distinction rest on writing, which I would say is an approach more literary than the symmetrical division of Testaments and parts, he could still preserve the theologian's conviction that biblical teaching taken as a

---

[81] See Ocker, "Fusion," p. 145.
[82] Nicolaus Eimericus, *Postilla super epistolam Pauli ad Galatos*, Barcelona, Biblioteca Nacional de Catalunya, Ms. 1280, 1:3v. His Matthew commentary exists in autograph (Barcelona, Biblioteca Nacional de Catalunya, Ms. 1278, vols. 1–3), and upon comparison with it, this seems to be an autograph as well. The Matthew commentary also gives better indication of its origins. It was begun at Barcelona and completed at Rome on 10 April 1377, according to the explicit (3:221v). At the incipit (1:1v), Francis Bonis, OP, explains that Eimeric wrote the text in his own hand; it came into Francis's possession because he had been the scribe to copy it for the convent library (presumably of Gerona, Nicolau's home convent, to which his books must have returned after his death). It was allegedly begun in 1367 as the first of the commentaries on the Gospels, written as the inquisitor travelled. See Klaus Reinhardt, "Das Werk des Nicolaus von Lyra im mittelalterlichen Spanien," *Traditio*, 48 (1987): 344–6, for a very good summary of Nicolau's exegesis (based on Seville exemplars), and p. 344 for the dates. The commentary on Luke was begun in Avignon on 1 May 1383 and completed in Gerona on 12 January 1387, according to its explicit: Barcelona, Biblioteca Nacional de Catalunya, Cat., Ms. 1287, f. 139r. See also Reinhardt, "Nicolaus," p. 345 n. 107.
[83] Ibid., ff. 187rb–188rb. Consider also the fifteenth-century exegete Alfonso Fernández de Madrigal el Tostado: Reinhardt, "Werk," p. 352.
[84] Dionysius Carthusiensis, *Enarratio in Genesim*, art. iv., *Opera* 1:13.
[85] Petrus Aureolus, *Compendium*, f. 6ra.
[86] Ibid. See also A. Teetaert, "Pierre Aureol," *DthC* 12/2: 1835–7.

whole had a single purpose and a single subject, in spite of the literary variety of its parts.

Religious doctrine was fused with literary description in the late medieval concept of the Bible as a book. This fusion of doctrine and criticism is also apparent in another aspect of the definition of scripture that I will discuss at greater length in chapter four.[87] In prefaces to their commentaries (these were sometimes expositions of the letter of Jerome that served as a preface to the Bible), following twelfth-century precedents again, theologians used Aristotle's four "causes" to describe scripture as literature, and this helped them clarify the importance of human, historical authors with circumstantial intentions that determined meanings, as Alastair Minnis has shown.[88] The "causes" always included divine authorship. The actual exegesis of people as scholastic as Thomas Aquinas (a champion of authorial intention) or as mystical as Meister Eckhart was extremely doctrinal, and this characteristic reflects their conviction that biblical language, with its distinctly religious purposes, informed their intellectual enterprise.[89] Preoccupations with technical theological subject matter are also reflected in the addition of "questions" and digressions within carefully executed works, like John Baconthorpe's commentary on the Gospel according to Matthew with its discussions of political theory, or Jacques Fournier's commentary on the same Gospel with its refutation of textbook heresies, and in hasty expositions, like Johann Müntzinger's gloss to the Lord's Prayer.[90] Such preoccupations are consistent, as I will explain in chapter four, with common opinions about the authority of scripture and with the desire, even among interpreters critical of the church, like John Wyclif, to find interpretations consistent with church tradition.[91]

---

[87] See pp. 123ff., below.

[88] Minnis, *Medieval Theory of Authorship*, and for sources in translation, Minnis and Scott, *Medieval Literary Theory and Criticism*.

[89] Thomas Domanyi, *Der Römerbriefkommentar des Thomas von Aquin* (Frankfurt am Main: Peter Lang, 1979); Aillet, *Lire*, pp. 89–98. Winkler, *Exegetische Methoden*, pp. 75–84.

[90] Beryl Smalley, "John Baconthorpe's Postill on St. Matthew," *Medieval and Renaissance Studies*, 4 (1958): 91–145, reprinted in eadem, *Studies in Medieval Thought and Learning* (London: Hambledon Press, 1981), pp. 289ff. For Aquinas, Domanyi, *Römerbriefkommentar*, p. 270. For early examples, de Lubac, *L'Exégése*, pp. 305ff. Jean de Hesdin's commentary on Titus goes so far as to make each word of the text the title of a theological subject: ibid., p. 312; Johann Müntzinger, *Expositio super oratione dominica*, Würzburg, Universitätsbibliothek, M.ch.f. 109, ff. 316r–328r.

[91] Conflicting interpretations could be adjudicated by appeal to the papacy, a general council, the consensus of patristic opinion, or the exegete; theologians disagreed. See Schüssler, *Primat der Heiligen Schrift*, pp. 294ff. For the way authorities helped negotiate differences in exegesis, consider Ocker, "Fusion," pp. 131–51. For Wyclif and his desire to interpret consistently with tradition, Benrath, "Traditionsbewußtsein." Jan Hus had the same desire, but Gabriel Biel, who

These various examples point to the diversity of interests evident in late medieval commentaries. To interpreters, the language of scripture embraced a realm of thought that invited abstraction and argument and debate. Aquinas once said, "every truth that can be adapted to the sacred text, without prejudice to the latter, is the sense of holy scripture." This reflects the fact that the Bible became a professional text for clergy and their teachers, whose culture was shaped by theological discourse. Exegesis became a workshop of ideas, be they the ideas of political or natural philosophy or the ideas of salvation and religious self-improvement.[92] This fusion of biblical text and questioning minds raises a number of issues, not least of which is the enormous matter of the translation of this scholastic and clerical exegetical imagination into popular culture, which I cannot address here.[93] My task in this book is to study how scholasticism shaped attitudes toward the text. What rational habits (not merely doctrines) are displayed in biblical commentaries? What, in particular, were their semantic and rhetorical assumptions?

unlike Hus held the papacy to be an infallible guide of the church's belief, did not describe the literal meaning of the Bible as consistent with papal opinion: Helmut Feld, *Die Anfänge der modernen biblischen Hermeneutik in der spätmittelalterlichen Theologie* (Wiesbaden: Franz Steiner, 1977), pp. 60, 69. Wendelin Steinbach equated scriptural and ecclesiastical authority, ibid., pp. 72–73. Consider also the political exegesis of Jean Major: A. Ganoczy, "Jean Major, exégète gallican," *Recherches de Science Religieuse* 56 (1968): 457–95, here 495. Jean Gerson assumed strong consistency between scripture and patristic opinion: Mark S. Burrows, "Jean Gerson on the 'Traditioned Sense' of Scripture as an Argument for an Ecclesiastical Hermeneutic," *Biblical Hermeneutics in Historical Perspective*, pp. 152–72.

[92] Thomas Aquinas, *On the Power of God*, trans. L. Shapcote (Westminster, Md.: Newman Press, 1952), ii.9; Froehlich, "Christian Interpretation," p. 546. Buc, *L'Ambiguïté du livre*; Christel Meier, "Argumentationsformen kritischer Reflexion zwischen Naturwissenschaft und Allegorese," *Frühmittelalterliche Studien* 12 (1978): 116–59; Karlfried Froehlich, "Saint Peter, Papal Primacy, and the Exegetical Tradition, 1150–1300," *The Religious Roles of the Papacy: Ideals and Realities, 1150–1300*, ed. Christopher Ryan (Toronto: Pontifical Institute of Mediaeval Studies, 1989), pp. 3–44.

[93] Anne Hudson, *The Premature Reformation. Wycliffite Texts and Lollard History*, (Oxford: Clarendon, 1988), pp. 228–77, summarizes the survey of 250 manuscripts of the Lollard Bible, including the glossed texts and the translations of Jerome's prologues. The glosses were carried out, notwithstanding the points of Lollard doctrine, in a typically scholastic fashion, drawing heavily from the Ordinary Gloss, Nicholas of Lyra, and a variety of orthodox theologians. James Morey has pointed out the availability of French and English paraphrases of the Bible in the twelfth through fourteenth centuries and the role of the *Historia scholastica* as source: "Peter Comestor," pp. 6–35. See also the chapters by Lockwood, Foster, and Morreale in *The Cambridge History of the Bible*, 2: 415–36, 252–65, 465–91. For learned cultures and folklore, consider also Michel Lauwers, "'Religion populaire,' culture folklorique, mentalités," *Revue d'Histoire Ecclésiastique* 82 (1987): 221–58, and Piero Camporesi, *Rustici e buffoni* (Turin: Einaudi, 1991), pp. 3–33. The role of visual images in devotion was directly analogous to the movement from scripture to religious knowledge. Consider Sixton Ringbom, *Icon to Narrative. The Rise of the Dramatic Close-Up in Sixteenth-Century Painting* (Åbo Akademi, 1965).

CHAPTER 2

Signification

This chapter looks more deeply at the signification of biblical language. It considers two distinct explanations for it, stressing the importance of an alternative to the Victorine view (section 1). It then considers how this alternative suggested that the Bible represents a world of thought (section 2).

1. SIGNIFICATION AND ALLEGORY

The medieval distinction between literal and spiritual meaning depended upon the rationale summed up in the sentence, "Not only words, but things also are representational."[1] Interpreters of the Bible often repeated and presupposed this hermeneutical theorem in the fourteenth and fifteenth centuries.[2] Where did it come from? It amounts to an

---

[1] Richard of St. Victor, *Excerptiones*, ii.3, *PL* 177:205; *De scripturis et scriptoribus sacris*, xiv, *PL* 175:20f. Ohly, "Vom geistigen Sinn des Wortes im Mittelalter," pp. 4–5 and n. 6, pp. 30–1. A distinct, more decidedly rhetorical approach was pursued by Abelard. Consider *Commentaria in epistolam Pauli ad Romanos*, prologus, CCL 11:41–44, translated in Minnis and Scott, *Medieval Literary Theory and Criticism*, pp. 100–05. But he exercised little immediate influence. David Luscombe, "The Bible in the Work of Peter Abelard and of His School," *Neue Richtungen in der hoch-und spätmittelalterlichen Bibelexegese*, ed. R. E. Lerner (Munich: Oldenbourg, 1996), pp. 79–93. Cf. M. T. Clanchy, *Abelard: A Medieval Life* (Oxford: Blackwell, 1997), p. 82, who downplays the significance of exegesis in Abelard's thought.

[2] The formula was repeated, for example, by Nicholas of Lyra in the first prologue to his *Postilla* before moving to his famous complaint of the neglect of the literal meaning in his second prologue, to which I will come in due course (*Glossa cum Lyra*, f. 3va; the definition of literal and spiritual meanings is also repeated in the so-called moral prologue, using the example of Jerusalem, ibid., f. 4rb); by Hermann of Schildesche (Zumkeller, *Schrifttum*, p. 23; L, f. 107vb–108ra; V, f. 132r; B, f. 134v–135r; M, f. 72r–72v [see selection 3 of the Appendix for the sigla]); by Heinrich of Langenstein (Henricus de Hassia, *Commentaria in prologis Biblie et Genesin*, Stadtbibliothek Mainz, Hs. I 449, f. 232rb–232va, an interesting passage on whether Latin can convey all the meaning of the Hebrew Bible); by Jan Milič of Kroměříž in a "sermon" that serves as a "compend of the ways sacred scripture can be expounded," with its thorough exposition of the standard four-fold division based upon the difference between the semantics of *vox* and *res* (Munich, Bayerische Staatsbibliothek, Clm 3097, ff. 240r–249v, here f. 241rb; the explicit gives the title), and by Denys the Carthusian (Dionysius Carthusiensis, *Summae fidei orthodoxae*, prima pars, art. 1, *Opera*

31

adaptation of St. Augustine's description of natural signification.³ According to it, biblical knowledge follows a progression from verbal sign to concept to thing:

signum (sign) → *dicibile* (concept) → *res* (thing)

The word "Jerusalem," to use an example that would become common in the Middle Ages, indicates the concept "Jerusalem," which indicates the actual city. This scheme seems to have been drawn from Stoic semantics, according to which a sign, σημαῖον (= *signum*), indicates "the thing being signified," τὸ σημαινόμενον or τὸ λεκτόν (= *dicibile*), which in turn indicates "what actually is," τὸ τυγχάνον (= *res*).⁴ As in Augustine, the Stoic sign is a linguistic entity that leads to a concept that represents the object of knowledge. In addition, Augustine distinguished between two kinds of signs, and here is where we will see how different the force of the Victorine theory was. "Natural signs" (*signa naturalia*), such as the smoke that signifies fire, signify automatically, without the imposition of human will or convention. The "natural sign" is a "symptom."⁵ "Given

---

17:27–28). Many authors also repeat other elements of the traditional rationale for allegory, for example, that spiritual reading is the goal of Bible study, no matter how much more certain the literal sense may be (Fournier, *Postilla super Mattheum*, f. 7ra, and Heinrich of Langenstein, text quoted at pp. 149–50, below); or that the rustic quality of biblical language requires allegory and was intended so to be read by God, who embedded spiritual truths in obscure speech (for example, Heinrich of Langenstein, text quoted at pp. 107–8, below). Each of these authors provided many allegorical readings in their commentaries, often to reinforce doctrinal themes that first appear in the literal sense: the letter is the foundation, and mystical readings add decoration. Mystical reading was accepted by the reformers who followed Jan Milíč's example in Bohemia, for example, Matthew of Janow and Jan Hus (e.g. Matthias de Janov, *Tractatus de Antichristo*, vii.1, in *Regulae Veteris et Novi Testamenti*, ed. Vlastimil Kybal, 4 vols. (Innsbruck: Libraria Universitatis Wagnerianae, 1908–13), 3:87; Jan Hus, 1 *Sent.* prol. ii., Joannes Hus, *Super IV. Sententiarum*, ed. Wenzel Flajšhans and Marie Komínková, vol. 2 of *Opera omnia* (Osnabrück: Biblio-Verlag, 1966 reprint of the 1905 edition) p. 35; Hus, *Leccionarium bipartitum pars hiemalis*, xlvi (dominica quarta in quadragesima), ed. Anežka Vidmanová-Schmidtová, vol. 9 of *Opera omnia* (Prague: Academia Scientiarum Bohemoslovacae, 1988), p. 431). Allegorical reading was also known in Lollardy (Minnis, "'Authorial Intention' and 'Literal Sense' in the Exegetical Theories of Richard FitzRalph and John Wyclif, *Proceedings of the Royal Irish Academy* 75C (1975): 1–30, here 17–18; Johannes Wyclif, *De ueritate sacrae scripturae*, vi, ed. Rudolf Buddensieg, 2 vols. (Leipzig: Dieterich, 1904), pp. 119–23; Hudson, *The Premature Reformation*, p. 272).

3 R. A. Markus, "St. Augustine on Signs," and B. Darrell Jackson, "The Theory of Signs in *De doctrina christiana*," *Augustine. A Collection of Critical Essays*, ed. R. A. Markus (New York: Anchor Books, 1972), pp. 61–147, esp. 136–7.

4 Jackson, "Theory of Signs," *passim*.

5 Markus, "St. Augustine on Signs." The distinction between conventional and natural signs corresponds to Aristotle's distinction between σημαῖον and σύμβολον, according to which σημαῖον signifies naturally and σύμβολον artificially. Aristotle, *De interpretatione* ii.16a19–29; Norman Kretzmann, "Aristotle on Spoken Sound," *Ancient Logic and Its Modern Interpretations*, ed. J. Corcoran (Dordrecht: D. Reidel, 1974), p. 8. Although Aristotle, in *De interpretatione*, is concerned to explain the analysis of conventional signs, Kretzmann has pointed out that a notion of natural signification seems to stand behind his notion of conventional signs: ibid., pp. 17–18.

signs" (*signa data*), such as words or gestures, by contrast, are made by a living organism to indicate a feeling, perception, or understanding, which Markus, using Aristotle's nomenclature,[6] calls "symbol." Augustine's theory appreciated both kinds of sign as vehicles of knowledge.

Although Augustine exercised a strong influence at St. Victor, as we would expect, it is difficult to say exactly how this theory arrived there.[7] The Victorines accepted Augustine's sense of hermeneutical priorities (scripture, like everything, should be used only for the enjoyment of God), reiterated his stress on "the multi-vocality of Scripture," followed his example as an interpreter, and adapted his use of "circumstances" as categories of analysis (I will turn to "circumstances" in chapter 3). Yet we lack any sure evidence that the Victorines used the key theoretical texts, most especially Augustine's *On Christian Doctrine*, as a source of their theory of biblical signification.[8] At best, the Victorines *adapted* Augustine because, as I will argue shortly, their theory of biblical signification assumes a distinct relationship between letter and meaning – religious and philosophical meaning, to be exact. The plausibility of the Victorine rationale for spiritual reading was surely reinforced by prevailing learned assumptions about knowledge and how people get it, which, unlike later Aristotelian views, alleged that the object of knowledge is an actual thing, *res*, in the intellect rather than a concept of it.[9] One knows a thing apart from its representation, even if some representation of it leads one to that experience. But because medieval scholars never explicitly linked discussions of the meaningfulness of biblical language to discussions of epistemology or, later, the representation of objects of knowledge in propositions, there is no *explicit* link between semantics in logic and attitudes toward signification in the Bible, not only at the school of St. Victor

---

[6] Kretzmann and Aristotle in the previous note.
[7] For the following, Matter, *The Voice of My Beloved*, pp. 52–8; Margaret Gibson, "The *De doctrina christiana* in the School of St. Victor," Grover A. Zinn, "The Influence of Augustine's *De doctrina christiana* upon the Writings of Hugh of St. Victor," English, *Reading and Wisdom*, pp. 41–60, and Michael A. Signer, "From Theory to Practice: The *De doctrina christiana* and the Exegesis of Andrew of St. Victor," ibid., pp. 84–98.
[8] Zinn, "Influence." Other texts relevant to Augustine's theory of signification are *On the Trinity* xv. 17–21, *Sermon* 228. 3–5 (*PL* 38:1304–8 on the relation of word and concept), and for his four-fold interpretation, *On the Usefulness of Believing* iii.5.
[9] Gabriel Nuchelmans, "The Semantics of Propositions," *CHLMP*, pp. 197–210, here 201–2; idem, *Theories of the Proposition* (Amsterdam and London: North-Holland Publishing Company, 1973), pp. 177–94. See also Brinkmann, *Mittelalterliche Hermeneutik*, pp. 3–51 for the philosophical background, pp. 74–153 for an overview of varieties of semantics of things, pp. 277–434 for an overview of the practice of interpretation in non-biblical commentaries; Christian Schütz, *Deus absconditus, Deus manifestus: Die Lehre Hugos von St. Viktor über die Offenbarung Gottes* (Rome: Pontificium Institutum S. Anselmi, 1967), pp. 167–252; Gibson, "*De doctrina christiana* in the School of St. Victor," p. 43.

in the twelfth century but at all schools where theology was studied until the end of the Middle Ages. Whether there be an *implicit* link between logic and scriptural hermeneutics (it seems that there must be), is a question I must leave to the historians of philosophy. We will concentrate on theories of biblical signification.

I turn, then, to the Victorine theory and, first, Cassian's often-used example.[10] The word "Jerusalem" represents to the mind a thing, a place – to be exact, the ancient city of the Jews. This thing, the ancient city of the Jews, represents to the mind other things more relevant to the soul in its quest for truth and more reflective of God's purposes: the means of salvation established in the church (allegory), the human soul itself (tropology), or the eternal communion of saints (anagogy).[11] According to the Victorine view of interpretation, a textual narrative conveys something like common sense knowledge of the world, "things" that are physical objects or tangible (historical) experiences that serve directly as the true objects of knowledge. The ambition of the mind is not to form a concept of such things – in Cassian's example, the historical city of Jerusalem – but to grasp or experience the truth of things – in Cassian's example, the means of salvation, the nature and needs of the soul, and the eternal communion of saints. In the case of the Bible, the goal of knowledge is not mundane but spiritual. Biblical knowledge, according to this theory, involves a progression from linguistic sign to created sign to the object of knowledge, following the hierarchical progression

$$verbum \to res^1 \to res^2,$$

in which res^1 is a natural object and res^2 is a no less real abstraction from res^1 that serves as the object of knowledge. This is, in effect, to subordinate biblical hermeneutics to a theory of natural signification: that in contrast to signs meaningful by convention, such as human speech, there are other signs the meanings of which are fixed by nature and cannot be attached univocally to particular words; the latter have the priority in the interpretation of the Bible.

In Hugh of St. Victor's scheme, *verbum* is pretty limited. Not only must it refer beyond itself to be meaningful, but its referent must also refer beyond itself. Hugh had a theological reason for alleging this sequence of thought. *Verbum* – in Cassian's example, the name "Jerusalem" – is merely

---

[10] See p. 21, above. Consider also Evans, *Language and Logic*, 1:51–9.
[11] Peter Lombard, at the beginning of his *Sentences*, also argued that all *res* serve as signs. Rather than treat this hermeneutically, he concentrated on *res* as the subject matter of theology: 1 *Sent.* d. 1. Peter Lombard, *Sententiarum libri quatuor* (Paris: Louis Vivès, 1892), pp. 9–14.

a collection of vocalizations granted a certain meaning by the agreement of people; it belongs to the realm of human convention. By contrast, *res¹* is a part of creation and belongs to the realm of divine artifice, which Hugh of St. Victor identified with revelation. One could say, *res¹* belongs to divine convention, and by this divine convention it represents the more celestial *res²*.¹² In addition, *res²* can be any number of celestial things, which most medieval Bible interpreters grouped under the three familiar headings of allegory, tropology, and anagogy.¹³ Revelation is associated with the knowledge of things because things, as part of creation, are intrinsically revelatory. Language has a crucial but limited role. The experience of knowledge is ultimately not at all linguistic: it begins with language but only succeeds when it goes beyond words to a kind of participation in the truth of things.

This progression beyond language distinguishes spiritual senses from metaphor, a point that Hugh made by drawing on a tradition that began with Origen and was amplified in the medieval west.¹⁴ According to this view, spiritual sense arises from the factual association of an abstract idea with the intrinsic qualities of a created thing, whereas metaphor rests upon the "improper" reference of words.¹⁵ The one is real, and the other contrived. That is, Hugh confined metaphor to the realm of human convention, for to him true knowledge was a kind of sharing between like things, the object of knowledge and the perceiving soul. Understanding occurs when successions of *res* provoked by texts are possessed by the mind, and the greater the affinity between these things and eternal truth, the greater the quality of understanding. People have, Hugh of St. Victor said, three "eyes" of cognition – fleshly, rational, and contemplative – by which they may proceed from phenomena to rational contemplation, and from reason to the contemplation of God.¹⁶ Likewise, there is a progression of textual reading from letter to sense to abstract thought, from the finite and definite to the infinite and

---

¹² Hugh of St. Victor, *De scripturis et scriptoribus sacris praenotatiunculae*, xiv, *PL* 175:20–1. Idem, *Didascalicon* v.3, trans. J. Taylor, *The Didascalicon of Hugh of St. Victor* (New York: Columbia, 1961), pp. 121–2. Yves Delègue, *Les machines du sens. Fragments d'une sémiologie médiévale* (Paris: Editions des Cendres, 1987), pp. 45, 57.

¹³ Hugh, however, grouped them under two headings, allegory and tropology: *Didascalicon*, vi.4–5, trans. Taylor, pp. 139–45.

¹⁴ Turner, *Eros and Allegory*, pp. 94–96, 111–12 for Origen's distinction, its problems, and its adaptation by Gregory the Great in his commentary on the Song of Songs.

¹⁵ Consider Paul Vincent Spade, "The Semantics of Terms," *CHLMP*, pp. 188–96, here 192–95.

¹⁶ *De sacramentis*, x, *PL* 176:328–9; Elisabeth Gössmann, *Glaube und Gotteserkentnis im Mittelalter*, vol. 1/2b of *Handbuch der Dogmengeschichte*, 4 vols. and numerous parts, ed. by Michael Schmaus et al. (Freiburg: Herder, 1971–90), pp. 28–30.

"undefined," culminating in meditation.[17] In this manner, the progression of thought from words to truth mirrors the activity of the contemplative soul in its quest for God.

The conviction that verbal representation was built upon natural associations between speech and nature, factual associations intrinsic to the objects under consideration, also pointed to the rational coherence of the created universe. The associations constituted a formal interdependence of exegesis (or natural philosophy) with theology, secular knowledge with revelation. They point to a poetic sensibility that is religious, that rests upon the sheer beauty and pleasure of rising above corporeal signs toward divine truth.

Among the Victorines, revelation was not associated with the literal sense of scripture, a point that markedly distinguishes the Victorine view from late medieval, scholastic approaches.[18] The intellect should focus its attention on what creation is communicating to it, even when one reads a book, like the Bible. This attitude (it was the soul's meditative posture) allowed twelfth-century intellectuals to describe a rational system for acquiring knowledge while preserving a characteristically monastic, mystical concern to limit the human mind, since according to these assumptions, sure knowledge, even if gained through reading and exegesis, involves a kind of submissive insight into God's creativity in the universe.[19]

The Victorine theory of biblical signification resembles Augustine's doctrine of biblical signification in the structure of its semantics and in its primary notion of the sign. The Victorine *verbum* corresponds to Augustine's given sign, and its res^1 corresponds to Augustine's natural sign. It differs from Augustine's theory by insisting that knowledge must be mediated through natural signs, which are, as res^1, real things external to the soul in nature and not concepts formed in the soul. The

---

[17] *Didascalicon* iii.8–10, trans. Taylor, pp. 91–2.

[18] Schütz, *Deus absconditus*, pp. 130–62. Marie-Dominique Chenu touched on this difference when he contrasted the Victorine stress on the "historical" basis of spiritual meanings (the "first age" of allegory) with approaches first achieving prominence in the thirteenth century (the "second age" of allegory), in which the meaning of the Bible was conceived as spiritual alone and by which there was a synthesis of scriptural and nature allegories: "Les deux âges de l'allégorisme scripturaire au moyen âge," *Recherches de Théologie ancienne et médiévale* 18 (1951): 19–28. But rather than representing "une extrapolation permanente du contenu littéral de la Bible" and "une évacuation de l'économie historique dont elle raconte les épisodes," second-age allegory can be seen as an attempt to reduce spiritual interpretations to literal meaning.

[19] Consider Chenu, *La théologie au douzième siècle*, p. 379. Bernard of Clairvaux's exegesis is an example of the synergy of rationalism and intellectual disability. See Gössmann, *Glaube und Gotteserkentnis*, p. 22.

Victorine theory did not explain how biblical narrative written in conventional language, Augustine's "given signs," could point directly to objects of religious or philosophical knowledge: the theory only says that such pointing occurs by "natural signs." This was especially important in the treatment of biblical metaphor. The Victorine view alleges that biblical metaphor does not merely substitute one word for another in accordance with some poetic purpose and human artifice: metaphor is rather meaningful insofar as it represents something that, according to divine artifice, represents a real entity of some further religious or philosophical significance. Human artifice is quite beside the point. In this way, biblical imagery and sacred literature were believed to depart always from secular poetry, where metaphor was limited to human contrivance. By contrast, Augustine's theory could allow one to interpret biblical imagery and secular poetry by the same rules, as for example Petrarch did on the semantic foundations laid down in Augustine's *De doctrina christiana*.[20]

Although scholars accepted the Victorine theory of allegory up to the seventeenth century, in the early thirteenth century there arose alongside it an old alternative, verbal signification, whose impact on the study of the Bible has never been fully appreciated.[21] The distinction between natural and verbal signification originated in Aristotle's *On Interpretation* and was emphasized in Boethius' commentary on it; it is also suggested by Augustine's *On Christian Doctrine*, in his distinction between knowledge of things and of signs.[22] I have just argued that the distinction in the hands of Hugh of St. Victor grants the priority to knowledge of things or natural signification. In the early thirteenth century verbal signification again appears in the context of biblical interpretation, in Thomas of Chobham's treatise on preaching, which he completed at Salisbury, England, by 1228.[23] Chobham elaborates on verbal signification in the Bible, although his sympathy with the Victorine priority of natural signification is clearly displayed in the insistence that only theology, the

---

[20] Quillen, "Plundering the Egyptians."
[21] I hope I'm not overstating it. Consider Minnis and Scott, *Medieval Literary Theory and Criticism*, pp. 204, 206; Evans, *Language and Logic*, 1:166–67. Meier, "Argumentationsformen," provides a detailed analysis of allegory through the Renaissance. See also Ohly's introduction to *Schriften* and "Sinn," p. 29; Christel Meier, "Überlegungen zum gegenwärtigen Stand der Allegorie-Forschung mit besonderer Berücksightigung der Mischformen," *Frühmittelalterliche Studien* 10 (1976): 1–69;" and idem, *Gemma spiritalis*, pp. 12–13.
[22] For Aristotle, p. 32 note 5, above. Boethius, *In librum Aristotelis de interpretatione*, i, De signis, PL 64:297C; Augustine, *On Christian Doctrine* i.2.
[23] Evans, *Language and Logic*, 1:57–58. Thomas de Chobham, *Summa de arte praedicandi*, ed. F. Morenzoni, CCM 82:xxxvii, for the date, and pp. 1–14 for his description of signification.

highest science, studies the significations of things. Accordingly, the four senses of the Bible correspond to the progression of knowledge from sense to wisdom. But he also noted that theology and natural philosophy alike study the conventional meanings of words. The theologians appeal to verbal signification in explanations of fable, argument, and history, the last of which employs both "proper" and "improper" uses of words. In these cases, the meaning of improper speech is discovered, he says, by the application of rhetoric. Over a century later, Hermann of Schildesche, as we will see in chapter 3, provided a more detailed analysis of literal meaning on exactly these lines.[24] But Chobham was only concerned to apply rhetoric and grammar to the historical sense, and their role in the attainment of religious knowledge remained auxiliary and limited. Rhetoric and grammar stand completely apart from and subordinate to the natural significations of things in mystical reading.

In the third quarter of the thirteenth century, the distinction between natural and verbal signification appears in the context of biblical hermeneutics again, in the work of Thomas Aquinas (see Fig. 1).[25] Whereas Chobham ultimately took rhetorical analysis as a tool of spiritual reading, Aquinas, as Yves Delègue has pointed out, presented the two theories, natural and verbal, as self-consistent alternatives. In Aquinas' statement of natural signification we meet no surprises. It accounts for mystical reading, by which *res*, "things," represent what one is to believe (allegory and anagogy) and do (tropology). But his statement of verbal signification expands the realm of literal meaning beyond "history" in the narrow sense to include metaphor more broadly and, potentially at least, all manner of figurative expressions, a point treated briefly by Hugh of St. Victor and Chobham but not presented as an alternative mode of analysis and explanation.[26] For Aquinas, verbal signification must be coherent and self-sufficient because theological argument stands on

---

[24] See pp. 93–106, below.
[25] The source could not have been Chobham, whose treatise had limited circulation, but must have been Aristotle's *De interpretatione* and Boethius' commentary on it, through which the distinction between natural and verbal signification had gained currency.
[26] Consider Hugh of St. Victor, *De scripturis et scriptoribus sacris praenotatiunculae*, v, *PL* 175:14. Delègue points out that his explanation of figurative meaning touches on the problem treated by Aquinas' "parabolic" sense, "non sans embarras": Delègue, *Les machines du sens*, p. 44 n. 1. Cf. Turner, *Eros and Allegory*, p. 96, who believes that Hugh and Aquinas shared identical semantic assumptions. I agree with many of Turner's observations about the tension between literary and spiritual explanations of metaphorical language, but it seems to me that the semantic differences suggested by Delègue stand behind the groups of scholars that Turner divides between "metaphoricist" approaches (biblical metaphor requires spiritual interpretation) or "anti-metaphoricist" ones (biblical metaphor can be understood literally), the former consisting of almost all interpreters and the latter consisting of Hugh of St. Victor, Thomas Aquinas, and Nicholas of Lyra.

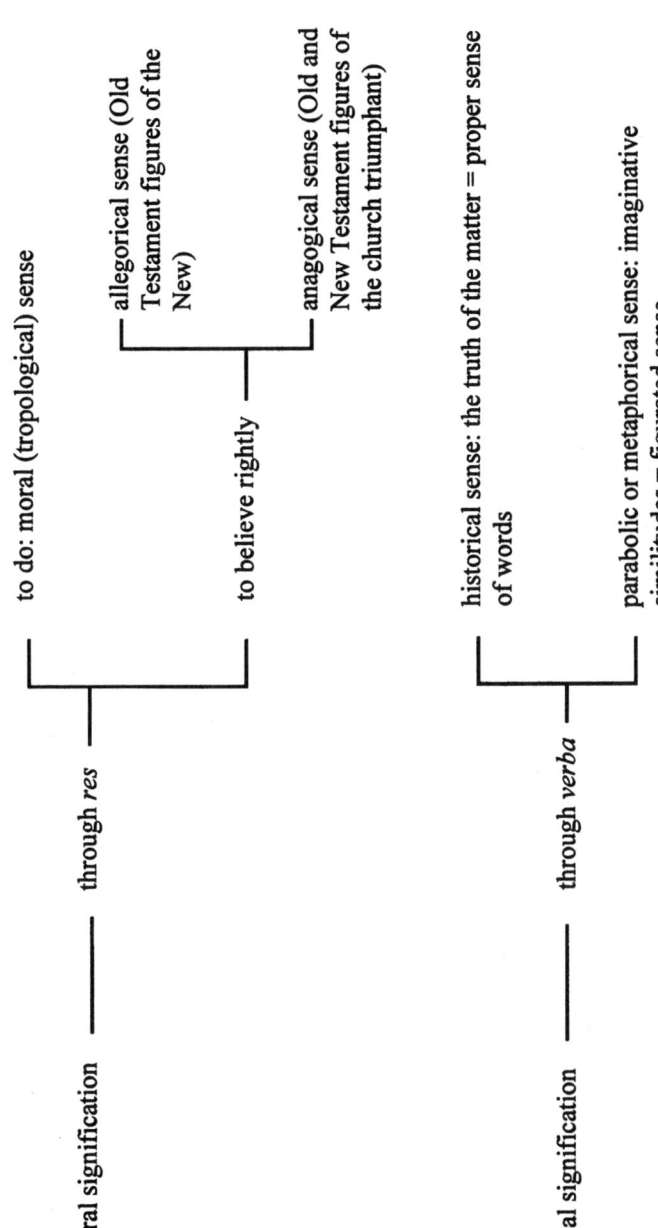

Figure 1. Natural and verbal signification according to Thomas Aquinas (adapted from Delègue, *Les machines du sens*, p. 20).

revealed principles, is fundamentally prophetic, and relies exclusively on the literal sense.[27] Built upon adaptations of Aristotle and theological presuppositions formulated earlier in the thirteenth century, the theoretical priority of literal meaning in argument became one of the most important innovations of thirteenth-century theology. Aquinas is justifiably famous for it, and we find it repeated in late medieval commentaries. His starting point sounds Victorine. The spiritual senses rest upon the literal, he noted. His conclusion, however, is not Victorine: "since all the senses rest on one, namely the literal sense, from this sense alone argument can be made."[28] Aquinas took this conclusion from Augustine, who made the same point in a letter to the Donatist Vincentius, which Aquinas, like Nicholas of Lyra after him, quotes.[29] In fact, Aquinas concluded, there is no necessary belief taught in the spiritual senses that is not also taught in the literal sense. The verbal signs of scripture, and not the "things" indicated by them, are revelatory – as words. The mind acting upon words constitutes religious knowledge, not mental acts reaching beyond words.[30] What is so important about Aquinas' use of verbal signification is this: it means that in addition to straightforwardly indicative or hortatory literal statements, there is a kind of figurative explanation that remains literal.[31] Figures may be far plainer than the classic Christian view of allegory would allow, so that the enigmatic qualities no longer need to propel the reader to non-verbal mysteries.

The emergence[32] of verbal signification in biblical hermeneutics must reflect, at least in part, the growing confidence of scholars in the face of new word-oriented analytical tools that emerged in the late twelfth and thirteenth centuries. The tools are surveyed by Gillian Evans: techniques to describe the imposition of meaning on words, grammar, and even dictionaries.[33] The emergence of verbal signification must also reflect the

---

[27] Chenu, *La théologie comme science au douzième siècle*, pp. 43–4.
[28] *ST* 1 a q. 1 a. 10 ad 1.
[29] Augustine, Ep. 93, *Letters*, 2:56–106. For Lyra, see p. 143, below.
[30] Marie-Dominique Chenu, "Histoire et allégorie au douzième siècle," *Glaube und Geschichte. Festgabe Joseph Lortz*, 2 vols. (Baden-Baden: Bruno Grimm, 1958), 2:59–71, here 62, 65–6. This is consistent with Aquinas' conviction that knowledge occurs when the mind perceives a subjective mental word that represents an object: Robert Pasnau, *Theories of Cognition in the Later Middle Ages* (Cambridge University Press, 1997), pp. 256–6.
[31] *ST* 1a, q. 1 a. 10 ad 3.
[32] One could call it a reemergence, since it did play an important role in Augustine's *On Christian Doctrine*, but it seems to me that its application in the late Middle Ages is quite different – less rhetorical and more dependent upon distinct theological themes, as I will argue in the next two chapters.
[33] Evans, *Language and Logic*, 1:72–100, 2:51–65. For the limited influence of rhetoric, see pp. 68–70, 73, below.

growing preoccupation of scholars with issues raised by the rediscovered corpus of Aristotle's writings, whereby his *On Interpretation* and *On the Soul*, among other things, provoked new and increasingly sophisticated logical discussions of the nature and truth value of mental concepts, their very existence, and their representation in speech.[34] Although neither Aquinas nor anyone else linked their discussion of biblical signification to their discussions of such problems of logic and epistemology, it seems likely that the stress on verbal signification in the Bible (it amounts to a claim that language-based knowledge is possible regardless of natural signification) was reinforced by the triumph of what A. C. Crombie once called the "logical culture" of scholasticism.[35] The effect of verbal signification as a foundation of Bible reading was to introduce a new definition of biblical discourse as a medium of religious knowledge; it was to open another avenue to the communion between the mind and God *within* biblical discourse, spiritual ecstacy regardless. If the words of scripture, as Aquinas taught, could signify in and of themselves, one must account for obscure language by means of rhetoric, that secular thing. To that end Aquinas offered the category of "parabolic" expression.[36] Obscure language can be seen as metaphor, the intellectual content of which may be explained in an entirely literal, not mystical, way.

The notion that biblical language is revelatory as such rested on the belief in its divine authorship, which we will consider in chapter 4.[37] I want here only to remind the reader in passing of two well-known features of Aquinas' Bible commentaries that reflect this elevation of biblical speech as the bearer of theological argument. His commentaries would call some things "parabolic" that earlier would have been called mystical (the same has been observed in the commentaries of Bonaventure), thus leaving symbolic meaning firmly in the context of the letter; and the commentaries emphasized doctrine, thus emphasizing abstractly the religious and intellectual purposes of biblical narrative.[38]

---

34 Nuchelmans, *Theories*, pp. 177–94. Idem, *CHLMP*, pp. 198–202. Pasnau, *Theories of Cognition*, pp. 254–89.
35 A. C. Crombie, *Augustine to Galileo*, 2nd revised edn., 2 vols. (London: Heinemann, 1952), *passim*.
36 *ST* 1a q. 1 a. 9.
37 See p. 123, below.
38 Mercker, *Schriftauslegung als Weltauslegung. Untersuchungen zur Stellung der Schrift in der Theologie Bonaventuras* (Munich: Ferdinand Schöningh, 1971), pp. 69, 216–18. Domanyi, *Römerbriefkommentar*, pp. 79, 268, 270. Winkler, *Meister Eckhart*, pp. 12–18. Franz Manthey, *Die Sprachphilosophie des heiligen Thomas von Aquin und ihre Anwendung auf Probleme der Theologie* (Paderborn: Ferdinand Schöningh, 1937), pp. 231–2, long ago showed the relation of spiritual senses to indirect forms of divine communication in Aquinas, which in turn allows a complex view of the intention of those who speak the word of God.

In Aquinas and throughout the late Middle Ages, verbal signification stood alongside natural signification. It is odd that discussions of these distinct but not necessarily incompatible approaches appear to have been so rare. Apart from Aquinas, the only clear presentation of the two theories I know is found at the beginning of Nicolas of Lyra's influential *Postilla*, in his first prologue.[39] Yet there is much reason to believe that the analysis of scripture along the lines of verbal signification was widespread, and that it created an unexpected duplicity of modes of explanation in commentaries. For on the one hand, scholars continued to pursue spiritual senses confidently and with some abandon. There is much in late medieval commentaries that looks and sounds Victorine. This was, of course, earlier true of thirteenth-century scholars like Aquinas, who allowed mystical senses in contexts other than the construction of doctrine or arguments, or Bonaventure, who insisted that spiritual meaning is intrinsic to the literal sense and manifests, to the intellect, the organic continuity of history and creation, to cite two well-known examples.[40] On the other hand, verbal signification allowed an integration of literal and spiritual meanings in exegesis, and that is what the rest of this book is about. It had the potential of making mystical reading a supplement to literal understanding, maybe even a luxury: the literal sense says everything that the spiritual senses say, Aquinas pointed out. "If we push this principle, stated so clearly by Aquinas, to its logical conclusion, allegory becomes at worst redundant and at best a pleasing (and persuasive) optional extra."[41] It required only a rationale against the multivalence of mystical reading to eliminate natural signification as an explanation of

---

[39] *Postilla super totam Bibliam* (Strasbourg, 1492), f. 1rb, at "Circa secundum considerandum."

[40] Thomas Aquinas, *ST* 1a, q. 1, a. 10. Domanyi, *Römerbriefkommentar*, pp. 47–76. M.-D. Mailhiot, "La pensée de saint Thomas sur le sens spirituel," *Revue Thomiste* 59 (1959): 613–63; Mercker, *Schriftauslegung*, pp. 16–37, esp. 16–20; 65–72, esp. 70–2. For the mystical aspect of Bonaventure's theory (and some successors, which included Pierre d'Ailly, Jean Gerson, and Denys the Carthusian), see Karl Rahner, "La doctrine des 'sens spirituels' au moyen âge en particulier chez saint Bonaventure," *Revue d'Ascétique et de Mystique* 14 (1933): 263–99. Roger Bacon, less curiously than some have thought, associated the literal sense with philosophy and allegories derived from natural objects: "In sensu litterali jacet tota philosophiae potestas in naturis et proprietatibus rerum naturalium, artificialium et moralium, ut per convenientes adaptationes et similitudines eliciantur sensus spirituales, ut sic simul sciatur philosophia cum theologia": *Opus tertium*, ed. J. S. Brewer (London, 1859), pp. 81–2 and quoted in Chenu, "Ages," pp. 26–7. See also de Lubac, *Exégèse*, 2/2:314–15. Henry of Ghent used Augustine's distinction of *signa* and *res* to distinguish the content of the Old and New Testaments. The Old Testament is the "figurated" doctrine of signs (or words and figures – employed synonymously), and the New Testament is the revealed doctrine of things (or the truth); together they comprise a unitary science that describes divine law (divine law is the natural law revealed in the decalogue). The distinction corresponds to two modes of cognition, sensual and spiritual: Henricus de Gandavo, *Lectura ordinaria super sacram scripturam Henrico de Gandavo adscripta*, ed. R. Macken, vol. 36 of Henricus de Gandavo, *Opera omnia* (Leuven: University Press and Leiden: Brill, 1980), pp. 9–27.

[41] Minnis and Scott, *Medieval Literary Theory and Criticism*, p. 204.

biblical knowledge. Such did not take hold before the Reformation. Verbal signification is a theory that nevertheless represents well a common feature of late medieval commentaries, namely the doctrinal preoccupations of the literal sense. A good example of this is provided by the late thirteenth-century Dominican Nicholas Gorran.

Gorran was the prior and teacher of the Dominican convent of St. Jacques in Paris and a confessor to king Philip IV of France. His commentaries probably originated as lectures in the Dominican "general school" of St. Jacques within the decade before his death in 1295.[42] He was an important interpreter in his day, as attested by the number of commentaries he produced and the number of extant manuscripts.[43] There are expositions of Genesis, Exodus, Leviticus, Numbers, Deuteronomy, the Psalms, Ecclesiastes, the Song of Songs, the Book of Wisdom, Isaiah, Daniel, Matthew, Mark, Luke, John, the Pauline letters, the seven Canonical letters,[44] and the Apocalypse, not to mention several additional commentaries wrongly attributed to him – misattribution itself being testimony to a reputation. Judging by the number of manuscripts known to Friedrich Stegmüller, Matthew and Luke were the most popular, with thirty-six and thirty-four manuscripts respectively, and several editions published from 1472 to 1617. A Psalms commentary follows with nineteen manuscripts, then Exodus (eleven) and Genesis (ten). The production of these copies throughout the late Middle Ages, including early editions, points to Gorran's ongoing reputation. When the early fourteenth-century Dominican William of Werda collected excerpts from commentaries for the use of Dominican preachers, he used Gorran along with the most famous postillators of the thirteenth century: Hugh of St. Cher, Albert the Great, and Thomas Aquinas.[45] We could think of him as one of such a number.[46] He provides testimony to the legacy of Dominican Bible study

---

[42] Smalley, *Study of the Bible*, pp. 273–74, 336. G. Gieraths, "Nikolaus von Gorran," *LThK* 7:986. J. Quétif and J. Echard, *Scriptores ordinis praedicatorum*, 4 vols. (New York: Burt Franklin, 1959 reprint of the edition of Paris, 1719–23), 1:437–44.

[43] The following is based on *RB* 4:28–47, 9:305–8, nos. 5740–5812.

[44] A transcription of this commentary may be found in Thomas Aquinas, *Opera omnia*, ed. R. Busa, 7 vols. (Stuttgart: Frommann-Holzboog, 1980), 7:361–99.

[45] Jean Longère, "La prédication en langue latine," *Le Moyen Age et la Bible*, pp. 522–23.

[46] I use his prologue and commentary on Genesis from Würzburg, Universitätsbibliothek, M.p.th. fol. 151, ff. 9v–36rb, 58vb–169vb. The published catalogue and Friedrich Stegmüller ascribed ff. 9v–169vb to Nicholas, but ff. 37ra–58va (which the manuscript, in a contemporary hand, incorrectly titles "prologus hystorie librum") actually contain Guillelmus Brito's commentary on Jerome's letter to Paulinus (Guillelmus' *Prologus historie librorum* is actually found on ff. 1vb–8ra of the codex). Moreover, ff. 9v–36rb contain Gorran's commentary on the prologues to the Bible and to the Pentateuch (ff. 9v–23rb) and the beginning of what appears to be an abbreviated or less complete version of Gorran's commentary on Genesis. The text of the complete commentary

in the tradition of Hugh of St. Cher at the end of the thirteenth century and, through the continued reading of his commentaries, beyond.⁴⁷

That Gorran was himself affected by the preoccupation with the conceptual bases of knowledge and their representation will not surprise, since, in the crude and general terms that are relevant to *biblical* hermeneutics, this was merely one of the most obvious characteristics of scholastic culture.⁴⁸ Neither is it suprising that as an interpreter, he upheld the distinction between literal and spiritual meanings.⁴⁹ In the light of Aquinas, it is unsurprising that he also saw the Bible as a fundamentally doctrinal book. Its basic division into two testaments, one of precepts and one of grace, reflects its purpose: to cultivate doctrinal knowledge and just conduct and to prepare readers for heavenly glory.⁵⁰

---

on Genesis begins on f. 58vb (it contains more extensive discussion of physics and philosophy). Cf. *RB*; Hans Thurn, *Die Handschriften der Universitätsbibliothek Würzburg*, 5 vols. (Wiesbaden: Otto Harrassowitz, 1973–94). A sample of his exegesis may also be found in three excerpts of his Romans commentary edited by Heinrich Denifle, *Die abendländischen Schriftausleger bis Luther über Justitia Dei (Rom. 1,17) und Justificatio* (Mainz: Franz Kirchheim, 1905), pp. 152–6. Beryl Smalley offers a different view of Gorran's exegesis from his commentary on Proverbs, but with a very thorough examination of his sources, in "Some Latin Commentaries on the Sapiential Books in the Late Thirteenth and Early Fourteenth Centuries," *Archives d'Histoire Doctrinale et Littéraire du moyen age* 18 (1950–51): 103–28, here 106–16. Minnis makes additional observations on Gorran's complex view of efficient causality in the Bible in *Theory of Authorship*, pp. 80, 81, 107, but ascribes a greater significance to human causality than I can find in the commentaries I have examined.

⁴⁷ Verger, "L'exégèse de l'Université," *Le Moyen Age et la Bible*, p. 205.

⁴⁸ There is to my knowledge no study of Gorran's philosophy or theology. We see a glimpse of this concept orientation in his treatment of cognition while commenting on the image of God in the Bible's creation story (Ge. 1.27), where it is clear that he holds an Aristotelian theory of the cognition of species similar to that of Aquinas, arguing that knowledge is attained by abstract comparisons of perceived objects with remembered ones. Würzburg, Universitätsbibliothek, M.p.th. fol. 151, ff. 61vb–62ra, says that the image exists in the natural qualities (*naturalia*) of people, for an image is a certain *representation* of a thing in right proportion to general and special conditions, a definition which Gorran then illustrates by a brief description of the physical and spiritual qualities of the Blessed Virgin in art. He then offers an explanation of Ge. 1.27 and its assertion of a human "likeness" to God that itself serves as an explanation of cognition, in which it becomes apparent that in Gorran's mind knowledge has not merely natural but also conceptual grounds. As in Aquinas, a thing known does not need to exist within the knower but can merely be represented there by its likeness. For Aquinas see Pasnau, *Theories of Cognition*, pp. 105–113, 195–219, 254–71.

⁴⁹ Seven questions are appended to his introductory lecture on the Bible (ff. 9v–11rb), of which the third and the fourth consider the senses of the Bible (f. 11rb). The third question names them: "hystoricus, qui narrat factum; allegoricus, qui perfectum signat intelligendum; tropologicus, quo signatur quid faciendum; anagogicus, quo signatur quid appetendum." The fourth question argues that the multiple senses require the service of the other sciences: grammar serves the *sensus proprius uel hystoricus*, while, according to Hugh of St. Victor, the other liberal arts serve the *sensus figuratiuus*, because *res – scilicet persona, numerus, locus, tempus –* are known under the other sciences, *et he habent figuras*. Grammar treats only *uocum significacio*, but the quadrivium treats *rerum significacio excellentior*. As Hugh of St. Victor said, grammar is ruled by convention, but the quadrivium by nature: "*illam usus instituit, istam natura dictauit*."

⁵⁰ Ibid., f. 9v: "Utilitas uero eius [i.e. scripture] est maxima, quia disponit ad uitam gratie. Johannes vi. [vs. 63], 'Uerba que ego locutus sum, uobis spiritus et uita sunt.' Item dirigit ad uitam iusticie.

Signification and allegory 45

His definition of the Bible according to five "causes," a type of literary definition that I will discuss in chapter 4, also points to the fusion of biblical literature and theology. The material cause is *res* and sign, to which the formal cause (or *modus agendi*) is closely aligned: proper (when words are taken according to their external sounds) and figurative (when they are taken otherwise). The final cause is knowledge and defense of the truth and love of the good.[51] But the principal cause is Christ (the human author is merely "moved;" he or she is a second-order efficient cause), beneath which the other causes stand. He concludes that the Bible is Christian theology in the form of simple narrative, whose subject is only distinguishable from the stuff of *Sentences* commentaries, the main literary genre of pure theology, in the style of its analysis.[52] Doctrine informs interpretation as much as the Bible informs doctrine.[53]

Nicholas included conventional mystical interpretations: for example, paradise as the soul inhabited by God or as the fountain of doctrine; the priest of Midian as Christ, whose seven daughters are the preachers (this was said to students of the Order of Preachers) who possess the seven virtues drawing the water of doctrine by scrupulous study and who dispense it by preaching.[54] He also liked to digress to questions in

---

Psalmus [119.93], 'in eternum non obliuiscam iustificaciones tuas, quia in ipsis uiuificasti me.' Item producit ad uitam glorie. Johannes vi. [vs. 68], 'Domine, ad quem ibimus, uerba uite eterne habes.' Ad hanc autem uitam scriptura ducit dupliciter, precipiendo per mandata que proponit, et hoc pertinet ad uetus testamentum. Item ad iuuandum per donum gratie, quod dat lator legis, quod pertinet ad nouum testamentum." For his division of the Bible into parts, see p. 27, above.

[51] For the "causes" of the Bible, see chapter 4, section 2, below. Christ is the cause "mouens et mota," whereas the human author is the cause "mota et non mouens." Ibid., f. 11ra (the second of the seven questions appended to the introductory lecture). Alastair Minnis has argued the importance of causal descriptions of the text, "'Authorial Intention' and 'Literal Sense,'" here pp. 11, 18–21, and idem, *Medieval Theory*. He observed a similar division of the efficient cause into principal (God) and secondary (a human author) in many thirteenth-century commentaries and in Nicholas of Lyra. Ibid., *passim*. Beryl Smalley found that Guerric of St. Quentin, a Dominican teaching at St. Jacques, 1233–4, was the first to apply the four causes to each book of the Bible (*Study of the Bible*, pp. 296–7). Minnis found no earlier evidence (*Medieval Theory of Authorship*, p. 79).

[52] The sixth question of the introductory lecture (f. 11rb): "In canone sacre scripture, id est in nouo et uetere testamentis, traditur theologia per modum simplicis narrationis, ueritatem simpliciter assendi. In libris *Sentenciarum* traditur per modum scrutationis ueritatem, inquirentis et defendentis compendiose, in moribus autem diffuse." For the distinction between narrative theology and defensive or rational theology, see Lang, *Theologische Prinzipienlehre*, pp. 174–5.

[53] In his commentary on Jerome's letter to Paulinus (f. 11rb): "*Taceo* [Hieronimus, Ep. liii.6; CSEL 54:452 line 7]. Hic ostendit per locum a minori quod doctrina est docta uia ad cognitionem sacre scripture, et ratio talis est: si alie scientie que sunt faciliores non possunt sine doctore, multo fortius theologia, que est difficillissima."

[54] The first example comes from his commentary on Ge. 2.8, f. 64rb. The second may be found in his *postilla* on Exodus, Ex. 2.16, Würzburg Universitätsbibliothek, M.p.th. fol. 155, ff. 2ra–113vb, here 5vb.

his commentary, many of which are exegetical, clarifying this or that point about the language of the text, but others of which explore theological themes liberally, like the action of the Holy Trinity in the work of creation considered at Genesis chapter one, or ecclesiastical offices at Luke chapter four (where Jesus reads the Torah scroll in the synagogue).[55] Such digressions point to his sense that what the church now knows to be true is true in biblical texts even when it is not explicit there, and what the church now knows is thus intrinsic to the meaning of those passages.

These spiritual interpretations are conventional enough. Beside them we find some interesting compromises of mystical exegesis, and these can suggest the force of verbal signification: that language can put a reader directly in contact with a realm of spiritual truths. Nicholas could distinguish between literal and spiritual, but then treat the "spiritual" sense in the grammatical terms proper to literal exegesis. For example, when the devil is condemned in paradise (Genesis 3.14), his condemnation is called the spiritual meaning of the text. The letter refers immediately to the snake alone, yet the point of the text is not the origin of creeping reptiles:[56]

All the days of your life. The words are thus explained according to the letter, concerning the penalty of the serpent. According to the spiritual sense the passage is explained so, concerning the penalty of the demon speaking in the serpent, for which reason [it says] *and the Lord said to the serpent*, that is the devil

---

[55] Another brief and incomplete version of the Genesis commentary in the same codex includes questions of a mostly (but not exclusively) exegetical character. After literal comments on Ge. 1 (ff. 23rb–26ra), fifteen questions appear (f. 26ra–27va), some of which narrowly pertain to the writing of the text (e.g., q. 1, how did Moses know of the creation?), and most of which narrowly pertain to its subject (e.g., q. 2 on creation and time; qq. 3 and 5 on the creative role of the second person of the Trinity; q. 4 on how the "beginning" pertains to God; and q. 7 on whether God created according to the divine essence or according to the person of the Father). The *postilla* on Luke relates Jesus' activity in the synagogue, along with other passages, to the lower offices of the church (on 4.17): Würzburg, Universitätsbibliothek, M.ch. fol. 277, ff. 3ra–297vb (the preface is missing in this manuscript), here f. 51va–51vb. Similarly, Lk. 9.1, "Conuocatis autem duodecim discipulis," provides instructions for the works of preaching and of prayer, that is, for the active and contemplative lives, which led Gorran to consider issues related to mendicant identity – the offices of apostles and preachers and personal property (ff. 11rb, 112ra–113ra). Gorran's *Euangelia et epistolae cum diuisionibus cum sermonibus* studies texts with attention to moral and allegorical matters, consistently presenting Old Testament texts as typologies of the advent, life, death, and resurrection of Christ: Stadtbibliothek Mainz, Hs. I. 153, ff. 4–65. See also *RB* 4:255–6.

[56] *Postilla super Genesim*, f. 32rb: "*cunctis diebus uite tue*. Sic exponuntur uerba secundum litteram de pena serpentis. Secundum sensum spiritualem exponitur sic, de pena demonis in serpente loquentis, unde sic, *et ait dominus ad serpentem*, id est dyabolum, qui loquebatur per *serpentem, quia hoc fecisti*, id est mulierem decepisti per tuam fraudem, *maledictus eris*, id est malo addictus, propter quod damnatus, quod hominibus mors est, angelis casus *inter omnia animancia et bestias terre*." Nicholas of Lyra argued similarly, but on a principle of double (literal) signification *Postilla super totam Bibliam*, at Ge. 3.14, "et terra commedes cunctis diebus vite tue." This is also noted by Fidelis Schwendinger, "De Vaticiniis Messianicis Pentateuchi apud Nicolaum de Lyra, O.F.M.," *Antonianum* 4 (1929): 3–44, 129–66, here 15–20.

who spoke through the serpent, *because you did this*, that is you [the devil] deceived the woman through your falsehood, *you are cursed*, that is addicted to evil, on account of which the devil was condemned; what is death to human beings is to angels a fall *among all the animals and beasts of the earth*.

The category of mystical meaning is here used to explain the complex referent of the term "snake," which in this context could be literally both the snake and the devil, but Nicholas is unable to distinguish theological allegory from metaphor.[57] At Genesis 22, he offers a conventional allegory of the sacrifice of Isaac: it refers to the passion of Christ. Yet he finds it difficult to distinguish the allegory from the events of the narrative because Abraham received a revelation of the crucifixion, and that is why he chose the mountain (to signify Calvary), used an ass (Christ's entry into Jerusalem), took two youths (the Jews and the Gentiles), collected wood (the cross), and waited three days (the resurrection).[58] Abraham's vision was an historical event, which allowed his equally historical intention to perform the sacrifice of Isaac in a way that was consistent with its allegorical meaning. If this is so, the allegory cannot be construed as remote from the historical narrative. The signs are historical. At Exodus 3, Nicholas discerns mystical meanings of the fire in the burning bush that pertain to the people of Israel in their early trials, but "this vision is called great on account of the great mystery," so that the fire also refers to the incarnation, the virgin birth, the birth of the church, its internal well being in spite of external tribulation, and the tribulation of a just person who burns with love.[59] Again, allegorical meaning in the passage of Exodus itself had reference to the original historical context of the text, as well as prophetic and contemporary references, as we will see.[60] To further blur the distinction between a historical, literal sense and allegory, Nicholas mentions, after offering the Christological allegories, that Moses, like Abraham, probably understood these mysteries. Hebrew patriarchs intended to convey Christian doctrine; they intended the mysteries of the covenant of grace.

---

57 The confusion may be partly due to the *Glossa ordinaria*, which referred to the meaning of "serpent" as "figurated": *Glossa cum Lyra*, 1:42rb–42va (also *PL* 113:94). Both Nicholas Gorran and the Gloss attribute the interpretation to Augustine. One might contrast Heinrich of Langenstein's interpretation, which follows Augustine's sense of figurative speech more carefully: Henricus de Hassia, *Commentaria in prologo biblie et Genesin*, f. 106ra–106rb, and Augustinus, *De doct. christ.* ii.16, CCL 32:49.
58 Nicholas de Gorran, *Postilla super Genesin*, ff. 106ra–106rb (Ge. 22.14): "*In monte* uisionis immolare uoluit quia Deus immolationem Christi reuelauit ei, uel in signum quod Christus pateretur in monte Caluarie." The other images follow, describing his actions as intended prefigurations.
59 The text is edited as selection 1 of the Appendix. It is translated at page 81, below.
60 See pp. 82 ff., below.

Nicholas assumed that biblical authors tinkered with language to make it suit the mystery it should convey. If the author is doing this intentionally, then mystical meaning belongs to the literal, not the spiritual senses.[61] All the language of the Bible is, after all, theology, even when, as here, an idea is not always called the literal meaning. While interpreters like Gorran would not reject allegorical interpretation, it nevertheless became difficult for them to distinguish allegory from literal meaning.

To give allegory such distinctly literal functions marks a notable departure from Victorine practice. In the next chapter, we will examine further evidence for the refiguring of biblical imagery in literal terms. My argument here is that verbal signification provides an adequate, if somewhat broad, rationale for it. As necessary as was the theoretical basis for such refiguring, the practice of reading could not really change unless some method to treat figurative speech as language were at hand. It would take some such discipline, for example rhetoric, to transform the act of reading into a textual experience distinct from that of earlier Bible readers. But the first thing to strike the student of late medieval Bible commentaries is not the presence of rhetoric but the attention to doctrine. There can be little doubt that in the minds of late medieval scholars biblical teaching belonged to a conceptual universe in which allegory and literal meaning were differentiated with difficulty, because the entire narrative of the Bible is a revelation that can and must be comprehended and argued. It would seem that the parameters of signification were not merely verbal but conceptual in some broader sense: that biblical language represented, for late medieval scholars, an entire body of knowledge.

2. THEOLOGY

To late medieval scholars, the Bible did encompass a body of knowledge, as we have seen.[62] In the previous chapter, I noted that when scholars

---

[61] At Ex. 12.6, on the lamb without spot, after notes on the figure of Christ, Nicholas de Gorran, *Postilla super Exodum*, ff. 31vb–32ra: "Et nota quod cum dicitur 'eum' singulare, ponitur pro plurali, et quelibet domus unum immolare tenebatur. Uel hoc dicitur propter mysterium ad signandum scilicet illum qui unus per multos figurabatur, unde non erat unus typicus, sed unus tantus uerus qui figurabatur." Alastair Minnis has noted an early example of the equation of allegory with figurative speech in William Brito: "Intention," p. 17. Suzanne Reynolds has demonstrated its prominence in twelfth-century commentaries on Horace's *Satires: Medieval Reading*, pp. 135–49. See also Evans, *Language and Logic*, 2:16, and Minnis and Scott, *Medieval Literary Theory and Criticism*, p. 205.

[62] See p. 25, above. There is no reason to dismiss the fusion of religious purpose and doctrine with exegesis as violations of "the accepted distinction between the study of Scripture or exegesis

distinguished the parts of the Bible, they tried to portray the religious content and purpose of the book as a whole. This was well represented in the scholarship of the twelfth century, not least in Hugh of St. Victor's *Didascalicon*.[63] One of the more important statements of the relation of the Bible to theology to appear later can be found in the influential commentary by Pierre Auriol, where it is combined with a typical scholastic statement of intellectual congruity between commentary and other theological work. Auriol wrote his *Compendium on the Literal Meaning of the Whole Bible* as the Franciscan regent master at Paris in 1318/19.[64] By then he had already established a reputation for himself in his religious order as a bachelor at Paris and a lecturer at the Franciscan general schools of Bologna and Toulouse, and as a defender of the immaculate conception of the Blessed Virgin and a promoter of the Franciscan doctrine of "poor use" (he may have influenced Pope Clement V's defense of the doctrine in the controversial and soon to be cancelled decree *Exivi de paradiso* of 6 May 1312).[65] According to Auriol, theology is a science of conclusions drawn from the articles of faith and scripture. It is a *habitus* of faith, a firm and repetitive action of the soul, by which what was written in the Bible is understood subject to the application of logic.[66] Theology therefore consists not of mere knowledge of the Bible but of deductions and conclusions drawn from it: a point of view that does leave some distance between theological subjects and scriptural narrative, but only while insinuating their relationship.[67] Theology is more than a rehearsal of narrative, biblical or otherwise, but Auriol took special care to give narrative its due. He gave it a historical frame. The ancient history of the Hebrews, over against ancient Roman history, conveys religious

and that of doctrine and theology": Beryl Smalley, "The Bible and Eternity: John Wyclif's Dilemma," *Journal of the Warburg and Courtauld Institutes* 27 (1964): 73–89, reprinted in eadem, *Studies is Medieval Thought and Learning*, pp. 270–1, here.

[63] See pp. 26–9, above.

[64] *Compendium literalis sensus totius divine scripture*, ed. Philibert Seeboeck (Quarracchi: Collegia S. Bonaventurae, 1896). I also have the text from Barcelona, Biblioteca de Universidad, Ms. 121, ff. 1ra–109va. For the manuscripts of his *Sentences* commentary, recent and ongoing studies of its philosophy and theology, and the preparation of a critical edition of Auriol's *Sentences* commentary, see Tachau, "Preparation of a Critical Edition," and Lauge Olaf Nielsen, "The Critical Edition of Peter Aureoli's Scholastic Works," *Editori di Quaracchi 100 anni dopo, bilancio e prospettive* (Rome: Edizioni Antonianum, 1997), pp. 212–225.

[65] A. Teetaert, "Pierre Auriol," *DThC*, 12/2:1810–81. Katherine Tachau, *Vision and Certitude in the Age of Ockham* (Leiden: Brill, 1988), pp. 85–112. William Duba, "The Immaculate Conception in the Works of Peter Auriol," *Vivarium* 38 (2000): 5–34.

[66] Petrus Aureolus, *Scriptum super primum Sententiarum*, ed. Buytaert, proemium, pp. 135–8, 148–50. For his view of natural knowledge, see Charles Bolyard, "Knowing *naturaliter*. Auriol's Propositional Foundations," *Vivarium* 38 (2000): 162–76.

[67] Petrus Aureolus, *Scriptum super primum Sententiarum*, pp. 151–54, 302–4, 324–25.

knowledge because of a better past, "not because those events [of ancient Israel] were revealed – no indeed, they were visibly seen and well remembered and faithfully committed to history books, as, too, were the deeds of the Romans – but because those events are traced back to God, who led and appointed the kings of the Jews and preordained or reproved the things that they did and not the things that the Romans did."[68] The events reflect a purposeful, intended arrangement of the historical world. Lyra soon after Auriol took the same confident, theological approach to history; we should remember it when we read his brief remark that the Bible's subject is God.[69]

At the beginning of his *Compendium*, Auriol offers a "special commendation of sacred scripture" that builds upon the text "Come, let us go to the mountain" (Is. 2.3 and Mic. 4.2), drawing his inspiration from Pseudo-Dionysius' "house of wisdom."[70] "Come, let us go" is an exhortation to stimulate the intelligence of "docile souls" that move from corporeal to spiritual, from mutable to unchangeable things, by meditation and the study of the letter, while moving from the term (*vox*) to the intellect, and through the intellect to the thing, and through the thing to reason, and through reason to the truth. It is not enough, Pierre says again, to know the Bible. Abstracted knowledge of its content will affect one's behavior (tropology) and one's aspirations (anagogy), and declare secrets (allegory). But all truth is gathered in the *literalis intellectus*, the *sensus hystoricus superficialis*, the *plana enunciatio*.[71] The literal narrative, with its peculiar rhetorical features (any rhetorical trope may be found in the Bible; Pierre names seven as common),[72] is identical with theological knowledge. In fact, every kind of knowledge – whether the histories of nations, mechanics, geometry, arithmetic, poetics, or philosophy – is found "carved in scripture in many ways."[73] Having said all this, the *Compendium* offers its straightforward scheme of a Bible divided into eight principal

---

[68] Ibid., p. 325: "non quia illa [gesta] fuerint revelata, immo fuerunt visa oculariter et retenta memoriter et fideliter historiis demandata, sicut et illa Romanorum, sed quoniam illa reducuntur in Deum, tanquam in gubernantem et destinantem reges Iudaeorum, et praeordinantem illa facta vel reprobantem, potius quam facta Romanorum."

[69] For theological and religious interests in Lyra's exegesis, see the essays by Patton, Smith, Van Liere in Krey and Smith, *Lyra: The Senses of Scripture*, pp. 19–81. For the subject of the Bible, see p. 25, above.

[70] Barcelona, Ms. 121, f. 2rb–3vb. Ps.-Dionysius, Ep. ix, *PG* 3:1103–14, here 1110, where divine speech serves as a vehicle of mystical knowledge.

[71] Ibid., ff. 2va–3vb.

[72] Ibid., f. 5ra (cythonomia, autonomasia, cathacresis, crethalensis, yperbacio, perifrasis, yronica).

[73] Ibid., f. 5ra–5rb. The point is defended from Jerome, *Commentarium in Isaiam*, prol., CCL 73: 1–2 (lines 30–1), and Augustine, *De doctrina christiana*, ii.39, CCL 32:64. Auriol also contends for the applicability of the Tyconian rules, following *De doctrina christiana*, iii.30, CCL 32:102–3.

parts, each part successively divided into books, each book divided into subdivisions, each subdivision divided into further parts, and everything following the overall thematic structure.[74] It is a thematic structure governed by theological expectations, by synchronic divine action dispersed over time. Implied by such convictions is this, and it is surely why Auriol mentions them at the beginning of a Bible commentary: the structure represents textually the convergence of revelation and literal meaning. It is a convergence intrinsic to the theory of verbal signification: that the language of the book as such portrays what God wishes to reveal.

True enough, Auriol is not attributing his description of the Bible to a theory of verbal signification but applying, in a beautifully compact way, exegetical methods and assumptions well known among the postillators of the thirteenth century.[75] All the better. My argument is not that a theory of biblical language *created* a method of reading but that it explained, to those who might want an explanation, how the letter immediately – not as medium – signifies what is revealed. It explained what was happening in their Bible commentaries. For that very reason the theory can, to us, represent a growing characteristic of late medieval Bible scholarship, with its own peculiar demands (it must be buttressed by new reading methods, the subject of the next chapter). To most scholars the Bible was a given; they opened it and lined up their books – the Ordinary Gloss, the *Historia scholastica*, a commentary by Bede or Hugh of St. Cher, a concordance, an index of the *Decretum* and decretals, whatever might be at hand – and worked their way through, passage by passage. As they did so, their assumption was: this is a document that feeds theological discourse; theology is a field of study that summarizes this document.

It is no accident that *Sentences* commentaries routinely describe theology as a rational discipline in expansive terms that implicate scripture. Albert Lang has studied these thoroughly and determined that there were three principal ways to describe the stance of theological writing toward the Bible in the late Middle Ages.[76] Theology, scholars alleged, consisted of either assent to scripture, a discursive explanation or defense of scripture, or speculations drawn from the articles of faith and scripture. Some theologians considered these to be three distinct enterprises (so thought the Dominican Durandus of St. Pourçain, the Franciscan William of Ockham, and the Augustinian Michael of Massa); others, three aspects of a single enterprise (so thought the Dominicans Hervaeus Natalis and Giovanni of Naples, the Franciscan Peter of Palude, the

---

[74] See p. 28, above. [75] See Smalley, Minnis, and Evans in the bibliography.
[76] Lang, *Prinzipienlehre*, pp. 169–75.

Augustinian Thomas of Strasbourg, and the secular theologian Heinrich of Langenstein). Franciscan theologians sometimes divided these aspects into four or five, adding immediate revelation as a form of theology (John of Bassolis and Francis de la Marche). Marsilius of Inghen and Heinrich Totting of Oyta stressed that assent, explanation, and the articles of faith arise from the revelational source of theology.[77]

Obviously enough, there is neither a Lollard nor a Protestant among these theologians: revelation is not *merely* biblical discourse. Nor did many a late medieval theologian follow the early fourteenth-century Dominican William of Crathorn to the opposite extreme, to say that theological knowledge was possible entirely apart from revelation, biblical or otherwise, by the power of reason alone; and even if that were so, it would seem an opinion irrelevant to Bible study.[78] The possibility of religious knowledge apart from the Bible is not my concern. My need is merely to know how such opinions about this source of theology rest upon assumptions about the Bible as a text, or as a cultural artifact, and my conclusion must be that biblical discourse was, in the minds of scholars, primarily about a present religious world of thought. This should be recognized as a major feature of biblical textuality. Any number of late medieval commentaries, even some parts of Nicholas of Lyra's *Postilla*, could prove the point.[79] One need only find a manuscript collection with a good number of commentaries from some late medieval monastery and begin to read. But let me illustrate the presence of this conceptual world in the text with just a few more examples.

The Dominican Robert Holcot wrote a famous commentary on the Book of Wisdom that survives in no less than 175 manuscripts, testimony to an imposing influence.[80] He wrote the commentary apparently as a convent lecturer, probably sometime after fulfilling his regency at Oxford in the mid-1330s, perhaps at the Dominican convent in Cambridge.[81] He

---

[77] Ibid., p. 175.

[78] F. Hoffmann, *Crathorn, Quästionen zum ersten Sentenzenbuch. Einführung und Text* (Münster: Aschendorff, 1988), pp. 17–20, 67–151, 152–205. Albert Lang found a similar view in Francis de la Marche and the Franciscan Richard of Conington: *Prinzipienlehre*, p. 188 n. 61.

[79] See the authors mentioned in note 69, above.

[80] Paul A. Steveler and Katherine H. Tachau, *Seeing the Future Clearly. Questions on Future Contingents by Robert Holcot* (Toronto: Pontifical Institute of Mediaeval Studies, 1995), pp. 2–3 and the literature noted there.

[81] It it is certain that Holcot's magisterial lectures on the Bible covered the Gospel of Matthew. Beryl Smalley, "Robert Holcot, O. P.," *Archivum Fratrum Praedicatorum* 26 (1956): 5–97, here p. 24. The commentary is now lost, but William Courtenay identified excerpts taken from it in Holcot's *Sentences* and quodlibets. W. J. Courtenay, "The Lost Matthew Commentary of Robert Holcot, O. P.," *Archivum Fratrum Praedicatorum* 50 (1980): 103–12, here 104–12. For the chronology of his studies at Oxford see Steveler and Tachau, *Seeing the Future Clearly*, pp. 3–27.

believed that theology, a science distinct from any other, was about the application of logic to revelation, and it seems to me rather consistent with that belief that Holcot's commentary should focus on the Bible's religious purpose.[82] Such a view had become well established in the thirteenth century.[83] He described this purpose somewhat cryptically according to four causes of its honor: a defense of majesty that magnifies (efficient cause), the foundation of firmness that ratifies (material), the complement of power that rekindles (formal), and the exertion of propriety that legitimates (final). Each cause requires a virtuous disposition of the auditor: the efficient cause, a simplicity of intention; the material cause, a humility of estimation; the formal cause, a liberality of communication; and the final cause, a conformity of operation.[84] There is thus a kind of anthropology corresponding to the nature of the biblical text, and this establishes the Bible's moral character. The Bible helps by disposing people to be governable, to resist evil, and to have a serious frame of mind.[85]

[82] F. Hoffmann, "Der Satz als Zeichen der theologischen Aussage bei Holcot, Crathorn und Gregor von Rimini," *Der Begriff der Repraesentatio im Mittelalter. Stellvertretung, Symbol, Zeichen, Bild* (Berlin: Walter de Gruyter, 1971), pp. 296–313, here 300–3. Idem, *Die theologische Methode des Oxforder Dominikanerlehrers Robert Holcot* (Münster: Aschendorff, 1972), pp. 139–40, 176–81.

[83] Minnis and Scott, *Medieval Literary Theory and Criticism*, pp. 200–1. Allen, *Ethical Poetic*, pp. 3–116.

[84] The preface is an exposition of "Dominus petra mea et robur meum," 2Rg 22.2 (= 2 Sam. 22.2). He describes the four causes after a brief account of the divisions of human science – civil or political, mathematical, philosophical or subtle, and servile or mechanical – according to which sacred scripture is a subtle science. Each cause corresponds to a word or words of the text–*Dominus*/efficient, *petra*/material, *robur*/formal, *mea* and *meum*/final. Robertus Holcot, *Postilla Super Librum Sapientiae*, Stadtbibliothek Mainz, Hs. II 480, ff. 1rb–2ra. The manuscript originated in the St. Jakob cloister in Mainz (noted at the explicit, f. 380va); it is written in a hand of the later fourteenth century. It numbers 211 lectures, and with the preface, we would have the 212 counted by Beryl Smalley (*Friars*, p. 140). It therefore appears to be complete. The script is neat, and the manuscript has obviously been executed with care (as the scribe hopefully wrote at the top margin of f. 1r: "Nutrix uerbigene michi confer scribere recte"). Balliol College ms. 27 in Oxford and Bodleian Laud Misc. 562 in London (the latter completed in Paris by a German friar in 1347) apparently preserve the earliest witnesses to the text (Smalley, "Robert," pp. 11–12), and Vienna, Nationalbibliothek, ms. 1513 could be an early German witness. I have seen none of these. I checked Mainz II 480 against another witness of the first third of the fifteenth century, Stadtbibliothek Mainz, Hs. I 26 (Gerhard List and Gerhardt Powitz, *Die Handschriften der Stadtbibliothek Mainz*, vol. 1 [Wiesbaden: Otto Harrossowitz, 1990] pp. 61–2), and against the edition of Peter Drach published at Speyer in 1483, both of which, excepting incidental omissions and changes of word order, very closely agree with Mainz II 480. The latter must at least represent a significant tradition, and perhaps an early and accurate one. William Courtenay once noted in passing that the commentary is neatly divided between literal and moral interpretations (Courtenay, "Matthew," p. 104). But after the introductory division of each chapter, the separation does not seem so strict. For Holcot's prologue, see Minnis, *Medieval Theory of Authorship*, pp. 178–9.

[85] Holcot, *Postilla super librum Sapientiae* Mainz II 480, ff. 5vb–6va. The association of politics and wisdom literature was well established by the time of Holcot: Smalley, "Some Latin Commentaries," pp. 120–5. See also Smalley, *Friars*, pp. 133–202; eadem, "Robert," 5–97; Judson Boyce Allen, "The Library of a Classicizer: The Sources of Robert Holcot's Mythographic Learning," in *Arts libéraux et philosophie au moyen âge*, pp. 721–9, esp. 723.

The 211 lectures on the text of the Book of Wisdom treat successive verses or phrases, with lavish digressions, questions, *dubia* (digressions on "doubtful things"), and examples, repeatedly drawing from the Bible and patristic authors (as well as classical and other sources). Each lecture begins with brief literal comments that often consist of little more than dividing the text into "parts" (that is, its implicit subject matter), followed by analysis with or without figurative examples, interspersed with "notes" and "doubts" that are almost always identified as *dubitaciones litterales*, "literal uncertainties." These prove to be questions only loosely connected to the literal narrative of the text, something that I think makes Holcot interesting. His figures seem extravagantly allegorical. His "literal" doubts seem theologically allegorical. Let us consider a case in point.

The ninth lecture, on Wisdom 1.11, "and spare your tongues of belittling, because dark speech will not go into the void," begins by setting this passage in the context of the previous lecture, and then analyzes it with an explanation of good speech, an explanation of bad speech, and "figures" drawn from secular authors and the Bible.[86] The explanations of good and bad speech build upon observations about the social character of the human being – an anthropological premise. As a social animal (*animal politicum*), a human being has the capacity not only of making sounds but also of self-expression (*opus locucionis*), which includes a reciprocity of feelings and desires between speakers, and it is here that the simple fact of speaking imposes moral obligation. Speech is a figure of the Holy Spirit, who is the love binding the Father and the Son in the Trinity, as Augustine taught. The figure is suggested by the "tongues of fire" at Pentecost, Holcot taking "fire" as a metaphor qualifying the tongues spoken at the event, so that the expression is an image of this figure. To this he adds historical figures, from Martial, the *History of Charlemagne*, and the Bible, which stress the moral conditions of friendship. A note then examines a figure of a belittler drawn from another book of the Bible (Daniel 7.5), the fourth beast of Daniel's vision, with three rows of teeth, to whom it is said, "Rise up! And devour much flesh!"[87] The three rows are figures of three ways to wrongly belittle someone (to diminish the good one has done, to make public a private moral deficiency, and to fabricate allegations altogether). In these examples, the "figures" expand the moral connotations of the passage and place those connotations in a broader literary context, biblical and secular. The "figures" signify verbally in that they have a rhetorical rather than a mystical function.

---

[86] Holcot, *Postilla*, ff. 26ra–27ra.   [87] Ibid., f. 27va–27vb.

Theology 55

Conspicuous is the lack of any indication that the figures should be taken as traditional allegory.

This is an important omission. Holcot's "figures," according to Victorine standards, would be called tropological interpretations, be they biblical or otherwise. They elicit moral doctrine, and it is injected into an argument about the letter of the text. What a Victorine reader would call the spiritual sense of allegory is inserted into a literal argument.[88] This move is not merely implied in the commentary, but is sometimes explicitly named. A fascinating set of four lectures, 24 to 27, assumes that the subject of the Book of Wisdom is an element of New Testament history, the passion of Christ. Holcot shows that the accusations and conspiracy of the Jews against Christ in the Gospels are described by Wisdom 2.14, 16, 17, and 19 – which again by a strict definition of meanings should be called allegory.[89] Holcot again fails to identify the interpretations as such, and indicates the opposite with the "literal uncertainties" raised by these verses: the *dubitaciones* treat questions of secret and independent revelations as well as the question of just how much the persecuting Jews in the passion narratives knew of Christ's divinity – all allegorical speculations, pertaining to prophecy and to life in the church.[90] Such *dubitaciones literales*, literal digressions, appear throughout the commentary, treating topics as diverse as wealth and poverty and the violence of Christ's death. His "figures" refer to analogies between a passage in Wisdom and other biblical and non-biblical stories, the kind of analogy that a preacher might want to use. They illustrate or elaborate the literal sense. Moreover, the literal sense included an extensive repertoire of biblical and theological themes.[91]

---

[88] Another example of this occurs in the seventy-eighth lecture, on Wisdom 6.8, "For the Lord will not humiliate himself to anyone, nor will he fear the greatness of anyone, because he has made the puny and the great, and equally is his the care of all; but the greater scrutiny pursues the greater." The lecture then examines the ethical values proper to Christian jurisprudence (ff. 193ra–194va), with particular attention paid to ecclesiastical prelates. Holcot's interpretation of this passage assumes that the judge mentioned in it is Christ and that the warning is for Christian prelates, who must exercise justice in all fairness. A strict definition would call this allegory and tropology, but Holcot does not attach these traditional names to it. Ibid., ff. 192vb–193ra: *"Non enim subtrahet personam cuiusquam dominus, qui est dominator omnium, nec uerebitur magnitudinem cuiusquam, dominus qui est dominator omnium, quoniam pusillum et magnum fecit ipse, et equaliter est illi cura de omnibus; forcioribus autem forcior instat cruciacio. Cum declaratum sit quod Christus iudicabit iniquos dominos et peruersos prelatos cum graui districtione, hic ostendit quod hoc [in marg add] fiet sine quacumque dissimulacione. Parcunt interdum iudices propter beneuolenciam, interdum propter impotenciam et interdum propter negligenciam, sed ista tria spiritus sanctus excludit a iudice christiano, primo et secundo subinfertur principalis, conclusio ibi forcioribus autem."*

[89] Ibid., ff. 65va–76va (each verse is the subject of a subsequent lecture).

[90] In lectures 24 and 26, respectively (ff. 67vb–68va, 71rb–72ra).

[91] Beryl Smalley noted a few theological themes (*Friars*, pp. 183–4), and Heiko Oberman translated

It is true that we may expect such an ambiguity in moral interpretation, in a book of the Bible whose literal meaning one would expect to be so overtly tropological, just as we have learned to recognize the ethical form of late medieval poetry.[92] But the same difficulty in making distinctions between literal and spiritual appears in other less "moral" contexts. Jacques Fournier, the Cistercian abbot of Fontfroide (1311), later bishop of Pamiers (1317), cardinal (1327), and finally pope Benedict XII (1334), produced his commentary on the Gospel according to Matthew as a cardinal and published it soon after assuming the church's highest office.[93] It is unusual in that he wrote it for no apparent academic purpose (the school of the papal court had its own specially appointed teachers).[94] He divided his commentary into tractates that expand themes suggested by the text, listing chapters at the beginning of each and adding an index at the end. In the first tractate alone, he piles onto exegetical matters a diverse array of themes: the love of God (it is discussed in the geneology of Christ), the manner of the Son's generation in the incarnation, prophecy, and ecclesiology. Another tractate treats the behavior of pastors and polemicizes against pagan poetry.[95] It

---

a piece on justification from the commentary: *Forerunners of the Reformation* (New York: Holt, Rinehart, and Winston, 1966), pp. 142–50. It seems safe to assume that the close association of text and thought contributed to the commentary's influence. The themes were catalogued in an index soon after the commentary was written, and it exists in several versions. One version exists in a fourteenth-century manuscript in Oxford (*RB* 5:146 no. 7416,8; Bodleian, Laud Misc. 562, ff. 189–93); there is at least one related version that circulated apart from the commentary in a codex of tables written in an early fifteenth-century hand, Stadtbibliothek Mainz, Hs. I 208, ff. 105r–130v. Another version of the index that I have seen may be found in Stadtbibliothek Mainz, Hs. I 26, ff. 337rb–355vb (= *RB* 5: 145–6 no. 7416,3), which is appended to the commentary. This version promises to index subjects alphabetically, but only some entries have those references, written in another hand. It provides a glimpse of the amalgamation of moral reflection, natural science, social doctrine, and formal theology as it was conveyed to readers looking for easy access to Holcot's imposing book. The index has doctrinal entries and entries that list natural phenomena and moral analogies to them. Topics range from just war (Stadtbibliothek Mainz, Hs I 26, f. 339ra) to grace (ibid., f. 343va). Smalley described another table of questions that may have originated very early: "Robert," p. 11.

[92] Allen, *Ethical Poetic*, *passim*.

[93] Noted at the end of the table of "capitula" of the first tractate (Barcelona, Biblioteca Nacional de Catalunya, Ms 550, f. 16va). The commentary was finally printed under the name of Nicholas Bocasinus (Benedict XI) at Venice in 1603: J. M. Vidal, "Les oeuvres du pape Benôit XII," *Revue d'Histoire Ecclésiastique* 6 (1905): 557–65, 785–810. Maier, "Der Kommentar Benedikts XII."

[94] Consider Agostino Paravicini Bagliani, "La fondazione dello 'Studium Curiae': una relettura critica," *Luoghi e metodi di insegnamento nell' Italia medioevale (secoli xii–xiv)*, ed. L. Gargan and O. Limone (Galatina: Congedo, 1989), pp. 57–81.

[95] Barcelona, Ms. 550, *passim*. Tractate 1 chapter 8 shows how the genealogy of Christ leads people to love God; chapter 9 explains how the Son of God is generated in the incarnation; chapters 12 and 13 examine the name "Christ"; chapter 22 discusses Christ's "dignities" as prophet, priest, and king; chapter 23 shows how the promise of Christ made to David concerns the person of Christ, whereas the promise made to Abraham pertains to his mystical body. Tractate 28 (on

seems to me important to acknowledge that these matters are not cut away from commentary but inserted in it. The simple and objective fact of the arrangement of the book reveals an important assumption about the text: that it is really about these things, and not so much – certainly not in any ultimate sense – about a remote history that belongs to others. In any event, heavy theology was not uncommon in commentaries.

John Baconthorpe, a Carmelite of conservative instincts who wrote a commentary on Matthew at Oxford or Cambridge in the mid-1330s that has been studied by Beryl Smalley, also accepted the four senses and associated them with an internal progression.[96] Yet it is clear that at an abstract level and in the very structure of Baconthorpe's biblical text, the letter and its spiritual meaning collapse into one another. This is clear in his commentary on book three of the *Sentences* (finished about 1325 while master at Paris), in his commentary on Matthew (finished about 1336 while lector at a Carmelite school of London or Oxford), and in his commentary on book four of the *Sentences* (finished about 1340, also as a lector at London or Oxford).[97] He approached the Bible within a theological framework of two covenants, the covenant of anticipation and the covenant of fulfillment, which is neatly sketched out at the beginning of his *Postilla* on Matthew and again at the beginning of each chapter of the Gospel, where the subject of every chapter is also examined in figures of the Old Testament.[98] In this way, Baconthorpe has every part of the Gospel prove that Jesus is the Messiah, and, chapter

---

Mt. 4.23–5.1) chapter 1 demonstrates how the passage portrays Christ gathering all peoples into the church; chapter 2 describes how curates of souls are to behave; chapters 3 to 6 describe the behavior of prelates; chapter 7 tells the difference between teaching and preaching; chapter 8 recounts how Christ preached to Jews in temple and synagogues; chapter 10 warns preachers to avoid fables and vanity, to proclaim only truth and rebuke iniquity for the approval of God and the well-being of hearers.

[96] Smalley, "Problems of Exegesis in the Fourteenth Century," *Antike und Orient im Mittelatter*, ed. Paul Wilpert (Berlin: Walter de Gruyter, 1962), pp. 26–74; eadem, "John Baconthorpe"; Walter Ullmann, "John Baconthorpe as Canonist," *Church and Government in the Middle Ages: Essays Presented to C. R. Cheney on His Seventieth Birthday* (Cambridge University Press, 1976), pp. 223–46; repr. in Ullmann, *Scholarship in the Middle Ages* (London: Variorum, 1978), nr. 10; Ocker, "Fusion," p. 138 n. 26 and the literature noted there. Johannes Bacon, *Questiones in quatuor libros Sententiarum Quodlibetales*, 2:225–26: IV *Sent.* prol., q. 1 (on Christ and the meaning of the Bible), art. 1 (on the senses of the Old Testament).

[97] For the dates, Beryl Smalley, "John Baconthorpe," pp. 295–6, 299, 302.

[98] The preface to the commentary contrasts this scheme with interest in fables, which Beryl Smalley showed to be a reaction to the use of classical fables as moral "pictures" by the likes of Robert Holcot, Baconthorpe's contemporary: Cambridge, Trinity College, James Ms 348, ff. 99ra–191ra, here 100ra–100rb, edited without the introductory invitation for papal correction in Smalley, "John Baconthorpe," pp. 306–8. See also James Ms 348, ff. 151ra–154ra (on Mt. 13) and Smalley, "John Baconthorpe," p. 308, for the distinction between parable and fable.

by chapter, he has the text describe the structure and composition of the church of his day. For example, chapter ten proves Christ to be the Messiah by the authority of his commission and the form of his transmission of power, which Baconthorpe shows to be the creation of the hierarchical church, to which Christ granted power first by preaching and miracles but now by the order of apostles, with Peter at the head, and by the current apostolic life of preachers (that is, among the members of the mendicant orders).[99] The chapter fulfills Exodus 15.25, where Moses commissions princes and centurions of the people as a figure of Christ, using the power which, according to Deuteronomy 18.15, was to be given to a successor of Moses (a prophecy whose conditions Christ fulfilled). In chapter ten, the power of Christ in the figure of Moses is transmitted to apostles and, thereby, to bishops (in contrast with Luke 10, where priests are commissioned in the persons of the seventy disciples), which also implies three grades of clergy – popes, bishops, and priests.[100]

Baconthorpe used traditional allegories to effect this synchronism of biblical narratives. Implicit in his allegory is the breakdown of old, Victorine distinctions. The patriarchs intended the allegories to break down the differences of times. The "doctors" of ancient Israel *chose* the name Elohim, with its plural ending, to convey the unity of God's essence and the plurality of the three persons of the Trinity.[101] There are other mysteries in Hebrew.[102] The "Chaldean" version of "the Lord said unto my Lord" (Ps. 109.1) expresses more aptly than the Latin how these words belong to the father speaking to the son, which points to the relation of father and son in the Holy Trinity.[103] These mysteries intended by human authors blur the distinction between literal (determined by authorial intention) and spiritual (that which pertains to the covenant of grace) in the Old Testament. Baconthorpe called the spiritual meaning "literal" when he found the allegory plainly apparent. Psalm 44 can only pertain to Christ, literally.[104] Hebrew patriarchs also taught the apostolic life displayed in the Gospels, which fact a Bible reader can discern by applying a simple rule: whatever cannot apply to prophets and doctors of the old

---

[99] James Ms. 348, ff. 143va–145vb.   [100] Ibid., f. 143rb.   [101] III *Sent.* d. 23, q. 1, a. 2; 2:150.
[102] "Sciendum quoque quod in hebraico mysteria abscondita et solum sapientibus nota ex modo scribendi in consueto frequenter designatur" (ibid., 2:151).
[103] III *Sent.* d. 23, q. 1, a. 3, 1:151. The conclusions are in the *Glossa ordinaria*, but the argument from "Chaldean," or Aramaic, comes from Lyra. *Glossa cum Lyra*, 3:251ra, 251va–251vb.
[104] III *Sent.* d. 23, q. 1, a. 3; 2:151, makes this point, referring to an extensive argument in his (now lost) commentary on Hebrews.

law must refer to the apostles "prophetically."[105] In the present, the role of doctors in the church assures the proper understanding of Christian doctrine taught obscurely in the Hebrew Bible.[106] But allegory, *contra* Aquinas, proves a theological point as well as history can, especially since allegory is considered the true meaning of past events.[107] The correct literal reading of the narrative of ancient Israel *is* allegory. The letter of the Hebrew Bible abundantly disproves rabbinic interpretations of Hebrew passages, but arguments drawn from allegories furnish equally valid refutations.[108] The challenge to Aquinas is not a challenge to literalism. It is a challenge to the clear distinction between literal and allegorical.

In addition, Baconthorpe believed that biblical exegesis and the abstract discussions of Peter Lombard's *Sentences* were closely related, for he placed questions taken from his commentaries on Matthew, Romans, 1 Corinthians, Galatians, and Hebrews in books three and four of his *Sentences* commentary.[109] He colored biblical interpretation with theological arguments as much as he used the Bible in theology.

Johannes Klenkok was an Augustinian Hermit much influenced by the theology of Gregory of Rimini, in particular his criticism of Franciscan doctrines of grace.[110] He achieved brief notoriety in the 1350s for his teaching on penance as a Parisian bachelor, for his opposition to Richard FitzRalph and Uthred of Boldon while regent master at Oxford in the late 1350s, and for his opposition to the first written code of German laws, the *Sachsenspiegel*, while professor in the "general school" of his order at Erfurt in the 1360s. At Erfurt he also lectured on the Acts of the Apostles.[111] The lectures display a remarkable sense of the coherence of an academic career, in that they include exhaustive cross-references to his earlier theological works in different redactions, the canon law, and philosophy – thorough and systematic links between these various writings, reflecting the diversity of subjects treated within the context of

---

[105] IV *Sent.* prol. q. 2, a. 2; 2:232–3. The point is of particular concern to a Carmelite who believed that his order was founded by Elijah on Mount Carmel. Robert Holcot once mocked the Carmelite account of their origins (Smalley, *English Friars and Antiquity*, pp. 187–8).

[106] IV *Sent.* prol. q. 2, a. 1; 2:231–2.   [107] Ocker, "Fusion," pp. 146–7.

[108] IV *Sent.* prol. q. 2, a. 1; 2:231–2, where Is. 48.16 is taken to describe the procession of son and spirit from the father within the Trinity, over against the interpretation of Rashi (Lyra made the same argument at length, without mentioning rabbis by name: *Glossa cum Lyra*, 4:82vb–83ra). IV *Sent.* prol. q. 1, a. 3; 2:230–1, after giving literal arguments against rabbinic interpretations of prophetic passages, presents arguments from the allegorical sense.

[109] B. Xiberta, *De Scriptoribus Scholasticis Saeculi XVI. ex Ordine Carmelitanorum*, (Louvain: Revue d'Histoire Ecclésiastique, 1931), pp. 185–6.

[110] Ocker, *Johannes Klenkok*, pp. 16–77.

[111] Eichstätt, Bayerische Staatsbibliothek, Ms. 204, ff. 117ra–192rb.

theological lectures in such schools.[112] In addition, Klenkok highlighted a set of intellectual issues related to Acts by beginning with twenty-nine introductory questions that focus especially on issues of apostolic authority and religious poverty, themes made acute by FitzRalph's recent campaign against the friars at the papal court; and such themes, among many others, appear throughout the commentary.[113]

To him the Book of Acts was less an historical artifact than a means to introduce his students to theological topics relevant now. The Bible should serve as an introduction to theology, as it did in the bachelor's curriculum at Paris, but in his own mind it meant that scripture and other sources of religious opinion made up a single intertextual body. How does biblical narrative converge with theological discourse? Klenkok had occasion to discuss this in his *Sentences* commentary. A fundamental principle of exegesis is that not every sentence of the Bible is to be taken the same way.[114] Thus, when from the cross Jesus said of Mary to John, "Behold your mother," the sentence is indisputably figurative, or tropological as Klenkok says. He must mean that it should be identified as a rhetorical trope, such as was listed in the grammars of Priscian, Donatus, Alexander of Villa Dei, and Evrard of Bethune.[115] But when Jesus said at the last supper, "This is my body," the sentence is not figurative but indicates the miraculous transformation of the substance of bread into the flesh of Christ while the "visible species" remain intact.[116] The Bible is a confusing book. It poses a sentence as if it possessed a particular logical form, when in fact it does not. The verses "God illuminates every person coming into the world," "God wills that every person be saved," or "All flesh shall see," sound like universal propositions – propositions making universally true claims rather than claims that are true under certain circumstances.[117] If so, they require universal premises: "every person" and "all flesh" must refer to everyone who did, does, or will exist. But

---

[112] Ocker, *Johannes Klenkok*, p. 17 n. 3.

[113] I intend to publish a monograph on this work in the near future that will provide a thorough account of these features.

[114] Klenkok identifies the opposite as the premise of an anonymous heretic heard at the court of Pope John XXII, that one literal sentence (*propositio*) of the Gospels cannot be more true than another, or in other words, that every sentence has an equivalent logical value: IV *Sent.*, d. 10, Erfurt, Wissenschaftliche Allgemeinbibliothek, Amplon. F. 117, ff. 42vb; Klosterneuburg, Stiftsbibliothek, Ms. 304, f. 159v; Siena, Biblioteca Comunale, G.V.16., f. 55rb.

[115] James L. Murphy, *Rhetoric in the Middle Ages*, (Berkeley; University of California Press, 1974), pp. 150–1. See also pp. 93–106, below, for the analysis of tropes according to Hermann of Schildesche.

[116] IV *Sent.*, d. 10, Ms. references as in note 114.

[117] IV *Sent.*, d. 15, Erfurt, Wissenschaftliche Allgemeinbibliothek, Amplon. F. 117, ff. 46rb; Klosterneuburg, Ms. 304, f. 166r; Siena, Biblioteca Comunale, G.V.16, f. 62rb.

scriptural language, Klenkok explained, frequently uses universal terms to refer to particulars, so that here "every person" and "all flesh" refer only to those who really will be saved (but to every one of them). He regards these examples as an instance of a fairly common problem of predication in the Bible and theology.[118]

Klenkok's *Postilla* on Acts offers two interesting opportunities to follow the movement from text to abstract thought at the level of word and sentence. One passage treats predestination and the other treats future knowledge. The first occurs at Acts 1.2, where the word, "chose" (for Jesus' choice of the twelve disciples) provoked Klenkok to attack Pelagius, the opponent of St. Augustine.[119] He began by summarizing the orthodox position. Augustine taught, "in all his sayings against Pelagius," "that divine election is the cause of all our merit."[120] Behind Pelagius was the point of view made famous by Ockham and disputed by Augustinian friars, that God elects on the basis of foreknowledge of future merits. That opinion led Klenkok to make a startling claim: the entire controversy between Augustine and Pelagius was about "the grace of predestination," not about "the grace placed as a quality in the soul."[121] To bear out the claim he rehearsed, in elementary and straightforward terms, the various uses of the term election and the problem of future contingency.[122] One

---

[118] The rules are derived from Gregory of Rimini and are discussed with regard to the unity of the divine essence in I *Sent*. d. 2, Erfurt, Amplon. F. 117, f. 4ra–4rb; Amplon. Q. 118, f. 121ra–121rb; Klosterneuburg, Ms. 304, ff. 68v–69v; Siena, G.V.16, f. 3va–3vb. Similar problems with the exclusive or general predication of terms are discussed with regard to the Trinity in I *Sent*., d. 21, Erfurt, Amplon. F. 117, f. 8va–8vb; Amplon. Q. 118, f. 128rb–128va; Klosterneuburg, Ms. 304, ff. 81v–82r; Siena, G.V.16, f. 11rb–11vb. Problems of predication, however, appear infrequently in his commentary on Acts. At Ac. 1.1, he considers the signification of the word *omne*: Eichstätt, Bayerische Staatsbibliothek, Ms. 204, f. 123va–123vb. At Ac. 2.17, he contrasts the positive use of the word *caro* with its negative use (as adversary of the spirit), and he clarifies the signification of the adjective *omne* which qualifies it, (Eichstätt 204, ff. 131vb–132ra): "*omnem*. Exponitur sicut prius [Ac. 1.1; f. 123vb] quod uult omnes homines saluos fieri [1 Ti. 2.4], uidelicet quod non uniuersaliter loquendo sed uniuersalis locuccio." At Ac. 8.9, he considers the predication of the term *magus*. Eichstätt 204, f. 158ra.

[119] For opposition to Pelagianism see Alister McGrath, *The Intellectual Origins of the European Reformation* (Oxford: Blackwell, 1987), pp. 86–93; C. Ocker, "Augustinianism in Fourteenth-Century Theology," *Augustinian Studies* 18 (1987): 81–106; and the essays gathered in *Via Augustini: Augustinianism in the Later Middle Ages, Renaissance, and Reformation* (Leiden: E. J. Brill, 1991).

[120] Eichstätt 204, f. 123vb–124vb, here 123vb: "Augustinus, *De predestinacione sanctorum* et in omnibus dictis suis contra Pelagium ostendit quod eleccio diuina sit causa tocius meriti nostri."

[121] Ibid., f. 124ra: "de ista gratia predestinacionis fuit inter Augustinum et Pelagium dissensio, non de gratia que ponitur qualitas in anima uel accidens." Klenkok holds the doctrine of created grace in conjunction with an Aristotelian psychology as perfectly Augustinian. For the distinction between created and uncreated grace, see Oberman, *Harvest of Medieval Theology*, pp. 160–72.

[122] Eichstätt 204, f. 124ra–124vb. For his treatment of future contingents, see also I *Sent*. d. 38, Erfurt, Amplon. F. 117, f. 12ra–12rb; Amplon. Q. 118, f. 132v–132vb; Klosterneuburg, Ms. 304, ff. 89r–89v; Siena, G.V.16, ff. 16vb–17ra (called distinction 37).

point of the argument was surely to introduce his students to the basics of analyzing terms and what was, by the 1360s, the well-known problem of future contingents. The other point was to draw a theological conclusion from the text of Acts. He showed through a theological digression that emerges from the literal exegesis of the text that divine foreknowledge, however perfect, has nothing to do with causality, or at least not always: moral behavior is a special case in which foreknowledge is joined to good deeds as a cause.

A second striking instance of the movement from text to abstract theology occurs at Acts 1.7 and the words "it is not yours," where Jesus tells the disciples that they may not know the time appointed by the Father for the restoration of the kingdom of Israel.[123] Klenkok associated the passage with Matthew 24.36 (where only the father may know the time of the restoration of Israel). Both verses, "in the manner of speaking of scripture," mean that information about Christ's future kingdom is not revealed to mortals.[124] A discrepancy between Jerome, as quoted in Peter Comestor's *Historia scholastica*, and Peter Lombard over Christ's knowledge occasions a cross-reference to Klenkok's commentary on the *Sentences*[125] and provokes reconsideration of Christ's knowledge of future contingents.[126] If the soul of Christ knew that the Antichrist would come, Christ had to know that it could not be otherwise, and hence Christ would have to assent to the proposition "there will be an Antichrist." But how can the soul of Christ assent to the Antichrist, which would be to assent to someone who is antithetical to himself in every way? The assumption is that knowledge is a form of assent to a mental proposition. Klenkok distinguished between the truth of the proposition and its actuality (its actuality depends upon future conditions). The soul of Christ, he said, only assents to its truth and has nothing to do with its occurrence. This is how Christ unproblematically knew what his disciples could not.

For my purpose, the most important conclusion to draw is a very simple one. Such theological digressions appear in a Bible commentary

---

[123] Eichstätt 204, f. 126ra–126rb.

[124] Klenkok claims to draw from the *Historia scholastica*, but takes very little; cf. Petrus Comestor, *Historia in Actus*, iii, PL 198:1646–7.

[125] III *Sent.*, d. 14, Erfurt, Amplon. F. 117, f. 33rb–33va; Klosterneuburg, Ms. 304, ff. 140v–141v; Siena, G.V.16, ff. 39vb–40va.

[126] Eichstätt 204, f. 126rb–126va. Klenkok then gives the discussion a more eschatological turn, first by raising the debate between Augustine and Hesichius (with specific reference to the interpretation of the weeks of years mentioned in Daniel, 126va–126vb, then by noting how apocalyptic passages frequently refer to events of Christ's life and passion (126vb–127ra) and returning to Daniel's prophecy (it was completed in the death of Christ and the destruction of Jerusalem; he concludes that Augustine's position is correct: 127ra–127va).

as biblical interpretation. They indicate the parameters of the thought-world of the text. The commentary helps establish just how wide that thought-world is.

Nicolau Eimeric was a Dominican inquisitor of the kingdom of Aragon, famous for his unpopular opposition to Ramon Lull. He wrote commentaries on the Gospels and the letters to the Galatians and the Hebrews as he travelled through Catalonia, Aragon, and Valencia from 1367 to 1376 and lived, exiled, at the papal court in Avignon.[127] At least one of the commentaries, written on paper, exists in his own hand.[128] It probably reflects his activity lecturing in the schools of the convents where he lived. Eimeric broke up the Gospels into particular aspects of Christ's identity and life: Matthew treated his humanity; John, his divinity; Luke, his passion; and Mark, his resurrection. It was a routine enough division of books into subjects. In his Matthew commentary theological questions are scattered throughout. At the end of the commentary an index catalogues them chapter by chapter.[129] To some extent the theological digressions may seem contrived to us, for example when in his discussion of Christ's geneology he discusses proofs of orthodox Christology.[130] It would not so seem to him. The text speaks in a present voice, for example the text of the Sermon on the Mount, where he noted that a verse was uttered to admonish squeamish prelates who should boldly teach in the face of persecution (Eimeric himself, though merely a friar and hardly a prelate, taught this at the papal court during his own exile from the kingdom of Aragon).[131] The apostles, he explained, were privileged to know the mysteries of the faith plainly by the gift of grace, whereas Christ hid these mysteries from the scribes and the Pharisees in parables.[132] This, then, is a condition of apostolic writing: it expresses

---

[127] He acquired two papal bulls against the works of Ramon Lull in 1372, which led to his exile by Père IV of Aragon in 1376. He took refuge at the papal curia: "Eimeric, Nicolau," *Diccionari Biogràfic*, vol. 2 (Barcelona: Alberti, 1968), p. 73; E. Mangenot, "Eymeric, Nicolas," *DThC*, 5/2:2027–8.

[128] See p. 28, n. 82.

[129] A catalogue of questions organized by chapters appears at the end of the commentary, Barcelona, Biblioteca Nacional de Catalunya, Ms. 1278 3:223r–279r. The head of each chapter notes the number of questions to the chapter. These total 1,665. Some may have been posed by auditors (e.g. 1:124r, "sed querendum nobis est . . .;" 1:118r, "sed querendum nobis occurrit . . .") or have simply come to mind (e.g. 1:14r, "sed hic questio dura animum nostrum pulsat . . .").

[130] Ibid., 1:5r–7r, where he "proves" the two natures of Christ, the double filiation of Christ (eternal and temporal), and the double passive generation of Christ. The questions which follow raise various exegetical problems, like the conflict between Matthew's genealogy and the Old Testament and why the subject matter of Matthew and of John differs (questions 1, 3, ibid., f. 7r–7v).

[131] At Mt. 5.14, 15 ibid., 1:88v.

[132] At Mt. 13.10–11: ibid., 1:134(6)r–134(6)v (six unnumbered folios stand between f. 134 and f. 135; I refer here to the sixth). After the passage, he continues to explain that the Jews did not understand the text of the prophets.

mysteries openly – the same fact suggested when scholars described the basic structure of the Bible as a book: the New Testament says plainly what the Old Testament predicts obscurely. And open mysteries meant a great deal of theological subject matter. At some times that subject matter was displayed in the thematic structure superimposed on the Bible, as in the cases of Auriol and Baconthorpe. At other times it was scattered in questions and digressions throughout the text, as in the cases of Holcot, Klenkok, and Eimeric.

Auriol, Holcot, Fournier, Baconthorpe, Klenkok, and Eimeric point to the simple fact that the play of ideas in the exegesis of scripture took place in diverse ways. It is enough to recognize, for my purpose, that such play of ideas, which would reflect the unique interests of particular theologians, was utterly commonplace in late medieval exegesis. As was the case in lectures on Peter Lombard's *Sentences*, a Bible scholar began with commentary; he focused on the criticism of ideas; and in most cases he expounded key doctrines, to some extent dialectically, but not as systematically as in the *Sentences* because the order was determined by the narrative, and the narrative was, after all, the Bible. The exposition did not need to be systematic. Its format was a given. Eberhard Winkler's conclusion regarding the controversial German Dominican theologian of the second quarter of the fourteenth century, Meister Eckhart, could to some extent apply to most Bible interpreters. Eckhart's exegesis, he observed, "not only performs the preliminary work of his theological system but contains it."[133] The presence of unique theological interests can be found in John Wyclif's commentaries. He found the humility of Christ portrayed everywhere in the Bible, the same humility that since mid-century had been the main theme in a rising crescendo of complaint against friars at the papal court, in England, and in Central Europe. (In Wyclif's polemical writings, the humility of Christ promised to divest the papacy and religious orders of their wealth.) In his commentaries, he also argued with his theological opponents in excursuses on predestination, law, and other doctrines.[134] We might be tempted to say that Nicholas of Lyra's *Postilla litteralis*, the most disciplined literal commentary of the late Middle Ages and certainly the most famous then and now, is the one exception to the rule that the Bible signified a present world of thought, had not a number of recent studies pointed out the opposite. His strict approach to literal exegesis served his preoccupation with convincing the Jews that Christianity fulfilled Hebrew prophecy: he

---

[133] Winkler, *Methoden*, p. 116.
[134] Benrath, *Wyclifs Bibelkommentar* (Berlin: Walter de Gruyter, 1966), pp. 17–18, 58–59, 73–75, 110–13, 198ff. *De ver. scrip.*, pp. 71–2. Walsh, *FitzRalph*, pp. 377–9 for the background of Wyclif's views.

Theology 65

clearly believed that his literal and historical work on the Bible furnished the proof. Anti-Jewish polemic appears in the work, which supports the Franciscan task of preaching and also a Parisian Franciscan master's contribution to discussions at the French royal court.[135] The *Postilla* also reflects Lyra's Capetian loyalties and the tendency among Bible commentators in the mendicant orders to defend hierarchical authority. One can read Lyra's commentary on the Books of Kings as a "Prince's Mirror."[136] Other aspects of his commentary touched on Franciscan controversies. The coming of the Antichrist, which he first addressed in a 1309 magisterial disputation, appears in the commentary; so too does the doctrine of religious poverty.[137] It was all consistent with Lyra's vocations as a theologian and a Franciscan, occasionally participating on theological commisions, teaching in the convent school, and surely sometimes preaching and hearing confessions.[138] Lyra meant his *Postilla* to throw light on Franciscan identity and Christian society. Exegesis was closely related to a theologian's intellectual profile.

The fusion of exegesis and doctrine corresponds to what scholars considered the more urgent need: to see the present within a biblical and divine framework. The thought-world touched by verbal signification in Bible commentaries is not ultimately the idea of the word or sentence, but theological science as a whole and the Christian universe that it was presumed to define.

A typical commentary facilitated the conversation between Bible and theological argument. It helped create the broad conceptual world implied by verbal signification and by the belief in revelation. The most eloquent statement of this fluid conversation is the rarest one in the fourteenth and fifteenth centuries. It is the gloss format, and an interesting specimen of it was authored by a scholar named Johann Müntzinger.[139] Müntzinger became a Bachelor in the Arts faculty at Prague in 1375,

---

[135] See the contributions of Patton, Smith, Van Liere, Krey, and Klepper in Krey and Smith, *Nicholas of Lyra*, pp. 19–81, 251–311.

[136] Philippe Buc, "The Book of Kings: Nicholas of Lyra's Mirror of Princes," *Nicholas of Lyra*, ed. Krey and Smith, pp. 83–109. See also idem, *L'Ambiguïté du livre. Prince, pouvoir, et peuple dans les commentaires de la Bible au Moyen Âge* (Paris: Beauchesne, 1994), pp. 298–9, 308-10, and *passim*.

[137] Michael A. Signer, "Vision and History: Nicholas of Lyra on the Prophet Ezekiel," Krey and Smith, *Nicholas of Lyra*, pp. 147–71; Peter Krey, "The Apocalypse Commentary of 1329: Problems in Church History," and Lesley Smith, "The Gospel Truth: Nicholas of Lyra on John," ibid., pp. 267–87, 223–49.

[138] For Lyra's biography, see page 6 note 23, above. Such things of Franciscan identity mattered to William of Ockham as well. Marilyn McCord Adams, *William Ockham*, 2 vols. (Notre Dame: University of Notre Dame Press, 1987), 2:903–1010, esp. 961–2, 979–1010.

[139] See page 13 note 23, above. He added vocabularies at the end of his comments on Romans and on the letters to the Corinthians: Johann Müntzinger, *Liber leccionum epistolarum sancti*, Basel, Universitätsbibliothek, A V 28, f. 179v.

attained the degree of Master of Arts there by 1378, and taught in that position until 1383, studying theology along the way, as was common in the late Middle Ages, but never taking a theological degree.[140] After Prague, he went to Ulm, where he directed the city school from 1384 to 1385. It appears that his lectures on Paul's letters were given at Ulm (there remains a chance that the lectures originated in his next job, at Rottweil). Topics that brought an angry accusation from the Ulm Dominicans and a subsequent investigation into his orthodoxy appear in his glosses on 1 Corinthians.[141] Even upon his exoneration by theological commissions at Prague and Vienna, he had to leave for another city. He became rector of the city school at Rottweil, continuing to work as a scriptural interpreter among other things (his commentary on the Lord's Prayer was subsequently translated into German).

Let us consider his interpretation of the story of the cornerstone of the temple at Ephesians 2.21.[142] The interlinear comments are here keyed to the biblical text with superscript letters, followed by the marginal comments, and a note:

[*text of the Bible*]

You are no longer[a] foreigners[b] and strangers[c], but you are citizens with the saints[d] and household servants of God[e], built[f] over the foundation of the apostles [and] prophets[g], with himself[h] as the highest[i] cornerstone, Christ Jesus in whom[j] the entire constructed[k] building[l] grows[m] into a holy[n] temple in the Lord.[o]

[*interlinear gloss*]

[a]All the gentiles always, that is, at the time of the receiving of faith. [b]That is, now more worthy than the Jews in faith, just as the others [were more worthy] in the law. [c]That is, strangers from God and his saints. [d]That is, of the same power and dignity in the house of God with the saints, because you are of that power and dignity by [spiritual] matrimony. [e]That is, servants received into the house of God, to whom the secrets are revealed. [f]That is, instructed and built up [ûfgebûwen] from the good into the better. [g]That is, I say always having been constructed upon the doctrine of the New and Old Testaments. [h]That is,

---

[140] Lang, "Johann Müntzinger," pp. 1200–1230. Georg Kreuzer, *Heinrich von Langenstein unter besonderer Berücksichtigung der Epistola pacis und der Epistola concilii pacis* (Paderborn: Ferdinand Schöningh, 1987), pp. 93–6.

[141] Bertrand Kurtscheid, "Die Tabula utriusque iuris des Johannes von Erfurt," *Franziskanische Studien* 1 (1914): 269–90; Norbert Brieskorn, *Die Summa confessorum des Johannes von Erfurt* (Frankfurt am Main: Peter D. Lang, 1980), 1:15–18.

[142] At 1 Cor. 10 and at the end of the epistle, he also wrote notes on the eucharist, the doctrine for which he was suspected of heresy: *Liber leccionum*, ff. 166v–167r, 167r–167v. For his eucharistic problems, see Lang, "Johann Müntzinger."

in Christ himself. ⁱAlways going forth. ʲThat is, through whom, through Christ. ᵏBoth from the Jews and from the Gentiles. ˡAlways through faith and of the faith of the fathers. ᵐAlways through the help of the virtues. ⁿThat is, until there be a holy temple. ᵒThat is, with the Lord working alongside.

[*marginal commentary*]

This portion is written to the Ephesians in the second chapter. The matter: the apostle makes a determination about the reception of the Gentiles to fellowship with God and the saints, and from so, *you are no longer*, etc. But caution: in 1 Peter it is said, "I beseech" you "as strangers and pilgrims"; is this therefore said wrongly, *you are no longer strangers*? It is answered that the saints are strangers to the world, not to God. Peter talks about the first, the apostle [Paul] about the second.

cornerstone. Note that it is said, in the building of the temple of Solomon there was a certain stone which time and again had been rejected by the builders, because there was no appropriate place where or to which it could be laid. Finally, since it was the best, it sits at the highest point of the building at the top of the arch; the two passing away into one church when they are joined together. It is well said in the Psalm [Ps. 117.22], "the stone which they rejected." And indeed, the apostle calls Christ the cornerstone. And it is called a cornerstone on account of its stability, because Christ himself constantly holds up the church, etc.

grows into a temple. Note on this, the Gloss says no one is so finished that he cannot grow. To the contrary, Christ cannot grow because he is full of all perfection. It is answered that the Gloss speaks about the perfection of someone who is purely a *viator* [a Christian in this life], but Christ was not purely a *viator*, but like a *viator* and someone who laid hold of that life. Indeed, he was not purely a human being but God and a human being at once, etc.[143]

---

[143] Johann Müntzinger's glosses on Eph. 2.19–21, Basel, Universitätsbibliothek, A V 28, f. 188v (the interlinear notes are followed by marginal comments):

[*textus bibliae*]

jamᵃ non estis hospitesᵇ et adueneᶜ, sed estis ciues sanctorumᵈ et domestici Deiᵉ superedificatiᶠ supra fundamentum apostolorum [et] prophetarumᵍ, ipsoʰ summoⁱ angulari lapide Christo Iesu in quoʲ omnis edificacioᵏ constructaˡ crescitᵐ in templum sanctumⁿ in dominoᵒ.

[*glossae interlineares*]

ᵃsemper omnes gentiles, bid est tempore accepcionis fidei. ᵇid est modo digniores iudeis in fide sicut alij in lege. ᶜid est extranei a Deo et sanctis eius. ᵈid est eiusdem uiris et dignitatis in domo Dei cum sanctis, quia estis de matrimonio earum. ᵉid est familiares in eccisiam [*sic*] Dei recepti quibus archana reuelantur. ᶠid est instructi et de bono in melium erecti ufgebowen. ᵍid est supra doctrina noui et ueteris testamenti [*sic*] semper edificati inquam. ʰid est in ipso Christo. ⁱsemper exeunte. ʲid est per quem Christum. ᵏsemper tam de iudeis quam de gentibus. ˡsemper per fidem et fidei patrum. ᵐsemper per augmentum uirtutum. ⁿid est quousque sit templum sanctum. ᵒid est domino cooperante.

[*commentarii marginales*]

Hec leccio scribitur ad Ephesios capitulo secundo. Materia, apostolus determinat de recepcione gentilium ad consorcium Dei et sanctorum et de sic, *iam non estis*, et cetera. Sed cautum [*sic*],

These casual teacher's comments, written in an equally casual Latin, will impress no one for their dialectics. They had the simpler ambition of creating a dialogue of literatures that digressed from the Vulgate to the vocabulary of Ephesians, to the reconciliation of apparent contradictions of little moment, to a legend that reinforces a theological, not historical point, to the resolution of another contradiction. We would expect commentary on a Pauline text to be doctrinal, and that quality seems naturally to carry over into this exposition of an Old Testament figure and Paul's own exegesis of it. The comments go much farther than Paul to say why Paul explained the figure, indicating various theological associations in what he and his auditors must have taken as a nitty-gritty way. Even the interlinear notes perform a reconciliation of the Pauline texts and the doctrine of cooperating grace (notes j and l) within the religious framework of moral and spiritual progress. The dialogue of literatures was the textual counterpart to the ideational character of biblical meaning.

The *literalizing* turn of commentaries – a difficulty in disciminating between literal and spiritual and the predominance of doctrine – received a theoretical explanation in the thirteenth century, namely verbal signification, and is quite evident in commentaries written then. The literalizing turn was well established in the fourteenth century. Can it be attributed to a particular philosophical movement? The diverse authors we have just studied could not be grouped under any single philosophical or theological umbrella. Was there nevertheless some broad trend in the teaching of the liberal arts that predisposed Bible interpreters to dwell on the letter? Speculative grammar, including that part of it called modal or modist grammar, transformed the study of Latin in the second half of the thirteenth century, while the Arts faculty of Paris became a

---

i. Petri dicitur [i. Pe. ii.11], "obsecro" uos "tamquam aduenas et peregrinos," igitur hoc male dicit, *iam non estis aduene*? Respondetur quod sancti sunt aduene quoad mundum, non quoad Deum. De primo loquitur Petrus, de secundo apostolus [Paulus].

Angulari lapi. Nota ut dicitur in edificaccione templi Solomonis fuit quidam lapis qui plures fuit reiectus ab edifficantibus, eo quod non conueniebat locum ubi uel cui applicabatur. Finaliter, cum aptissimus, sedit in summitate edificij in angulo, duos perientes in unam ecclesiam coniungentes. Bene dicitur in Psalmo [Ps. cxvii.22], "lapis quem reprobauerunt." Et immo Christum nominat apostolus lapidem angularem. Et dicitur lapidem angularem propter firmitatem, quia ipse Christus firmiter sustinet ecclesiam, et cetera.

Crescit in templum. Nota super hoc dicit glossa nemo tam perfeccius est quam non possit crescere. Contra, Christus non potuit crescere quia omni perfeccione repletus. Respondetur, quod glossa loquitur de perfeccione puri uiatoris, sed Christus non fuit purus uiator sed similis uiator et conprehensor. Immo non fuit purus homo sed Deus et homo simul, et cetera.

"veritable faculty of philosophy."[144] The origins of speculative grammar go farther back, to the late twelfth century, and at least one scholar has speculated that it then contributed to historical exegesis and interpretation: "The new emphasis on the historical and literal meaning of the *littera* coincided with the development of speculative grammar, which advocated strict rules governing philosophical and theological language. These grammarians distinguished between concrete and abstract terms and defined their functions within the framework of a logically construed sentence," and the rules could apply to any written document. True enough, but they very seldom were.[145] The study of written documents in the late twelfth and early thirteenth centuries depended on an earlier tradition of grammatical *enarratio* – precisely the grammatical tradition displaced, among scholastic writers at least, by speculative grammar in the second half of the thirteenth century.[146] Among the speculative grammarians, the *modistae* believed that the mind apprehends the particular "modes of being" of things and then ascribes those modes to uttered noises, which transforms them into dictions and parts of speech that represent the qualities of things.[147] Other speculative grammarians relied less on such an extreme realism. Their rise is evidence of how logic dominated the trivium by eclipsing rhetoric and invading grammar. With logic dominating their background in the trivium, theologians may have been encouraged to move from biblical narrative to ideas, but there is no evidence that speculative grammar dominated or shaped biblical reading *per se*.[148] Speculative grammar, after all, generally assumed that the signification of words was an elementary issue to be superceded by a preoccupation with what the words actually denoted.[149] Biblical

---

[144] The phrase is Claude Lafleur's: "Les 'Guides de l'étudiant' de la faculté des arts de l'Université de Paris au xiiie siècle," *Philosophy and Learning. Universities in the Middle Ages*, ed. M. J. F. M. Hoenen, J. H. J. Schneider, and G. Wieland (Leiden: E. J. Brill, 1995), p. 139, and p. 156 for the first appearance of modist grammar in a Parisian collection of questions in the second quarter of the thirteenth century (p. 144 for the date of the collection).

[145] Häring, "Commentary and Hermeneutics," p. 195. Froehlich ("Christian Interpretation," p. 507) has noted a single anonymous example from the twelfth century. See also Franco Guisberti, *Materials for a Study on Twelfth-Century Scholasticism* (Naples: Bibliopolis, 1982), pp. 87–109; idem, "A Twelfth-Century Theological Grammar."

[146] Murphy, *Rhetoric in the Middle Ages*, p. 156. This corresponds to the eclipse of rhetoric in the trivium by grammar at Paris and Oxford in the early thirteenth century. Gordon Leff, "The *trivium* and the Three Philosophies," *History of the University in Europe*, p. 308.

[147] Murphy, *Rhetoric in the Middle Ages*, pp. 155–6.

[148] The method of rhetorical invention provided a more direct link with methods of interpretation. Copeland, *Rhetoric, Hermeneutics, and Translation*, pp. 151–78.

[149] Joseph Mullally, *The* Summulae logicales *of Peter of Spain* (Notre Dame: University of Notre Dame Press, 1945), pp. 3–5. Alfonso Maierù, *Terminologia logica della tarda scolastica* (Rome: Edizioni dell'

language was significant at that elementary level, representing literally the very doctrines argued logically in theological texts.

An emphasis on the verbal sign accelerated in the early fourteenth century, as "terminism," another aspect of speculative grammar that also had its origins in twelfth-century trends, provided a method of analysis that gradually displaced the "modes of being." Terminism focused on the analysis of the properties of terms (it should not be confused with the narrower doctrine of "nominalism," a name so fraught with misunderstandings that it is best avoided).[150] William J. Courtenay pointed out that "as of 1330 the potentiality was there for using *sophismata*-solving techniques based on terminist logic to solve theological problems, not simply by creating and applying a 'new logic' in theology but by analyzing biblical and patristic statements according to supposition and context. It was, in theory at least, a major exegetical tool."[151] The use of this technique in debates over the Trinity, the eucharist, and the problem of future contingents, which was provoked in various ways by the teachings of John Duns Scotus and William of Ockham, is well known. But the consequences of this trend for biblical interpretation were meager. Of the commentaries we have just considered, only one, Klenkok's *Postilla* on Acts, uses such a technique, and that unimpressively. Other commentaries where we might expect the influence of terminism to be obvious, like Robert Holcot's commentary on the Wisdom of Solomon, bear out Courtenay's point that terminist techniques had "far less of an effect on biblical commentaries" than on commentaries on the *Sentences*, "perhaps because of the restricting weight of traditional exegesis."[152]

What exactly was that exegetical tradition? We have seen in this chapter that interpreters in the middle of the thirteenth century had begun to associate biblical meaning with a kind of literary analysis compatible with their generally conceptual approach to knowledge, as is clear in Thomas Aquinas.[153] In fourteenth-century commentaries, the assumption that

---

Ateneo, 1972), p. 93. The elementary form of signification should not be confused with "modes of signification," which refer to various additional uses of a term in a proposition.

[150] The best overview is Courtenay, *Schools and Scholars*, pp. 221–40, for terminism, and pp. 193–218 for the various doctrines that were associated with Ockham, pp. 198–201 for his nominalism. For problems with the use of the categories "nominalism" and "Ockhamism" in this context, see also H. Schepers, "Holcot contra dicta Crathorn," *Philosophisches Jahrbuch* 77 (1970): 320–54, 79 (1972): 106–36; here, 77: 320–1. Terminism was used as an epithet for nominalism in the fifteenth century, from which the confusion of terminism, nominalism, and the *via moderna* has arisen. Neal Ward Gilbert, "Ockham, Wyclif, and the 'via moderna,'" *Antiqui und Moderni*, ed. A. Zimmermann (Berlin: Walter De Gruyter, 1974), pp. 117–19.

[151] Courtenay, *Schools and Scholars*, p. 261.   [152] Ibid., p. 262.

[153] See also Frans van Liere, "The Literal Sense of the Books of Samuel and Kings: from Andrew of St. Victor to Nicholas of Lyra," in Krey and Smith, *Nicholas of Lyra*, pp. 70–81.

verbal meaning in the Bible represents the things argued by theologians appears to have been commonplace. If so, we should consider the ambition to abstract ideas from narrative as a predominant feature of late medieval Bible scholarship (overagainst, for example, the historical ambition to reconstruct the past). A number of additional commentaries and texts examined in the remainder of this book should bear this out. Abstracting knowledge from biblical narrative implied a synergy of Bible commentary and scholastic theology. It went both ways. Abstractions from the Bible, scholars assumed, inform theology, but theological truth sheds light on biblical meaning. They were happy to import and export good ideas. The fact reflects only a most general feature of scholasticism, its logical culture and the compatibility of Bible reading with it.

CHAPTER 3

Rhetoric

This chapter examines rhetoric in late medieval interpretation. It shows that a specific adaptation of classical rhetoric, mediated through Augustine, was available to medieval scholars, but it exerted little influence on late medieval Bible study (section 1). The Victorine tradition of biblical allegory was held by late medieval interpreters, but it implied less of a broad outlook on the world in the face of the new, verbal alternative studied in the previous chapter. This may have been related to changing sensibilities about tradition itself (section 2). It is clear that late medieval interpreters had difficulty distinguishing literal and spiritual interpretations, a distinction that was fundamental in the Victorine view (section 3). To what extent, given the limited rhetorical tools available to them, could scholars provide a verbal, grammatical account? Hermann of Schildesche's *Compend on the Senses of Scripture* is a unique text from the middle of the fourteenth century that shows the extent to which one could rely on paltry rhetorical tools to develop a method of "grammatical" reading (section 4). The experiment is impressive enough, and – more than he or any theologian of his day would venture to know – its success could undermine the fundamental conviction that religious and poetic knowledge, like religious and poetic literature, are qualitatively distinct. A rhetorical method of reading could allow biblical and pagan poetry to be read alike.

Theologians evaded this implication. Instead, they recontextualized Victorine and patristic concepts of the biblical image in the intellectual environment of verbal signification, which I will explore in the cases of the late fourteenth-century Vienna professor Heinrich Langenstein and the late fifteenth-century Tübingen professor Wendelin Steinbach (section 5). The next chapter is, in a sense, a continuation of the study of this recontextualization, which relied on a number of concepts (simplicity, causality, prophetic inspiration) to describe the context of biblical literature as human life. While this chapter studies the limited tools of grammatical reading and the late medieval view of biblical imagery, the next chapter surveys the religious ideas that shaped the late medieval sense of the Bible as a text.

1. RHETORIC

Insofar as intellectuals in medieval Europe were concerned, Augustine was the first to adapt rhetoric to Bible reading. He did this in a specific way. He applied the classical method of "invention" to exegesis. "Invention" in classical rhetoric, as first taught by Aristotle and later explained by Cicero and Quintilian, was a procedure "to formulate and establish proofs that are extracted methodically from existing signs and existing regions of argument, or topics."[1] It was performed both in dialectic (the formulation of logical arguments) and in rhetoric (the formulation of persuasive arguments). Invention refers to an orator's or logician's building of proofs, a "discovery," *inventio*, of arguments that best suit one's purpose. In Augustine's *On Christian Doctrine*, some of the topics of invention were systematically applied to the treatment of scripture, and this effected an important conversion of rhetorical work. What applied to speaking now applied to reading.[2] Rhetorical *inventio* became the process by which a reader makes use of a text, discovers its meaning, merging with the process of exposition earlier classified under the field of grammar.[3] In the Middle Ages, as Rita Copeland pointed out, this conversion of a rhetorical function to reading practice had no effect on the academic study of rhetoric, but it did influence the concept of poetry as an art defined in the field of grammar. This inclusion of the art of poetry in grammar reflects an expansion of grammar in the twelfth century and its encroachment on the "rhetorical."[4] The transfer of poetry to grammar, however, had limited influence in the late medieval interpretation of the Bible. By the second half of the thirteenth century, with the rise of speculative grammar, logic supplanted rhetorical subjects in the arts faculties, in the grammatical lectures taking place there. This further restricted scholars' knowledge of rhetoric.

In addition to the conversion of invention from a method of oratory to a method of criticism, Rita Copeland noted that a specific aspect of

---

[1] Copeland, *Rhetoric, Hermeneutics, and Translation*, p. 151.
[2] It was anticipated by classical grammar. Kathy Eden, *Hermeneutics and the Rhetorical Tradition* (New Haven: Yale University Press, 1997), pp. 20–63.
[3] See Copeland, *Rhetoric, Hermeneutics, and Translation*, pp. 155–56 and the literature cited there.
[4] Ibid., pp. 158–78. For the distinction between rhetoric and grammar and the classification of poetry, Murphy, *Rhetoric in the Middle Ages*, pp. 135–8.

invention, the doctrine of circumstances, was adapted to a method of criticism. In Cicero, circumstances comprise one of several categories of topics.[5] Boethius reduced these to seven (who, what, where, when, why, what manner, what means) and made them the cornerstone of rhetorical invention. With the conversion of invention to a form of criticism, the "circumstances" assume a pronounced hermeneutical role, in that

> they define rhetoric by constituting its basic procedure, topical invention.... The individual interpretive act is defined by its historicity, by the historical situatedness of understanding, and this circumstantiality of interpretation also defines the exegetical process in general, to render it something of 'an independent productive act,' on the order of rhetorical invention or argument. With this in view we can see how the historicity of the hermeneutical act corresponds to the circumstantiality of the rhetorical act.[6]

Although this adaptation was first propagated in rhetorical commentaries, it survived only in the context of grammar's study of poetry, where invention had become a grammatical (expository) category,[7] at least until the rise of speculative grammar.

An adaptation of rhetorical invention and the doctrine of circumstances can be found in Hugh of St. Victor, as I briefly noted in chapter 2.[8] The adaptation suggests the influence of Augustine on medieval heremeneutics, but that influence can easily be exaggerated. Hugh assumed that exegetical rhetoric is fundamentally distinct from, even if parallel to, the methods applied outside sacred literature. His six "circumstances" (physical objects as such and their properties, persons who signify mysteries in their deeds and experiences, numbers in their various arrangements and computations, places, times, and events) applied, as we have seen, to the significations of "things," not words. That is, to Hugh a process of "invention" and the study of "circumstances" helped an interpreter move from literal to allegorical, away from the text toward God. The "circumstances" showed that the circumstantiality of the text is the created universe, not the history of human authors. This adaptation of rhetorical doctrine certainly appreciated Augustine's conviction that the text must be, can only be, an instrument for enjoying the divine. But it also limits the method of invention as a textual tool. To

---

[5] For this and the following, Copeland, *Rhetoric, Hermeneutics, and Translation*, pp. 67–72. For an introductory summary of the doctrine and its place in Cicero's *Topics*, Murphy, *Rhetoric in the Middle Ages*, pp. 15–16.
[6] Copeland, *Rhetoric, Hermeneutics, and Translation*, pp. 70–72.
[7] Ibid., pp. 161–78.   [8] See p. 33, above.

Augustine, it had been a way of calculating the force of a text's words as language. To Hugh of St. Victor, it became a way to cross from words over to extra-textual meanings: it helped displace meaning from the text. Hugh's doctrine of invention exercised little influence, and Augustine's doctrine, it would appear, was forgotten. This chapter will show that when scholars explored critical approaches oriented toward the letter as such in the late thirteenth and fourteenth centuries, they drew not from the procedure of invention but from the background of verbal signification discussed in the previous chapter. The adaptation of rhetorical invention to the grammatical study of poetry had little influence on the late medieval study of the Bible – which is not surprising, given the absence of rhetoric as a discipline and the importance of logic-oriented speculative grammar in late medieval scholasticism. Logic was almost the only tool of textual analysis available. Its influence on Bible commentaries was indirect, as I argued in the previous chapter. The great and minimally dialectical commentaries – the Ordinary Gloss, the *Historia scholastica*, and the *Postillae* of the thirteenth century – were still the models of exposition.

The absence of rhetoric in late medieval schools was a significant handicap to literal analysis, but not a fatal one. The following sections of this chapter will study aspects of literal reading in the absence of rhetoric as a systematic field. In the background is the question: to what extent could scholars approach a kind of textuality that humanist rhetoric could seem to redeem? I doubt that I need to convince the reader that we should care whether late medieval scholars anticipated the humanistic exegesis of the sixteenth century. If Protestantism were an unprecedented revival of New Testament religion or an unprecedented abandonment of Catholic culture, the question would be truly pointless, but who today would assume such a miraculous, not to say parochial, view of the Reformation? The question is really whether, beneath the obvious intellectual differences of late medieval Catholics and early Protestants, there might have been some broader continuity of perspective and attitude, and whether it might have touched something so fundamental as Christianity's most authoritative book? We will return to this in chapter five.

2. THE DIFFERENCE BETWEEN LITERAL AND SPIRITUAL

We could call the Victorine definition of natural signification a tight theory, comprehensive and internally consistent. It relied on natural signification, and it implied that natural signification was an especially wonderful way to get the knowledge that belongs to spiritual adepts. Old definitions, including the Victorine rationale, were repeated often in late medieval commentaries,[9] but did this repetition imply an unadulterated continuation of the twelfth-century background?

Tradition was a compelling authority. Interpreters believed that spiritual exegesis, as it was defined by the Victorines and expressed in the common distinction of one literal and three spiritual meanings, had been the standard practice of sacred writers at least since the time of the apostle Paul.[10] The Victorine rationale for it, the theory of natural signification, seemed to be a constituent part of the "glorious repository" of Christian literature.[11] I suggest, and through the accumulated evidence of this book I hope show, that the continuation of allegorical exegesis expresses the force of tradition minimally, in repetition. For the theoretical foundation of allegorical exegesis was first the theory of natural signification, yet interpreters had been drifting from the implications of natural signification – implications of spiritual expertise, privilege, and insight that is neither literal nor secular – since the thirteenth century, even when they repeated it and took it for granted as a quality of sacred literature. In other words, they repeated the traditional definition of spiritual meaning, and they did not restrict themselves to it.

This may reflect a changing sense of tradition itself. The great, sacred repository of Christian literature, dominated by the apostle Paul, Augustine, and Pope Gregory the Great – who were all known as allegorical interpreters – commanded assent. For the monastic writers of the eleventh and twelfth centuries, this assent occurred in contemplative reading of their books, out loud in the refectory and privately. Its framework was not really an idea but an attitude of compliant thinking with ancient saints, a shared frame of mind. By contrast, in the thirteenth, fourteenth, and fifteenth centuries, the authority of tradition was an idea articulated in legal and systematic, dialectical frameworks. From the first compilations of books of *Sentences* and the debates over theological heresy in the late twelfth century, the canon law and theology of late medieval schools formalized and to an extent reified tradition as an idea, by the techniques of debate, not in singular viewpoints or doctrines.[12] By then,

---

[9] See p. 31, above.   [10] As Thomas Aquinas argued: *ST* 1 a q. 1 a. 10.

[11] To identify tradition with the whole of a literature beyond repetition is to adapt T. S. Eliot. See the interesting discussion by Sunhee Kim Gertz, *Poetic Prologues* (Frankfurt am Main: Vittorio Klostermann, 1996), p. 16.

[12] This important point was made by G. R. Evans, "Exegesis and Authority in the Thirteenth Century," *Ad Litteram*, ed. M. D. Jordan and K. Emery (Notre Dame: University of Notre Dame

the idea of tradition implied doctrinal positions and arguments, rather than, as it earlier had, a reader's stance toward his predecessors. There were three main late medieval views of the location of religious authority, as is well known. One located it in the teaching office of the papacy, another in the councils of the church, and another in the consent of all the faithful. These three alternatives were strongly contested, especially after the papal schism – so much that it would be difficult to say that any one position dominated late medieval schools. They were all orthodox. They all admitted the authority of tradition. John Murdoch's observation, that the unity of late medieval scholasticism rested on method rather than material agreement, applies.[13]

With this diversity of viewpoints, the texture of the idea of authority changed. With the dialectical definition of tradition's authority in the late Middle Ages, around debates over a set of ideas (the definition of apostolic authority or the nature and extent of corporate authority), "tradition" no longer relied on monastic reading practices (nor did the monastic sense of reading with previous saints rely on traditional allegorical reading). Tradition was no longer about what one does but about what one accepts.

We may be witnessing one facet of this ossification in the unchanging definition of allegory. A theologian could repeat the definition of the four-fold sense without fully or exclusively embracing the attitude and presuppositions from which that notion emerged. The proof is in late medieval reading habits, where we see that the theory of natural signification described only the most conventional spiritual interpretations, while the theory of verbal signification can account for the tendency to merge literal and spiritual meanings.[14] The theory of verbal signification suggested a different approach to literary representation. It suggested that representation was built on the closeness of verbal figure to reality.[15]

Press, 1992), pp. 93–111. Jean Leclercq, *The Love of Learning and the Desire for God*, trans. C. Misrahi (New York: Fordham University Press, 1982), pp. 71–150.

[13] John E. Murdoch, "*Mathesis in philosophiam scholasticam introducta*. The Rise and Development of the Application of Mathematics in Fourteenth Century Philosophy and Theology," *Arts libéraux et philosophie au moyen âge* (Paris and Montréal, 1969), p. 247. Idem, "From Social into Intellectual Factors: An Aspect of the Unitary Character of Late Medieval Learning," *The Cultural Context of Medieval Learning*, ed. J. E. Murdoch and Edith Dudley Sylla (Boston: D. Reidel Company, 1975), pp. 272–75, 303.

[14] See p. 38, above.

[15] This is apparent in Thomas Aquinas' and Bonaventure's definitions of a human being as an "image" and "likeness" of God, as Denys Turner pointed out. Although Aquinas and Bonaventure disagreed on the relation between these terms, they agreed that either or both terms locate the power of representation in a sharing of form (*conformitas*), the participation of human nature in the divine nature that it represents (Turner, *Eros and Allegory*, pp. 145–49). Turner identifies Hugh of St. Victor's very brief treatment of the *imago Dei* in his *De sacramentis*

3. THE BIBLICAL IMAGE

According to verbal signification, an image could be immediately evocative and meaningful as such, as word or speech-act. The theory of natural signification, by contrast, subordinated texts to an experience of the revelatory, created world. In the late Middle Ages, biblical readers tended to locate the experience of revelation in the text itself, which we will consider in the next chapter; but this included a tendency, seen in many commentaries, to put spiritual meaning in a literal framework. The distinction between literal and spiritual began to break down, which is to say scholars believed that the ability of the text to excite, to cause insight, and to overwhelm the reader with truth was intrinsic to the letter. The Bible became more like poetry.

In part the combination of literal and spiritual was spontaneous, and we will notice it only by remembering the Victorine contextualization of literal meaning in a historical past. The fusion of literal and spiritual is implied, for example, in a commentary by the Augustinian Hermit Heinrich of Friemar on the Decalogue. He was a contemporary of the more famous Franciscan John Duns Scotus at the university of Paris. Later, in 1324, he lectured on the ten commandments in his order's general school at Erfurt. The commentary soon circulated under various names, including Nicholas of Lyra's, and became one of the most widely disseminated Bible commentaries of the late Middle Ages.[16] Heinrich doubted the necessity of historical context for understanding the Mosaic

---

I.vi.2 as the source of this idea. See Hugh of Saint Victor, *On the Sacraments of the Christian Faith*, trans. Roy J. Deferrari (Cambridge, Mass: Mediaeval Academy of America, 1951), p. 95. There, Hugh juxtaposes the divine image to the divine likeness in a human being in these terms: "image according to reason, likeness according to love; image according to understanding of truth, likeness according to love of virtue; or image according to knowledge, likeness according to substance; image, because all things in it are according to wisdom; likeness, because it is itself one and simple according to essence; image because rational, likeness because spiritual; image pertains to figure, likeness to nature." The final clause provides the clue: it is not that likeness is *participatory*, as Turner argues, and image is not. Since image/reason, in Hugh's theory of knowledge, participates in the divine source of truth to some degree when it knows truth, both are participatory. The analogy between image to likeness is that of figure to nature, and that, as the fact that this is a description of creation suggests, is the result of affinities between figure and nature that are natural. Turner's conclusion (*Eros and Allegory*, pp. 149–56), which he admits "is but a speculation," applies the distinction between image (non-participatory) and likeness (participatory) to Song of Songs exegesis, in which the text's sexual imagery is held apart from its non-sexual meaning. The analogy seems to work, but there is no reason to assume that a definition of *imago Dei* functions as a definition of literary imagery.

[16] Clemens Stroick, *Heinrich von Friemar. Leben, Werke, philosophisch-theologische Stellung in der Scholastik* (Freiburg: Herder, 1954), pp. 12–20, 34, 38, 59. Bertrand-Georges Guyot, "Quelques aspects de la typologie des commentaires sur le *Credo* et le *Décalogue*," *Les genres littéraires dans les sources théologiques et philosophiques médiévales. Définition, critique et exploitation* (Louvain-la-Neuve: Institut d'Etudes Médiévales de l'Université Catholique de Louvain, 1982), pp. 239–48.

law. His reason was philosophical. A universal, natural law implied that the decalogue could be both the precepts given to ancient Israel and the law common to all peoples.¹⁷ The decalogue has no historical particularity (and we could reasonably speculate that, in his mind, even the particularity of ceremonial and national laws in the Old Testament served the universal purpose of the ten commandments by foreshadowing a covenant of universal grace).

An obscure Franciscan lector of the fourteenth century, Johann Michael, wrote his lectures in the margins of his Bible.¹⁸ His notes on passages are first literal, then moral, with the literal meaning directly corresponding to the moral sense. So, for example, he explains that the story of Abraham and Lot in Genesis 13 is about the resolution of the conflict between them, which the text of the Bible, according to Michael, treats in three stages that precede the restoration of their friendship: a choice, a separation, and a performance of reconciliation, supported by the divine promise, tested and increasing hope. The same stages and the same promise, Michael points out, apply to progress through penance among those who seek perfection.¹⁹ Michael does distinguish between the literal and tropological/moral stages of his interpretation. But the moral exegesis is a kind of replication of the literal. The letter is certainly not the discarded symbol of spiritual referents. It refers directly to spiritual and moral subject matter, and vice versa: moral meaning elaborates historical experience, insofar as the story of Abraham and Lot becomes a moral tale.

It was possible to identify moral and allegorical meaning as literal, as happened, for example, throughout Robert Holcot's commentary on

---

¹⁷ Henricus de Frimaria (attr. Nicholas of Lyra), *Preceptorium divinae legis* (Cologne, 1477 or 1497), f. 8r–8v.
¹⁸ Munich, Bayerische Staatsbibliothek, Clm 9411, ff. 7r–288v (= *RB* 9:215 no. 4783f, cf. *RB* 3:382f no. 4783f). The glosses are fairly extensive up to the Book of Joshua. The title is given on f. 6vb, top margin: "Incipit lectura fratris Michaelis ordinis minorum super bibliam."
¹⁹ Clm 9411, f. 12r, at Ge. 13.1: "*Ascendit ergo*, et cetera. Hic ostenditur Abraham fuisse ordinatus quoad proximum in prosperis habuit, enim primo pacem in prosperis et secundo pietatem in aduersis capitulo xiv. Circa primum propter opulenciam orta sedicione facta est separacio inter ipsum et Loth, et immo primo traditur materia contencionis, secundo forma separacionis, ibi *eleuatis igitur* [Ge. 13.10], tertio gratia consolacione, ibi *dixit dominus ad Abraham* [Ge. 13.14]. Circa primum nota quod occasio contencionis fuit primo ex opulencia. Secunda causa fuit ex familia, ibi *unde facta est rixa* [Ge. 13.7], tertio effectus in eorum consciencia quem precauent, ibi *dixit ergo Abraham ad Loth* [Ge. 13.8]. Quoad secundum ubi ponitur reparacio, primo ponitur electio, secundo Loth egressio, ibi *eligitque sibi Loth* [Ge. 13.11], tercio executio uel habitacio, ibi *Loth uero moratus est* [Ge. 13.12]. Circa consolacionem primo notatur promissio Dei, secundo probacio rei, ibi *surge perambula* [Ge. 13.17], tertio progressio spei, ibi *mouens igitur Abraham* [Ge. 13.18]." Then follows an application of the stages of Abraham's progression to the penitential life and the progress of those who seek perfection.

the Wisdom of Solomon, where tropology is identified as literal.[20] This was a reflection of an "ethical poetic." We see it applied not only to pagan literature but also to scripture. It reflects the inability of medieval scholars to treat poetry as an independent literary category.[21] But it could also suggest the convergence of theology and poetry. It was, as Beryl Smalley emphasized in her study of the classicizing friars, among whom Holcot was prominent, an extension of the preacher's art. In the same way, the fusion of tropology and the letter stood behind the expositions of the Bohemian reformer Jan Milič. His preliminary exegesis of texts rehearsed the exemplary deeds and qualities of saints as sermonic tropes.[22] In tropology, the spiritual meaning of the text reiterates the literal sense.

The first ambiguity of spiritual and literal was, then, tropology, which we should consider in late medieval commentaries as the belief that the letter was clearly moral at the top layer of meaning. The second ambiguity had to do with a sense of history as a theater of divine action. This anticipates the problem of prophetic inspiration, which we will consider in the next chapter.[23] I would like here to restrict myself to the problem of time. Literal meaning could not be restricted to the past, nor could spiritual meaning be restricted to the present. We can see the collapse of time clearly illustrated in Nicholas Gorran's commentary on Exodus 3 (where God appears to Moses in a burning bush), which I already mentioned.[24] We must look at this passage closely. In addition, the violation of times has an anthropological aspect, which will be considered at greater length in the next chapter. I may introduce it here from Gorran and two later commentaries, Heinrich of Langenstein's prologues commentary and Denys the Carthusian's commentary on Genesis. At issue right now is

---

[20] See pp. 52–55, above.
[21] As Judson Allen wrote almost hyperbolically, by reducing the poetic sentence to ethical subject matter, scholars of the thirteenth century obliterated poetry as a medieval category. Allen, *Ethical Poetic*, p. 18.
[22] This is particularly evident in feast day sermons. Consider the sermon for Cathedra Petri (p. 31 note 2, above). A sermon for the feast of St. Nicholas on Ps. 110.4, *Tu es sacerdos in eternum* (Clm 8864, ff. 17rb–20ra = *RS* 3:589 no. 139) begins by explaining that the text shows that a preacher or teacher must have a perfect life, clear and sound doctrine, and charity. St. Nicolas had them, and so should all prelates and preachers. The sermon proper (ff. 17rb–20ra) begins by noting that the letter of the passage refers to Christ, whom every priest, like St. Nicolas, should imitate. The substance of the sermon consists of Milič's elaboration of three reasons for imitation: to do so is of greater authority, greater honesty, and greater piety in the world. St. Nicolas furthermore commends the priesthood, Milič notes, by the essential dignity of the honor, the durability of election, and the sanctity of justice. A similar use of a saint as an example in conjunction with a biblical text may be found in the sermon for the feast of St. Martin on 1 Ti. 3.2 (Clm 8865, ff. 126vb–129va = *RS* 3:599 no. 237).
[23] Pages 149–61, below.   [24] Page 47, above.

how the experience of prophetic writers and the atemporal facts of biblical narrative comprised, for scholars, a textual fact. This is not something they talked about much, but Jacques Fournier's treatment of the fourfold sense in his commentary on Matthew can give us some indication of what interpreters assumed, and I will turn to him in due course.

Nicholas Gorran believed that the historical Moses, whom as the Hebrew lawgiver we might expect to know Christian truth only in allegorical shadows, had intellectual experience of the new covenant comparable to that of the apostles. This is the passage:[25]

And the Lord appeared to him in a flame, which was done, as Andrew[26] says, lest they make a statue of him. A flame is in constant motion, and thus one cannot make an image of it. Because God might be depicted in an image, God has to be [represented] under certain terms of fire, which was done by means of his greatest active power, so that thus he might show himself to be above the Egyptians, just as fire is above all the elements. Deuteronomy 4 [verse 24], "Our God is a consuming fire." *From the middle of the bush*, to signify that he will appear for the sake of driving on a people humble and afflicted. For a humble bush is a vile bush, and it signifies the people of the Hebrews to be a bush humble and of little worth. Whence the flame in the bush is the help-bringing power of God in the midst of the people. And in this he reveals himself to the Hebrews as the Lord of a people about to be liberated from the burning captivity of the Egyptians. Deuteronomy 4 [verse 20], "the Lord bore you and led you from the furnace of Egypt."

And note that although God may appear in all creatures through the effect of the power of his wisdom and goodness, nevertheless spiritually he is said to appear to some particular person for the showing of some notable effect, like here, *and he* [Moses] *saw that the bush burned, and it was not burned up*, in which is signified that through the flame of affliction the people were not consumed but rather were warmed [that is, encouraged]. Above in chapter 1 [verse 12], "for as much as they [the Egyptians] oppressed, so much they [the Jews] multiplied and grew." Or in this it was signified that God, while existing amidst the Hebrew people in the bush, did not consume in them the thorns of sin, even though he would afflict them like a flame of fire through the oppression of the Egyptians. Or in this it is signified that a law was to be given to the people that would illuminate like a flame, and yet he would consume the thorns of sins by the fire of charity. *Therefore Moses said*, that is he deliberated with himself, *I will hurry*, namely to inquire, *and I will see this great*, that is shown of someone great, *vision*, the miraculous sign, *why the bush is not burned up*. Note that this vision is called great because of the greatness of the mystery.

For the fire in the bush is the divinity [of Christ] in the humanity [of his physical body]. John 1 [verse 14], "the Word was made flesh." *Burned and was*

---

[25] The Latin text is edited as selection 1 of the Appendix.
[26] Andrew of St. Victor, *Expositio super Heptateuchum*, on Ex. 3.2, CCM 53:98.

not burned up, because the humanity is not destroyed by the divinity. Again, *fire in the bush*, born of the virgin, she *burned* inwardly with charity *but was not burned up*, that is, the bush that Moses saw was not violated in the birth of the church, etc. Again, *fire in the bush*: tribulation *burned* in the church because the church is tormented externally *but is not burned up* because it is not consumed internally.

And if it is asked whether Moses might have understood those mysteries, I respond: it is believed that he probably did, just as it is told of Abraham, John 8 [verse 56], "Abraham exulted that he would see my day," etc.

Or so, *fire in the bush*: the tribulation in a righteous man who *burns* with charity *but is not burned up* by tribulation or by charity.

However the Lord seeing, that is an angel in the person of the Lord, *that he* [Moses] *came closer to see*, namely the miraculous sign, *called out to him from the middle of the bush*, namely wanting to speak about the common good, *and said, Moses, Moses*.

And note that he named him twice because he was summoned to a double understanding, namely spiritual and literal, or because two things were about to be completed by him among the people, namely leading the people from Egypt and leading them into the desert. The Psalm [77.20], "you led your people like sheep by the hand of Moses and Aaron."

The exegesis begins with an explanation of the historical phenomenon, God's appearance to Moses at a particular place, in a bush (first paragraph). But soon the sites of literal and spiritual meaning become reversible. First, the commentary historicizes the significations of *res*, things that appear in the text. The bush is a sign for the abject people of Israel who are about to be led out of Egypt; the flame is divine power, by which God will lead them, for fire is a stronger element than the fire of the furnace of Egyptian bondage. These metaphors are named spiritual significations, and indeed, although put in the historical frame of Israel's past experience, they point to moral and Christological interpretations. Yet they were deliberately revealed to Moses "for the showing of some notable effect" (second paragraph). Thus, the flame represents *to Moses*, as well as to Gorran's reader, the affliction of the Jews in Egypt, and the unconsumed bush shows its positive effect on them. It represents *to Moses*, in light of the new, Christian covenant, the limitations of God's covenant with ancient Israel, where the "thorns of sin" were not completely purged (as they are in the church through the gift of charity in baptism), a point that in spite of its historicized form suggests a tropological, penitential interpretation. This experience communicated more than the limitations of knowledge before the advent of Christ. *Moses* pondered the mysteries revealed to him in the sign of the bush.[27] "*Therefore Moses said*, that is, he

---

[27] Contrast Denys the Carthusian, who in the fifteenth century separated the "historical" question of exactly how God appeared in the bush and the Christian allegories of bush and fire that point to the incarnation: *Ennaratio in Exodum*, iii. art. 5, 6, *Opera* 1:494–95, 502–3.

deliberated with himself, *I will hurry*, namely to inquire, *and I will see this great*, that is, shown of someone great, *vision*, the miraculous sign, *why the bush is not burned up*. Note that this great vision is mentioned because of the greatness of the mystery." Indeed, the "vision" touches the greatest mysteries of the Christian faith, the incarnation and the virgin birth, as Gorran explained. He seems to justify his conflation of allegory and the letter of the text when he raises the question "whether Moses might have understood those mysteries," and answers, "it is believed that he probably did, just as it is told of Abraham, John 8, 'Abraham exulted that he would see my day.'" After adding a traditional tropological interpretation that associates the bush with tribulation and the perseverance of charity, he again mentions Moses' "double understanding," spiritual and literal: it was the historical Moses who understood the bush in both ways. By considering the experience of Moses, Gorran conflates the images of Israel's historical perseverance with the perseverance of charity in the new covenant, God's appearance to Moses at Sinai with the incarnation of Christ, and so forth. The text of Exodus thus literally narrates this conflation *in Moses' mind*. The distinction of literal and spiritual as qualitatively dissimilar contexts of meaning (historical and spiritual) has thus disappeared.[28]

How innovative is this interpretation? Much of its basic content is taken from the margin of the Ordinary Gloss: that the burning bush had the purpose of thwarting idolatry, that it may represent Israel's sin or the church's persecution.[29] The Ordinary Gloss's interlinear comments provide initial allegorical links (the flame is the word of God, the bush is Jewish sin, burning and not consumed "because through the law the sins of the people were not purged"), and there is no conflation of Moses' experience with the prophetic and allegorical meaning of the words.

[28] This conflation is related to the problem of the "double literal" sense. Nicholas of Lyra's well-known discussion of double literal sense in his second prologue to the Bible seems to assume a sharp difference between historically and theologically literal meanings, or at least, this is how it is usually taken. Consider, for example, James Samuel Preus, *From Shadow to Promise Old Testament Interpretation from Augustine to the Young Luther*. (Cambridge, Mass.: Harvard University Press, 1969), pp. 68–9. It is important to realize that other theologians, like Gorran here and Hermann of Schildesche in the next section of this chapter, considered the problem of recognizing the theological referents of historical speech more thoroughly than Lyra did. Lyra, *Postilla*, prologus secundus (Strasbourg, 1492), vol. I, f. 2ra. The passage is omitted from the selection translated by Minnis and Scott, *Medieval Literary Theory and Criticism*, pp. 268–70. The double literal sense in Lyra is described very well by Philip D. W. Krey, *Nicholas of Lyra's Apocalypse Commentary* (Kalamazoo: Medieval Institute Publications, 1997), pp. 18–19.

[29] To these things, the margin of the Ordinary Gloss adds the comment that Moses, having been among the Egyptians, "quasi uigilabat mundo," did not hear the voice of God until after fleeing the Egyptians into the desert, since the divine word can only penetrate a mind quieted from external things (*Glossa ordinaria*, 1:116 at Exodus 3.2).

What distinguishes Gorran's interpretation from the Gloss most strongly is not merely the more elaborate interpretations he provided, but the recontextualization of allegory into the literal history of Moses.

A similar perspective on the mind of Hebrew patriarchs can be found near the end of the fourteenth century in a fascinating commentary by Heinrich of Langenstein. Langenstein had already been a prominent professor of philosophy and theology at Paris, vice chancellor of the university, outspoken conciliarist, and mystical writer when he was called to Vienna as professor of theology by Duke Albrecht III in 1384.[30] In 1388 he became dean and, for 1393 and 1394, rector of the university. His principle work as a Master of Theology at Vienna was a massive commentary on Genesis, which he began by commenting on Jerome's prologues to the Bible and the Pentateuch. The commentary on the prologues is one of the two longest hermeneutical works of the Middle Ages (the other is John Wyclif's *On Sacred Scripture*). The commentary proper made full use of Langenstein's expertise in natural philosophy.[31]

Langenstein explained in his commentary on Jerome's prologue to the Bible how Abraham knew the future, according to Christ's declaration in the Gospel according to John:[32]

> While God simultaneously revealed it as an intellectual vision in the intellect, he [Abraham] knew the future time of the New Testament through Christ, which time is nevertheless like a "day" [John 8.56] with respect to the entire preceding time in which those heavenly secrets clearly revealed by Christ and his people were hidden and obscure in various figures.

Again, the historical patriarch was privy to a revelation that allowed comprehension of things that had been deliberately hidden in figures. The prophetic experience of the historical person passes over the distinctions of times.

---

[30] Goerg Kruezer, "Heinrich von Langenstein," *TRE* 15:11–13; C. J. Jellouschek, "Heinrich Heimbuche von Langenstein," *LthK* 5:190–91; Michael Shank, *"Unless You Believe, You Shall Not Understand." Logic, University, and Society in Late Medieval Vienna* (Princeton University Press, 1988), *passim*; Nicholas Steneck, *Science and Creation in the Middle Ages: Henry of Langenstein (d. 1397) on Genesis* (Notre Dame: University of Notre Dame Press, 1976), pp. 9–24. For his study of prophecy, Marjorie Reeves, *The Influence of Prophecy in the Later Middle Ages* (Notre Dame: University of Notre Dame Press, 1969), pp. 425–8.

[31] Steneck, *Science and Creation*, studies the commentary's natural philosophy.

[32] Stadtbibliothek Mainz, Hs I 449, f. 98rb: "Deo reuelante intellectuali uisione cognouit tempus noui testamenti futuri per Christum, quod tempus est tanquam *dies* respectu tocius temporis precedentis in quo clausa et obtenebrata fuerant in diuersis figuris illa archana celestia, que per Christum et suos clare sunt patefacta."

Denys the Carthusian (otherwise known as Denys van Leeuwen, a Carthusian of Roermond) entered the university of Cologne in 1421, studied the works of Thomas Aquinas already as an arts student and became acquainted with the theologian Rutgerus Overhach (he later drew from Overhach's literal exegesis in his own Bible commentaries), attained the degree of Master of Arts in 1424, and then entered the Charterhouse of Roermond in 1424 or 1425.[33] He spent all but a few years of the rest of his life (he died in 1471) in the cloister. Denys's seclusion allowed for unprecedented productivity as an author. Kent Avery's list of authentic works includes 184 titles, forty-three of which are biblical commentaries.[34] The commentaries were written over a twenty-three-year period, from 1434 to 1457, purely independent of any academic requirements, which is very unusual for late medieval commentaries. Even so, Denys's commentaries, like all his works, have a spiritual and doctrinal quality that would render them popular among fifteenth-century readers. The practical quality of his thinking earned him a place beside Nicolaus of Cusa in Cusa's famous reforming tour of the Low Countries and Germany in 1451 and 1452.[35]

According to Denys the Carthusian, writing a generation after Heinrich of Langenstein, the Abraham narratives in Genesis record the deeds of an obedient and faithful man, who was, in Genesis 22, tested by God for the sake of trying and "crowning" him while edifying others. Denys's comments followed the historical notes of the *Historia scholastica*, Nicholas of Lyra, and Paul of Burgos (who is called "Rabbi Paulus"), but he nevertheless conceded that Abraham bound his son Isaac for the sacrifice to represent the nailing of Christ to the cross, while also indicating his own constancy and obedience.[36] The point is consistent with the prophecy of the New Covenant that Denys sees in God's promise to Abraham, that his seed will multiply.[37] Likewise, Jacob's prophecy in Genesis 49 predicts the time of the Messiah and not merely the creation

---

[33] Kent Emery, ed., *Dionysii Cartusiensis Opera Selecta*, vol. 1, *Bibliotheca manuscripta* (Turnholt: Brepols, 1991), pp. 15–38. Idem, "Denys the Carthusian and the Doxography of Scholastic Theology," Jordan and Emery, *Ad Litteram*, pp. 327–59. A. Stoelen, "De Chronologie van de Werken van Dionysius de Karthuizer: De eerste Werken en de Schriftuurkommentaren," *Sacris Erudiri* 5 (1953): 361–401. Lorna Shoemaker, "Denys the Carthusian," *Historical Handbook of Major Biblical Interpreters*, ed. D. K. McKim (Downers Grove: Intervarsity, 1998), pp. 95–9.

[34] *Bibliotheca manuscripta*, pp. 218–54.

[35] Convenient summaries of his thought may be found in Emile Brouette, "Dionysius der Kartäuser," *TRE* 9:4–6, and "Denys le Chartreux," *DthC* 4/1:436–48.

[36] *Enarratio in Genesim*, xxii., art. lxii., *Opera* 1:289.

[37] Ge. 22.18, cf. 17.1–8. *Enarratio in Genesim*, xvii., art. liv., *Opera* 1:244; ibid., xxii., art. lxii., *Opera* 1:291.

of a Hebrew nation from the twelve tribes that will arise from the progeny of his sons.[38] The fact of the revelation forces the spiritual meaning of the figures into a historical frame, which provokes theological questions not merely about the nature of God's voice in past experiences, but also about the purpose of such speech and its relation to hearing: it is ultimately a matter of the coordination of intentions and soul-conditions of authors and auditors, which was known in classical rhetoric and among Christian writers of late antiquity as "accommodation."[39] This came with a Christian emphasis on reciprocity, God accommodating divine speech to human auditors and sinful human beings accommodating themselves to divine communication by holiness. The bridge between Jewish antiquity and the Christian present was created in part by sanctity – that of patriarchs and that to which students of scripture in the late Middle Ages aspired. If it involved sanctity it involved a concurrence of historical wills, of ancient and erstwhile saints and of God. And this required theological explanations, as we will see in the next chapter. With the concurrence of historical wills came a particular experience of reading, one in which the reader is invited to return to the great sacred moments of the past and experience them in the present.[40] Literal reading is empathetic. A textual past likewise elevates present experience; Christian beliefs and practices, especially the practice of penance, are ennobled by relocating them in the ancient history of the Jews.

Behind these anthropological and theological assumptions that will occupy my next chapter – the condition of readers and writers, the nature of prophecy and divine agency – is what scholars assumed to be a textual fact. One knows ancient history by reading, and the textual documents of revelation past are shaped by past experiences of Christian mysteries. The mysteries are embedded in the literature, as Gorran, Langenstein, and Denys the Carthusian imply. If so, what are the stylistics of these documents of revelation? This is a question I wish late medieval scholars talked about more, but lacking the field of rhetoric, how could they address it? The prologue literature of the thirteenth century treated this topic under the heading *forma tractatus*, and it was influential in thirteenth-century poetics as well.[41] In late medieval Bible commentaries, the *forma tractatus* sometimes gets mentioned, but little else.[42] Theology bears the

---

[38] This receives lengthy consideration. *Ennaratio in Genesim*, xlix., art. c., *Opera* 1:437–48.
[39] Dionysius Carthusiensis, *De coelesti hierarchia*, art. viii., xli., *Opera* 15:37–8, 147.
[40] A similar effect can be observed in passional devotion. Consider Ocker, "Ritual Murder and the Subjectivity of Christ," *Harvard Theological Review* 91(1998):176–92.
[41] Minnis, *Medieval Theory of Authorship*, pp. 145–59. Allen, *Ethical Poetic*, pp. 117–78.
[42] Chapter 4, section 2, below.

burden of accounting for style, insofar as style was considered at all. Jacques Fournier provides an especially rich example of it. Since he became a pope taking special aim at philosophical speculation among the theologians,[43] his sense of biblical style may be of particular interest. The question of style is obliquely treated in two difficult chapters of the preface to his commentary on the Gospel according to Matthew. There he addressed the question of the relation of spiritual comprehension to historical contexts, building his account out of an image, the image of a square table. The passage begins at the top of his twenty-fourth chapter, and I will quote it at length.[44]

[Chapter 24]
Why the evangelists are called square tables, chapter 24. Where it is considered that the manner in which the Gospels were written is plain; with regard to history and precepts, the style is dedicated; with regard to the promises and deeds of Christ for our sake, the style is manifold and obscure insofar as mystical and divine things are concerned. Which is all signified in the source: the [form of] understanding mentioned before, its plainness, is expressed in *table*, but its dedicatedness in *sacrifice*, and its multiplicity in *four-sided stones*. Therefore he says *square tables*.

By table, scripture is understood to be a level surface, for just as a table is level and overflows at banquets, so that a person standing at the table can receive the food that suits him or her, so also scripture is in certain places plain and open and for the sake of its comprehension, as it were, serves up spiritual food. Whence Augustine in the letter to Volusianus says, "that manner of speaking in which the Gospel is constructed" is "accessible to everyone. The things that it contains openly, it speaks openly to the heart of the unlearned and the learned like a familiar friend without pretence, even those things that it hides in mysteries lest it arouse proud speech, which a sluggish and boastful mind dare not approach, like a poor man coming to a rich man; but it invites everyone with humble language, whom it not only feeds openly but also exercises in secret truth." "By these, the depraved are corrected, the little ones are nurtured, and great geniuses are entertained," concerning which table it is said in the Psalm [Psalm 23.5], "you prepare before me a table against those who persecute me." Moreover of this table either it is said it is square or it is said that it has four corners, according to that saying of Exodus 25 [verse 26], "you will prepare four gold rings, and you will attach them to the four corners of the table at each of the feet." Whence the interlinear Gloss says, "the Gospels" are four "books, through the faith of which the entire sacred scripture is read and understood throughout the world." And at the passage, "at each of the feet," the Gloss says, "the table of the tabernacle has

---

[43] Chapter 4, section 1, below.
[44] The text is edited as selection 2 of the Appendix. I have not found Fournier's reference in the prologue to the Gospels in the Ordinary Gloss, so I am not sure on what text he is basing this. The table refers to the table of the ancient Jewish Tabernacle.

four feet because the words of the heavenly oracle are taken either historically or allegorically or tropologically, that is morally, or anagogically." Whence also the square table represents the four contents that scripture contains relating to moral things, for according to Jerome on Matthew, "there are four qualities from which the holy Gospels are constructed: rules, commands, testimonies, and examples; that is justice in the precepts, charity in the commands, faith in the testimonies, and fulfillment in the examples."

Insofar as the historical sense is concerned, there are four modes of speaking in the Gospel, namely historically, prophetically, proverbially, and doctrinally. The last three of them are expressed [to us in the New Testament] by the evangelists by means of history, and in the mode of history things may be spoken prophetically, proverbially, or as straightforward doctrine, as is clear concerning prophecy when it is told that Elizabeth said, "why has this happened to me that the mother of my Lord should come to me" [Lk. 1.43] and concerning proverb, when many parables spoken by the Lord are told by the evangelists, and in the same way concerning straightforward doctrine, which the evangelists report the Lord to have spoken.

From which it is clear that fittingly the table is four-cornered or is four-fold, because since those men would tell everything historically, yet those things which they told are either simply historical or prophetic or proverbial or straightforward doctrine. And because it [that is, everything told by the evangelists] is so manifold – its narration is historical and is plain in all things – it is apparent that the table can well be called square. For these tables anyone who seeks can find, as Chrysostom says in the commentary on Matthew while explaining the passage, "send his servants to call those who have been invited to the wedding banquet" [Mt. 22.3]. Like a royal meal adorned with many kinds of food, so is the feast of the scriptures decorated with different kinds of statutes. And on that passage, "I have prepared my meal" [Mt. 22.4], I adorned the tables of the scriptures from all the law and from all the prophets. And on the passage, "all things are ready" [Mt. 22.4], what is asked for salvation's sake has already been fulfilled entirely in the scriptures. The ignorant man finds there what he ought to learn. The man stubborn and a sinner finds there the future lashes of judgment, which he ought to fear. The laborer discovers there glorious promises of unending life, which he eats and is at the same time more thoroughly roused to work. The man cowardly and weak finds there the simple food of justice, which while it may not render his constitution fat, it nevertheless does not permit him to die. The generous and faithful man discovers there spiritual food more constituent of life, which food leads him specifically toward the constitution of angels. The man devil-struck and drunken in sins discovers there medicinal food, which prepares him through penance for salvation. There is therefore nothing less on this table than what is necessary for human salvation. Whence also the evangelists are suitable stewards at these tables, so that each and every one may take what one wants from this table, according to the passage of Esther [Esther 1.8], "the king gave orders telling all his princes that each should take what he wishes."

Fournier summarizes his argument at the head of chapter 24: he will show that the Gospels are written in plain speech and explain the extent to which the texts are literal (as history and precepts) and the extent to which they are figurative of divine mysteries. In the terms of traditional interpretation, as it was elaborated in the twelfth century, he will explore the difference between literal and spiritual interpretation of the Gospels. His image of the square table is treated as an allegory in the old-fashioned sense, to explain allegorical in the old-fashioned sense. A square table with four corners points to four-fold interpretation. But the image is problematized by the layers of narrative that get superimposed within the Bible. For scripture is a site of lavish nurture, where people receive what suits them, "in certain places" without any interpretive complications. Fournier then quotes Augustine, who appeals to scriptural rhetoric: the Gospel speaks unpretentiously as though to a familiar friend, which masks its mysteries for a purpose, "lest it encourage proud speech, to which the mind, sluggish and ignorant, like a poor man to a rich man, dare not approach." This is a restatement of patristic teaching on the purpose of biblical language.[45] Rather than pose a straightforward opposition between the Old and New Testaments – an Old Testament of shadows and a New Testament of transparent revelations – Fournier argues that the text is plain and obscure at the same time, open to some and concealed to others. Different experiences issue from different human vantage points, which is to say that spiritual people exploit hidden truth in the simple language of the Gospels while others hit against a wall, according to the ancient Christian idea, precisely because the language is crude. In his appeal to this ancient Christian literary ideal, Fournier had a choice. He could explain the different experiences of the text anthropologically, in terms of the variable conditions of human wills, or textually, in terms of the characteristics of the writing itself. Here, Fournier attempted a textual explanation.

The Ordinary Gloss lists the traditional four meanings in its exposition of the table of the tabernacle, "the table of the tabernacle has four feet because the words of the heavenly oracle are taken either historically or allegorically or tropologically, that is morally, or anagogically." The biblical quadriga carries over to the New Testament. The meaning of the Gospels, which teach plainly throughout the world the faith portrayed throughout the Bible, can be classified differently, as, according to Fournier, Jerome explained: "there are four qualities from which the holy

---

[45] See pp. 112–23, below.

Gospels are constructed – rules, commands, testimonies, and examples; that is justice in the precepts, charity in the commands, faith in the testimonies, and fulfillment in the examples." The narrative is constructed out of the qualities of justice (in the genre of precepts), charity (in the genre of commands),[46] faith (in the genre of report), and obedience (in the genre of example). Jerome's is a statement about literature. The diverse implications of the Bible come not from its ability to refer beyond the letter but from ethical qualities inherent in the forms of literature therein contained. Fournier makes this point by drawing his readers' attention to the rhetoric of Christian antiquity.

Fournier now succumbs to the medieval penchant for developing alternative lists from a single number, without clearly explaining the connection between them, perhaps assuming our own readiness to search out such analogies. In the Gospels, the historical sense possesses four styles – history, prophecy, proverb, and doctrine; but the distinction is strained, for "the last three of them are related [to us in the New Testament] by the evangelists by means of history." When a pregnant Elizabeth greets her pregnant cousin Mary, she utters a prophecy, "why has this happened to me that the mother of my Lord should come to me." But Luke writes historically. Prophecy is embedded in the historical narrative. When Jesus tells parables, the text speaks parabolically, while the evangelist writes historically. When a character in the narrative teaches doctrine, there occurs both doctrinal and historical communication. The diversity of meanings is therefore restricted to the historical narrative. "And *because* it is so manifold – its narration is historical and yet is plain in all things – it is apparent that the table can well be called square."

Fournier gives his evangelical paradox (a Gospel that is transparent to all but meaningful in diverse ways) a moral spin. The diversity of meanings does express accommodation to the variety of readers, after all, who range from the dumb, the timid, and unsteady, devil-struck men to moral hard-laborers and souls that follow a diet for an angelic life. They come to the feast of Bible study, and they take what they want from the diverse foods on the table, according to their own spiritual capacities. This variety of fare is intrinsic to biblical literature according to the letter. One could say, it is intrinsic to the rhetoric of the letter.

The twenty-fifth chapter of Fournier's commentary on the prologue lends further clarity to his contrast between Old and New Testaments, and it is here that he is most traditional.

---

[46] This is an allusion to Matthew 22.37–38, Mark 12.30–31, Luke 10.27.

[Chapter 25]
Why all the things said and done by the Lord in the Gospels were put there to provoke devotion, and they are effective insofar as within himself a person is a sacrifice to God. Chapter 25.
For a sacrifice follows. Where it is shown that this scripture agitates to devotion, with regard to those things that the Lord does for us, even his promises. For in the Old Testament there are many histories that do not provoke the mind to devotion, but rather some provoke the mind to lust, as is clear in many stories; some even provoke the mind to an upset stomach, as is apparent in many stories; some even provoke the mind to savagery, as is clear in many places. All the history of the New Testament provokes people, if they carefully pay attention, to devotion, and especially the things of the Lord done for our sake and the promises. Whence Bernard in the sermon for the eighth Sunday of Epiphany says, "since in Christ it is obvious that he is entirely sweet, entirely wholesome, entirely desirable, entirely delightful, you should reproduce his works." For that surface considered from the outside is exceedingly beautiful, but if anyone will break the nut, inside he will find it is happier and much more delightful. You will not find it among the fathers of the Old Testament. For also in their works the mystical signification is beautiful and delightful, yet if those things are considered by themselves, they sometimes will be found less worthy, as are the deeds of Jacob,[47] the adultery of David, and many similar things. Precious indeed are the foods, but the vessels are not so precious...

Where again we might expect a simple contrast between hidden and transparent meaning, allegory and the letter, Fournier seems concerned not to present the Old Testament as a book more demanding and, because of its allegories, more sophisticated than the New. His reader is permitted frank disgust at the Old Testament's occasional eroticism and violence, which "provoke the mind" the wrong way. This of course had long been a ground for allegorical interpretation among Christian interpreters. Here it becomes a ground for reassessing the multivalence of the New Testament. The New Testament letter never provokes the mind wrongly; every word of it provokes piety, and even at its surface, seen from the outside, every word "is exceedingly beautiful." But the reader of it can still "break the nut" and see that inside it is better than would appear from the outside. A reader can find pleasure in deeper meanings. Both the Old and New Testaments offer their readers a deeper, spiritual world, but in the New Testament, that representation is always consistent with the historical narrative. Spiritual pleasure belongs to the New Testament letter.

---

[47] That is, his subversion of his brother's place before his father, Ge. 27.1–38.

Behind this is an assumption of the purposefulness of the text, which thirteenth-century interpreters had often identified as its "final cause," the effect that the text intends for the soul.[48] But Fournier (like most late medieval interpreters, as I hope is becoming obvious) assumed that this quality was not merely a condition of readers; it was a condition of the literary genres of the Bible. In the case of Fournier, the Bible's moral purpose is apparent in the distinct kinds of verbal representation that one finds in the Old and New Testaments. To make the point he appeals to rhetoric, even though his use of it is indirectly winnowed from quotations of Jerome and Augustine, and the rhetoric is not developed systematically. Had Fournier been writing this commentary on a book of the Old Testament, he might have considered whether his sharp distinction between genres so uniformly applied. Did not saints of the ancient Hebrews also speak prophecy, proverb, and doctrine: were those not also frank representations of profound spiritual truth? His general distinction is drawn from grossly limited evidence.

There was, as Fournier admitted, a similarity between the language of the Old and New Testaments. The evangelists also wrote enigmas.[49] Fournier resolved them according to a simple rule of Gospel writing. The method, he said, is plain and clear insofar as it pertains to history and precepts; it is "gracious" and devout insofar as it pertains to the things Christ has done for the church; and it is secret and dark insofar as it pertains to the mystical sacraments.[50] This division more than faintly resembles the distinction between literal (plain and clear) and spiritual (gracious and secret) meanings, but Fournier has discovered a way to explain the difference within the parameters of literal understanding. Contrast the Old Testament, some of whose letter, he insists, is really crude and misleading and demands mystical exegesis.

If nothing else, it should be apparent that by the early fourteenth century interpreters could no longer assume that the *contrast* between

---

[48] The "causes" of the Bible are treated in chapter 4 section 2, below.

[49] Barcelona, Biblioteca Nacional de Catalunya, Ms. 550, f. 12rb–12va, lists six matters "que sunt ualde occulte ad intelligendum ac etiam ad loquendum": the mystery of the Trinity; the unity of flesh, rational soul, and sensitive soul in Christ; the miracles of the Lord, the resurrection, and the ascension (which all exceed human intelligence, he reminds us); what pertains to the apostles alone, and what to those who follow after them; how the eternal foreknowledge, creation, sustenance, and future of creation are "in God"; the obligations imposed by grace, the beginning of good works, and the consequences of sin.

[50] After a quotation of Gregory the Great on faith, life, patience, and kindness as the foundations upon which the church is built, ibid., ff. 12vb–13ra: "Ex quibus patet modus tractandi quem habent sancta euangelia, quia est planus et lucidus quantum ad hystoriam et precepta, est graciosus et deuotus quantum ad Christi pro nobis facta, est secretus et occultus quantum ad mistica sacramenta."

literal and spiritual meaning was a uniform feature of biblical literature, nor could they assume that a single theory of representation summarized the Bible's hermeneutic. There was the ambiguity of tropology, the ambiguity of history, and the possibility of giving textual grounds – classifications of genre – for the differences of spiritual content in the parts of the Bible. One had to consider the literary conditions of the parts. The most obvious place to begin was the distinction between Old and New Testaments, related to each other as promise and fulfillment, where methods of representation were relative to the peculiar purposes of God with ancient Jews and the Christian church. This followed divisions of the Bible as a book that could be found discussed in Pierre Auriol's *Compendium* and in other late medieval commentaries.[51] Verbal ambiguities might justify traditional allegories, but alongside this justification of mystical reading was the possibility of verbal signification and a textual assumption: that the mind, at least in specific literary contexts, should discover theological meaning in the letter. In the latter case, the verbal sign functioned less as an icon. This suggests a changed stance toward contemplation, and it forces us to ask what, in these attempts at literary explanation, could compete with the spiritual amazement that accompanied traditional allegorical interpretation as its reward?

4. FIGURATIVE EXEGESIS

The expansion of the literal sense first stood alongside spiritual amazement. The well-known "parabolic" sense of Aquinas, Bonaventure, and Meister Eckhart was a step toward the discovery of historical and historically metaphorical meanings in passages that were spiritually and theologically rich according to the letter, passages whose imagery enhanced rather than led away from literal meaning.[52] What other techniques of verbal interpretation did scholars have? From handbooks of grammar and encyclopedic reference works like the *Etymologies* of Isidore of Seville, interpreters had lists of tropes that they used to classify figurative nouns. They were encouraged to use this paltry vestige of classical rhetoric by Aquinas' recognition of poetic metaphor in the Bible, as Alastair Minnis has recently explained upon the example of two fifteenth-century Dominicans, Alfonso de Madrigal and Girolamo Savanarola.[53] The lists

---

[51] For the division of scripture, see pp. 26–29. [52] See p. 21, above.
[53] A. J. Minnis, "Fifteenth-Century Versions of Thomistic Literalism," *Neue Richtungen*, ed. Lerner, pp. 166–78.

allowed interpreters to see the transference of meaning in verbal images without recourse to natural signification. But to what extent could scholars reconceive the text rhetorically?

I know one treatise that provides extensive evidence with regard to this question, Hermann of Schildesche's *Compend on the Meanings of Sacred Scripture*. Hermann was an Augustinian Hermit who had taught in his order's schools at Magdeburg, Erfurt, and Herford before entering the university of Paris in 1330, becoming master in 1334, and returning to Germany as prior provincial of the Saxon-Thuringian province of the Augustinians.[54] In 1338, he participated in the delegation of German bishops trying to mediate a settlement between Ludwig of Bavaria and the papal court. He was later recruited by the bishop of Würzburg to help educate priests. From 1340 until his death in 1357, Schildesche served in the offices of general vicar, penitentiary major, and cathedral lecturer of the diocese of Würzburg. His lectures on the interpretation of scripture, given at the cathedral school of Würzburg between 1345 and 1350, are preserved in his *Compend*, which he intended to expand into a longer treatise; but if he did, it is not known to have survived.[55]

The first half of these remarkable but neglected lectures treats figurative exegesis (he later explains the Victorine approach), and it merits a careful review. After an introduction, Schildesche's second chapter begins with distinctions of historical and figurative representation in the literal sense. It will be best to hear Hermann speak at length for himself.[56]

The literal sense is when either something performed or not performed is told or when something is commanded or forbidden to be done, according to what Augustine says around the beginning of *On the Usefulness of Believing*. And according to this, at first glance, the literal sense is divided into a historical sense in which the deeds of certain people are told, as in the book of Genesis the deeds of Adam, Noah, Abraham, Isaac, Jacob, and the other patriarchs are told, and in the other books of Moses the deeds of the sons of Israel are told; in the books of Joshua and of Judges, the deeds of Joshua and of the judges of Israel; in the books of Kings and Paralipomenon, the deeds of the kings of Israel and Judah and so on concerning the other books which are called historical.

Second, the literal sense is divided into non-historical, and so it is in all those books where according to the letter something is prohibited and commanded to

---

[54] A. Zumkeller, *Schriftum und Lehre des Hermann von Schildesche O.E.S.A. (g. 1357)* (Würzburg: Augustinus-Verlag, 1959), pp. 1–3, 89–91; consider also pp. 134–5.

[55] Zumkeller, *Schriftum*, p. 23. Zumkeller considered it a disappointing and unoriginal work (ibid., pp. 26, 95–6).

[56] The Latin text is edited as selection 3 of the Appendix.

be done, as in the wisdom books and in many prophetic books and in the letters of Paul. For all that, it poses no problem when in the same book there should occur the literal historical sense and the non-historical, when some deed is told and according to the letter something is commanded and prohibited to be done, as in the book of Exodus, where the deeds of the sons of Israel in Egypt and their exodus from Egypt are told, and yet they are commanded to do many things there, like the ten commandments of the law, and many things are prohibited at the same place, and that is also the case in many other books of Moses and of the prophets. The same thing happens in the four Gospels, where both the deeds of Christ and the apostles are told, and many things are commanded and prohibited. That is therefore the first division of the literal sense, which is something historical, something non-historical.

The second division of the literal sense is that some of those parts are subdivided according to proper and figurated. For the literal historical sense is proper when under proper words someone's deeds are told, as in the book of Judges chapter 9 [verses 1–5]:[57] the deeds of Abimelech are told under proper words, where it is said how he killed seventy-two sons of Jerubaal, his brothers. He who was illegitimate wanted to reign in Shechem. But the non-proper historical sense is when someone's deeds are told figuratively, namely parabolically or enigmatically, as in the same place in the ninth chapter [verses 8–15], where under the figures of a riddle almost poetically they [the lords of Shechem] are told about him, that "the trees of the forests went out that they might anoint over themselves a king, and then they said to the bramble, rule over us!," through which tree he was represented [verse 14].

We also have an example of this in the eleventh chapter of 2 Kings [2 Samuel 11. 1–17], where those things that David did with Bathsheba and with Uriah her husband are told properly, how he had lain with her and ordered her husband to be put to the destruction of death through Joab. But his same deeds are again told figuratively under a parable, which in the twelfth chapter the prophet Nathan proposed to David, about a certain rich man who had many oxen and many sheep and about a poor man who had but one little lamb that he raised at his side, and how the rich man took that single lamb of his and ate it with a certain guest who came from a journey. That sense is therefore a certain literal sense, historical yet not proper, because what was done is not told with proper words but with transferred and figurative words.

The literal sense, non-historical proper, is when something is commanded or prohibited with proper words. Commanded, as in Deuteronomy 6 [verse 5], "love the Lord your God with the entire heart," etc.; prohibited, as in the Psalm [81, verses 8–9], "Israel, if you heed me, God will not depart from you, and you will not worship a foreign god."

---

57 This example was discussed by Augustine (*Contra mendacium*, xiii.28, CSEL 41:508–9), Henry of Ghent, Pierre Bersuire, Boccaccio, and Nicholas of Lyra. Minnis and Scott, *Literary Theory and Criticism*, pp. 209–10. Turner, *Eros and Allegory*, pp. 106–7, 391, 393, for Lyra, who mentions the passage in the preface to his moral exposition as evidence of the need for spiritual interpretation, then in his Song of Songs commentary discusses the passage in terms of the literal sense.

Figurative is when in proper and transferred words something is commanded or prohibited, as in the Apocalypse [chapter] 3 [verse 18], "anoint with salve the eyes," that is, you shall heal the internal eyes of your mind with a soothing poltice. For there are two eyes of the mind, intellect and affect. At first, the intellect illumines and the affect inflames, as the Gloss says at that place. Something is also prohibited by transferred words, for example, Matthew 7 [verse 6], "Do not give what is holy to dogs," that is, to sinners, or "cast pearls before swine," that is teach precious doctrine to piglike and carnal people who are not capable of it. In which books of sacred scripture there may be literal senses, historical, proper, and non-historical is sufficiently clear from what has already been said. The figurative are especially in the Song of Songs, where the love of Christ for the church or for the devout soul is introduced under the figure of the groom and bride.

Schildesche understood that literal expression in the Bible had to encompass more than the report of events, for the obvious reason that much direct speech is about things that happen at no particular time. There are also moral commands and instruction, whose meaning is absolute and universal and not to be drawn with reference to a particular historical context. This establishes the difference between the literal-historical and the literal-non-historical. With the distinction he classifies biblical literature. The letter is a straight narrative of events in some books (the Pentateuch, Joshua, Judges, Kings, Paralipomenon), which he calls historical literal literature. The letter is not straightforward in other books (the Wisdom literature, the prophets, and the Pauline letters), which he calls non-historical-literal literature. Yet some books are mixed (Exodus, with deeds, laws, and the decalogue; other Mosaic books; prophets; and Gospels).[58] Other books are, he mentioned in the remainder of chapter 2, literally figurative (the Apocalypse, the greater part of Ezechiel, Zachariah, and scattered sections of other books of the Bible, including the parables of Jesus). "From what has been said it is clear that those who call each literal sense historical do not speak properly, because many literal senses are not historical."[59] Within both literal frames, the historical

---

[58] Contrast an anonymous treatise on the four senses that has been edited from a fourteenth-century manuscript, where it served as a preface to Rabanus Maurus' *Allegoriae*, in Jean Baptista Pitra, *Spicilegium Solesmense*, vol. 3 (Paris: Didot, 1855; reprinted Graz: Akademische Druck- und Verlagsanstalt, 1963), pp. 436–45, here 438–9 (xii). The historical sense is divided into historical and non-historical, but rhetoric is not applied. Metaphor is the spiritual sense (xiii, p. 439; cf. xxxiv, p. 445). Christel Meier dated the treatise to the mid-fourteenth century (the approximate date of Pitra's manuscript), "Überlegungen," p. 17. The text relies heavily upon Hugh of St. Victor's *Didascalicon*, cites Joachim of Fiora favorably (but uncontroversially), and does not mention a single author more recent than the twelfth century. It may therefore be a twelfth or thirteenth-century piece.

[59] M (for sigla see Appendix, p. 224), f. 136v, "Ex hijs que iam dicta sunt patet eos non proprie dicere qui omnem sensum literalem uocant hystoricum, quia multi literales non sunt hystorici."

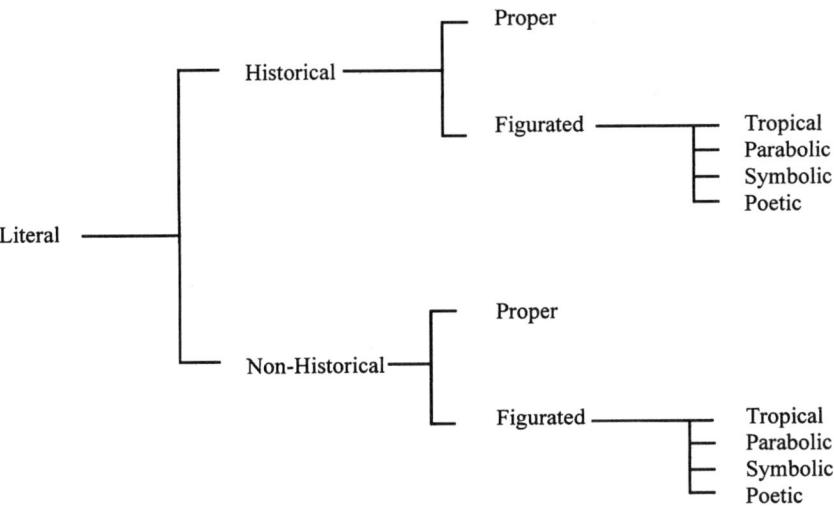

Figure 2. The literal senses in Hermann of Schildesche.

and the non-historical, Schildesche recognized a distinction of language, that terms are sometimes used "properly" and sometimes with a transfer of meaning. This is nothing but the classical rhetorician's distinction between the proper reference of words and metaphor, in which meaning is "transferred" from the proper referent of a word to something else. *Pratum ridet*, "the meadow laughs." A human act is transferred to a meadow.[60] Metaphor stands firmly within Schildesche's conception of literal reading.

In the third chapter, Hermann looked more closely at literally figurative meaning (see Fig. 2).[61] Now, he commented, he enters new ground. His sources, both ancient and modern, give little guidance on the "reduction" of figures to the letter and on the difference between figurative and mystical meanings (although, he admits, there may be many works he has not seen).[62] He fills the gap by distinguishing four figurative senses: tropical, parabolic, symbolic, and enigmatic or poetic. Each sense presents progressively more difficult challenges. The figurative sense expresses events, commands, or prohibitions (the substance of his definition of literal meaning in chapter 2) with "improper and translated words," for example, Matthew 7.6, "Do not give what is holy

---

[60] Quintilian, *Institutio oratoriae*, VIII.ii.6. Curtius, *European Literature*, p. 128.
[61] The first half of the chapter is edited as selection 4 of the Appendix.
[62] See the Appendix, selection 4, lines 4–9.

to dogs," which is a prohibition against giving holy things to sinners, nor "cast pearls before swine," which is a prohibition against teaching spiritual doctrine to carnal people who are not capable of understanding it. These are hortatory statements that include metaphors (dogs, pearls, and swine). When such metaphors appear within a narrative in which most words are "proper," and the proper sense is not obscured by figurative locutions, the meaning is tropical. Pointing to Isidore of Seville and Evrard of Bethune, the authors of widely used grammars,[63] Hermann expressed strong confidence in lists of tropes to clarify metaphorical expressions: "in trope the modes of locution make a comparison of a proper signification to a non-proper signification, of which it is difficult to list all the names."[64] Indeed it was, and not only because the names were customarily given in Greek. Evrard listed 103 figures in the first three chapters of his *Graecismus*.[65] Alexander of Villa Dei listed an only slightly more modest eighty figures; Donatus was the most manageable with thirty-three.[66] Hermann offered a typical definition of trope, but he seems to restrict it to single nouns, even though these, like other figures in Evrard, could apply to entire phrases and sentences: a tropical noun improperly signifies something else, Hermann said, but always within an otherwise straightforward statement.[67] Tyconius' seven rules apply to this sense.[68] The appearance of these rules in the context of grammatical exegesis poses an interesting contrast with Hugh of St. Victor. For Hugh, Tyconius' rules function much like the six circumstances noted in his *De scripturis et scriptoribus sacris praenotatiunculae*. They provide a springboard for spiritual allegories. They begin a train of significations that extend beyond the text and toward God.[69] They do not

---

[63] Murphy, *Rhetoric in the Middle Ages*, pp. 76–138, 151–52, 182–92. Medieval rhetorical manuals concentrated on figures of speech and gave little attention to disposition or delivery. Peter Mack, *Renaissance Argument: Valla and Agricola in the Traditions of Rhetoric and Dialectic* (Leiden: Brill, 1993), p. 5. But Evrard's work reflects the late twelfth-century continuation of "the disciplinary contest over literary, figurative language that characterised the relationship of the language arts in Roman antiquity": Reynolds, *Medieval Reading*, p. 27. Absent was the clear distinction between verbal allegory (*allegoria* as trope) and factual allegory (allegory as the referent of things), introduced by Bede and serving as the basis of theological allegory and *allegoresis* as a method of reading (ibid., pp. 139–40).

[64] Appendix, selection 4, lines 14–24.

[65] Eberhardus Bethuniensis, *Graecismus*, i–iii, ed. J. Wrobel (Breslau: G. Koebner, 1887), pp. 3–15.

[66] Murphy, *Rhetoric in the Middle Ages*, pp. 150–51.

[67] Eberhardus Bethuniensis, *Graecismus*, i, pp. 8–10.

[68] Appendix, selection 4, lines 61–79. In Tyconius and Augustine, however, the rules apply to entire locutions and not merely to figurative nouns. Augustine, *De doctrina christiana* iii. 42–56; *On Christian Doctrine*, trans. D. W. Robertson, pp. 104–17.

[69] *Didascalicon* v.4, trans. Taylor, pp. 122–5. Cf. *De scripturis et scriptoribus sacris praenotatiunculae* xv., PL 175:22–3.

help fix meaning in the letter of the text. For Hermann of Schildesche, the rules do not move beyond the letter; they help fix meaning in the letter.

Parabolic meaning, on the other hand, occurs in texts that are frankly obscure because of the complexity of verbal transference in them. Hermann reflects thirteenth-century views of parable. Literary definitions of it only emerged then, whereas earlier medieval writers described parable as akin to theological allegory, as a transgression of literal meaning.[70] Hermann said parabolic meaning occurs when a possible but imaginary story illustrates something else, as in the parables of Jesus, where a story from daily life illustrates some other moral or doctrinal point. Thus in parable, a kind of improper signification characterizes not just a noun (as in Hermann's view of trope) but an entire narrative. Symbolic meaning occurs in texts that employ analogies that are impossible in nature, like the trees and brute animals that speak (as in the examples he gave in chapter two), God's "wings" in the Psalms, or the "flying" angels of Isaiah 6.[71] It occurs whenever physical characteristics are attributed to pure spiritual beings, like God and the angels. The most extreme type of symbolic meaning occurs when spiritual or rational qualities are attributed to irrational things, like the trees that anoint a king or speaking animals, and this Hermann calls "poetic sense."[72] Poetic meaning depends upon such a literal "falsehood" (*fictus*), the falsehood that occurs when you read the sentence "The trees anointed a king" as a logical proposition.

Each of the four types of figurative meaning – tropical, parabolic, symbolic, and poetic – relies progressively on what Hermann regarded as greater distortions of the words that form a sentence. In his mind, they violated the proper signification of words. This is precisely the kind of negative judgment that led earlier theologians to see metaphor as a movement away from literal meaning, suggesting the need to rely on natural signification: the distortion of nouns and phrases in metaphorical expression implied movement through nature to a supra-literary context, a spiritual context where the mind grasped truth more directly than by means of verbal signs. Hermann, by contrast, realized that a fiction,

---

[70] Brinkmann, *Hermeneutik*, pp. 166–8.
[71] Contrast the treatment of Henry of Ghent on Judges 9.8, who notes the role of trope and metaphor but describes them as "prophetical speeches." The distinction between figurative literature and spiritual allegory seems less clear in his mind. Minnis and Scott, *Medieval Literary Theory and Criticism*, pp. 209–10.
[72] Other authors, such as Thomas Aquinas, had also regarded parable as a form of poetic expression. Brinkman, *Hermeneutik*, pp. 166–8.

although a violation of proper signification, may remain a meaningful verbal sign in the Bible.

Chapter four treats the "reduction" of these four figurative senses to the literal sense.[73] The relation of tropical to literal meaning is fairly transparent, Hermann explained, because it involves single metaphors in an overtly literal context, where tropes are embedded in both historical and non-historical literal narratives.[74] The parabolic sense, on the other hand, tends to have a historical meaning. Thus the majority of Jesus' parabolic and figurative sayings speak literally about the deeds of the Jews, as Hermann argued on the evidence of the parable of the wicked husbandman, in which Jesus compared the persecution of servants to the rejection of prophets in ancient Israel.[75] Parables occasionally bear non-historical literal meaning when they insinuate religious standards of human behavior, as for example in the parable of the ten virgins, which teaches, according to Hermann, that the joy of doing good should proceed from the internal desire of the conscience and not from the desire for the good opinion of other people.[76] Nevertheless, such a moral point may have historical reference, insofar as Christ refers to what still was, at the time he told the story, future. The foolish virgins of the parable, who were unprepared for the coming of the bridegroom and who found themselves excluded from the marriage, would thus refer to the Jews, who Hermann believed did all their deeds only for the sake of human regard.[77] Hermann seems to have believed that tropes are, as it were, carried along by their literal contexts, so that he has no need to explain further the semantics of metaphors.

Symbol, his third type of figure, required something like a semantic explanation. It is, thought Hermann, the abstractions, the qualities, shared between a symbolic "thing" and the spiritual object to which it refers that link symbolic and literal meaning. A symbol-thing and a spiritual referent share "true properties" that exist in the nature of a particular *res* and in God or in spiritual angels (one manuscript adds spiritual substances to the list), but the similarities are "remote and very strange."[78] This distance between symbol-*res* and spiritual referent is what distinguishes the reading of symbols from mystical reading. The characteristics shared

---

[73] Edited in the Appendix, selection 5, lines 1–68.   [74] Appendix, selection 5, lines 5–13.
[75] Appendix, selection 5, lines 15–22. Mt. 21.33–41, Mk. 12.1–9, Lk. 20.9–16. Hermann also cites the parable of the laborers in the vineyard (Mt. 20.1–16) (although Jesus does not explicitly add an anti-Jewish interpretation to it) and the parable of Nathan the prophet on David's adultery.
[76] Appendix, selection 5, lines 25–32.   [77] Appendix, selection 5, lines 32–41.
[78] Appendix, selection 5, lines 43–54.

between the symbol and its spiritual referent are really in the nouns that indicate the *res* rather than in the *res* itself. In Hermann's mind, this constituted a literary definition over against the theological definition of allegory, hence symbol remained within the parameters of the literal. In anticipation of the next chapter, where he treats the difference between literally figurative and mystical, he added that because the similarities between noun and spiritual referent (God or angels) designate *ad litteram* divine or angelic nature, symbolic narratives are a form of literal expression. These are finely drawn distinctions that try to account for mounting degrees of obscurity in language. It therefore seems a little defensive when he turns to the more abstract poetic sense and alleges that its historical aim must be obvious, for example, in the imagery of trees crowning a king in the story of Abimelech or in the riddle of Samson in Judges 14. The riddle refers to a strange event reported in the book of Judges. Samson killed a lion with his bare hands, and later, passing by the corpse, he found a beehive in the lion's mouth, so he reached in and ate its honey.[79] Whereas we might be tempted to take this strange story as an author's poetic extravagance, Hermann took the narrative at face value as an event, and he regarded the non-metaphorical riddle, "food came out of the one who eats, and from the strong one came sweetness," which has no imagery, as poetic. The obscurity of the referents of "the one who eats," "the strong one," "food," and "sweetness" implied to Hermann a condition identical to poetic imagery: the referents of the verbal signs are hard to identify; they require more thinking. Their meaning is indirect and hence in Hermann's terms, "poetic." Nevertheless the "poetic" riddle functions within historical narrative. Poetic expression may also point to non-historical literal meaning, as in the Psalms and even in the Song of Songs, a book whose eroticism was often evaded by mystical exegesis.[80] He noted that this subject must be treated at greater length in his other, longer treatise on interpretation, but whether that treatise was ever written is unkown.

To this point, Hermann has made it clear that figurative language involves a process of remote reference. Verbal signs point beyond their most immediate significations. But the Victorine theory of mystical meaning also assumes a process of words pointing beyond their immediate significations: "not only words but also things are representational."

---

[79] Judges 14.8, 14. Appendix, selection 5, lines 55–68.
[80] Max Engammare, *Qu'il me baise des baisers de sa bouche. Le Cantique des cantiques à la Renaissance* (Geneva: Droz, 1993), pp. 39–60. Consider also ibid., pp. 322–38, for grammatical methods producing a non-erotic reading among early Protestants.

Hermann realized that the traditional view of mystical meaning is extremely close to his discussion of literally figurative senses. Indeed, according to Isidore of Seville and Evrard of Bethune, the two rhetorical sources from which he repeatedly drew, allegory is a type of trope: "Why then does the tropical sense pertain to the letter and the allegorical to the mystical senses?" Hermann asked.[81] Again, Isidore wrote that enigma is a type of allegory, so "Why should the two enigmatic senses, namely symbolic and poetic, pertain to the literal sense?"[82] Hermann's fifth chapter gives the grounds for differentiating figuratively literal senses from mystical interpretation.[83] The difference, he wrote, is five-fold.

First, significations in the mystical senses have their basis in historical things. Jerusalem, the pascal lamb, and the stone on which Jacob rested his head to sleep are all actual things that allegorically represent the church (in the case of Jerusalem) or Christ (in the cases of the pascal lamb and Jacob's stone pillow). Literally figurative senses, by contrast, have their basis in fictions: the trees that elect a king in Judges 9.10 are not real trees, nor is the fatted calf slaughtered in the parable of the prodigal son a real calf. As Augustine said, "the narrative of the Lord, that is the parable of the prodigal son, was about something that never actually happened, yet the things that are mentioned in the speech could seem to have literally happened."[84]

Secondly, the words of scripture can be interpreted mystically in many ways from case to case, "so also any sound meanings can depart from the literal sense and move into the mystical sense," because the words of the Bible have been so endowed by God.[85] An abstract "characteristic," which Hermann earlier showed to be the basis of comparison between a figurative image and its improper referent, is not as multivalent as the "characteristic" behind mystical meaning: the figurative "characteristic" refers to specific subject matter, as for example the parable of the wicked husbandmen discussed in his previous chapter, which is about the Jews crucifying Christ.[86]

Thirdly, the mystical senses are products of divine providence, insofar as the Old Testament is an image of the New Testament and everything within the old law is a figure of the good things that were to come.[87] The figurative senses, on the other hand, are, Hermann alleged,

[81] Appendix, selection 5, lines 71–6. [82] Appendix, selection 5, lines 76–9.
[83] Appendix, selection 5, lines 69–211. [84] Appendix, selection 5, lines 84–108.
[85] Appendix, selection 5, lines 109–16. [86] Appendix, selection 5, lines 117–20.
[87] Appendix, selection 5, lines 124–37.

accidental and issue from human intellectual disability, because the divine ray of light can only illuminate human beings when it is enveloped in metaphors, according to (Pseudo) Dionysius the Aereopagite. Alfonso de Madrigal would make the same point a century later.[88] Metaphors also serve to get people's attention. Hermann clearly regarded the basis of figurative language to be human and not divine, and this human foundation does not express the structure of salvation history, as theological allegory does. Figurative exegesis does not necessarily require divine revelation.

The fourth difference expands upon this point.[89] Literally figurative meaning occurs in poetry and pagan literature as well as in the Bible.[90] Augustine, drawing on Terence, said that the nine muses were not produced by the god Jove and the goddess Minerva but were rather the product of mere artists' genius, carved by three sculptors. The number, three sets of three, was to reflect the universal structure of music.[91] Other poets knew that Neptune was not a god but represented all water taken together – the sea, the rivers, and gushing springs. These poetic figures (*figmenta*) are "meticulously and properly" discovered in pagan literature, but as the food of swine and not of "holy men," as Augustine said.[92] Whereas pagan literature is rich in figurative meaning, it is empty of mystical meaning because it fails to tell "properly" any allegory of Christ and the church, any tropology of the holy soul, or any anagogy of eternal life. Hermann went so far as to say that Christ and the apostles "discovered" the spiritual method of interpretation, and so too did the saints, by divine inspiration, even if, as Augustine said, some Gentiles – the Sybil, Ovid, and the scriptural Balaam (Numbers 23) – prophecied openly of Christ and Christian times (other Gentiles, Hermann noted, obscured the prophecies).

It is possible for figuratively literal meaning in the Bible, however, to serve as the foundation of mystical interpretation, which Schildesche explained as the fifth difference between figurative and mystical.[93] Hermann read mystical (namely, tropological) interpretations of the parables in Pope Gregory the Great, yet he himself suggested that

---

[88] Minnis, "Fifteenth-Century Versions of Thomistic Literalism," *Neue Richtungen*, p. 176.
[89] Appendix, selection 5, lines 138–68.
[90] Hermann excludes symbolic meaning from poetry and pagan literature, presumably because it pertains to the description of God and spiritual substances, subjects that to him were the theologian's prerogative. He apparently did not entertain the idea that non-religious poetry and pagan literature would also require metaphor to describe God and spiritual substances.
[91] Augustine, *On Christian Doctrine*, pp. 53–4.   [92] Ibid., p. 85.
[93] Appendix, selection 5, lines 169–80.

parables should rather be historicized to refer to the Jews. In the fifth difference between figurative and mystical he simply claimed that Gregory's tropologies are built upon a figurative-literal sense. The figuratively literal meaning may serve as the literal basis of mystical interpretation.

In this way, Hermann believed that his five-fold comparison of biblical imagery with mystical meaning reinforced the traditional, compatible relationship of literal and spiritual interpretations. Could he have been uneasy with this? The chapter ends by returning to the question of allegory as a trope, which he handled clumsily.[94] Hermann noted that the term "allegory" may refer to both a particular grammatical trope and a method of spiritual reading. A term, for example "animal," used "absolutely," refers to an irrational animal, but it may also refer to a rational animal, a human being. The term "body," used "absolutely," refers to an inanimate body, but it may also refer to a living body. Hermann's meaning seems to be that in the case of "animal" for human being, something is added to the class "animal," namely a rational soul. In the case of "body" for a living body, something is added to the class "body," namely a living soul. It is an argument about supposition, and it reflects relations of genera and species outlined in "Porphyry's tree."[95] Similarly, enigma can only be called a species of allegorical trope grammatically and not theologically. The grammatical and the theological differ in that grammatical allegory has "a certain double power under another thing indicating something else figuratively." That is, using the term *animal* to refer to a human being involves a transfer of meaning, like the transfer of meaning in figurative language. This underscores the fact that grammatical allegory can be explained at the level of words, and it explains the relation of enigma to grammatical allegory (it is a form of grammatical allegory).

Schildesche insisted that figurative speech in the letter of the Bible cannot undermine spiritual exegesis. He argued that they have distinct foundations, and his exploration of non-historical literal meanings tried to prove this. The basis of figurative meaning is human, whereas the basis of spiritual exegesis is divine. He also seemed to believe that figurative meaning tends to be fixed, whereas there is tremendous freedom in spiritual exegesis, and interpretations within a basic scheme of promise-fulfillment, Old and New Testaments can vary. But were

---

[94] Appendix, selection 5, lines 181–211.
[95] For definitions of supposition see Maieru, *Terminologia logica della tarda scolastica*, pp. 87, 93. Mullally, *The* Summa logicales *of Peter of Spain*, p. 13. William of Sherwood, *Introduction to Logic*, trans. N. Kretzmann (Minneapolis: University of Minnesota Press, 1966), p. 54.

literally figurative and mystical forms of exegesis in fact so very distinct? To Hermann, both literally figurative and mystical readings were theological, when all was said and done. Figurative speech in the Bible answered the inability of human beings to understand God and spiritual substances directly, whereas mystical interpretation revealed meanings hidden in the text by God. Patristic theologians, like Augustine,[96] and (as we will see in the next chapter) Jerome, found both theological assumptions, the anthropological assumption of figurative reading and the supernatural assumption of mystical reading, intricately related. The fact that God spoke in veiled language first justified spiritual exegesis to medieval interpreters, in the sense that obscure and even grotesque speech in the Bible required an enlighted, mystical interpretation by spiritual people. Hermann was aware of this connection between veiled language and mystical reading. So, for example, when he revived two rhetorical categories that he had learned from Augustine's *On True Religion*, aetiology and analogy, Hermann took them to be applicable to both literal and mystical readings.[97] In spite of instances such as this one in which a rhetorical explanation applies to both literal and spiritual senses, his was a stronger distinction between the rhetorical and the mystical than patristic and medieval interpreters before the thirteenth century could have allowed.

It seems to me that Hermann's extensive discussion of figurative language could have displaced mystical reading altogether. At the level of signifying, his views of figurative and mystical interpretations work much the same way. They both rely on a transfer of meaning: the verbal sign points to a "thing" that in turn represents something else, the fact that allowed Augustine to see spiritual interpretation as a kind of intensified and advanced rhetoric, an interpretative technique superior to those used in the reading of pagan literature.[98] Hermann explored the possibility of treating figurative language in a more strictly rhetorical way. In Jesus' sentence, "Do not give what is holy to dogs," the word "dogs" is, to Hermann, a trope for sinners because the reader can identify a similarity between sinners and dogs.[99] A dog is unworthy of precious things; a

---

[96] *On Christian Doctrine*, ii. 62–63, pp. 76–8. Augustine, Ep. 137, Saint Augustine, *Letters*, 6 vols., trans. W. Parsons and R. B. Eno (Washington, DC: Catholic University of America Press, 1951–89), 3:32–4.
[97] *De vera religione*, 1.99, PL 34:166. Zumkeller, *Schrifttum*, pp. 37–40. They are particularly useful, he says, for showing the relation of the two Testaments, which he then argues in a nuanced criticism of Joachim of Fiore's method of correlation.
[98] Augustine, *On Christian Doctrine*, iii.40, pp. 102–3.
[99] Appendix, selection 3, lines 54–61.

sinner is unworthy of holy things. An abstract quality, unworthiness, connects the noun "dog" with the noun "sinner." Hermann believed that this connection was purely verbal. A mystical reading of a sentence required, he argued, a more specific historical setting. To return to Cassian's popular example, the literal meaning of Jerusalem is not figurative but a real city. It seems to me that something is overlooked here, and that is the simple fact that Jerusalem, in spite of the fact that it is a real city, could be a metaphor at the literal level, just as dogs, which he assumes to be unreal in Jesus' sentence, could refer to real animals. If one accepts this fact, then one cannot say, as Hermann did, that a noun such as "Jerusalem" with specific historical reference in biblical history is never figurative because history makes its remote reference mystical. The process of signification is the same in both nouns, "dogs" and "Jerusalem." One should say that both are figurative in grammatical terms.

It seems to me that the difference Hermann wanted to allege between grammatical and mystical reading at the level of signification is not very strong. What was implied to him by the difference? The difference was the range of interpretations. A reader can find any mystical meaning in any biblical text, whereas figurative meaning is specific to particular passages that employ certain forms of language. Contrary to our own assumptions about poetic expression, Hermann allows the theological conviction, that literal theological meaning is unambivalent, to color his view of figurative language in the Bible. Figurative exegesis discovers fixed, literally true meaning. Mystical exegesis uses scripture to launch the mind into spiritual mysteries, and therefore it can discover myriad meanings in the text. With this difference in mind, we can see that figurative exegesis must have seemed too narrow a method to replace the spiritual amazement experienced in mystical reading.

Still, he showed how rhetoric could explain difficult and crude passages of the Bible without departing from the literal sense. He pointed out how this *method*, although identical with that used in the interpretation of secular literature, was useful in the interpretation of scripture. Any potential incompatibility between rhetoric and mysticism was concealed by the desire for mystical experience, perhaps in part because Hermann did not know how rhetoric – a rhetorical method of invention, to be exact – might help an interpreter see the text as possessing a complete and inherent intellectual context. A handy list of tropes, a catologue from which one could pull out an explanation for an obscure word, would not accomplish that.

5. BIBLICAL RHETORIC

There was a "grammatical" explanation of the biblical image, yet scholars like Schildesche were reluctant to juxtapose it with the traditions of spiritual interpretation. The technique of identifying tropes was applied in a minimal way, to convert figurative nouns to direct language, as has been observed in the exegesis of the famous German Dominican Meister Eckhart and can also be seen in Johannes Klenkok's *Postilla* on Acts.[100] Grammar does not seem to have led theologians to a stylistics of the Bible. When Schildesche recognized the similarity of biblical to poetic language, his context was really a logical one – supposition – and not the rhetorical context of style and argument. But theologians did have a discourse of biblical style. It drew on Victorine and patristic concepts. Those concepts were removed from the earlier context of monastic reading and placed in the scholastic context of literal argument. I would like to consider in conclusion to this chapter this recontextualization at the end of the fourteenth century and the end of the fifteenth century, in Heinrich of Langenstein and Wendelin Steinbach.

Langenstein, like Schildesche, placed mystical and literal methods side by side, also adapting a patristic view of biblical literature. The Bible's language is utterly different from the vain embellishments of rhetoric, he said. It possesses a unique rhetoric, humble, yet concealing tremendous mysteries:[101]

And in this the humble speech of holy scripture differs from the sublime and polished speech of human tradition, so that suddenly, as if just under a golden

---

[100] Winkler, *Methoden*, pp. 85ff. In Klenkok's *Postilla* there are ten instances in which his explanation of a passage appeals to a rhetorical trope. An additional forty-three instances in which he examines *figurae* seem to function much the same way.

[101] Stadtbibliothek Mainz, Hs. I 449, f. 95va–95vb: "Aut quod fuerit eius sentenciarum profunditate uacuus, quamquam non fuerit humano modo rethoricis coloribus fucatus aut expolitus, unde quamuis sacra scriptura humili et uulgari sermone plurimum decorat, tamen ubique excellentibus misterijs et profundis intelligencijs est grauida, que misteria spiritus sanctus, qui locutus est in talibus scripturis quadam humilitate, uoluit obumbrare, ut confunderet superbiam sapientium huius mundi. Et in hoc differt sermo humilis sacre scripture a sermone sublimi et polito humane tradicionis, quod subito, quasi sub aurea superficie, latet luctum et sepe falsitatis uenenum. E conuerso autem sub sermone sacre scripture, quasi sub inculta superficie aut rudi cortice latet aurum multiplicitas spiritualis intelligencie. Et redolet mira celestium misteriorum suauitas. Et ob hoc ualde attendendum est, ut ponderandus sermo et modus loquendi sacre scripture et usque ad minima discuciendus est. Et omnis apex ipsius uentilandus est, attento quod ipsa est dictata a subtilissimo et sapientissimo doctore scilicet spiritu sancto, qui usus est non solum communi significacione terminorum et oracionum, sed et omnibus methaphoricis locucionibus et significacionibus rerum et uocum usus est, ad latenter representandum altissima celestium misteria propter quod recte dixit Christus judeis Johanne v. [Jn. 5.39] 'scrutamini scripturas, quia in ipsis putatis uitam eternam habere.'"

cover, there is hidden sorrow and the poison of lies. On the other hand, beneath the speech of holy scripture, as if under an unrefined cover or a crude shell, there is hidden an abundance of the gold of spiritual understanding. The wonderful fragrance of heavenly mysteries is there. And for this reason it is very important to pay attention; the speech and the manner of speaking of holy scripture is to be pondered and to be discussed down to the little details. Every letter is to be investigated, having considered that holy scripture was dictated by the most subtle and wise teacher of all, namely the Holy Spirit, who used not only the ordinary signification of terms and of utterances, but also all metaphorical locutions and significations of things and of words, for the sake of secretly representing the highest mysteries of heaven, on account of which Christ rightly said to the Jews, "search the scriptures, because in them you think you have eternal life" [Jn. 5.39].

This is a restatement of the teaching handed down from Augustine's *On Christian Doctrine* and adapted by the Victorines, with its distinctions between sacred and profane literature, its reliance on the language arts of the trivium (grammar, rhetoric, and dialectic), its distinction between the significations of words and things, and its notion of metaphor as the vehicle of heavenly secrets. Heinrich observed professorially that the Holy Spirit surely knew the arts of language better than any of us. What were those arts? There is an intriguing conflation of rhetorical and logical language in this passage. Langenstein raises the elementary issue of signification (what actually is represented by the text?) and rhetorical tropes (metaphorical locutions), and he conflates these secular categories of analysis with natural signification (significations of things).[102] He is listing the various ways he knows to decipher the meanings of words, and it is clear that a rhetorical approach seems to be just another method of dealing with hard terms. But the methods nevertheless allow the Holy Spirit's meaning to be found in a literal understanding of the sentence.

A rhetorical analysis of language is really quite different from a logical one, and this is the recognition we miss in late medieval commentaries. Even so, biblical language signified verbally in the late Middle Ages. When we encounter patristic and Victorine language in a scholar like Langenstein, it is important to remember how vastly different his mind was from the mind of Hugh of St. Victor. The soul no longer moved beyond discourse when it comprehended. One did not necessarily pray to gain knowledge. One read and argued. Traditional concepts have been recontextualized in an environment of language analysis.

---

[102] In his commentery on the prologue to the Pentateuch he lists vocabulary, etymology, grammatical accidents, number, case, gender, syllables, and modes of locution as conditions of meaning. Ibid., f. 191 va–b. For supposition theory, Maieru, *Terminologia logica della tarda scolastica*.

Thus scholars felt free to adapt traditional distinctions in original ways. One such adaptation can be found in Nicholas of Lyra's *Postilla*, in his commentary on Hebrews, where he distinguished between figures that signify by history and those that signify by convention.[103] It is a curious distinction because the Victorine attitude toward the text has, as one of its premises, the semantic likeness of history and convention, according to which history, like conventional language, is a human realm, and nature is the sphere of revelation. In Lyra's *figura*, history belongs to the sphere of revelation, which could overthrow the Victorine metaphysical ranking of low historical and high spiritual meanings. Wendelin Steinbach, in his twenty-third lecture on the Epistle to the Hebrews, delivered at the University of Tübingen in the academic year 1516–1517 (the same time as Philip Melanchthon was reading Agricola's *On Dialectical Invention* there for the first time),[104] recognized that Lyra here regarded history as a form of natural signification, and he tried to expand upon the idea.

Steinbach's text was Hebrews 4.11, "Let us hasten to enter into that rest, so that no one sets an example of faithlessness such as theirs." The author of Hebrews argued that the sabbath rest promised by God to the Jews was not accomplished by their entrance into the promised land but only in the new, Christian covenant. Steinbach turned to Nicholas of Lyra and the question he raised at this place: "Whether the *rest* of the blessed was figurated by the rest of the sons of Israel in the land of promise."[105] This is a problem because the point of Hebrews is that the Jews did not enter into continuous rest, since they were repeatedly exiled and their land was, as Steinbach knew, eventually destroyed. How then is their entrance into the promised land a figure of the new covenant? Lyra argued that "rest" could be taken in the sense of either physical or spiritual rest. Insofar as spiritual rest is concerned, Lyra said that it is a figure "mediated" by the New Testament, indicating the eternal peace of the saints. It is not an unmediated figure, a figure meaningful, for example, simply by virtue of the Jews having possessed a land.

Steinbach took this as an opportunity to define "figure" more sharply in defense of Lyra's notion of a "mediated figure." There are figures, he explained, that communicate naturally, and there are others that

---

[103] Nicholas of Lyra, *Postilla*, at Hebrews 4.3, *et quidem operibus*.
[104] Melanchthon received a copy of Agricola's *De inventione dialectica* from Johannes Oecolampadius in that year. Schneider, "Hermeneutics," p. 26. Mack, *Renaissance Argument*, pp. 261, 321. For Steinbach's life and works, Wendelin Steinbach, *Opera exegetica*, ed. H. Feld, 3 vols. (Wiesbaden: Franz Steiner, 1976–1987), 1:xi–xlv.
[105] Steinbach, *Opera exegetica*, 2:208.

communicate conventionally, by meanings ascribed to them, and this beyond the significations of words:

> just as grammar puts out words (*voces*) and signs to signify something at the pleasure of the person using them, so also some things are created at the pleasure of him in whose hand all things are and depend for their existence [namely God], to be made and to continue to exist at some time or other to signify something, or they are given the function of signifying after they had already been made, created, or fashioned, and this happens either by the authority of scripture or by the church and the holy fathers.... That signification happens by a natural similitude, by an obvious arrangement, or by voluntary usage of either God or the author of scripture or of the holy fathers.[106]

The scriptural figure of rest in the land of promise may therefore refer to the "thing" itself, that is, Jews living in the land of Israel who, according to Deuteronomy 32.15, grew fat and bloated there and abandoned God by committing idolatry (in Lyra's sense, an "unmediated figure"). Or, just as literally, other Old Testament passages may refer to eternal rest, for example, Ezechiel 43.7, "Son of man, this is the place of my throne and the place of the tracks of my feet, where I reside in the midst of the people of Israel forever." The reference to divine feet indicates that the literal text employs figurative language, namely a figure of eternal rest, not according to nature (since God's nature includes no feet) but according to ascription (Lyra's mediated figure). Both forms of signification may occur at once, for example in every instance in which God promises peace to the children of Israel in the land of promise as the reward of virtuous behavior while promising the expulsion of the enemies who possessed the land. Rest in the land of promise is thus a figure of peace in the land of the living and the peace of the saints. This ambivalence of representation allowed Steinbach to suggest that Moses does not serve as a figure of Christ in all respects. He, after all, did not lead the people into the land of promise.[107]

Here, as in Lyra, history stands with nature in the realm of divine, not human convention. Letter and allegory, convention and nature, history and revelation, all belong to the realm of literal analysis, which is the main point of my chapter. Not only was it possible to violate the distinction of literal and mystical interpretations; it was also possible to read without soul travel. The realms of divine agency (nature) and history (convention) have merged. In addition, the method of understanding has become

---

[106] Ibid., p. 210.   [107] Ibid., pp. 212–13.

universal and textual. Scholars elevated language alongside nature as a more or less transparent representation of divine truth.[108]

The burden of this chapter is only to show how this possibility existed. We have seen the elevation of language alongside revelatory nature in the classification of historical and non-historical figures, in the faint recognition that biblical imagery did not require metaphyscial reading. Hermann of Schildesche demonstrated the extent to which the Bible could be interpreted as a body of literature composed of historical, non-historical, mixed, and figurative narratives.[109] The secret meanings of biblical writing could succumb to verbal interpretation. In the sixteenth century, interpreters, using a Ciceronian method of invention, were able, as it were, to normalize biblical images by recognizing their literary place within a piece of writing as a whole. Within an over-arching argumentative structure, they discovered, images and unadorned speech could share the same literary goals (chapter 5, below). Late medieval Bible scholars labored without the benefit of this discovery, even though the classical system of invention was known to medieval scholars from such standard works as Isidore's *Etymologies*. Biblical commentators ignored it. Before the revival of classical rhetoric and the reconciliation of rhetoric and dialectic in the early sixteenth century, as we will see, interpreters rediscovered the literary context of the image in theology.

We have an incomplete picture. We have seen how the distinction between poetry and the Bible was no longer absolute, even without a systematic application of rhetoric to interpretation. But what was biblical language? Where did it come from? And how did it work?

---

[108] This conclusion about late medieval exegesis agrees with Peter Harrison's conclusion about Reformation exegesis in *The Bible, Protestantism and the Rise of Natural Science*.

[109] Compare Henry of Ghent, p. 42, n. 40, above, and Nicholas Gorran, p. 44, n. 49, above.

CHAPTER 4

Divine speech

This chapter examines several ways that theological ideas contributed to the late medieval understanding of the Bible as a text.[1] There was, at least to some extent, an expectation that the simplicity of scripture should characterize other discourse about revelation, that this textual quality of the Bible pointed to a broader literary style (section 1). Theology took a particular approach to defining the Bible as a book (section 2). Theology also attributed two characteristics to divine speech and its textual manifestation: "verbalness" (section 3) and subjectivity (section 4). Given these characteristics, interpretation became a process of translation, and Heinrich of Langenstein, in particular, tells us much about it (section 5). Finally, these characteristics also point to the limits of historical interest in late medieval Bible study (section 6).

I. SIMPLICITY

Jerome's letter to Paulinus, the preface that circulated with the Vulgate, extols simplicity as a unique quality of biblical literature. It was a common patristic teaching.[2] In his letter, Jerome advocated a Christian

---

[1] Other authors have treated the problem of biblical authority, most importantly Schüssler, *Primat der heiligen Schrift*. See also Evans, *Language and Logic*, 2:9–14. Biblical authority is more an issue for theology (is the Bible an exclusive source of it, and how does the Bible relate to other sources of knowledge?) than for biblical commentary, in which the issue is really the expressiveness of the text *per se*. See also pp. 51–2, above.

[2] Karlfried Froehlich, "Bibelkommentare – zur Krise einer Gattung," *Zeitschrift für Theologie und Kirche* 84 (1987): 465–92, here pp. 472–4, 478. For simplicity as a rhetorical feature, consider E. Auerbach, *Literary Language and its Public in Late Latin Antiquity and the Middle Ages*, trans. R. Manheim (New York: Pantheon Books, 1965), pp. 27–66; idem, "Sacrae scripturae sermo humilis," *Neuphilologische Mitteilungen* (1941): 57–67, reprinted idem, *Neue Dantestudien*, vol. 5 of İstanbul Yazilari (Istanbuler Schriften) (Istanbul: Ibrahim Horoz Basimevi, 1944), pp. 1–10 (which is here used). G. J. M. Bartelink, "Sermo piscatorius. De 'vissertaal' van de apostelen," *Studia Catholica* 35 (1960): 267–73 (for the contrast between the [biblical] speech of fisherman and rhetorical oratory); R. Macmullen, "A Note on Sermo humilis," *Journal of Theological Studies* ns 17 (1966): 108–12 (alleging a role among lower social classes). Heiko A. Oberman, *Contra*

confrontation with classical culture, and in the process he asserted biblical wellsprings of intellectual attitude and literary style. Scripture was, he realized, written in a crude and ungainly Greek, a fact all too obvious to learned pagans. He therefore insisted, in an ironic passage, "really, holy boorishness is only good for itself, and, insofar as it builds up the Church of Christ out of the dignity of a life [namely, the life of Christ], so does it do harm, if it does not withstand those who contradict it."[3] The humility of Christ and the apostles is the core of the wisdom that pagan intellectuals overlook, as the Bible suggests (1 Cor. 1.18–25), and it is the basis of Christian learning, which builds a noble culture that resists pagan insults. "Do you see how distant righteous simplicity and learned righteousness (*iusta rusticitas et docta iustitia*) are from one another?" They are not distant at all.[4] The apostles Peter and John, however backward their origins, grasped the wisdom that is Christ. Jerome cited, among other things, John's use of the term λόγος, which recognized philosophical nuances of this word known to Plato and Demosthenes; but John progressed far beyond Greek philosophers by associating these connotations with the Son of God. It was, Jerome felt, remarkable for an untutored fisherman. The simplicity of biblical language mysteriously communicates truths that elite scholars failed to perceive. Jerome then offered Paulinus a compact review of biblical literature.[5]

This letter was widely known by medieval scholars as the first prologue to the Bible. A reader of the Ordinary Gloss or many other Bibles and commentaries would often find this letter on the first page of the codex. Numerous authors wrote commentaries on it or appealed to its sense of style. For example, in the early fourteenth century, Jacques Fournier wedded pragmatic, pastoral assumptions about the purpose of theological study to the ideal of biblical simplicity at the beginning of his commentary on Matthew, which he published as Pope Benedict XII, shortly before promoting educational reforms at Paris. He would follow, he said, Jerome's example and chose a simple over an ornate style because it is more accessible and therefore more useful (but this was not to put down those who choose more lavish writing).[6] Near the end of the century,

---

vanam curiositatem, vol. 113 of Theologische Studien (Zürich: Theologischer Verlag, 1974), esp. pp. 33–8.

[3] Hieronymus, Ep. 53, iii.4, CSEL 54:447: "sancta quippe rusticitas sibi soli prodest et, quantum aedificat ex uitae merito ecclesiam Christi, tantum nocet, si contradicentibus non resistit."

[4] Ep. 53, iii.6–7. Ibid., p. 448–9.

[5] Ep. 53, viii–ix. Ibid., pp. 454–63. Consider also Ep. 57, ix–xii, ibid., pp. 518–26, which discusses problems of language and exactitude in connection with translation.

[6] *Postilla super Mattheum*, Barcelona, Biblioteca Nacional de Catalunya, Ms 550 (which contains only twenty-seven of the original 132 tractates), ff. 1ra–364va, here from the preface, f. 2ra:

when the Church seemed riven with heresy and schism, Heinrich of Langenstein, in his commentary on the first prologue, pressed Jerome's *sancta rusticitas* into his own un-radical reformist mold, arguing that here Jerome taught bishops and priests to reform their offices by studying theology and knowing scripture (the two belong together), which will restore their pastoral office and renew Christendom.[7]

Lacking in both Fournier and Langenstein is a clear sense of simplicity as an element of style. In the late Middle Ages the value of simplicity had connotations beyond the literary. It was dialectical simplicity that scholars valued. William Ockham, who some theologians wrongly alleged had encouraged an impractical lust for speculation, believed that intellectual authenticity rested on the usefulness of theological ideas.[8] The value of dialectical straightforwardness was often expressed in the pregnant adverb *simpliciter*, by Bible scholars like Nicholas Gorran, Jacques Fournier, and Nicholas of Lyra.[9] Theologians recognized a need to keep logic

"Quantum uero potui sensum meum uerbis simplicibus expressi, non curans de ornatu uel pompa uerborum aut ritimis que ut frequenter magis sententias ueras solent occultare quam manifestare. Cum enim simplicibus meis similibus loquerer, simplicia uerba omnibus intelligibilia accepi, ut pluribus hoc opus utile esse possit, quod feci etiam quia in uerborum ornatu tritus non sum, cum nec de hoc a iuuentute mea curauerim, et tamen nunc minus michi conuenit in senectute. Scripture etiam expositioni hoc non congruit, dicente Jeronimus secundo libro super Ysayam: 'finito primo uolumine in Ysaya, quod ut potui, non ut uolui celeri sermone dictaui sensum potius scripturarum quam composite orationis uerba, perquirens nunc transcendam ad sensum.' Et in principio viii. libri dicit idem, 'qui flumen eloquentie et concinnas reclamationes desiderant legant Tullium, nobis propositum est Ysayam per nos intelligi et nequaquam sub Ysaye occasione nostra uerba laudari.' Hoc autem non dico uolens detrahere illis, qui in uerborum ornatu student, sed meam insufficientiam recognoscens, cum ego tales ornatus non ad plenum intelligam, et immo nec in eis delectari, quod enim bene intelligimur, bene proferimur, et econtra." The citations of Jerome may be found in CCL 73:41 and CCL 73:315, respectively. Fournier then explains his attempt to conform to doctrinal truth and submits his commentary to the correction of the Roman church and his readers (f. 2rb). He later (f. 2va–2vb) associates the childishness of biblical speech with God's condescension to inferior, human minds, in order to raise them to sublime knowledge. The simple language, he says, is therefore received by the church and her doctors, along with sublime sayings, for the nurture of the faithful.

[7] Stadtbibliothek Mainz, Hs. I 449, ff. 87va–93rb. A more conventional interpretation is provided ibid., ff. 94vb–95vb, and an explanation of the proper application of the liberal arts, ff. 101ra and following. A similar contrast of biblical simplicity and sophistry may be found among neo-scholastics (and in a singular qualification of pope Leo XIII's praises of Thomas Aquinas) in the nineteenth century: P. J. FitzPatrick, "Neoscholasticism," *CHLMP*, pp. 838–52, here 843.

[8] *Guillelmi Ockham elementarium logicae*, ed. E. M. Buytaert, *Franciscan Studies* 25 (1965): 170 and cited in Jürgen Miethke, *Okhams Weg zur Sozialphilosophie* (Berlin: Walter De Gruyter, 1969), pp. 428–9 n. 2. Consider also the preface to the "Thesaurus philosophorum" and its Pseudo-Albertine version in comparison with commentaries on Aristotle, in the actual standards of argument proposed. Lambert Marie de Rijk, *Die mittelalterlichen Traktate De modo opponendi et respondendi. Einleitung und Ausgabe der einschlägigen Texte* (Münster: Aschendorff, 1980), pp. 69–72, 109, 195–6. For the constructive role of speculative philosophy among fourteenth-century theologians see Hoffmann, *Robert Holcot*, pp. 16–79, esp. 18–20, and Courtenay, *Schools*, pp. 219–306.

[9] See the Latin texts of these authors cited at pp. 25, 45, 222.

within constructive bounds. John Baconthorpe, a critic of speculative learning who lectured in the Carmelite school at Cambridge or Oxford about 1340, explained the point. *Sophismata* are valid as exercises for schoolchildren (they study deceptions in the use of terms) and as a tool in philosophy (it resolves doubts). But in theology, *sophismata* are superfluous and only cause heresy, as Baconthorpe endeavored to prove at length.[10] Whereas arguments based on the analysis of absurdities could clarify the use of terms, in the light of theological truth absurd propositions were plainly false.[11] What, then, was the purpose of entertaining them in theology beyond the clarification of a logical problem? The dialectician was supposed to do more than hack out good syllogisms. He avoided sophistry, the art of mere appearances.[12] We should understand blanket condemnations of logic against the background of its controlled use.[13]

The scholastic value of simplicity implied several things: the practical nature of theological knowledge (scholars learned it from Jerome at the beginning of their Bibles); a desire for straightforward argumentation that leads to positive assertions of doctrine; and the conviction that the sources of religious knowledge should be treated without violence. This last item, combined with a worry that speculative thinking was about to ruin theology as a discipline, is especially displayed in the educational legislation of religious orders in the first half of the fourteenth century.[14]

---

[10] IV *Sent.* prologus q. 8. Bachon, *Questiones in quatuor libros Sententiarum Quodlibetales*, 2:253–57. For the date see Smalley, "John Baconthorpe," pp. 295–6, 302. The same sentiments were expressed some years earlier in the *postilla* on Matthew (ibid., p. 312). For *sophismata* as pedagogy and a literary genre, see Martin Grabmann, *Die Sophismataliteratur des 12. und 13. Jahrhunderts mit Textausgabe eines Sophisma des Boetius von Dacien* (Münster: Aschendorf, 1940), pp. 1–77. For the use of *sophismata* in the late Middle Ages see Murdoch, "Social," p. 303.

[11] Bacon, *Quaestiones*, article 3, 2:254–56. Baconthorpe was uncommonly severe in his judgment against any use of "dialectics," by which he meant terminist logic (ibid., article 4, 2:257). Accordingly, his commentary on the *Sentences* was constructed of biblical (as well as patristic and canonistic) arguments, some of which (particularly in books 2 and 3) he lifted from his Bible commentaries (Xiberta, *Scriptoribus*, pp. 185–6).

[12] Lafleur, "Les 'Guides de l'étudiant,'" p. 153.

[13] Courtenay, *Schools*, pp. 261–2.

[14] The best records come from the Dominicans. Bible teachers should expound the literal sense (1321), staying close to the text and its glosses, just as lecturers on the *Sentences* should stay close to the text of Peter Lombard (1354). Dominican teachers and students were to refuse "useless discourse" (1307, 1346) and take a practical approach that prepared them for preaching and confession, as well as scholastic disputation (1315). Among the fourteenth-century records ominously warning of the impending collapse of Dominican education, one finds frequent demands that lectors perform their jobs (1328, 1335, 1337, 1339, 1346, 1347, 1352), a demand for more lectors (1341, 1346, 1347) and, in one instance, for more Bible teachers (1308): *Acta capitulorum generalium ordinis praedicatorum*, ed. B. M. Reichert, 3 vols. (Rome: Typographia polyglotta s.c. de propaganda fidei, 1989–1900), 2:34–42, 179, 229, 245, 252–3, 271; 3:308, 313–14. They were also to study "our doctors" rather than entertain any proposition contrary to the church (1354) and replace logical and philosophical disputations with theological and moral ones (1357): (ibid.,

Stay close to the text of Peter Lombard's *Sentences* and the Bible, avoid useless speculation, and follow the official teachers of our order, the missives said. Such protective admonitions promoted educational values well established in the thirteenth century, and they complement the markers of a teacher's authority – moral stature and social responsibility – long promoted in the standard-setting environment of universities.[15] Popes John XXII, Benedict XII (Jacques Fournier), and Clement VI added their own warnings. The first came in 1317 in a letter of John XXII to the masters and students of Paris that takes special aim at the Arts faculty, but it worries about theologians, too: "even some theologians, having put aside and neglected the required canonical, useful, and edifying doctrines, get mixed up in curious, useless, and incredibly empty philosophical questions and subtleties."[16] The concern appears six years before William Ockham was first investigated by his Franciscan province in England, only after which his case came to the attention of the apostolic see; this was twenty years before there is definite evidence of Ockham's influence on the continent.[17] When Ockham's influence was first officially

---

2:24, 38, 78–79, 313, 359; 3:315). Thomas Aquinas, who presented nothing but the plain truth of scripture, sacred doctors, and approved philosophy (1344), was to replace vain science in Dominican education (1315, 1346, 1347, 1352, 1353, 1355): ibid., 2:81, 313, 341, 350–1, 367; 3:308. (Admonitions to study Thomas, in 1309 and 1361, should probably be taken to presuppose the same sense of the security of his doctrine, rather than a sense of its intellectual superiority; ibid., 2:38, 391.) The 1315 admonition may have had something to do with the condemnation of eight articles composed by a bachelor applying a Scotist principle to the doctrine of the Trinity at Oxford. However, the university regent masters, in condemning those articles, did not use rhetoric critical of speculative thinking and in defense of traditional sources: William J. Courtenay, "The Articles Condemned at Oxford Austin Friars in 1315," *Via Augustini. Augustine in the Later Middle Ages, Renaissance and Reformation*, ed. H. A. Oberman and F. A. James (Leiden: Brill, 1991), pp. 5–18. The Carmelites issued a warning against speculation in theology just when Nicolas of Autrecourt was lecturing on the *Sentences* at Paris and when Michael de Massa contested the implications of Ockham's doctrine of categories for logic and physics: *Antiquas Ordinis Constitutiones, Acta Capitulorum Generalium*, ed. B. Zimmerman, vol. 1 of Monumenta historica Carmelitana (Lirina: Ex Typis Abatiae, 1907), pp. 126–7. Zénon Kaluza, *Nicolas d'Autrecourt. Ami de la vérité*, vol. 42/1 of *Histoire littéraire de la France* (Paris, 1995), pp. 35–8, 55, 62, 74, 186. William J. Courtenay, "Was There an Ockhamist School?," *Philosophy and Learning. Universities in the Middle Ages*, ed. M. J. F. M. Hoenen, J. H. J. Schneider, and G. Wieland (Leiden: Brill, 1995), pp. 276–91 here p. 279 n. 50.

[15] Mulchahey, *First the Bow Is Bent*, pp. 134–41, 180–83, 340–44, 380–2, 480–526. Verger, "Teachers," in De Ridder-Symoens, *Universities in the Middle Ages*, pp. 162–3.

[16] CUP 2:200 nr. 741. This followed the retractation made in the Cistercian house of Paris by a certain friar Bartholemew, who had argued, as Ockham would later in clearer language, that a *relatio* was according to its genus merely an *ens rationis*, a rational construct. He also insisted, against common scholastic opinions, that the Trinity could be rationally demonstrated, while the unity of God could not. Konstanty Michalski, "Les courants critiques et sceptiques dans la philosophie du xive siècle," *Bulletin International de l'Académie Polonaise des Sciences et des Lettres, classe d'histoire et de philosophie* (1925): 192–3.

[17] Franz Ehrle, *Der Sentenzenkommentar Peters von Candia* (Münster: Aschendorf, 1925), p. 114, where he wrongly places the 1317 decree in the context of debate over nominalism. See Gilbert, "Ockham,

protested at Paris, in the Arts faculty in 1339, at issue was his treatment of Aristotelian subject matter.[18] Only with the proceedings against Nicholas of Autrecourt at Paris and Avignon from 1340 to 1347, and against Jean of Mirecourt at Paris from 1345 to 1347, does the concern with overly subtle thinking at Paris get associated with Ockham, but by now it is clear that people had been worrying about speculation for some time, and Ockham could not have been the original cause.[19] But worry over Ockham was growing. In 1340, a year after the Arts faculty prohibited private instruction in Ockham's doctrine under pressure from pope Benedict XII, a statute of the university of Paris complained that in the faculty of Arts some people posed a threat to theology, for they were "striving to disseminate certain less sound views from which intolerable errors not only about philosophy but even concerning divine scripture may arise in the future."[20] At issue, as J. M. M. H. Thijssen recently pointed out, was a belief that Ockham's method led to too narrow an interpretation of sources, too directly associating the properties of speech with its subject matter.[21] In 1345, while the proceedings against Nicholas of Autrecourt at the papal court were drawing to a close, the general chapter of the Augustinian Hermits, under the leadership of Thomas of Strasbourg, a theologian with strong Aristotelian sympathies, forbade by papal mandate adherence to or teaching of any doctrines in philosophy or theology that contradicted the canonical scriptures, "canonical" doctors, or the works approved by the Roman church.[22] On 20 May 1346, soon after Nicholas of Autrecourt's revocation of errors, pope Clement VI wrote to the university of Paris warning against those whose speculative philosophy departed from the text of the Bible and the expositions of the saints and doctors, abandoning the good, old philosophy and using vain philosophy in its stead.[23] Don't use Ockham's logic, Thomas of Strasbourg ordered at the Augustinian general chapter in 1348.[24] Worry over the uses of *sophismata* reveals an awareness that logic could undermine orthodoxy when terminism exceeded its accepted function as a tool to defend biblical and patristic statements and became the means to assert and defend positions that contradicted traditional doctrines.[25] It seems

---

Wyclif, and the 'via moderna,'" p. 92; J. M. M. H. Thijssen, *Censure and Heresy at the University of Paris, 1200–1400* (Philadelphia: University of Pennsylvania Press, 1998), pp. 14–15, 59–63; William J. Courtenay, "Erfurt CA 2 127 and the Censured Articles of Mirecourt and Autrecourt," *Die Bibliotheca Amploniana. Ihre Bedeutung im Spannungsfeld von Aristotelismus, Nominalismus und Humanismus*, ed. A. Speer (Berlin: Walter De Gruyter, 1995), pp. 341–52, here 342–3 n. 4.

[18] Thijssen, *Censure and Heresy*, p. 63. See also Courtenay, "Was There an Ockhamist School?"
[19] Thijssen, *Censure and Heresy*, pp. 73–89.   [20] Ibid., pp. 63–6.   [21] Ibid.
[22] Ocker, *Johannes Klenkok*, p. 16 n. 1.   [23] CUP 2:587–90 no. 1125.
[24] Ocker, *Johannes Klenkok*, p. 16 n. 1.   [25] Courtenay, *Schools*, pp. 261–2.

that the commotion may have inspired new interest in Bible study in some places.²⁶ It also gave Ockham an undeserved reputation. But at issue was something else, portrayed in an intriguing vespers disputation of about that time that may have been composed by Mirecourt. It asked the question "Whether through the work of theological study the fruit of catholic activity could be diminished?"²⁷ This was what unnerved theologians. It would have unnerved Ockham, too. The answer seemed to be retrenchment, keeping logic and philosophy out of one's theology lectures.²⁸

Of course, the use of logic in theology was universal, and worry over it means only that theologians wanted to use it well. The worry also marks a convergence, at least, of a value associated with biblical doctrine and a value widely accepted in theology. A biblical culture, Jerome had taught, will prize intellectual humility and simplicity of expression. Simplicity became one of the sticks regularly used by angry scholars to beat their opponents, and that includes some very angry scholars indeed: Richard FitzRalph, archbishop of Armagh and enemy of the friars in England and at the papal court in the middle of the fourteenth century;²⁹ Matthew of Janow, Bohemian priest and popular preacher before the Hussite Revolution;³⁰ and the revolutionaries themselves, for example, Jerome of Prague.³¹ Then there was Wyclif, whose strident view of biblical authority insisted that scripture is by virtue of its speech, *de virtute sermonis*, eternally true in every respect, and logic can only uphold that truth. Anything else, said Wyclif, was an abuse of logic.³² Wyclif, Jerome of Prague, and even Janow could mislead us into believing the old Protestant fallacy that biblicism and theological simplicity inspired radical reformers. Their appeal to simplicity rather expresses a common desire to retrench theology in sources free of the destructive

---

²⁶ Ibid., pp. 368–9, 373–4.   ²⁷ Courtenay, "Erfurt CA 2 127," pp. 348–50.
²⁸ As in a Paris statute of 1366. CUP 3:144; Murdoch, "Social," pp. 276, 364 n. 20.
²⁹ Beryl Smalley, "Jean de Hesdin O. Hosp. S. Ioh.," *Recherches de Théologie Ancienne et Médiévale* 28 (1961): 285–330, reprinted in eadem, *Studies in Medieval Thought and Learning*, pp. 345–92, here 369. J. I. Catto, "Theology after Wycliffism," *Late Medieval Oxford*, ed. J. I. Catto and R. Evans, vol. 2 of *The History of the University of Oxford* (Oxford: Clarendon, 1992), pp. 264–5.
³⁰ *Tractatus de Antichristo*, ix. 1, in Matthias de Janov, *Regulae Veteris et Novi Testamenti*, ed. Vlastimil Kybal, 4 vols. (Innsbruck: Libraria Universitatis Wagrerianae, 1908–13), 3:147–50. But consider also *Tractatus de abominatione desolationis in loco sancto*, xxi, xxxi, and li, in *Regulae*, 4:88, 130–1, 237 (the last reference complains of students who, for love of ingenuity and eloquence, abandon theology and study canon law). He also frequently refers to scripture as divine speech (e.g. *Regulae*, 1:197; 2:12; 3:163, 192, 336, 338; 4:36, 55, 379).
³¹ According to testimony at a trial of his views in Vienna, 1410/12. Gilbert, "Ockham, Wyclif, and the 'via moderna,'" p. 106 n. 58.
³² Ibid., pp. 101–5. For the phrase *de virtute sermonis* see Courtenay, *Schools*, p. 238 n. 37.

questions that, according to some, philosophy supplied. We accordingly find the rhetoric of simplicity used by Gerhard Groote, the founder of the Brethren of the Common Life who studied at Paris and after three introspective years in the monastery of Munnikhuizen decided, in 1379, on the advice of John Ruysbroek, to preach against very many things. In a letter of that year to an archdeacon of Lüttich, he railed against the academics who had captivated Europe with their hybrid mixture of scripture and the Siren songs of philosophers; they are shipwrecked between Scylla and Charybdis, he said.[33] By the time Peter of Candia lectured on the *Sentences* of Peter Lombard at Paris between 1378 and 1381, theologians there were divided between two competing forms of speculative theology, the one Scotist and the other Ockhamist.[34] It was then that the unabashedly old-fashioned Jean Gerson developed a taste for the metaphysics of Albert the Great. He also insisted that biblical logic was entirely distinct from the speculative kind.[35] Both "Scotists" and "terminists" were undermining piety at the university, he said at the end of the century, reflecting truths that were by then over fifteen years old.[36] The threat, thought Gerson, was an exaggeration of Aristotelian distinctions by Scotists who thereby opposed the solid Augustinian and Dionysian metaphysical assumptions that agreed with patristic tradition (all pious minds accepted these, he said); it was a transgression of the boundaries of speculation by terminists.[37] He at least could name what he thought went over the edge of piety and intellectual propriety.

There was, in the fifteenth century, other grist for the polemical mill: the conflict at the universities of Germany and Poland between the two "ways," the *via antiqua* and the *via moderna*, the meaning and evaluation of which has turned out to be far more complex than scholars have often believed;[38] the conflict between "realists" and "nominalists" at Paris in

---

[33] Ep. 9, *Gerardi Magni Epistolae*, ed. Willelm Mulder, vol. 3 of Tekstuitgaven van Ons Geestelijk Erf (Antwerp: Uitgever Neerlandia, 1933), pp. 23–36. See also R. R. Post, *The Modern Devotion. Confrontation with Reformation and Humanism* (Leiden: E. J. Brill, 1968), pp. 81–2.
[34] Zénon Kaluza, *Les querelles doctrinales à Paris. Nominalistes et realistes aux confins du xive et du xve siècles* (Bergamo: Pierluigi Lubrina, 1988), p. 64. Ehrle, *Sentenzenkommentar*, p. 62.
[35] For Gerson, see pp. 165–9, below.   [36] Kaluza, *Les querelles*, pp. 43–62.
[37] Ibid., pp. 46–60. Elisabeth Gössmann, *Antiqui und Moderni im Mittelalter* (Munich: Ferdinand Schöningh, 1974), pp. 109–16.
[38] Gilbert, "Ockham, Wyclif, and the 'via moderna,'" pp. 85–125. Even the "ancients," followers of the great thirteenth-century Dominican masters Albert the Great and Thomas Aquinas, could pose a threat to orthodoxy. So in 1426, during the Hussite Crusade, the electoral princes worried that the dangerous innovations of the *antiqui* at the university of Cologne, who were realists, would prevent the introduction of the more orthodox teachings of the *moderni* at the university. By then it was well known that Hussites, following Wyclif, not only held heretical views of the church and society but also held extreme realist positions, Wyclif's realism having been

1471, leading to king Louis XI's 1474 decree prohibiting nominalism at his university (but it only remained in effect until 1481). The controversy at Paris in the 1470s suggests that arguments had to some extent degenerated into name calling. The parties scarcely mentioned the contested doctrines – universals, necessary and intemporal propositions, and the Scotist doctrine of forms – each instead documenting the unorthodox lineage of the opposing party, which in turn helped create the image of established and continuous traditions of realist and nominalist schools going back to the early fourteenth century (it was this late fifteenth-century allegation of nominalist and realist academic genealogies that led scholars, eighty years ago, to believe late medieval scholasticism was shaped by the conflict over nominalism).[39] We are told that these debates reflect the declining centrality of Paris in late medieval theology, the institutionalization of philosophical doctrines around schools or *bursae* within schools (the university of Cologne is a notable case in point), and the growing self-confidence in the Arts faculties where philosophers now managed their own schools of thought.[40] But again, the excitement of condemning should not obscure the fact that the ideal of simplicity was universally held.

In fact, the condemnations of speculative thinking were a little strange, as John Catto pointed out with regard to the theologians of Oxford. Who were they complaining about? No fifteenth-century theologian seems even remotely as speculative as some of the scholars of the second quarter of the fourteenth century.[41] Catto's conclusion could easily apply to the most "nominalist" of fifteenth-century theologians, for example, the extremely pastoral, practical Gabriel Biel. Theologians argued for simplicity whether their peers were speculative or not. There is no evidence of an explosion of speculative theology in the century before the

---

debated by Jerome of Prague at Paris and Heidelberg in 1406 and condemned at the university of Heidelberg in 1412. The orthodoxy of realists remained suspect at mid-century Heidelberg. Zénon Kaluza, "La crise des années 1474–1482: l'interdiction du nominalisme par Louis XI," Hoenen, Schneider, and Wieland, *Philosophy and Learning*, pp. 293–327 (here pp. 299–306).

[39] Gilbert, "Ockham, Wyclif, and the 'via moderna,'" pp. 94–7; Kaluza, "La crise des années 1474–1482," pp. 307–27; Courtenay, "Was There an Ockhamist School?," p. 263. See also Kaluza, *Les querelles*, pp. 87–106 and 124–5, where he suggests that the new Albertism was less tolerant of other theological and philosophical sects than fourteenth-century adherents of a particular school of thought.

[40] There were distinct Thomist and Albertist *bursae* at Cologne at the end of the fifteenth century: M. J. F. M. Hoenen, "Late Medieval Schools of Thought in the Mirror of University Textbooks. The *Promptuarium argumentorum* (Cologne 1492)," Hoenen, Schneider, and Wieland, *Philosophy and Learning. Universities in the Middle Ages*, pp. 331–2. For Arts faculties see Kaluza, "La crise des années 1474–1482," p. 296.

[41] J. I. Catto, "Theology after Wycliffism," *Late Medieval Oxford*, ed. Catto, vol. 2 of *The History of the University of Oxford* (Oxford: Clarendon, 1992), pp. 264–5.

Reformation, nor is there evidence that interest in the Bible declined. To the contrary, we know that bachelors and masters of theology were still required to lecture on the Bible everywhere, as they were also required to lecture on Peter Lombard's *Sentences* and to perform disputations well into the sixteenth century. In at least some places, like the university of Oxford, interest in Bible study seems to have grown.[42] Although fewer sources survive from fifteenth-century Cambridge, the university continued to require Bible lectures, and the same situation existed at Paris.[43] Likewise in Central European universities German masters continued their biblical lectures until finally, at the end of the fifteenth century, professors of the Bible were routinely appointed alongside professors of theology (the best known is the biblical professor of the new university of Wittenberg, Martin Luther).[44]

Apart from the sheer mental goodness of simplicity, theologians may also have been motivated to assert the need for it because they believed simplicity served the consensus. Truth is neither egotistical nor controversial. Theologians reflected the practical orientation of lawyers, like Johannes Andreae, whose popular handbook on marital cases, the *Summa de sponsalibus et matrimonio*, completed about 1309 and used, like all canonistic handbooks, as a theological and exegetical sourcebook as well as a casuistic and legal one well into the sixteenth century, placed the scholar's need to be useful in the context of consensus: the consensus of the church was practical. His compilation, he assured the archbishop of Bologna in his dedication, contained nothing subtle or new, only what was commonly approved.[45] It is therefore not surprising that some interpreters

---

[42] Ibid., pp. 29–30, 196–98, 257, 267–68, 271, 279, 473.

[43] Damian Riehl Leader, *The University to 1546*, vol. 1 of *A History of the University of Cambridge* (Cambridge University Press, 1988), pp. 173–4, 185–8.

[44] Erich Meuthen, *Die alte Universität*, vol. 1 of *Kölner Universitätsgeschichte* (Vienna: Böhlau, 1988), pp. 27, 142–3. Isnard Frank, *Hausstudium und Universitätsstudium der Wiener Dominickaner bis 1500* (Vienna: Böhlau, 1868), pp. 173–4.

[45] *Summa de sponsalibus et matrimonio* (Cologne: n.p., 1505), f. 1r–1v. Schulte, *Geschichte*, 2:215. Consider also his introduction to his additions to Guillaume Durand, *Speculum Guilhelmi Durantis cum additionibus Johannis Andree* (Cologne: Antonius Koberg, 1486), f. 1r. For the use of canonistic handbooks by theologians see Ocker, "Fusion." Similarly, spiritual writers would criticize lecturers whose science overlooked self-renunciation, drawing on well-known mystical reservations about science. Consider Tauler: "Liebenkinder, die grossen pfaffen und die lesemeister die tispitieren weder bekentnisse merre und edeler si oder die minne. Aber wir wellen nu al hie sagen von den lebmeistern. Als wir dar komen, denne súllen wir aller dinge warhe wol sehen. Unser herre sprach: 'eins ist not.'" Ferdinand Vetter, *Die Predigten Taulers*, vol. 11 of Deutsche Texte des Mittelalters (Zürich: Weidmann, 1968), p. 196 lines 28–33 (I am grateful to Blake Hefner for calling this passage to my attention years ago). Gerhard Groote's letter to Guillaume of Sarvavilla uses the criticism against friars (for their subtle and vain questions) and jurists (for their litigiousness): Ep. 9, *Gerardi Epistolae*, pp. 23–36, esp. 27–8, 29, 33.

insisted that conflicting interpretations should be decided by religious authority (for example, Nicholas Gorran) or by following the techniques and principles of canon law (Jacques Fournier).[46] Or they simply assumed, like Jean Gerson, that the literal sense of the Bible was identical with the cumulative sense of the "decrees, decretals, and codices of the councils."[47] Some interpreters had discovered broad agreement between the church's legal literature and the Bible, encouraged by the biblical-canonistic concordances of the fourteenth-century canonists Jean of Nivelles and Johannes Calderinus, while others insisted on the convergence of interpretation and tradition against the supporters of oral tradition.[48] Subjecting interpretation to papal authority or the canon law had its rationale. The existence of an intellectual continuum between the Bible and the government of the church rested upon the clarity and usefulness of scripture. The Augustinian friar Agostino of Ancona, famous for his papalism, warned in the 1320s that curious science belongs to those who would rather be seen than see, be known than know. This bad science, he continued in a chivalrous image of church fidelity, employs methods that attack the bride of Christ, but the doctors – theologians, the knights of Christ – offer the various books they have written on the basis of scripture, like all the horses of Solomon from all over the earth, to the pope.[49] Interpretation defends Christ with devotion rendered to the papacy. Such correspondences between biblical literature and theological writing, Christian service and papal authority, were crucial to the orthodox majority. Speculation undermines the holy consensus that, as a matter of principle, always exists in the church.

What we lack is any evidence that the Bible really stood in opposition to late medieval scholasticism in any definite way. If we could know that Gerhard Groote was reacting to an actual neglect of Bible study we might conclude otherwise, but that seems impossible. Wyclif's contrast of biblical orthodoxy with the positions of his scholastic opponents depends entirely on his idiosyncratic view of biblical language. Moreover, by the days of Wyclif and Groote, the most speculative of late medieval theologians were dead. We have, instead, just the rhetoric of simplicity.

[46] Ocker, "Fusion," pp. 135–6.
[47] See the eighth point of Gerson's *De sensu litterali sanctae scripturae*, Gerson, *Œuvres complètes*, 10 vols., ed. P. Glorieux (New York: Desclée et Cie, 1962), 3:336. Mark S. Burrows, "Jean Gerson on the 'Traditioned Sense' of Scripture as an Argument for an Ecclesial Hermeneutic," *Biblical Hermeneutics in Historical Perspective*, pp. 152–72.
[48] See Ocker, "Fusion," pp. 140–51; Oberman, *Harvest of Medieval Theology*, p. 372.
[49] Augustinus de Ancona, *Summa de potestate ecclesiastica* (Augsburg: Johannes Schüssler, 1473), f. 1r. The work was completed in 1326. Michael Wilks, *The Problem of Sovereignty in the Later Middle Ages* (Cambridge University Press, 1963), p. 6.

Jerome's letter to Paulinus was always there to remind scholars that simplicity was not only practical, convenient, and churchly, but also biblical and at the foundation of Christian culture in the west. His was a description of style merged with literary purpose and the integrity of readers' minds. Late medieval scholars understood the connection of simplicity with purpose and integrity, but they did not understand well its connection to style. To explain the Bible as literature, they relied on theology. Theology provided a hybrid view of authorship (section 2, below). It emphasized the synergy of divine and human in both writing and reading (sections 3 and 4). It required the presuppositions of verbal representation and an exegetical procedure that had as its goal the conversion of biblical into theological discourse (section 5). It minimized the remoteness and otherness of the past (section 6).

2. CAUSALITY

The Bible required a hybrid view of authorship, as Jerome's letter to Paulinus and Augustine's *On Christian Doctrine* implied: the Holy Spirit, they said, embedded secrets in biblical speech, and its style therefore reflects divine purposes. It is obvious that the Bible could not be attributed exclusively to a divine origin, since its literature presents itself as the writing of human beings – unlike, for example, the Qur'an, whose divine words were dictated to Muhammed by an archangel. Christian interpreters stressed this human source by identifying authors of even anonymous books in scripture according to traditions widely accepted by Jews and Christians since late antiquity. So for example, Moses was believed to have written the first five books of the Bible, the Pentateuch (excepting the conclusion to Deuteronomy, which records his death), even though only one of these books, Deuteronomy, suggests Moses as its source.[50] Medieval theologians always assumed that scripture was the word of God, yet they could not imagine the text apart from human agents. They therefore explained biblical authorship in ways

---

[50] For the ancient idea, Otto Eissfeldt, *The Old Testament. An Introduction*, trans. P. R. Ackroyd (San Francisco: Harper and Row, 1965), pp. 158–60. Although questions were raised time and again by Jews and Christians about the plausibility of Mosaic authorship (prompted by questions over the morality of some of the record attributed to him and by the final chapter of Deuteronomy, which recounts his death), it was not systematically criticized until the seventeenth century, by Thomas Hobbes. Henning Graf Reventlow, *The Authority of the Bible and the Rise of the Modern World* (Philadelphia: Fortress, 1985), pp. 216–17, points out Hobbes's ambivalence: he criticizes Mosaic authorship while also insisting on the authority of received opinion in the church of England (by which he means to insist that the law of the Old Testament binds kings). For Hobbes, church authority, rather than authorship, makes a book canonical.

that encompassed both human and divine activity within a theological frame.

It is easy to miss this simple fact by limiting one's attention to medieval theories of inspiration and authority or by focusing on human authorship. The term "origin" may itself be misleading. Medieval intellectuals did not rely exclusively, or even primarily, on a temporal beginning point or spatial relationships to explain the source or character of something. Rather their account of "causes" gave reasons for the actuality of a thing that involved both physical and non-physical factors.[51] Our own commonsense notions of "cause" are mechanical. No "cause" of a piece of literature could be more compelling to our common sense than the mind of the person whose hand moved the pen that composed the text. Medieval intellectuals took causality to be a broader explanatory device. It could include, for example, definition of natural and supernatural features of the Bible together. Scholastic assumptions about causality shaped late medieval views of authorship and prevented theologians from seeing biblical authorship as a form of human creativity. It is therefore important to explain causality at greater length, in order to identify general aspects of late medieval discussions of causality that are relevant to the definition of the Bible as a book.

Late medieval theories of causality were intended to give an account of existence by focusing not on static being but on change, which intellectuals tried to put in quantitative terms and subject to theorems developed to address all cases of specific kinds.[52] All change, as Aristotle taught, could be reduced to a simple logical transition, the transition from potentiality to actuality and vice versa. Any physical "substance" was a combination of "matter" (potentiality) and "form" (actuality).[53] In the case of the substance "this particular statue," clay is the matter of the form, sculpture; in the case of the substance "a living human being," body is the matter of the form, soul. This is obvious enough. A particular

---

[51] Michael Frede, "The Original Notion of Cause," *Doubt and Dogmatism*, ed. M. Schonfield *et al.* (Oxford: Clarendon, 1980), pp. 217–49. Some intellectuals, like Richard Rufus of Cornwall, used causal language in distinct ways – logical, evidentiary, metaphysical, or demonstrational – and distinguished the evidentiary causes that serve as the basis of knowledge from metaphysical causes that serve as the basis of being. Rega Wood and Robert Andrews, "Causality and Demonstration: An Early Scholastic *Posterior Analytics* Commentary," *The Monist* 79 (1996): 325–56. Because discussions of authorial causality apply causal theory generally, no distinction between evidentiary and metaphysical causes appears in them. Evidentiary and metaphysical causes are considered together.

[52] This was especially the case after the early fourteenth century, once the influence of English theologians who mastered these techniques was felt on the continent. Courtenay, *Schools*, pp. 241–9.

[53] Causation as such was explained in Aristotle's *Metaphysics* and applied to both his natural and his practical philosophies.

clay statue must consist of both clay and a particular shape. A human body is not a living body unless it is animated by the biological, rational, volitional, and emotive powers that are bundled together under the name "soul." The transition from potentiality to actuality occurred according to the categories not only of substance (generation and corruption), but also of quantity (quantitative increase and decrease), quality (intensive increase or decrease), or place (the most basic form of movement). In addition, change in any of these categories was considered in terms of mover, the thing moved, and the end of movement: change was considered to encompass all three, including the end (although there was some debate over whether the "end" was distinct from movement in both essence and being or just in essence, a point that need not detain us). Therefore, change could be explained in four related ways, namely the famous "four causes" of Aristotle (material, formal, efficient, and final), to which I will return in a moment. Because it was a logical rather than a purely physical account of causality, this method of explanation could be applied to things that we would consider in vastly different ways. It applied to a physical object, for example a sculpture, but also to an immaterial or mixed thing, for example a human being or a literary work like the Bible. It could account for spatial movement, metaphysical entities (like God or the soul), and immaterial things (like speech or an idea).

As Anneliese Maier pointed out long ago, this approach to change and movement has certain affinities with modern ones, insofar as physical objects are concerned, in particular, affinities with the principle of inertia in Newtonian physics (the property of matter by which it remains at rest or in uniform motion in the same straight line unless acted upon by some external force).[54] Most late medieval scholars believed that spatial movement was somehow an inherent characteristic of the thing moved, yet it had some independent existence; it was itself a thing. In the Newtonian principle of inertia, by comparison, movement is a kind of characteristic or condition of the thing moved, and once it has been shared with a body, it exists on its own apart from a continuously working, moving power. Most late medieval intellectuals preferred to think of movement as a path or succession of particular moments of change caused as the continued effect of some agent. The agent must be constant and not remote. Each point in this series was an end, or *terminus*, in itself.[55] Most scholars

---

[54] Anneliese Maier, *Die Vorläufer Galileis im 14. Jahrhundert* (Rome: Edizioni di Storia e Letteratura, 1949), pp. 9–25.

[55] Similar questions and solutions were explored in discussions of light and the transmission of the image of an object to the eye. Consider Tachau, *Vision and Certitude in the Age of Ockham*,

believed motion was a comprehensive idea that included outcomes as much as origins and means. Why? Because change was about an entire succession of points that characterized a thing, not merely the individual points along the path of its existence. It is the way their explanations of cause, of the process of coming to be, included origins and outcomes as well as means that is especially relevant to the causal definition of the Bible.

Typical medieval approaches to causation gave comprehensive account of potentiality, actuality, origins, and outcomes together. The four aspects of explanation are Aristotle's four causes: material (potentiality), formal (actuality), efficient (physical origins), and final (outcomes). The four causes united physical and metaphysical explanations, and although challenged in the seventeenth century, the combination of physical and metaphysical, particularly final causes, continued to exercise a strong appeal even after Galileo.[56] Two of Aristotle's causes pertain to substance, material and formal, and accordingly they are not *effective* principles in and of themselves but refer rather to the potentiality (matter) and actuality, condition, or state of being (form) of a thing. Both the material and formal causes indicate the metaphysical significance of an object. They do not contribute to a strictly physical explanation of nature, but most medieval intellectuals were not interested in strictly physical or mechanical explanations. The final cause, which indicated outcomes, was metaphysical, like the material and formal causes. Only one cause

pp. 3–81. William Ockham is best known for this theory, but his account of movement as a series of consecutive points, which was generally held by philosophers and theologians in his day, was not his invention. Ockham's unique contribution was the argument that each moment in the series was nothing other than the thing moved, and so each *terminus* existed only in the mind, thus rendering "movement" not a thing, as scholars generally believed, but only a name. After Newton, motion became the *condition* of an object caused when another object (which has in turn experienced a previous change of condition) acts upon it, and this *condition* will continue uniformly until yet another object exercises some force upon it, just as a body's lack of motion is a condition that continues uniformly until some other object exercises some force upon it. In medieval scholasticism, uniform movement is the result of the constant exercise of the force of a moving thing, a *movens*, in the absence of which change does not occur (Maier, *Vorläufer*, p. 55). On the limits of Ockham's influence see Tachau, *Vision*, pp. 157–312, and for the absence of his influence at Paris, ibid., pp. 315–52.

[56] Margaret J. Osler, "From Immanent Natures to Nature as Artifice: The Reinterpretation of Final Causes in Seventeenth-Century Natural Philosophy," *The Monist* 79 (1996): 388–403. Bacon, *De augmentis scientiarum* iii.4–5, and *Novum organum* ii.2–17, in Basil Montagu, ed., *The Works of Francis Bacon*, 16 vols. (London: William Pickering, 1825–34), 8:162–98, 9:287–328. Enrico de Angelis, *La critica del finalismo nella cultura cartesiana. Contributi per una ricerca* (Florence: Le Monnier, 1967), pp. 49–50, 108–15. Osler, "From Immanent Natures," pp. 396–403. Malebranche, *De la recherche de la vérité*, i.8–20, ed. Jules Simon, *Œuvres de Malebranche*, 2 vols. (Paris: Charpentier, 1855, first published 1674), 2:59–118. Leibniz, *Monadology* xii, Leibniz, *Discourse on Metaphysics. Correspondence with Arnauld. Monadology*, trans. G. R. Montgomery (La Salle, Illinois: Open Court, 1950), p. 253; *Monadology* xvii, ibid., p. 254; lxxvii–xc, pp. 268–72.

pertained to external forces that induce change, that is, "cause" in our sense: the efficient cause. Thus seen together the four causes provided a logical, metaphysical, and physical account of an object. It must have been the ability to balance a universal and metaphysical, even supernatural, context of a thing's existence with its particular physical origins that rendered the four causes so appealing to theologians.[57]

Late medieval discussions of the efficient cause have drawn most scholarly attention because it is obvious that efficient causation alone describes the physical and mechanical operations that became the central preoccupations of modern physics. Efficient causality has been the focus of attention in the study of theories of authorship, too, as we will see. Anneliese Maier, and more recently Amos Funkenstein, have argued that fourteenth-century scholars increasingly emphasized efficient causality, such that it "came to be the prime meaning of causality," while natural processes came to be seen as an inviolable system that operated of its own "necessity."[58] Both the emphasis on efficient causes and the view of nature anticipate the idea that the universe is ordered in a predictable fashion that can be explained mathematically. Yet only a small number of English scholars, following the lead of William Ockham and anticipating the arguments of Descartes, reduced all causality to the efficient cause and argued against the viability of the other causes.[59] However much the majority of scholars emphasized efficient causality, it was never to the exclusion of the other causes.

How, after all, did interest in the three metaphysical "causes" decline? It declined first because the notion of efficient causality was expanded to include metaphysical concerns. In the thirteenth century, efficient causality could be ascribed, beyond physical sources, to psychological, cosmic, divine, and occult things.[60] If God is in fact the cause of all matter, such that no other material cause could exist apart from God, and is also the formal and final cause of everything (as Thomas Aquinas for example had said), it can hardly surprise us that God or any entity from within

---

[57] One might say that the theologians balanced a heterogeneous approach to nature characteristic of Aristotle against a homogenous approach characteristic of Stoicism and the neo-Platonism of patristic theology. Consider Amos Funkenstein, *Theology and the Scientific Imagination* (Princeton University Press, 1986), pp. 35–42.

[58] Ibid., pp. 144–5. Maier, *Vorläufer*, pp. 219–50.

[59] André de Muralt, "La causalité divine et le primat de l'efficience chez Guillaume d'Occam," *Historia Philosophiae Medii Aevi. Studien zur Geschichte der Philosophie des Mittelalters*, ed. B. Mojsisch and O. Pluta, 2 vols. (Amsterdam: B. R. Grüner, 1991), 2:745–69. Muralt points out that Ockham's motivations were theological and identical with those of Thomas Aquinas and John Duns Scotus, who defended the Aristotelian causes.

[60] Maier, *Vorläufer*, p. 54.

the full range of psychological or cosmic creation could also exercise efficient causality, including angels, heavenly bodies, internal properties of natural objects, and so forth.[61] By the end of the thirteenth century, scholars realized that God, an infinite and primary being, could be seen as the *efficient* cause of everything,[62] which attributes in some sense all change to God – a possibility that encouraged theologians in the first half of the fourteenth century to explore the predictability of nature in long discussions of necessity and contingency (which was done with the help of the well-known distinction between absolute and ordained powers of God, God's absolute power working as the guarantor of contingency).[63] It gave William of Ockham the opportunity to criticize the possibility of any but the efficient cause, but this view, however correct it would eventually prove to be, did not achieve a consensus.[64] In the discussions of the efficient cause of the Bible, the role of divine agency was pronounced, too, as we will see. Even in more strictly physical explanations of phenomena, the broadening concept of efficient causation in the fourteenth century tried to do some of the work of the final cause by accounting for things like gravity.[65]

The fact that there was a burst of academic speculation on these problems in the first half of the fourteenth century is remarkable, but the fact that interest faded surely reflects limited interest in purely mechanical explanations and an abiding interest in the nature and effect of God's volitional power and agency.[66] Although the preoccupation with efficient causality points to what Amos Funkenstein has called the secularization of theology, it reminds us that scholars were motivated by their desire to understand divine activity rather than undermine it.[67] With the ascent of physical explanation, God seemed to drift closer to their world.

Was there, then, a secularization of scholastic concepts of authorship?[68] Medieval commentators adapted a late antique tradition. Like the fourth-century grammarian Aelius Donatus, they introduced their

---

[61] Thomas Aquinas, *ST* I, q. 44, aa. 3–4.
[62] John Duns Scotus, *De primo principio*, iii.7–45: *A Treatise on God as First Principle*, trans. A. J. Wolter (Chicago: Franciscan Herald, 1966), pp. 44–62. But see also *Quaestiones quodlibetales* ed. and trans. Felix Alluntis (Madrid: Biblioteca de Autores Cristianos, 1968), q. 7, art. 2, iv.–v. conclusiones.
[63] Funkenstein, *Theology*, pp. 124–152.   [64] Muralt, "La causalité divine," pp. 746–47.
[65] Maier, *Vorläufer*, pp. 59–78; see also pp. 132–54.
[66] When Newton did this, it was not to restrict God's action to the design of matter and the principles of motion that, rather than inhering as qualities within particular bodies as scholastic natural philosophy taught, exist as laws of nature whose causes are unknown. He believed that God's will could alter those laws arbitrarily. Isaac Newton, *Opticks* (New York: Dover, 1952), pp. 401–2.
[67] Funkenstein, *Theology*, pp. 3–9. Muralt in note 64, above.
[68] Minnis, *Medieval Theory of Authorship*, p. vii, "*auctoritas* moved from the divine realm to the human."

work with prologues that stereotypically summarized the object of commentary.⁶⁹ In the twelfth century, prologues usually did this under the categories: title of the work, name of the author, intention of the author, subject matter of the book, manner of proceeding, order of the book, utility, and "to what part of philosophy" the work belongs. Within these headings, they acquainted the reader with a work's subject and ideas, and they stressed ideas above historical circumstances:

> there was rarely any attempt (at least, not until very late in the Middle Ages) to relate a person's purpose in writing to his historical context, to describe an author's personal prejudices, eccentricities and limitations. The commentators were more interested in relating the work to an abstract truth than in discovering the subjective goals and wishes of the individual author.⁷⁰

Accordingly, twelfth-century prologues to biblical commentaries point out the thematic coherence of a book within the overall subject matter of the Bible. They also describe the "intention" of the writing as a disposition of the soul to the particular spiritual teachings of the book.⁷¹

In the thirteenth century, Aristotle's four causes came to dominate the shape of these prologues: beginning at Paris, but also at other places, commentators described the material, formal, efficient, and final causes of a book. In both the twelfth and the thirteenth-century prologues, their goal was "to lead the listeners or readers into authoritative texts."⁷² But whereas twelfth-century commentaries on theological texts denied the significance of human authors (as grammatical texts did, too) and emphasized a uniform message within the Bible, the new Parisian prologue, with its systematic use of Aristotelian causality, tried to consider the human author and the circumstances of his authorship.⁷³ Alastair Minnis, in his important study of these introductory sections of commentaries, has shown that the causal approach of thirteenth-century commentators facilitated a literary method that recognized differences among biblical books, the distinct purposes of authors, and the unique features of separate literary genres.⁷⁴ Minnis contended that it was their appeal to the "efficient cause" of scripture that played the crucial role in developing a literary over against a purely theological awareness, and that their treatments separated the roles of God and human beings in the

---

⁶⁹ Ibid., pp. 15–72.   ⁷⁰ Ibid., pp. 20–21.
⁷¹ Ibid., pp. 49–57. The exception was Abelard's commentary on Paul's letter to the Romans, where he shows greater interest in the coming of Christianity to Rome, Paul as a writer, and rhetorical features of the work. Ibid., pp. 59–63.
⁷² Ibid., p. 30.   ⁷³ See the detailed investigation by Minnis, ibid., pp. 36–72.
⁷⁴ Ibid., pp. 73–159.

production of scripture. By identifying human beings as efficient causes, he argued, they elevated human authors as writers composing literature within particular historical circumstances.

There can no doubt that the causal approach elevated the literary sensibilities of commentators and allowed them to improve their systematic methods for treating biblical literature, as Minnis emphasized. This in itself is an important discovery. But to what extent did the development of a literary sensibility depend upon the systematic analysis of *human* authorship? Aristotelian prologues by scholars in the Arts faculty at Paris showed pronounced interest in the formal cause and only passing interest in the efficient cause. Some also divided the efficient cause into two, external and internal, and used this distinction to integrate it with formal and final causes of a work.[75] When theologians first adapted causal explanation, they also multiplied or divided the efficient cause. Hugh of St. Cher's commentary on the Gospel of Mark noted that the apostle, the grace of God, or a request of Peter's disciples could all be the efficient cause, whereas the material cause is Christ, the formal cause is a mode of treatment of few words with many profundities (recalling a feature of the patristic idea of biblical rhetoric), and the final cause is salvation. Guerric of St. Quentin, Richard Fishacre, anonymous commentaries on the Psalms and the Apocalypse, Nicholas Gorran, and Nicholas of Lyra all distinguished between a moving efficient cause (the Holy Spirit or God) and an efficient cause that moves but is also acted upon (the biblical authors, or for example in the case of the visionary Apocalypse, the apostle John, the angel who appeared and talked to him, and Christ, who also spoke in the vision).[76] Thomas Aquinas added to this division a description of the loving cooperation between the human author and the divine Spirit. Such cooperation indicated the material, formal, and final causes of the writing, which were also shared by the author.[77]

---

[75] A certain Master Jordan, Robert Kilwardby (when still in the Arts faculty), two anonymous commentaries on Aristotle, a Dominican named Elias (perhaps Elias Brunetti). Alexander of Hales followed the tradition already established in the arts faculty in his *Summa theologiae*. Ibid., pp. 75–8.

[76] Ibid., pp. 78–81.

[77] The part played by "human feelings and emotions" (ibid., p. 80) involves the reciprocity between a human being and God that is characteristic of a saint, that is, an individual who has experienced salvation, as Minnis notes (ibid., p. 81) but downplays. It is true that "divine omnipotence no longer interfered with the integrity of the human *auctor*" (p. 82), if theologians ever thought that it did. My argument is that theologians, rather than seek a human explanation for literary features, were more preoccupied with the synergy of divine and human authorship, such that it was the grace of God in the saint that established the integrity of the human author. Consider also Giles of Rome: Minnis and Scott, *Medieval Literary Theory and Criticism*, p. 201.

As we saw in discussions of causality *per se*, increasing sophistication in the treatment of efficient causality did not displace God or the metaphysical issues of material, formal, and final causes (their potential so to do was not realized until the seventeenth century). Precisely the same is suggested for the causes of the Bible on Minnis's evidence. The efficient cause was conceived in such a way that it included divine agency and remained congruent with the other causes. Theologians believed that efficient causality of any kind was ultimately attributable to God, who nevertheless set in motion intermediate powers that exercised their own effects.[78] As I noted above, this played an extremely important role in late medieval discussions of contingency, and it reflects the close association of human agency with divine existence in the late Middle Ages.[79] In the case of the writing of the books of the Bible, the intermediate agent was the human author, who possessed certain powers in the soul, most importantly the powers of intellect and will. The coordination of that intellect and will with the efficient causality of God was consistent with the material, formal, and final causes of the Bible. Lyra, who has been identified as the culmination of medieval causal definitions of the Bible, found the material cause (that is, the potentiality) of the Psalms to be Christ, the formal cause (their actuality) to be the structure of the book and a worship-style in it (literary features), the efficient cause to be principally God and instrumentally David, and the final cause to be the promotion of salvation.[80] Likewise in a preface seldom noticed, his preface to the letters of the apostle Paul, Lyra identified effective (efficient), "subjective" (for material), final, and formal causes of Paul's doctrine. I would like to consider this preface in detail.

In the preface to the letters of Paul, Lyra first explained at some length the nature of the efficient cause. He emphasized not the personal interests of the apostle but the divine origin of his teaching. This comes in the form of an exposition of Proverbs 22.20, "Behold, I wrote it for you three-fold, in thoughts and knowledge":

Concerning the first cause, it is to be noted that although Paul was the writer of this doctrine, which is meant when it says, *behold I wrote* [Prov. 22.20], he was the writer ministerially [i.e. as an unfree servant], but Christ principally, wherefore he says in Galatians 1 [verses 11–12], "I made known to you, brothers, the gospel of Christ that was preached by me, because it is not according to a human being nor did I receive it from a human being nor teach it except

---

[78] Minnis, *Medieval Theory of Authorship*, p. 83.
[79] Cf. Ockham in Muralt's account, "La causalité divine," pp. 762–9.
[80] Minnis and Scott, *Literary Theory and Criticism*, pp. 272–4.

through the revelation of Jesus Christ." Indeed, when he, while Christ was revealing and speaking, explained this doctrine congruently [i.e. in agreement with Christ's speech], he could say the word of Baruch that is recorded in Jeremiah 36 [verse 18], "from his mouth he spoke to me as though reading all those words from a book, and I wrote in the book with ink." Baruch, which means blessed, was a figure of the apostle, who obtained the mercy and blessing of God. Jeremiah, which means high to God, is a figure of Jesus Christ, whom God afterward exalted and gave "to him a name that is above every name," as it says in Philippians 2 [verse 9]. Indeed, Paul the apostle could well say concerning Christ, "from his mouth he spoke to me as though reading from a book," that is, distinctly and openly revealing to me, and I wrote according to his revelation "in a book with ink." For Paul wrote his letters, at least some or a certain part of them, by his own hand, whence he says correctly at the end of the letter to the Corinthians [1 Cor. 16.21], "my greeting by the hand of Paul," written in completion of the letter. For in this manner he signs his letters taken by a scribe, lest letters written by false apostles under his name would be believed to be from the genuine book.[81]

Paul wrote *ministerialiter*, as a servant whose service is owed, not free. The conclusion reiterates this sense of Paul's authorship by reflecting worry over forged documents, a preoccupation of the royal, baronial, and noble adminstrators who made up the bulk of the literate and more learned laity. It encourages us to think of Paul's agency as that of a bailiff serving documents. What makes his action authoritative is the authenticity of the documents he serves, although he genuinely bears that authority in his person. He speaks while Christ speaks but authenticates the writing with his own hand, as a servant. It seems clear that in his discussion of

---

[81] Nicholas of Lyra, *Postilla super totam Bibliam* (Strasbourg, 1492), unfoliated, vol. 4, at the beginning of the Pauline letters, from Lyra's "Prohemium in epistolas Pauli" (this is presented as an exposition of Proverbs 22.20, *Ecce descripsi eam tibi tripliciter, in cogitationibus et scientia*): "Circa primum, est notandum quod licet Paulus fuit scriptor huius doctrine, quod notatur cum dicitur, *ecce descripsi* [Prov. 22.20], hoc tamen fuit ministerialiter, Christus autem principaliter, propter quod dicit ad Galatos i. [Gal. 1.11–12], 'notum uobis facio fratres euangelium Christi quod euangelizatum est a me, quia non est secundum hominem neque enim ego ab homine accepi illud, neque didici, sed per reuelationem Iesu Christi.' Et immo quando Christo reuelante et dictante hanc doctrinam descripsit conuenienter, dicere potuit uerbum Baruch quod habetur Hieronymus xxxvi. [Jer. 36.18], 'ex ore suo loquebatur ad me quasi legens in libro omnes sermones istos, et ego scribebam in uolumine attramento.' Baruch, qui interpretatur benedictus, figura fuit apostoli, qui consecutus est misericordiam et benedictionem Dei. Jieremias, uero qui interpretatur excelsus Deo Iesum Christum figurauit quem Deus post exaltauit et dedit 'illi nomen quod est super omne nomen,' ut dicitur Philippenses ii. [Phil. 2.9]. Et immo bene potuit dicere Paulus apostolus de Christo, 'ex ore suo loquebatur ad me quasi legens in libro,' id est distincte et aperte mihi reuelando, et ego scribebam secundum eius reuelationem in uolumine atramento. Epistolas enim suas saltem aliquas uel pro aliqua parte earum manu propria conscripsit, unde in fine proprie epistole ad Corinthios dicit, salutatio mea manu Pauli supplens scripta est. Hoc enim modo signabat epistolas suas per notarium conscriptas, ne sub nomine eius epistole a falsis apostolis scripte a fido libro reciperentur."

the efficient cause, Lyra's intention is to stress Paul's cooperation with divine efficiency.

Lyra's discussion of the material cause moves his students to an increasingly abstract, even metaphysical description of scripture. Lyra called the material cause "subjective," which he means in the late medieval sense of an extra-mental reality.[82] He associated it with natural philosophy, with basic assumptions about motion, to be exact:

> Concerning the second cause, it is to be understood that just as in natural philosophy a movable body is a reality under an absolute reason, yet in particular books [of Aristotle's natural philosophy] a reality under determined reasons (such as a body moving to a position in the *Book of Heaven and Earth* and a body moving to a form in the book *On Generation and Corruption*), so too the subject of sacred scripture is God under an absolute reason, in its parts under determined reasons, as in the Old Testament under the reason of the creator and of government and in the New Testament under the reason of redemption in general, in the epistles of Paul under a more determined reason, namely under the reason of redemption by Christ's passion (as Paul says in the letter to the Corinthians [1 Cor. 1.23–4], "we preach Christ crucified, to the Jews a scandal, to the gentiles foolishness"). Therefore this wisdom of the doctrine of Paul, which is the subjective cause, is touched upon when Acts 13 [verses 32–3] says, "we preach to you that which was promised to our fathers" concerning Christ who will suffer for the salvation of the world.[83]

Paul's preaching Christ as "that which was promised" to the ancient Jews refers to the "determined reasons" of the Old and New Testaments. I am especially intrigued by the analogy Lyra draws with natural philosophy. By associating the "subjective cause" with theories of movement in natural philosophy, Lyra reminds his reader that "subjective" is a pregnant term, not merely the casual "subject" of common English usage, "the subject of a book." It means that and more. It refers to an objective

---

[82] What we now would ordinarily call "objective." See Tachau, *Vision and Certitude*, p. xxii and *passim*.

[83] Nicholas of Lyra, *Postilla super totam Bibliam*, vol. 4, Lyra's "Prohemium in epistolas Pauli": "Circa secundum, sciendum [est] quod sicut in philosophia naturali corpus mobile est subiectum sub ratione absoluta, et in partialibus [*sic*] libris sub rationibus determinatis, ut corpus mobile ad situm in *Libro celi et mundi*, et corpus mobile ad formam in libro *De generatione et corruptione*, sic Deus sub ratione absoluta est subiectum in sacra scriptura, in partibus uero eius sub determinatis rationibus, ut in ueteri testamento sub ratione creatoris et gubernationis, et in nouo sub ratione redemptionis in generali, in epistolis uero Pauli sub ratione magis determinata, scilicet sub ratione redemptionis per suam passionem, immo dicit Paulus ad Corinthios i. [1 Cor. 1.23–4], 'predicamus Christum crucifixum iudeis quidem scandalum, gentibus autem stulticiam. Ipsis autem uocatis iudeis atque grecis filium Dei Christum Dei uirtutem et Dei sapienciam.' Hec igitur sapiencia doctrine Pauli que est causa subiectiua tangitur cum dicitur eam de qua dicit Actus xiii. [Ac. 13.32–3], 'nos uobis eam annunciamus que ad patres nostros repromissio facta est' de Christo pro salute mundi passuro."

condition of nature – in this case, the nature of the book – and it is connected to its efficient and formal causes.

It is good to linger a little over Lyra's analogy, lest his references to Aristotle seem pointless and affected, before I summarize Lyra's definition of subjective cause. The "subject" of natural philosophy is not merely a theme or topic. It is a particular potentiality in nature, namely moveable bodies. The reality of this thing may be determined absolutely, in the sense that a body moves to a position, such as the movement of heavenly bodies described in Aristotle's *On Heaven*, where the movements of heavenly bodies are derived from a general theory of corporeal movement. The reality of moveable bodies may also be determined particularly, in the specific sense of a body's attainment of a particular form, which is the passage from potentiality to actuality, such as the movement from matter to form described in Aristotle's *On Generation and Corruption*. There, too, Aristotle built upon a general theory of change, of coming to be and passing away, or in other words, movements more complex than the simple movement of bodies in lines, circles, or a combination of the two that form the backbone of *On Heaven*. In both the absolute and the particular cases, the student confronts two varieties of the same subject matter, the one more general and the other more particular. The distinction between general and particular, however, is some real thing in nature, namely distinctions of motion.

So too, the "subject" of the Bible is not merely a theme, but an objective (in our sense) being, namely God. The conditions described here are logical, not necessarily physical, and this is how Lyra could define Pauline doctrine in terms analogous to natural philosophy. The subjective (material) cause of scripture, which determines the potentiality of the Bible as a thing, is both general, insofar as the Bible is holy, and specific in particular parts, namely creation and governance in the Old Testament and redemption in the New Testament. The potentiality of the Old Testament thus rests on the fact of creation and divine governance. The potentiality of the New Testament rests on the fact of redemption. The subjective (material) cause of Pauline doctrine is only slightly narrower. It is the particular wisdom of Paul's preaching, a stumbling block to the Jews, foolishness to the Greeks, but salvation to the church. This wisdom was of course, in Lyra's mind, historical, a true feature of Paul's preaching. But its own place within the literary parts of the Bible is established by its connection with broader theological facts, facts about God's existence relative to the world, human society, redemption, and preaching.

The final cause is a statement of the purpose of biblical doctrine. It is the usefulness of this doctrine to all Christian people:

> Concerning the third cause, it is to be considered that the final cause of this doctrine is the benefit of the entire church, which is noted when it says, "to you," that is for your benefit, because through this doctrine, understood and carried out by work, the life of grace is attained in the present and the life of glory in the future, concerning which what is said in Proverbs 3 can be taken, "let your heart keep my commandments," for they will appoint to you length of days and years of life and peace. He says years of life [compare Prov. 3.10] with regard to the life of grace, and the length of days with regard to the life of glory, which includes eternity, and peace [verse 27], that is, rest from desire, because, concerning the reason of the ultimate end, it is that it puts desire completely to rest.[84]

It is a little odd that Lyra introduces the final cause between the material and formal causes, which complement each other so obviously; but then again, all the causes together are assumed to be complementary. The final cause reinforces the character of the doctrine Lyra mentioned in his definition of the "subjective" or material cause. He then turns to the formal cause.

The formal cause describes the actual configuration of Pauline doctrine, but not in terms of its intellectual content, which is adequately described by the subjective (material) cause. Lyra says the formal cause is doctrine in two respects, as it is organized within the Pauline letters (the "form of the treatise") and as it is to be handled by an interpreter (the "form of treating"). He was compelled, like most commentators who offered causal definitions of the Bible, to see both the literary structure of ideas in the texts and a method of analysis used by theologians as intrinsic to biblical literature:

> Concerning the fourth, namely the formal cause, it must be understood that the form of doctrine is two-fold, namely the form of the treatise and the form of treating. The form of treating is the procedure [to be followed], which is triple according to the philosophers, namely definitive, divisional, and probative, and this triple procedure the apostle uses from another direction. Whence in the letter to the Hebrews [Heb. 11.1] he defines faith, saying, "faith is the substance of things

---

[84] Ibid.: "Circa tertium, considerandum [est] quod causa finalis huius doctrine est utilitas totius ecclesie, que notatur cum dicitur, 'tibi,' id est ad utilitatem tuam, quia per hanc doctrinam intellectam et opere adimpletam habetur uita gracie in presenti et glorie in futuro, de quo potest accipi quod dicitur Prouerbia iii. [Prov. 3.1–27], 'precepta mea cor tuum custodiat,' longitudinem enim dierum et annos uite et pacem apponent tibi. Dicit annos uite [vs. 10] quantum ad uitam gracie, et longitudinem dierum quantum ad uitam glorie, que eternitatem includit a parte post, et pacem [vs. 27], id est quietem appetitus, quia de ratione finis ultimi est, quod quietet totaliter appetitum."

hoped for, the argument of things that do not appear." Similarly 1 Corinthians 12 [verses 4, 8], he divides grace, saying, "moreover there are divisions of gifts, but the same Spirit," and he adds, "indeed to another the word of wisdom is given by the same Spirit," etc. Similarly 1 Corinthians 15 [verses 12–22], from the resurrection of Christ he proves that there will be a general resurrection of the dead, as is possible in such a case. And this formal cause is treated when it is said, "three-fold," concerning which what Ecclesiasticus 4 says can be taken, "the triple cord is hard to break." The form of the treatise consists in the division of doctrine. All of doctrine is divided into three parts, according to the fact that he writes to the three main nations. First to the Romans, who excelled the other nations in power; secondly to the Greeks, who excelled the other nations in wisdom; third to the Hebrews, who excelled in the knowledge of the divine law. Yet he writes to the Romans one letter which is explained first, since it is first with respect to the other letters.[85]

Paul's actual treatment of doctrine in his letters, which is the formal cause or actuality of the New Testament books ascribed to him, reinforces the continuities of authors (divine and human) and readers. Lyra thought that Paul handled the text in the scholastic way indicated here, and this underscores the correspondence between the divine and human features of the text, commentary on it, and religious discourse.

Lyra's causal description thus creates an overall picture of the Pauline letters. It begins with the co-agency of Paul and Christ in physically moving the doctrines into existence. It assumes that the material cause of scripture consists of general theological facts, the relation of the creator to the world he governs and the work of redemption. The purpose that defines the existence of Pauline doctrine is its usefulness to those who are being redeemed. And the actuality or form of it is its structure in particular Pauline letters and a routine scholastic method of definition, division, and proof. Both the efficient and formal causes define Pauline doctrine

[85] Ibid.: "Circa quartum scilicet causam formalem, est sciendum quod duplex forma doctrine, scilicet forma tractatus et forma tractandi. Forma tractandi est modus agendi, qui est triplex apud philosophos, scilicet diffinitiuus, diuisiuus et probatiuus, et hoc triplici modo utitur aliunde apostolus. Unde in epistola ad Hebreos [He. 11.1] fidem diffinit, dicens, 'fides est substantia rerum sperandarum, argumentum non apparentium.' Similiter i. ad Corinthios xii. [1 Cor. 12.4, 8] graciam diuidit dicens, 'diuisiones autem graciarum sunt, idem autem spiritus,' et subdit, 'alii quidem per spiritum datur sermo sapientie,' et cetera. Similiter i. Corinthios xv. [1 Cor. 15.12–22] ex Christi resurrectione probat resurrectionem generalem mortuorum esse futuram, sicut possibile est in tali materia. Et hec formalis causa tangitur cum dicitur 'tripliciter,' de quo potest accipi quod dicitur Ecclesiasticus iv 'funiculus triplex difficile rumpitur.' Forma uero tractatus consistit in diuisione doctrine. Diuiditur autem tota doctrina in tres partes, secundum quod tribus precipuis gentibus scribit. Primo romanis, qui precellebant alias gentes in potentia, secundo grecis, qui precellebant alias gentes in sapiencia, tertio hebreis qui recellebant [leg. precellebant] in diuine legis noticia. Romanis tamen scripsit unam epistolam que primo exponetur, sicut est prima respectu aliarum." For *forma tractatus* and *forma tractandi*, see Minnis, *Medieval Theory of Authorship*, pp. 119–59.

by a correspondence of divine and human speech, both in the co-agency of Paul and Christ as authors, and in the correlation of a method believed to underlie both Pauline literature and the work of scholastic interpreters. The existence of these letters as literature is thus dependent upon gigantic realities: creation and redemption and a basic, perhaps in his mind universal, method of scholastic analysis. The circumstances that brought the letters into physical existence had to be directly linked to a universe through subjective, formal, and final causes. Paul had to be a scribe, and an author only in this restricted sense. It is obvious that the framework of authorship could not be restricted to history.

How was this causal definition of scripture received? Lyra's account of the "subjective" cause may have seemed unnecessarily complicated, in comparison with the simple definitions of material cause available in thirteenth-century commentaries. (It is also reflected in Lyra's prologue to the Psalms.) In fact, Lyra adapted the theory of motion in its broadest, even crudest terms: given his literary and exegetical purpose, he could ignore the particular debates over motion – real or apparent, general or local, successive and eternal, as a thing or a relation – that occupied Parisian theologians in his day.[86] Others would prefer a yet simpler causal definition, as we can see in one fourteenth-century reader of Lyra, the rector of city schools at Ulm and Rottweil, Johann Müntzinger. Müntzinger's glosses on Paul's letter to the Romans turn to the thirteenth-century Franciscan Peter of Tarantasia (who first wrote his commentary on Paul's letters between 1259 and 1269 and who later, in 1275, became pope Innocent V) for an uncomplicated definition of the material cause. He uses Lyra to supplement Peter of Tarantasia's account of the final cause:[87]

> Again concerning the causes of the science of this book, it is asked what they might be. It is answered, speaking liberally about the causes, especially material and formal, that the causes of the doctrine of this book are four, namely efficient, material, final, and formal. The efficient cause was the apostle Paul, less principal, taught by our Lord Jesus Christ. But the principal efficient cause was Christ... But the material cause, as master Peter of Tarantasia recounts,[88]

---

[86] Tachau, *Vision and Certitude*, pp. 85–112, 135–48, and *passim*. Maier, *Vorläufer Galileis*, pp. 11, 201–15, 267.

[87] For Peter of Tarantasia, see Minnis, *Medieval Theory of Authorship*, pp. 132, 249 n. 17, and H.-D. Simonin, "Les écrits de Pierre de Tarentaise," *Beatus Innocentius V (Petrus de Tarantasia O.P.). Studia et Documenta* (Rome: S. Sabina, 1943), pp. 163–335, here 213–31.

[88] Peter of Tarantasia did not attribute this account of the material cause to the Ordinary Gloss, although elsewhere in his Pauline commentaries he discusses interpretations taken from it. I.-M. Vosté, "Beatus Petrus de Tarentasia Epistularum S. Pauli interpres," *Beatus Innocentius V*, pp. 337–412, here 340–1.

is according to the Ordinary Gloss the doctrine of the savior specially handed down, which is contained in the Gospel. The final cause according to the same Peter was the illumination of the gentiles because Paul was principally the apostle of the gentiles. Moreover master Nicholas of Lyra said that the final cause is [its] usefulness for all of Christianity because through this doctrine, understood and fulfilled by work, the life of grace in the present and the life of glory in the future is obtained. And concerning the formal cause, it is to be understood that it is a double form of doctrine, namely the form of treating and the form of the treatise. The form of treating is the manner of proceeding, which is threefold among the natural philosophers, namely definition, division, and proof, and the apostle sometimes does not use these. The form of the treatise is the division of the book, about which I spoke above.[89]

Tarantasia's final cause was fairly historical, in that it referred to a particular historical role of the apostle Paul as preacher to the gentiles. Lyra's final cause, by contrast, assumed the broadest theological frame, and even the particular people addressed by Paul Lyra saw in a general, abstract way: the Romans whose empire excelled all others in power, the Greeks who excelled all others in wisdom, and the Hebrews who excelled in knowledge of the divine law. His formal cause, which Müntzinger slightly modifies (the apostle does *not* always follow the philosopher's "form of treating"), was literary, but not, as I pointed out before, because of any presumption of authorial creativity. Lyra's formal cause rather indicated a structural organization common to both the biblical writer and theologians here and now. It was an intellectual condition of these two kinds of religious discourse, scripture and theology. The formal cause touches on features of the text that humanists would later treat as a writing's *dispositio*, "disposition," argumentative structure. Lacking is any vestige of the treatment of *dispositio* in poetic commentary established over a century before.[90]

---

[89] Basel, Universitätsbibliothek, A V 28, ff. 146r–226v, here f. 146rb–146va: "Item queritur de causis sciencie huius libri, quod sint. Respondetur large loquendo de causis precipue materiali et formali quod doctrine huius libri quattuor cause scilicet efficiens, materialis, finalis et formalis. Causa efficiens fuit Paulus apostolus minus principalis edoctus a domino nostro Iesu Christo. Sed principalis causa efficiens fuit Christus ... Sed materialis causa, sicut recitat magister Petrus de Tarantasia, est secundum glossam ordinariam doctrina saluatoris specialiter tradita, que continetur in ewangelio. Causa autem finalis secundum eumdem Petrum fuit gencium illuminacio, quia ipse principaliter gencium fuit appostolus. Magister autem Nicolaus de Lira ait quod causa finalis est utilitas tocius christianitatis, quia per hanc doctrinam intellectam et opere ad impletam habetur uita gracie in presenti et uita glorie in futuro. Sed de causa formali, sciendum est quod duplex est forma doctrine scilicet forma tractandi et forma tractatus. Forma tractandi est modus agendi, que est triplex apud physicos scilicet diffinicionis, diuisionis et probacionis, et hoc triplici non utitur aliquando apostolus. Forma uero tractatus est diuisio libri, de qua supra dictum est."

[90] For which see Allen, *Ethical Poetic*, pp. 130–3.

There were other commentaries after Lyra that also produced conventional, causal definitions of biblical literature, but the few that I have seen suggest that these definitions were less common in the late Middle Ages than in the thirteenth century. A good example from later in the fourteenth century is provided by the Dominican Nicolau Eimeric in the preface to his commentary on Galatians, which he addressed to the former abbot of San Cugat del Vallés. He began with a description of divine self-expression, a chaste language (*eloquia casta*) that is more precious than gold, silver, and gems. Then he continued,

> Because such are the expressions of the Lord, such (and a great cause) are the expressions of the apostle Paul. The expressions of Paul are the expressions of the Lord Jesus Christ, since he learned the Gospel of Christ neither from man nor through man but through the revelation of Jesus Christ, as he says [Gal. 1.12], and he adds, "Or do you seek proof that it is Christ who speaks in me" [2 Cor. 13.3]. Therefore the expressions of Paul's letters are the expressions of Christ's letters. And if all the epistles of Paul are the expressions of the Lord Jesus Christ, all the letters of Paul – the one to the Hebrews, to Titus, to the Galatians – are collectively in some extraordinary way the expressions of the Lord Jesus Christ. In these three letters of Paul, the signs of figures are revealed, the oracles of the prophets glitter, the winds of the scriptures shine forth, and the miracles of nature become evident.[91]

The idea of the equivalence of the speech of Paul and of Jesus is further explained in the introductory questions which serve as the prologue proper of the commentary (f. 6r–6v): Paul's eloquence, *eloquentia*, came from the "third heaven" that he visited (2 Corinthians 12.2), just as Peter's special wisdom came from the superior revelations he received. The eighth question treats the efficient cause:

> Surely therefore Paul was not the efficient and principal cause of this Epistle to the Galatians. To be sure, the Lord Jesus Christ was the principal cause, but Paul himself also was an instrumental and less principal cause. The Lord Jesus

---

[91] Nicolau Eimeric, written while he was apostolic penitentiary in Avignon according the passage preceding this one, in his preface to the commentary on Galatians (Biblioteca Nacional de Catalunya, Ms. 1280, f. 3r): "Et quia talia sunt eloquia domini, talia et causa grandja [*sic*] sunt eloquia apostoli Pauli. Eloquia namque Pauli eloquia sunt Domini Iesu Christi, nam euangelium Christi neque [ab] homine neque per hominem ipse didicit, sed per reuelationem Iesu Christi, ut idem ipse inquid, qui et subjungit, 'an experimentum queritis eius qui in mihi loquitur Christus.' Ergo eloquia epistolarum Pauli eloquia sunt epistolarum Christi. Et si omnes epistole Pauli sunt eloquia domini Iesu Christi, sunt et quodam modo singulare cuncte epistole Pauli, quam ad Hebreos, quam ad Titum, quam ad Galatos, eloquia Iesu domini Christi. In hijs enim tribus epistolis Pauli patent signacula figurarum, fulgent oracula prophetarum, splendent spiracula scripturarum, et clarent miracula naturarum."

revealed the Gospel to Paul, and he had it not from another man nor from him [Jesus], as he says in the chapter above, he [Jesus] revealed to the Paul who wrote this letter; he imprinted in his heart those things which he aroused in his heart when he spoke. "Or do you seek proof that it is Christ who speaks in me," 2 Corinthians, and Hebrews 1 [verse 2], "he [God] has spoken to us in the son." And was the Holy Spirit also the agent of the cause of this letter? Certainly he was, for all the prophets, all the teachers of sacred theology spoke while inspired by the Holy Spirit, whence 2 Peter 1 [verses 20–1], "understanding this, that all prophecy of scripture is not made for private interpretation, for at no time has prophecy come forth by human will, but people of God spoke while the Holy Spirit inspired them." Whence Hebrews 3 [verses 7–8], "Therefore, as the Holy Spirit says, today, if you should hear his voice, do not harden your hearts." And Hebrews 5 [verse 6], "as the Holy Spirit also says in another place, 'you are a priest forever according to the order of Melchisadek.'" Therefore everything of sacred scripture is revealed by the Holy Spirit. And Wisdom 9, "for who can know the counsel of God, and how can he judge what God wills? Who can know your meaning unless you [God] give wisdom and send your Holy Sprit from on high?" And 1 Thessalonians 1 [verse 5], "our Gospel was not among you in speech only, but in truth and the Holy Spirit." The active cause of this evangelical letter is therefore the Holy Spirit.[92]

Question 8, with its appeal to revelation and prophetic inspiration, preserves the standard doctrine of co-agency in the efficient cause. The other causes are equally conventional and may simply be mentioned. Question 12 names the Gospel of Christ as the material cause.[93] Question 13 names the division of the epistle into six chapters as the formal cause.[94] Question 14 names conversion and perseverance as the final cause of the letter.[95] Such conventional causal definitions may also be

---

[92] Ibid., f. 6r–6v: "Num ergo Paulus huius epistole ad Galatas fuit causa efficiens et principalis? Sane dominus Iesus Christus fuit causa principalis, sed ipse Paulus tam fuit instrumentalis et minus principalis. Dominus Iesus Paulo euangelium reuelauit, nec ab homine alio non ab eo habuit, ut ipse infra capitulo dicit, ille eidem qui hanc epistolam scripsit, reuelauit [quod] in corde suo infixit, in corde suo loqutus excitit. 'An experimentum eius queritis qui in michi loquitur Christus,' ii. Cor. xii. et Hebreos i., 'loqutus est nobis in filio.' Et num et spiritus sanctus, actor cause huius epistole fuit? Utique fuit, nam omnes prophete, omnes doctores sancte theologie spiritu sancto inspirati sunt loquiti, unde ii. Petrus i., 'hoc intelligentes, quod omnis prophetia scripture propria interpretatione non fit, non enim uoluntate humana allata est aliquando prophetia, sed spiritu sancto inspirante loquti sunt sancti Dei homines.' Unde Hebreos iii., 'quapropter, sicut dicit spiritus sanctus, hodie si uocem eius audieritis, nolite obdurare corda uestra.' Et Hebreos v., 'quemadmodum et in alio loco dicit spiritus sanctus, tu es sacerdos in eternum secundum ordinem Melchisedech.' Omnia ergo sacre scripture sunt a sancto spiritu reuelata. Et Sapientia ix., 'quis enim poterit scire consilium Dei, atque qualiter poterit iudicare quod uelit Deus, sensum autem tuum quis sciet, nisi tu dedis sapientia et missis spiritum sanctum tuum de altissimis.' Et i. Thessalonienses i., 'euangelium nostrum non fuit apud uos in sermone tantum, sed in ueritate et spiritu sancto.' Est ergo causa huius epistole euangelice actiua spiritus sanctus."
[93] Ibid., f. 6v.   [94] Ibid., ff. 6v–7r.   [95] Ibid., f. 7r.

found in Denys the Carthusian's early fifteenth-century commentaries on Proverbs and Luke.[96]

Eimeric stressed that feature of authorial co-agency most obvious to a scholastic theologian. The intention of authors was in fact the intention of saints, be they Hebrew patriarchs, prophets, or apostles – people who expressed in their bodies and actions the nearness of God to the world. Hence their co-agency with God as efficient cause was consistent with their identity, just as it was consistent with the other three causes that together defined the Bible as literature. Causal explanations showed that writers were taken beyond themselves. There is no reason to conclude that Lyra or anyone saw "the literal sense as the personal meaning of the human *auctor.*"[97] Quite the opposite is indicated by the material and final causes: the literal sense is the message of God given for a specific purpose. It is not a personal, or for that matter historically circumscribed, piece of literature; rather, the circumstances of writing can and must be shown to fit a universal framework. Any interest in historical particularity dwindled beneath the universal, theological framework of meaning. As important as this anti-historicizing move was, it is equally important to see that it was anti-allegorizing, too. Because literal exegesis did not depend upon the idea that a book of the Bible expressed the literary interests of a human author, but rather depended upon the congruence of authorial interest with divine interest, literal exegesis could assume many of the theological functions exercised by allegorical exegesis in the twelfth century. Likewise, history, for example the history of Solomon and the Shulamite woman, whose love affair interpreters assumed the Song of Songs to record, could literally be an allegory of the history of Israel – as Nicholas of Lyra may have learned from an anonymous thirteenth-century Latin adaptation of Rashi's commentary on this book – and not the sensuous poem that to us it obviously is.[98]

In this way causal definitions of the Bible reflected the movement of the divine realm to the human. Richard FitzRalph could have spoken for many when he said that no human being could claim to be the author of scripture in the truest sense, in that its assertions originate with God.[99] In his *Summa on the Questions of the Armenians*, composed at the papal court in 1349/50, FitzRalph noted that any narrative of someone speaking

---

[96] *Enarratio in Proverbia, Opera,* 7:203, and the prologue to the *Enarratio in Lucam,* ibid., 11:363.
[97] Minnis, *Medieval Theory of Authorship,* p. 86.
[98] Turner, *Eros and Allegory,* pp. 114–17, but assuming the distinction between typology and allegory that I reject. See also p. 18 n. 43, above.
[99] Minnis, *Theory of Authorship,* pp. 94–103, esp. 100–1.

could be attributed to the authorship of the speaker, the narrator, or both, but properly considered, a real *auctor* must be both speaker and narrator. In the Bible, only God, who reveals the text, is author in this sense.[100] Accordingly, the Bible is really about the knowledge of God – theology.[101]

3. DOUBLE-LITERAL AND PARABOLIC MEANING

Human authorship proved itself ambivalent. God was author, too, and his purposes were not limited to the objectives of individual writers. This implied that the meaning of biblical literature could vary, that it was not fixed to one thing determined by a human writer's intention. Under what conditions did interpreters imagine this variety to occur? They traced it to the nature of language, the condition of readers, and the broad intellectual context to which the Bible as a book and theology as an endeavor of the human mind belonged. Biblical meaning was verbal, anthropological, and, in the broadest sense, intellectual, three characteristics that theologians separated with difficulty. Parabolic meaning emphasized the first characteristic, the "verbalness" of biblical meaning.

Nicholas of Lyra, in a part of his second prologue to the Bible that also circulated independent of his *Postilla*, explained that some texts, particularly those commonly regarded as Messianic prophecies, could have two literal meanings, one pertaining to the immediate circumstances of their original narrator, and one pertaining to the remote future.[102] In his comments on Tyconius' third rule, "on promises or the law," which

---

[100] Minnis, "Authorial Intention," pp. 5–10, and *Medieval Theory of Authorship*, pp. 100–2. The definition of authorship raises a problem: whether the sense of the human author and that of the divine author might disagree. FitzRalph appeals to New Testament interpretations of passages with prophetic meaning, in effect limiting authorship as a determinant of meaning to God's activity. Also cf. Katherine Walsh, *Richard FitzRalph in Oxford, Avignon and Armagh* (Oxford University Press, 1981), p. 171, which provides (pp. 159–81) a thorough analysis of the polemical arguments of the treatise.

[101] Minnis, *Medieval Theory of Authorship*, pp. 85–94, on Thomas Aquinas, Nicholas Trevet, and Nicholas of Lyra. See also pp. 118–59 for the congruence of the Bible's literary structure, with its doctrine and religious purpose, with the style of the authors of particular books.

[102] Stadtbibliothek Mainz, Hs 177, ff. 274r–275v, Anonymous, *Clauis sacre scripture*, is written in a cursive gothic hand of the late fourteenth or early fifteenth century on paper in a volume of mostly sermons written by several contemporary hands, from the library of the Carthusians of Mainz. It is copied from Nicholas of Lyra's second prologue to the Bible. Lyra claims that he has Tyconius' rules from Isidore, *De summo bono* (i.20 *Glossa cum Lyra*, 1:3vb), but Lyra's version is expanded. The Mainz *Clauis* was not known to Stegmüller, but *RB* 6:148 no. 8848 (Breslau Univ. 328, ff. 89–91) is apparently another adaptation of Isidore and Hugh's version of the seven rules or an excerpt from Lyra's prologue. The third rule, from Lyra's version, is found on f. 274v (also *Glossa cum Lyra*, 1:3vb–4rb; the variations of text are very minor and noted with the sign L [=Lyra] in the critical notes following the selection). Lyra's treatment of the rule of Tyconius is omitted

according to Augustine can also be called "on the Spirit and the law," Nicholas explained that the traditional distinction between historical and spiritual meaning is unnecessary:

The third rule concerns the letter and the spirit, that under the same letter the historical and mystical sense is taken, because the truth of the story is to be maintained, and yet referred to a spiritual understanding. This is the way the letter is commonly explained. But it can be explained otherwise, so that it is referred to the literal sense as well as the others, concerning which it is to be considered that the same letter at times has a double literal sense. An example: 1 Paralipomenon 17 [verse 13]. The Lord says concerning Solomon, "I will be to him a father, and he will be to me a son," and it is interpreted to be about Solomon according to the letter, insofar as he was made a son of God by adoption in his youth. On that account Nathan the prophet called him "dear to the lord," as 2 Kings 12 [verse 25] says. The aforementioned text, "I will be to him a father," etc., is introduced by the apostle, Hebrews 1 [verses 4–8], as though it were said about Christ according to the letter, which is clear from this, because the apostle introduces the case to prove that Christ was greater than the angels. Such an argument cannot be made with the mystical sense, as Augustine says against Vincentius the Donatist, as has been alleged above.[103] For the aforementioned text had been fulfilled according to the letter in Solomon, all the same, less perfectly, because he was the son of

> from Minnis and Scott's selection, *Medieval Literary Theory*, pp. 269–70: "Tercia regula est de spiritu et littera et secundum quod accipitur sub eadem littera sensus historicus et misticus, quia ueritas historie est tenenda, et tamen ad spiritualem intellectum referenda. Hoc modo exponitur ista littera communiter. Potest eciam aliter exponi, ut referatur ad sensum litteralem tamen sicut et alie, circa quod considerandum quod eadem littera aliquando habet duplicem sensum litteralem. Uerbi gratia. i. Paralipomenon xvij [1 Para. 17.13]. dicit dominus de Salomone, 'ego ero illi in patrem, et ipse erit michi in filium,' et interpretatur de Salomone ad litteram in quantum fuit filius Dei per adopcionem in iuuentute. Propterea Nathan propheta nominauit eum 'amabilis domino,' ut habetur ii. Regum xij [2 Rg. 12.25]. Predicta eciam auctoritas, 'ego ero illi in patrem,' et cetera, inducitur ab apostulo ad Hebreos i [He. 1.4–8], tanquam dictum de Christo ad litteram, quod patet ex hoc, quia apostolus inducit causam probandum quod Christus fuit maior angelis. Talis autem pro causa non potest fieri per sensum misticum, ut dicit Augustinus contra Uincentium donatistum, ut supra allegatum est. Predicta enim auctoritas impleta fuit ad litteram in Salamone minus tamen perfecte, quia fuit filius Dei per graciam solum, in Christo autem perfectius, qui est Dei filius per naturam, licet autem utraque expositio sit litteralis simpliciter. Secunda tamen que est de Christo spiritualis est et mistica, secundum quod in quantum Salomon fuit figura Christi."
>
> secundum quod] secundum hoc L. referenda] est referenda L. ista littera communiter] communiter illa regula L. interpretatur] intelligitur L. Propterea] Propter quod L. nominauit] uocauit L. amabilis] amabilem L. ut habetur] *ms. supersc.* dictum] dicta L. causam] eam L. quod Christus] *ms* quod Christum. filius Dei] *trans* L. est et mistica] *trans* L. Salomon] *leg* Solomon.
>
> Contrast the anonymous treatise probably of the thirteenth century (p. 96 note 58, above), where divine authorship is associated with the spiritual senses. *Spicilegium*, pp. 439–40 (xiv).

[103] Near the beginning of his second prologue Lyra refers to this letter and Augustine's assertion that only the literal sense may be admitted in argumentation. See Augustine, Ep. 93, *Letters*, 2:56–106.

God only by grace, but in Christ more perfectly, who is the Son of God by nature, although both expositions are simply literal. Yet the second which is about Christ is both spiritual and mystical, insofar as Solomon was a figure of Christ.

The prophets knew the figures. Through them they could achieve an understanding of the divine essence and, with it, of God's foreknowledge, as if they were reading from the book of God's mind.[104] Alongside the reduction of prophetic meanings to the consciousness of the author in the double-literal sense, Nicholas added the "parabolic," which he discussed in the "moral prologue." Parabolic passages are those in which the immediate referents of words do not provide the principal meaning. In a parabolic passage, figurative expressions carry a single literal meaning.[105] Both the double-literal sense and the parabolic sense provide literal categories for passages that would otherwise have been interpreted mystically. Bonaventure, Aquinas, Meister Eckhart, and Matthew of Janow also appealed to the parabolic sense.[106]

Scholars were reluctant to accept Lyra's point that parabolic meaning is univocal. This was in part due to their recognition that the meaning of words could scarcely be restricted to an author's wishes. In the fifth century, Hilary of Poitiers noted that the meaning of a word might suggest something other than an author's intention.[107] In the twelfth century Gilbert de la Porrée, among others, showed that the distinction between authorial and grammatical meaning could further subvert the dominance of authorial intention, by arguing from the fallibility of human judgment and intellect. An act of speech, *sermo*, cannot adequately express an object of knowledge, *res*. The finite human mind cannot grasp the *res* in its entirety, and its ability to express even what it does grasp in language is more inferior still. To Gilbert, "linguistic expression lags

---

[104] *Glossa cum Lyra*, f. 3rb. See also the examples considered by Schwendinger, "De Vaticiniis," pp. 8, 22–23, 29, 37–42, 131, 140, 145, 155, 156–61. Schwendinger's preoccupation with the validity of Lyra's interpretations, and his constant comparison with Catholic exegetes of the nineteenth and early twentieth centuries, can be ignored for the sake of his minute examination of Lyra's commentaries.

[105] *Glossa cum Lyra*, f. 4rb–4va.

[106] Winkler, *Methoden*, pp. 52–54. Donald F. Duclow, "Meister Eckhart on the Book of Wisdom: Commentary and Sermons," *Traditio* 43 (1987): 215–35. Matthew of Janow, *Tractatus de abominatione desolationis in loco sancto*, xxxi (see also lxii), in *Regulae*, 4:142, 279–80. This is an interpretation of Gog and Magog in the Apocalypse. Gog refers parabolically to people in religious orders, and Magog refers parabolically to the remaining clergy and laity. Appeal to parabolic meaning is unusual in Matthew of Janow's exegesis. He prefers to call the mysteries hidden in the Bible signs and figures. For the parabolic, see also page 21, above.

[107] *De Trinitate* ii.3, PL 10:51. Häring, "Commentary and Hermeneutics," pp. 195–6.

behind both reality and our understanding," as Nikolaus Häring once explained.[108] We also find late medieval scholars like Meister Eckhart, who gave authors little regard.[109] For others, the literal meaning of a text evaded *any* singular intention. John Wyclif upheld the possibility of passages with an "equivocal" literal sense, which was, in effect, a double-literal meaning.[110] He also experimented with multiple literal interpretations, for example at Genesis 1.1, where he identified six literal senses (and three allegorical, six tropological, and two anagogical ones).[111] Multiplicity is most apparent in prophetic passages, where the letter may refer to Christ, Christ and ancient Israel, or Christ and future glory.[112] With regard to authorial intention, the prophets themselves could intend such variety.[113] A parabolic sense "is mystical enough," but may be attributed to the letter rather than to allegory, as Thomas Aquinas had done.[114] In fact according to Wyclif, all the mystical senses may be literal or non-literal. When allegory, tropology, or anagogy are "immediately" conveyed by the language of scripture, they are actually literal.[115] Wyclif finally concluded that the distinctions between meanings and the intentions of human authors are irrelevant; the "manner of speaking" (*modus loquendi*) is "superfluously onerous"; all that matters is "the aggregate of that [divinely intended sense] and our mode of understanding."[116] The effect of the text upon the soul, the intention of the divine author, is everything.[117]

Wyclif's intellectualizing was consistent with earlier causal definitions of the Bible and the increasing association of theological truth with literal narratives. Jan Hus was a student of arts and then theology in Prague at the turn of the fourteenth to fifteenth centuries, and he was among the

---

[108] Häring, "Commentary and Hermeneutics," p. 196. Gilbert de la Porrée, *The Commentaries on Boethius*, ed. N. Häring (Toronto: Pontifical Institute of Mediaeval Studies, 1966), p. 67.
[109] Winkler, *Methoden*, p. 79.
[110] Workman, *Wyclif*, 2:152. Wyclif, *De civili dominio*, iii.21, ed. J. Loserth (London: Trübner and Co., 1904), *Latin Works*, 4:443. Benrath, *Wyclifs Bibelkommentar*, p. 69 (a double-literal sense in Is. 7.14).
[111] Benrath, *Wyclifs Bibelkommentar*, p. 65.
[112] Especially in the commentary on Isaiah. Ibid., pp. 69–71.
[113] Ibid., pp. 75–6 n. 176.
[114] *De veritate sacrae scripturae*, vi, pp. 122–3. Although Lyra is frequently cited in the commentaries (see p. 281, below), his prefaces are not used in Wyclif's discussion of parabolic meaning. Parable is also regarded as a form of literal-figurative speech, ibid., iv, 1:65–67 (defined from Aquinas; cf. "fictive locution," which is subject to a definition in keeping with mystical interpretation). Consider also Wyclif's *principium*: Smalley, "John Wyclif's Dilemma," p. 292. An example of a parabolic-historical sense may be found in *De veritate sacre scripture*, iv, 1:77. In other places, Wyclif tends to regard parable as a form of non-literal speech subject to mystical interpretation: ibid., iv, 1:73 (also from Aquinas), 74–5.
[115] Ibid., vi, 1:123.   [116] He says this while justifying his earlier exegesis. Ibid., vi, 1:124.
[117] Ibid., vi, 11:124–6. Minnis, "Authorial Intention," pp. 26–7.

students there influenced by Wyclif's realist metaphysics and doctrine of the church. We might expect him to replicate Wyclif's exegesis. Hus used the "parabolic sense" from Thomas Aquinas to defend the truth of all of the Bible's parts, even those that seem to contradict Christian morals and doctrine.[118] Adapting the argument from divine authorship, Hus built upon the conviction that the book objectively displays the word of God, which Christ has given to people.[119] Parabolic meaning in scripture points to divine authorship, in that the variety of literal meaning is established by human and divine co-agency.

Heinrich of Langenstein pressed the hermeneutics of the parabolic a little further. If the scriptural letter is polyvalent, then polyvalence must be true of other literature as well. The category of parabolic meaning resolves linguistic and semantic difficulties in scripture, but applying parabolic interpretation to secular literature endangers Christians, who might then regard the fables as inspired, like scripture. Heinrich discussed the danger of people who, without any other qualification, use "spiritual revelations and inspirations given to them by the Holy Spirit ("spirituales reuelaciones uel inmissiones eis a spiritu sancto facte") to interpret "the simple and rustic sense of scripture" contrary to the common mind of the church handed down by the holy doctors. He allowed for the possibility of such special interpretation, but it must be tested by examining its effect on the interpreter's soul. Does it incite vanity or holiness? If it incites holiness and its divine source is thus proven, it may yet be a meaning that extends beyond the intention of the Holy Spirit in scripture:

It is to be recognized that divine scripture is interpreted sometimes according to the meaning intended by the Holy Spirit and sometimes according to a meaning not intended by the Holy Spirit. And this second thing is to be understood in two ways, because either it leads to false meanings or to certain true meanings which the Holy Spirit did not intend through scripture.

For the parabolic locutions of holy scripture can be applied as signs and figures to many virtues concerning human and divine things, for the signifying of which truths the Holy Spirit neither dictated nor ordained the scriptures. An example. Just as it often happens that someone offers a saying or pronounces some speech univocally (*ad unum sensum*), that saying carefully examined and taken apart is found to introduce by addition other adjacent, unintended true meanings, on account of a multiplicity in the signifying of terms and on account of the variety of the construction and supposition of terms, or on account of

---

[118] Joannes Hus, *Super IV. Sententiarum*, pp. 15–16. For Wyclif's influence at Prague and Hus's partial dependence on him see Matthew Spinka, *John Hus' Concept of the Church* (Princeton University Press, 1966), pp. 35–41, 52–53 and *passim*.
[119] *Super IV. Sententiarum*, pp. 14–15.

a remote property of a single thing. Hence it is that many fables of Ovid and others can be adapted as figures and parables to those things which Christ did. And so, as though allegorically, one explains either certain moral or other true meanings to apply, which Ovid never understood when he fashioned the fables in this way.[120]

The extension of meanings beyond authorial intention is allegorical, and it may arise from the complex reference of things, established by an analysis of their properties. So much Langenstein concedes to the tradition of mystical interpretation. But he also refers generally to the syntax and supposition of terms, using language that his readers knew from their elementary study of Latin and logic.[121] Meaning beyond authorial intention – allegory – was thus drawn into literal speech, and the analysis of terms could account for it. Langenstein then added that such exposition of fables is dangerous, because weak Christians might think that if the poets can be so taken to mean what they did not intend, so too the Christian religion may rest insecurely on unintended meanings of the Bible.[122]

---

[120] Stadtbibliothek Mainz, Hs. I 449, ff. 139vb–140ra: "Est tamen advertendum quod scriptura diuina exponitur quandoque ad sensus intentos a spiritu sancto et quandoque ad sensus a spiritu sancto non intentos. Et hoc secundum est duplex intelligendum, quia uel ad falsos sensus uel eciam ad aliquos ueros sensus, quos spiritus sanctus non intendebat per scripturam. Possunt enim parabolice locuciones scripture sacre adaptari tanquam signa et figure multis uirtutibus circa humana et diuina, ad quas tamen ueritates significandas spiritus sanctus scripturas non dictauit nec ordinauit, uerbi gracia, sicud et sepe accidit quod aliquis proponit unum sermonem uel profert aliquam oracionem ad unum sensum, et tamen ille sermo diligenter inspectus et discussus inuenitur eciam importare alios sensus ueros adicientes non intentos et hoc propter multiplicitatem insignando terminorum et propter construccionis et supposiccionis terminorum uarietatem uel propter diuersam unius rei proprietatem. Hinc eciam est quod multe fabule Ouidii et aliorum possunt tamquam figura et parabole aptari ad ea que Christus gessit. Et sic quasi allegorice [aliquis] exponit uel aliquos sensus morales uel alios ueros applicare, quos Ouidius nunquam intellexit fingens huiusmodi fabulas." At ff. 143va–144va Langenstein again considers the question whether the person who interprets scripture according to a sense not intended by the author sins. He answers from the implications of the interpretation: it is sinful if it leads to error. This means that it is dangerous for those inexpert in theology to depart from the interpretations offered by the best-known theologians. Langenstein also associates such interpretation with the "secta Begkardorum et aliquorum hereticorum" (f. 144rb).

[121] For the difference between signification and supposition see Joseph Mullaley, *The Summulae logicales of Peter of Spain* (Notre Dame: University of Notre Dame Press, 1945), p. 3.

[122] Stadtbibliothek Mainz, Hs. I 449, f. 140ra, immediately following the passage given in note 120: "Et periculosa est huiusmodi fabularum exposicio de Christo propter duo. Primum, ne simplices audientes quomodo proprie tales fabule correspondent facto Christi uel ueritatibus fidei credant forte illos uanos poetas fuisse prophetas. Secundum ne surripiat [leg. succurrat] infirmis christianis cogitacio quod sicud fabule poetarum preter eorum pertinentem intencionem et colorate exponuntur de Christo, quod ita preter intencionem spiritus sancti et prophetarum eorum figure et parabole exponuntur forte de Christo et factis religionis christiane et quod sit propter ambiguitatem et diuersitatem sensuum scripture religio christiana non sit secure fundata."

His reference to the properties of things points to the limited approach to metaphor that existed in late medieval commentaries and was examined in the previous chapter, and it raises an interesting problem. Langenstein did not perceive the difference between a logician's view of language and a traditional view of mystical exegesis. Was Augustine's *On Christian Doctrine* sending him to the text or beyond it? Exegesis relied on both the "conditions of things" and the "meanings of terms."[123] All the figurative expressions commonly taught by grammarians are in the Bible, hence grammar is "most useful for understanding the divine scriptures, because in holy scripture not only words signify but also things and their conditions signify higher mysteries."[124] We are then reminded of the doctrine of *circumstantiae*: through the liberal arts, one may consider the disposition, condition, property, and order of things, which Augustine insisted was necessary for the unraveling of obscure figures.[125] Langenstein then adds that logic and metaphysics help one treat theological problems like predestination, future contingents, and the question of the necessity of the past; the liberal arts help one struggle against heretics and unbelievers and embellish theology with beautiful language and moral illustrations.[126] Canon law should serve as practical theology.[127] Without the auxiliary sciences, Augustine pointed out, some biblical expressions cannot be understood.[128] This all sounds very Victorine, except for one thing. The mysteries of which Langenstein is speaking are not necessarily allegorical at all. They may be based on the strictly literal meaning of terms. This raises the possibility that in Langenstein's mind the metaphysical properties of things have to do not with allegorical but with literal meaning. And in fact, we know this to be the case because Langenstein's commentary on the text of Genesis is a very long study

---

[123] But Langenstein considered it sinful to impute such meanings to the author. If the text is knowingly interpreted against the intention of the "doctor," the interpreter incurs mortal sin, as do the "secta Begkardorum et aliquorum hereticorum." Ibid., f. 143vb–144va.

[124] After explaining that grammar is useful in Bible reading because it explains the figures of speech commonly used, he adds: "[grammatica] utilissima sit ad intellegenciam diuinarum scripturarum, secundo quia in scriptura sacra non solum uoces significant sed et res et earum habitudines alta significant misteria." Langenstein refers to Augustine's claim in *De doctrina christiana* (iii.29, CCL 32:100–1) that all rhetorical figures are found in the Bible (Hs. I 449, f. 106ra–106rb).

[125] Ibid. and Augustinus, *De doctina christiana* ii.16, CCL 32:49.

[126] Hs. I 449, f. 106va–106vb.

[127] Ibid., f. 110ra: "sciencia juris canonici nondum plene segregata erat a sciencia theologyca, cum sit quasi una species theoloyce practice ut uidebitur."

[128] Ibid., f. 106rb: "Et est intencio Augustini quod nisi rerum quibus fit figuratiua locucio proprietates et condiciones cognoscantur misteria, talibus locucionibus designata intelligi non possunt. Et ita est necessaria rerum cognicio ad intelligendum scripturas sacras, que plurimi talibus locucionibus utuntur."

of natural philosophy in the literal sense. Augustine implied something quite different to Langenstein than he did to Hugh of St. Victor. He reinforced the belief that interpretation occurs in two places: in the language of the text and in the knowledge of the universe. Literal meaning was controlled by universal truth. But it was, as Lyra, Eckhart, Wyclif, and Langenstein recognized, also found in parabolic expressions, in the verbal meaning of obscure speech. A sentence, an expression as such, possessed diverse significations.

4. INSPIRATION

Inspiration emphasized the anthropological aspect of biblical meaning, as Langenstein explained. Verbal meaning was mutable and not really under the control of human authorship. But Langenstein did not regard textual meaning as arbitrary. The reader prevented the cascade of subjective interpretations, because he or she stood within a continuum of experience: the reader was inspired by the Holy Spirit and in communion with reading and writing saints.[129] Inspiration characterized the oral, human context of biblical meaning.

Allegorical reading required an anthropology (anthropology in the theological sense), and Langenstein appealed to it. Jerome explained that the wisdom of God, which is Christ, is hidden in mystery and prefigured in the law and the prophets,

whence the prophets were called seers, because they saw him whom others did not see. Abraham saw the day of Christ and rejoiced. The heavens opened to Ezechiel, which were closed to a sinful people. "Take the veil," said David, "from my eyes, and I will consider the marvelous things of your law"; for the law is spiritual, and it requires unveiling, so that it may be understood and, when the face of God has been unveiled, we may contemplate glory.[130]

Langenstein commented upon this passage:

Take the veil from my eyes by removing the said darknesses and blindnesses or by opening the figures of the law of Moses. And why did he say here *prophet*? Surely

---

[129] A similar point was made by Langenstein when he rejected the prophecy of Joachim of Fiore. Reeves, *Influence of Prophecy*, p. 426.
[130] Hieronymus, Ep. liv., 4.3–4, CSEL 54/1:450: "unde prophetae appellabantur uidentes, quia uidebant eum, quem ceteri non uidebant. Abraham uidit diem eius et laetatus est. aperiebantur caeli Ezechieli, qui populo peccatori clausi erant. 'Reuela,' inquit Dauid, 'oculos meos, et considerabo mirabilia de lege tua'; lex enim spiritalis est et reuelatione indiget, ut intellegatur ac reuelata facie dei gloriam contemplemur."

because that *law is spiritual*, as it is said in Romans 7 and 2 Corinthians 3, "the letter kills, but the Spirit gives life." And so it appears that spiritual marvels are contained in the law under figures and mysteries, which cannot be understood without spiritual revelation, nor without such spiritual revelation are we able to make manifest those marvelous things that God to his glory arranged to be appointed to be contemplated in the old scripture [that is, the Old Testament]. And therefore for the sake of the comprehension of the godly scriptures, the work is by revelation, which conclusion is intended by St. Jerome here, from which it appears that where the earliest doctors touched on the high and deep spiritual senses while explaining the holy scripture, in this they had been spiritually steered and aided by God. For if God was once so generous and kind to illuminate men that he even deigned to reveal to a person looking for lost jack asses where they were, as is apparent in chapter 10 of 1 Kings,[131] why therefore would he not reveal his glory to a teacher anxious to discover and declare salutary glory to the Jewish people and open up the truth and the mysteries of the scriptures?[132]

This is a defense of spiritual interpretations, as Langenstein knew them in patristic sources or perhaps as these were excerpted in the Ordinary Gloss, but the conditions of spiritual learning existed within the history of the Bible itself, since patriarchs, prophets, and apostles wrote and understood their own writings under divine influence.

Can one understand the letter by natural ability, without the Spirit? This question was presented, in Langenstein's mind, by Jewish readers, who could understand without the Holy Spirit's inspiration, but who he believed did not possess reliable religious knowledge. This was, he recognized, also a question about literal comprehension in general:

And I said with emphasis the spiritual senses "deep and high" because indeed through proficiency and study of the divine scriptures teachers can attain the scriptures' many true and spiritual senses by a human process of expounding. That is clear on the one hand because otherwise it would seem pointless to study

---

[131] 1 Rg 10.14–16.
[132] Stadtbibliothek Mainz, Hs. I 449, f. 98va–98vb: "*Reuela* inquid scilicet *oculos meos* removendo dictas [f. 98vb] tenebras et cecitates, uel aperiendo legis Moyses figuras. Et quare dixit hic *propheta*? Certe quia *lex* illa *spiritualis est*, ut habetur Ad Romanos vii. capitulo et ii. Ad Corintheos iii., 'littera occidit, spiritus autem uiuificat.' Et ita apparet quod in lege sub figuris et misterijs spiritualia continentur *mirabilia*, que absque reuelacione spirituali intelligi non possunt nec sine tali possumus in scriptura ueteri reuelata facere illa magnalia que Deus ad gloriam suam fieri disposuit contemplari. Et ergo pro intelligencia diuinalium scripturarum, opus est reuelacione, que conclusio est beati Jeronimi hic intenta, ex qua apparet quod ubi doctores maxime primitiui exponentes sacram scripturam tetigunt sensus altos et profundos spirituales sensus spiritualiter in hoc directi et adiuti fuerunt a Deo. Si enim Deus ita largus et benignus fuit olim ad illuminandum hominem, quod eciam querenti asinos perditos reuelare dignatus fuit ubi essent, ut patet i. Regum capitulo decimo, quare ergo doctori sollicito de inueniendis et declarandis salutaribus ueritatibus ad salutem populi judei gloriam non indicaret [et] ueritatem et abscondita aperiret scripturarum?"

the holy scriptures and on the other hand because even Jerome said, about these matters, that whatever human effort yielded to diligent students of the law [of Moses], this the Holy Spirit revealed to the apostles. And consequently, expertise in the holy scriptures could achieve, even by means of a human method of learning, a certain true comprehension of them, which comprehension was revealed to others. It was so before the coming of Christ and before the dissemination of the scriptures through him, as was evident concerning Paul. He, very learned in the law, could attain a deep understanding of the scriptures through study and diligent exercise. [Yet] it could not so have been achieved before Christ was presentially exhibited to the human study of the sciences and of the scriptures, because it is easier after the fact to apply the signs to the things signified [and] the figures to the things figurated than [to apply them] before the positioning of the things figurated that accompanied the property [of the figure] . . .[133]

Scriptural knowledge attained without revelation, such as the knowledge gained by Jewish scholars of the law, was therefore true insofar as it agreed with revelation. One could judge the knowledge gained by human prowess by testing the correspondence of its signs against the things signified in subsequent revelation, and its figures against the things figurated in subsequent revelation. The constant element in this passage is its presumed definition of reading comprehension. The association of signs and things signified produces comprehension. It is a statement of verbal signification. An uncertain signified meaning becomes definite when it is confirmed by more certain revelation, which is of course a restatement of Augustine's famous "analogy of faith." Langenstein described signification as verbal, and he insisted that it stand alongside subjective revelation.

It was subjective by divine action, along a continuum of readers. The incarnation and the New Testament restrict personally inspired reading within the conventions of the established church. The point is to read charismatically, if you will, and communally at the same time. To

[133] Ibid., ff. 98vb–99ra: "Et dixi notanter sensus spirituales profundos et altos, quia eciam per exercicium et studium diuinarum scripturarum doctores possunt processu humano expositorio attingere multos ueros et spirituales sensus scripturarum. Istud patet tum quia alias frustra uidetur studium poni in scripturis sacris tum quia eciam Jeronimus super is dixit quod quidquid humana exercitacio contulit studiosis in lege, hoc spiritus sanctus reuelauit apostolis. Et per consequens exercicium in sacris scripturis peruenire poterat eciam humano modo discendi ad aliquem ueram earum intelligenciam, que intelligencia alijs reuelabatur. Et si sic fuit ante aduentum Christi et ante aspersionem scripturarum per ipsum, sicud superius patuit de Paulo docto in lege multo forcius modo per studium uel exercicium studiosum in scripturis profundum earum intellectum spiritualem attingere potuisset, qui antequam esset Christus presencialiter exhibitus humano studio scienciarum seu scripturarum sic attingi non poterat, quia facilius est ex post facto applicare signas signatis [et] figuras figuratis quam ante posicionem rerum figuratarum inesse qualitatem . . ."

make his point, Heinrich appealed to a common allegation made against heretics. Heretics regard scripture as obscure and on that pretext distort its definite, orthodox meaning. Because Langenstein admitted the possibility of actual meanings beyond the Holy Spirit's intention, this is a significant problem. How does one know that the heretics are wrong? Figurative and parabolic meanings of scripture beyond the intention of the Holy Spirit or the prophets may not provide a firm foundation for Christian religion, Langenstein explained,

> And on that account, those people are to be reproved, who relying on the subtlety of their own ingenuity explain the meanings of the divine scriptures as varied, diverse, and even contradictory, leading the simple to believe that sacred scripture almost does not have a fixed meaning and leading them to say that it may have a wax nose, equally bendable to the right and to the left. They ought to know that holy scripture has not a wax nose but an iron nose, a fiery nose, or surely blessed Jerome would not have said, as Gratian alleges, that "whoever understands scripture otherwise than the Holy Spirit emphatically demands could still be called a heretic, even if he did not leave the church." And Jerome on Isaiah says, "they are drunk with wine" who understand the holy scriptures wrongly or pervert them. And again he says that we ought to consider as false prophets those who take the words of the scriptures in ways other than what the Holy Spirit has spoken. And the savior says in the fifth chapter of Matthew [Mt. 5.18] that "no letter and no stroke of a letter will be taken away from the law until all things are fulfilled." And at another place [Mt. 24.35], "heaven and earth will pass away, but my words will not pass away." And it is said at Deuteronomy 4 [verse 2], "you must not add to the word that I speak to you nor take away from it." And in the last chapter of the Apocalypse [Apoc. 22.18], "if anyone should add to this, let God put upon him the plagues," etc.
>
> From these things it is clear that the divine scriptures contain the most definite meaning and irrefragable truth and even an unmovable and inflexible understanding intended in them by the Holy Spirit. It is therefore clear that scripture does not have a wax nose but an iron and a fiery nose. It is also clear that they do not sin lightly who, having found or wrenched out diverse, strange, and foreign things by their own ingenuity, are responsible for the fact that sacred scripture is accustomed to be defamed in the said manner, namely [when it is said] that it has a wax nose. It is therefore clear that sacred scripture is not to be dragged to that meaning that each and every interpreter presumes for himself, but is to be handled according to the traditions of the fathers and from the circumstances of scripture itself: the meaning of the truth ought to be investigated from people, places, and times; from the situations of speaking, from the ways of speaking the languages or language in which it has been published.[134]

---

[134] Ibid., f. 140ra–140rb, following the passage given at note 122, above, after explaining that figurative and parabolic meanings beyond the intention of the Holy Spirit and the prophets do not provide a firm foundation for the Christian religion: "Et propter idem reprehendendi

Langenstein returns us again to historical and linguistic circumstances, but it is his presuppositions about the history of spiritual teachings that render true interpretations ironclad. Theologians belonged, in his mind as in the minds of sixteenth-century interpreters later, to a continuum of meaning that included Hebrew patriarchs, prophets, apostles, and saints. The inspired meaning of the text is consensual.

The meaning of pagan, or classical, poetry could evade the intention of poets and receive a Christian interpretation, but because the poets did not share the experience of prophets and apostles, such interpretation was also tenuous. Christian exegesis of ancient poets (Langenstein named Homer and Virgil) and philosophers could not, to him, obscure the fact that those authors lacked revelation. Christian interpretations of pagan literature therefore rely, he said, upon the coincidental similarity of pagan and Christian ideas.[135] What makes it arbitrary? Missing, Langenstein believed, is a common understanding shared between poet and believer. Nevertheless, while error in theology could lead to spiritual death, mistakes in the liberal arts were of little consequence.[136]

These are intriguing claims. Langenstein was no classicist. His outside field, if you will, was natural philosophy, and unlike the small group of English friars of the beginning of the fourteenth century studied by

> sunt illi qui subtilitati ingenij sui innitentes scripturarum diuinarum uarios et diuersos et quandoque aduersos exponunt sensus, facientes credere simpliciores, quod quasi scriptura sacra non habeat determinatum sensum et dicere quod habeat nasum cereum ad dexteram et sinistram eque flexibilem. Illi scire debent quod sacra scriptura non habet nasum cereum sed ferreum, ymo calidum, alias utique beatus Jeronimus non diceret, ut allegat Gracianus,[a] quod 'qui scripturam aliter intelligit quam spiritus sanctus efflagitat, licet ab ecclesia non recesserit, tamen hereticus appellari potest.' Et Jeronimus super Ysaiam dicit, 'uino inebriantur' qui scripturas sanctas male intelligunt atque peruertunt.[b] Et iterum dicit quod pseudo prophetas eos debemus accipere qui aliter scripturarum uerba accipiunt quam spiritus sanctus sonat. Et saluator dicit Matthei v.[c] quod 'jota unum aut unus apex non preteribit a lege donec omnia fiant.' Et alibi,[d] 'celum et terra transibunt, uerba autem mea non transibunt.' Et Deuteronomij iv.[e] dicitur, 'non addetis ad uerbum quod uobis loquor nec aufferetis ex eo.' Et Apokalipsis ultimo,[f] 'si quis apposuerit ad hoc apponat Deus super illum plagas,' et cetera.
>
> "Ex quibus manifestum est quod diuine scripture continent determinantissimum sensum et irrefragabilem ueritatem atque inmobilem et inflexibilem intelligenciam a spiritu sancto in eis intentam. Patet ergo quod non habet nasum cereum sed ferreum ymo calidum. Patet eciam quod non mediocriter peccant qui uarijs extraneis et peregrinis exposicionibus suo ingenio inuentis uel extortis sunt in causa quod scriptura sacra dicto modo diffamari consueuit, uidelicet quod habet nasum cereum. Patet ergo quod sacra scriptura non est trahenda ad eum sensum, quem sibi uniusquisque presumit, sed est tractanda secundum tradiciones patrum aut ex ipsius scripture circumstanciis: ex personis ex locis, ex temporibus, ex causis dicendi, ex modis loquendi lingwarum uel lingwe in qua est edita inuestigari oportet sensus ueritatis."
>
> a. Gratianus, *Decretum*, C XXIV.iii.39, CICan 1:1006. b. Cf. Jerome, *Commentariorum in Esaiam*, prol., CCL 73:1–4, et cf. Eph. 5.18. c. Mt. 5.18. d. Mt. 24.35. e. Deut. 4.2. f. Apoc. 22.18.

[135] Ibid., ff. 140vb–144va.   [136] Ibid., f. 144va.

Beryl Smalley, for him the beauty of classical literature, with its fables and demons masquerading as gods, had no power. Yet he, with his exaltation of revealed truth over pagan learning, was hardly as shrill as critics of the classicizing friars, like the Carmelite John Baconthorpe, who mark the rapid decline of sympathy with pagan literature among theologians in the middle of that century.[137] The classicizing friars, Smalley taught us, were a curious English prelude to humanism, and they had no connection with it. Langenstein, writing at the end of the century and in the new Central European university of Vienna, reveals something else – a certain ambivalence toward classical erudition, a relaxation of intolerance. He has, in fact, placed the reader of holy scripture and pagan poetry in a position between revelation and individual rational power, and not merely because scripture is revealed and poetry is not. To the contrary, he is well aware that, in certain respects, the conditions of reading poetry are identical with those of reading the Bible. A person may understand scripture on the strength of individual rational power, just as that person may understand pagan literature. So the interpretations must be judged by their correspondence to revealed truth, which is truth revealed in biblical writing and also revealed in biblical reading.

Spiritual reading was reading with the authors of scripture and the divine author of regeneration. Before Langenstein, John Wyclif and Matthias of Janow had argued for its necessity.[138] After him, Agostino Favaroni and Denys the Carthusian insisted that the Holy Spirit's influence was evident when interpretations conformed to received tradition and confirmed the Christian faith.[139] When meaning corresponds to tradition, reading corresponds to authorship. We usually think of this in the context of doctrinal problems like the connection of revelation and tradition. Langenstein's position, that revelation confirms true interpretation and that the correspondence of meaning can extend to pagan as well as sacred literature, is in broad agreement with the well-known position of Robert Holcot, who argued in his *Wisdom* commentary that revelation confirms the teachings of Hermes and Aristotle.[140] But the hermeneutic of consensus did not belong to any one position on that debate. One could be as extreme as Holcot's contemporary Jacques Fournier. One

---

[137] Smalley, *English Friars*, p. 299.
[138] Matthias of Janow, *Tractatus de Antichristo*, vii.1, in *Regulae*, 3:87. Wyclif, *De veritate sacrae scripturae*, ix, 1:194–202, esp. 201–2.
[139] Agostino Favaroni, in Willigis Eckermann, *Wort und Wirklichkeit. Das Sprachverständnis in der Theorie Gregors von Rimini und sein Weiterwirken in der Augustinerschule* (Würzburg: Augustinus-Verlag, 1978), p. 290; and Denys the Carthusian, *Enarratio in Genesim*, *Opera* 1:15.
[140] Oberman, *Harvest of Medieval Theology*, pp. 238–43.

could face off scripture and pagan learning:

> Because therefore those things which are principally treated in scripture are such that they cannot be known by human investigation, a human being who knows everything and more, but is without knowledge of those things, is considered a nobody, according to Wisdom 9 [verse 6], "even someone made perfect among the sons of men, if your wisdom be absent from him, he will be counted for nothing," and in the same book, chapter 13 [verse 1], "vain are all people in whom there is no knowledge of God."[141]

The final cause of scripture always determined that this literature would affect the soul. Biblical reading implied communion. According to Jacques Fournier in his commentary on Matthew,

> nothing tyrannical or crude is admonished in this scripture, but whatever is taught in it is easy and delightful to the well-disposed soul, and this especially in the New Testament. For the Holy Spirit who created and breathed it into the souls of the holy prophets (with regard to the Old Testament) and of the apostles (with regard to the New Testament) is a gentle Spirit loving the good, kind toward human beings, as it is said in the seventh chapter of Wisdom [Wisdom 7.22–3] and as it is said in the same book, chapter 1[Wisdom 1.6.], "kind is the Spirit of wisdom."[142]

The thematic structure and unity of the Bible reflect the experience of holy writers, which in turn reinforces its subjective purpose. It is this subjective, consensual requirement that Langenstein emphasized, but it belonged to the most basic anthropological convictions of late medieval theologians. Holy writers had, as holy readers should, a well-disposed soul – a soul whose will was habitually trained on God, bent on openness to divine influence, and committed to doing good. No one thought of this synergy of readers, writers, and divine source as embracing an exaggerated confidence in human ability. It was not, in scholars' minds, the ancient heresy of Pelagius. From the twelfth century and until the Reformation, all theologians, however variously, believed that good behavior

---

[141] *Postilla super Mattheum*, f. 4va: "Quia ergo illa que principaliter tractantur in scriptura sunt talia que non possunt per humanam inuestigacionem sciri, et sine quorum scientia homo omnia etiam alia sciens pro nichilo reputatur, secundum idem Sapientie ix. [Sap. ix.6], 'si quis erit consummatus inter filios hominum, si abfuerit ab illo sapientia tua in nichilo comparabitur,' et eodem libro xiii. [Sap. xiii.1], 'uani sunt omnes homines in quibus non subest scientia Dei.'"

[142] Jacques Fournier, *Postilla super Mattheum*, f. 6vb: "in hac scriptura nichil tyrannicum uel crudele precipitur, sed totum quidquid in ea precipitur est facile et delectabile anime bene disposite, et hoc maxime in nouo testamento. Spiritus enim sanctus qui eam creauit et inspirauit in animis sanctorum prophetarum quantum ad uetus testamentum, et apostolorum quantum ad nouum testamentum, est spiritus suauis amans bonum, humanis benignus, ut dicitur Sapientie vii.[vs. 22–3] et ut dicitur in eodem libro capitulo i. [vs. 6], 'benignus est spiritus sapientie.'"

was based upon a cooperative, reciprocal relationship between human beings and God, whether it be expressed as an ontological connection between the soul and divine grace or as a contract between human beings and the creator.[143] Late medieval theologians who hoped to root out Pelagianism accepted these premises as much as any of the admirers of Franciscan doctrines of free will.[144] Inspiration implied the synergy of divine and human lives that was intrinsic to late medieval notions of grace.

To late medieval interpreters, biblical literature was correlated with human needs and the divine plan of redemption. This seemed obvious in the division of the Bible into Old and New Testaments, a division basic to any structural description of the Bible as a book and expressing, in the strongest terms, confidence in the Christian fulfillment of prophecy and God's plans for the human race; or, as Langenstein said, the New Testament is "the final intention and will of God over everything that God ordained in heaven and on the earth."[145] Salvation was more narrowly coordinated with individual parts of the Bible, as for example the Augustinian friar Heinrich of Friemar demonstrated in his extremely popular commentary on the ten commandments.[146] The two tables of the decalogue reflect the structure of religious life. According to diverse positions (*status*) in life, the first table pertains to the contemplative life, and the second to the active. According to diverse ends, the first table orders human beings with respect to God, and the second with respect to other human beings. According to diverse formal objects by which people are ordered to God (first table) or to their neighbor (second table), the commandments have five divisions (the first three commandments pertain to the worship of the members of the Trinity; the fourth commandment determines benevolence to one's neighbor; the fifth to tenth commandments stipulate innocence toward neighbors).[147] This structure

---

[143] Bernd Hamm, *Promissio, Pactum, Ordinatio. Freiheit und Selbstbindung Gottes in der scholastischen Gnadenlehre* (Tübingen: J. C. B. Mohr, 1977), pp. 438–62. This includes the radical critics of "condign merit," John Wyclif and Jan Hus (ibid., p. 461).

[144] For synergy among the anti-Pelagians see Ocker, "Augustinianism in Fourteenth-Century Theology," pp. 87–95. These notions of reciprocity were only challenged by Martin Luther, although he drew on certain aspects of the doctrine of grace of his Augustinian superior, Johannes Staupitz. Markus Wriedt, *Gnade und Erwählung. Eine Untersuchung zu Johann von Staupitz und Martin Luther* (Mainz: Philipp von Zabern, 1991), pp. 78–80, 231–3.

[145] "finalis intencio et uoluntas Dei super omnibus que disposuit in celo et in terra." Hs. I 449, ff. 185vb–187rb.

[146] Friemar was also one of the first Augustinians to reject John Duns Scotus' controversial doctrine of merit: Adolar Zumkeller, *Erbsünde, Gnade, Rechtfertigung und Verdienst nach der Lehre der Erfurter Augustinertheologen des Spätmittelalters* (Würzburg: Augustinus-Verlag, 1984), pp. 15–16.

[147] Heinrich of Friemar (Henricus de Frimaria), *Praeceptorium divinae legis*, f. 7r–7v.

arises from the decalogue's purpose. The souls of all human beings are corrupted by the sin of Adam. For this reason the divine precepts must be written back onto souls and into outward behavior, to counteract the prevailing carnal desires and sinful actions of people.[148] The decalogue answers the crippled condition of the mind and soul – confused, concupiscent, and helpless to detest evil.[149] And it does not work alone. For healing the wound of the intellect, God has prepared "in the pharmacy of divine goodness by the craft and artistry of eternal wisdom" a triple antidote made from the three extraordinary herbs of divine mercy, mellifluous doctrine, and inspired grace.[150] The ten commandments contribute to a three-stage movement toward perfection. They take the mind from outward appearances, turn it into itself, and teach it to pursue contemplation.[151] Commandments are thus an antidote to the corrosive force of natural instinct, which interrupts the mind's unity with a riot of visual impressions, mental images, and words that are all empty and unreal, swelling the mind with pride and snuffing out its love for God.[152] Readers must not merely learn the words and sentences of the commandments. They must desire while they meditate and rewrite the precepts internally upon the heart and upon an obedient body.[153] Interpretation is consuming work.

Literary structure leads us back to the subjective goals of divine speech and inspiration. The danger was, as Langenstein had explained philosophically, inspiration without consensual reading or without reading at all. An anonymous treatise apparently of the late fourteenth century, *On the Rational Formation of the Individual from Scripture*, insists that a sweet, gentle, and good-hearted person ('ein susser senftmutiger gûthertziger mensche') can preserve a clear understanding only through the Bible or

---

[148] Ibid., ff. 2r–7v.

[149] The commentary begins with Deut. 6.3, which declares three things: that the commands are to be joyfully heard, committed to memory, and eternally rewarded. The first consists in three things: the cure of sin, the love of the highest good (over against concupiscence), and irascibility (over against a debilitated capacity for detesting evil): *Preceptorium*, ff. 2r–3r.

[150] Ibid., f. 3r: "Nam ad sanandum vulnera nostre mentis pigmentarius Deus ipse in apotheca diuine bonitatis, per artem et magisterium sue sapientie increate, conficit unguentum et triplex antidotum peroptime sanatiuum. Et hoc ex herbis nobilissimis adinuicem permixtis, ex diuina scilicet misericordia, et ex eius melliflua doctrina, et ex gratia diuina inspirata. Hec autem artificio diuine sapientie sibi inuicem permixta, illud unguentum sanatiuum conficiunt."

[151] Ibid., f. 3r–4v.

[152] Robert G. Warnock and Adolar Zumkeller, *Der Traktat Heinrichs von Friemar über die Unterscheidung der Geister. Lateinisch-mittelhochdeutsche Textausgabe mit Untersuchungen* (Würzburg: Augustinus-Verlag, 1977), pp. 194–235, esp. 205–35 for the role of contemplation in combatting the "natural instinct." For the epistemology behind this see Stroick, *Heinrich von Friemar*, pp. 102–8, 128–30, 134–9.

[153] *Preceptorium*, f. 4v–5r.

rational doctrine.[154] But in the treatise's radical view, this involves interpretation without exegesis. It requires the formation of reason through faith, illumination, the removal of internal hindrances to God, and the like. Such implications, explored in late medieval German mysticism, were also traced out in the early Reformation, most notably by Thomas Müntzer, who juxtaposed prophetic inspiration to the arid learning of Dr. Martin Luther.[155] But one need not be a mystical extremist to insist on the role of subjective insight and experience, as we have seen in Heinrich of Friemar and as one could also observe in Johann Müntzinger's commentary on the *Pater noster*, in the commentaries of Meister Eckhart, and in works of diverse authors, including Luther.[156] To John Wyclif, the purpose of the Bible was the production of virtuous behavior.[157] Heinrich of Langenstein argued that unlike any other science, the divine scriptures are fully sufficient to govern human life to salvation. Sufficiency rests upon the Holy Spirit, who taught the apostles everything they needed to know of philosophy necessary for a proper understanding of virtue, vice, and salvation.[158] Jan Hus could similarly define the Bible's moral purpose, although he seems to have preferred doctrinal definitions.[159] In the case of each theologian examined in this section of the chapter, the approach to biblical literature was conditioned and restrained by a technology of the soul, however a particular theologian may have conceived of it – a soul that was being trained and, the theologians did not need to say, was an object of priestly care.

Biblical inspiration was about spiritual regeneration. The correlation of regeneration and literature that we have just examined in

---

[154] *Über die vernünftige bildung des Menschen aus der Schrift*, Stadtbibliothek Mainz, Hs. I 65, ff. 311ra–311va, here the incipit: "Ein susser senftmutiger gůthertziger mensche sol ein innerlichen iamer han, nach dem daz er von der gescrifte oder von uernunftigen leren nît versatus." The text is written in a slightly cursive gothic hand on paper. Several dates in the manuscript suggest that the collection was made in the late fourteenth century. There is no indication of authorship or origin.

[155] Karl Holl, "Luther und die Schwärmer," *Gesammelte Aufsätze*, 1:432–3. See also *Le temps des Réformes et la Bible*, pp. 316–20.

[156] Müntzinger's middle high German *Expositio super oratione dominica* also proposes an equation of reason and scripture and reason with sanctity in the opening lines: ff. 316r–328r, here 316r and, similarly, 318v–319r. For Eckhart see Winkler, *Methoden*, pp. 103–06. For Luther, p. 202, below.

[157] Smalley, "Wyclif's Dilemma," pp. 272, 288, 292.

[158] Mainz, Stadtbibliothek, Hs. I 449, f. 94vb.

[159] "Dominica ii in adventu," *Leccionarium*, p. 59. Contrast his I *Sent*. d. 1, 3–4, pp. 38–9, where he borrows the reduction of all doctrine to signs and things from Augustine (*De doctrina christiana*, I.ii.2, CCL 32:7) and associates the two types of doctrine with the content of the entire Bible, so that all scripture is doctrine. See also II *Sent*. inceptio, 1.1–4; pp. 189–91 and IV *Sent*., inceptio, 1.1, p. 501.

Inspiration 159

Langenstein, Fournier, and Friemar was consistent with the general trend of scholastic doctrines of prophecy, the machine of inspired speech. Patriarchs, prophets, and apostles were holy people, influenced by the Holy Spirit. This could mean that inspiring biblical writers was simply an extension of work that God routinely did among human beings. There were those who argued as much as early as the late twelfth century: that prophecy was a habit of the soul, linking it more generally to the Spirit's formation of sanctity within a person. *Habitus* could help explain, as it did for John Duns Scotus at the beginning of the fourteenth century, the very close relation of prophets to God and the infallibility of a prophet's knowledge.[160] Prophecy was a subjective condition in the prophet – subjective in the modern sense of internal to the self, just as revelation in scripture had subjective outcomes. The point was entirely consistent with what the earlier Franciscan Alexander of Hales had taught about revelation in the Bible: that the central teaching of scripture, namely the incarnation of Christ, illumines the intellect and moves the soul to believing consent and to the emotion of love, which happens progressively, stage by stage, in salvation history.[161] An alternative, less subjective view was offered by the influential Bible scholars Hugh of St. Cher and Thomas Aquinas, who argued that prophecy was a particular gift of grace, *gratis data*, given without necessarily making the recipient gracious.[162] Their view emphasized the supernatural quality of revelation and distinguished its mechanism from ordinary sanctity. Even so, inspiration was added on to the normal process of cognition, and the primary agent of sanctity and of prophecy remained the Holy Spirit, the agent routinely active, theologians hoped or insisted, in the church through the sacraments and through the church's hierarchy.

Inspiration determined that the effect of reading was subjective, where it could be misconstrued. Clergy anxious to promote the experience of regeneration among the widest group of people could teach them to apply the methods of a new literature "On the Discernment of Spirits." Treatises on spiritual discernment, in widely circulating Latin and

[160] Seybold, *Offenbarung*, p. 142; see also Froehlich, "Christian Interpretation," pp. 523–5, and the literature noted there.
[161] Seybold, *Offenbarung*, pp. 120–1. See also Minnis and Scott, *Medieval Literary Theory*, p. 205.
[162] Jean-Pierre Torrell, *Théorie de la prophétie et philosophie de la connaissance aux environs de 1230* (Louvain: Spicilegium Sacrum Lovaniense, 1977), pp. 155, 279, 281–4 and *passim*. Nicholas of Lyra's view, stated in his first prologue to the Bible, that revelation rendered the passive intellect of the prophet active, allowing the perception of truths in images that appear in his or her imagination, seems likewise to stress the particular divine intervention. Delègue, *Les machines du sens*, pp. 102–3.

vernacular editions, taught readers how to distinguish divine apparitions and inclinations from demonic or natural ones in their everyday lives. Heinrich of Friemar wrote the text that commonly served as the model for these treatises, and Heinrich of Langenstein wrote one of the most influential of them.[163] Bible reading did not figure here, as it eventually would in the Protestant view of spiritual discernment.[164] The reliability of biblical meaning was determined not by a reading method but by consensus, as we have repeatedly seen. The saints confirm the interpretation of revelation, said the thirteenth-century Dominican professor Albert the Great.[165] The fathers of the church received a special revelation of the Bible's meaning, Bonaventure added.[166] Special revelation or not, all interpreters agreed that the subjectivity of the text included the inter-subjectivity of consensus.

The consensual authority of the church seems like such an impersonal, institutional thing. But theologians wanted their work to address the subjectivity of their audiences. They wanted revelation to continue among themselves and their publics. It belonged both in the fixed, literate realm of scripture and patristic writings and in the contestable realm of oral tradition. Revelations had not ceased in the remote past but continued and would continue beyond their own day, as theologians learned from William of Ockham, whose enumeration of Catholic truths (scripture, apostolic oral tradition, custom, conclusions drawn from the first three, and new revelations) late medieval theologians generally accepted.[167] Giving evidence of the importance of contemporary revelations to writers who were nevertheless suspicious of claims to prophecy, Jean Gerson listed personal inspiration with two other first-order sources of truth: scripture and tradition.[168] The control of subjectivity was consensus, defined and argued by theologians and, one way or another, guaranteed by the hierarchical church. As Hermann Schüssler explained, theologians aimed to show that truth known from sources outside the Bible agreed with it, the force of which was to argue, as John Duns Scotus early did,

---

[163] Thomas Hohmann, *Heinrich von Langenstein: Unterscheidung der Geister, lateinisch und deutsch* (Munich: Artemis, 1977); see pp. 2–18 for a survey of the most important treatises, pp. 39–48 for the transmission of Langenstein's text.

[164] Consider Zwingli, pp. 202–4, below.   [165] Seybold, *Offenbarung*, p. 119.   [166] Ibid., p. 127.

[167] Schüssler, *Primat der heiligen Schrift*, pp. 81–91. Guillelmus de Occam, *Dialogus de imperio et pontificia potestate*, I.ii.5, in William Ockham, *Opera plurima* (Lyon, 1494–6; réimpression en facsimilé avec un tableau des abréviations, London: Gregg Press, 1962), f. 9v. It was adapted by writers as diverse and as influential as the late fourteenth-century Heinrich Totting of Oyta and Jean Gerson: Ehrle, *Der Sentenzenkommentar Peters von Candia*, pp. 141–3 n.10.

[168] Schüssler, *Primat*, p. 88. James Connolly, *John Gerson. Reformer and Mystic* (Louvain: Libraire Universitaire, 1928), p. 239.

that the traditions of interpretation that prevailed in the church agreed in principle with biblical teachings.[169] In the fourteenth century, these issues involved a number of extremely intricate debates over the nature of revealed knowledge. They were also closely tied to arguments over epistemology and John Duns Scotus' distinction between intuitive and abstractive cognition and Ockham's challenge to the notion that species serve as the object of knowledge.[170] The details of these arguments contributed little or nothing to attitudes toward scripture as a text, but a general agreement about divine agency in human life, associated with the Holy Spirit, did. Theologians could assume the agreement of scripture, oral tradition, and established interpretations because of the divine point of contact between the human actors in all three cases. The Holy Spirit united the ancient people who first perceived divine truths with those who afterward wrote and transmitted them. As Johannes Staupitz taught at the end of the fifteenth century in terms redolent of German mysticism, divine speech must be identified with the distribution of the Spirit, by which God's word is experienced.[171] The belief in inspiration established the broad continuity of divine language in historical, written, and oral realms. Inspiration was about a shared, supernatural subjectivity.

5. LOGIC

I have surveyed evidence of two features of biblical meaning that arose from a foundational conviction that the text is divine speech: it is verbal (section 3, above) and consensual or, we could say, inter-subjective (section 4). Both features characterize the late medieval text, which is why definitions of the Bible as a book and beliefs about inspiration are so important. This is what scholars thought the book was: an object with intrinsic goals and qualities that reflect its past and present human contexts. The means by which scholars established the connections between the text and its human contexts, its universal meaning, was a process of abstraction, or I should say, translation.[172] Biblical narratives are full

---

[169] Schüssler, *Primat*, p. 91. For Scotus, Seybold, *Die Offenbarung*, p. 143.
[170] Ibid., pp. 138–52 and the literature noted there. Tachau, *Vision and Certitude*, pp. 72 and 177 for Scotus and John of Reading. Pasnau, *Theories of Cognition*, pp. 161–94 for the challenge to the idea that species are objects of knowledge.
[171] Wriedt, *Gnade und Erwählung*, p. 42.
[172] This has also been called a basic hermeneutical conviction of confessional exegesis after the Reformation. Interpreters were not producers of meaning but miners of the Bible's doctrinal bedrock: *Le temps des Réformes et la Bible*, p. 253.

of "improper" language. They cannot be taken at face value, even according to the letter. Figurative language, as William of Ockham once explained, should be translated to its underlying literal equivalents.[173] This really amounts to translating biblical narratives into sentences than can be subjected to logical analysis.[174] Most interpreters did this intuitively in their Bible commentaries, by spontaneously discussing a theological or philosophical idea within the exposition of a passage or by digressing from a particular passage to a theological or philosophical question.

Wyclif, more explicitly than most late medieval theologians, gave a rationale for translating biblical to mental language, and for that reason, it is helpful to begin briefly with him, and then turn to Jacques Fournier, Jean Gerson, and Heinrich Langenstein, who each illuminate aspects of this textual conversion. The principle for understanding biblical language, he said, is the truth which lies beneath the whole.[175] He then nailed down this general conviction by collapsing biblical speech and logic. The truth of the whole is eternal, past-less, and therefore every idea of the Bible is contemporaneous, its realm, eternity.[176] The Bible was uniquely connected to eternal truth, and it thus stood above the "periodic" academic fashions of Oxford schools; to understand it, one need simply apply the rules that apply to the analysis of truth.[177] Accordingly, individual terms and phrases in a biblical passage could be understood as though they were logical statements, not poetic ones. In this way, Wyclif resolved contradictory and problematic passages by treating them as logical fallacies and by expanding the nuances of apparently restrictive terms, sequences, times, or modes, in the manner of a logician. As Gillian Evans pointed out, these argumentative techniques had been commonly taught in the elementary course of logic since the end of the thirteenth century.[178] But with his doctrine of the eternity of the true referents of biblical language, he stated more boldly than his contemporaries the conviction that the context of exegesis is purely intellectual. The text mirrors eternity, and the literal sense is historical only insofar as readers exist in

---

[173] Minnis, "Authorial Intention," pp. 22–23. Cf. Michalski, "Les courants critiques," pp. 178–9, which notes some other instances of the distinction between literal meaning and *virtus sermonis* in Ockham.

[174] Consider Adams, *Ockham*, 1:289–97, 342–6, esp. 290–1.

[175] *De veritate sacrae scripturae*, pp. 73–4, 79–80, 189. The principle takes precedence over textual factors (ibid., pp. 234–36).

[176] Smalley, *Studies in Medieval Thought and Learning*, pp. 409–10.

[177] *De veritate sacrae scripturae*, iv, pp. 82–3; iii, pp. 52–4.

[178] Gillian Evans, "Wyclif's *Logic* and Wyclif's Exegesis: The Context," *The Bible in the Medieval World. Essays in Memory of Beryl Smalley* (Oxford: Blackwell, 1985), pp. 286–300.

time.[179] Yet "the logic of scripture stands in the form of the words and the manner of speech."[180]

Wyclif's predecessors and contemporaries would agree with his general conviction that invisible things mattered more than empirical ones. In the third chapter of his prologue to the Gospel of Matthew, Jacques Fournier explained that the subject of biblical knowledge exceeds human reason and involves a correlation of authorial ambitions. The facts of the Bible's regenerative purpose and inspired consensus drove the reader of the letter to invisible things:

Therefore it was fitting that the divine scripture was handed down through the God who knows all things and through the creature who understands God, lest human nature had been ordained to some other purpose. Whence Augustine in book 11 of *On the City of God* in chapter 3[181] says, "Christ, speaking first through the prophets, then through himself, afterwards through the apostles, showed what was sufficient [for human beings]. He made scripture, which is called canonical, the highest authority, by which we have faith concerning those things that we need to know and that we are incapable of knowing by ourselves." "Just as concerning visible things that we have not seen, we believe people who have seen them, so too with regard to those things that are perceived by the soul and the mind, that is concerning invisible things that are absent from our sense to comprehend, it is fitting that we believe those people who learned in that incorporeal human soul the things that have been distributed or who perceive those vestiges that remain." These people were the holy prophets and apostles and even the angels through whom holy scripture was, by their service, handed down, by God, to other human beings. As Peter says in his second Epistle, chapter 1 [verses 20–1], "knowing this first, that every prophecy of scripture does not have its own interpretation. For no prophecy has been given by human will, but holy people of God have spoken, inspired by the Holy Spirit." The Gloss says at this passage, no one of the saints and of the prophets preached from their own interpretation to the people the dogmas of life, but those things that they had learned from God in secret, these they delivered to the people of God to be observed. But the divines of the gentiles composed from their own heart, which is obvious because prophecy is not written in such words and in such manner of expression as secular people use in their speech and as secular writings are composed and interpreted. So therefore the principal author of holy scripture is God, and Christ is immediately the author of the New Testament, because "in manifold and many ways God once spoke to the fathers and the prophets, but in these last days he spoke to us in the Son, whom he appointed heir of all things everywhere, through whom he also made the worlds," Hebrews 1 [verse 2], because even if he did not write the New Testament, yet did he teach it in word

---

[179] Thus *De veritate sacrae scripturae*, iv, pp. 82–3, insists that the signs of scripture are true only because God has intended them to adequately convey the truth.
[180] Ibid., iii, p. 52.   [181] *De civitate Dei*, xi.3.

and deed, and he fulfilled it in deed, and because it is God himself by whom wisdom and truth are appropriated, therefore in the New Testament, just as there can be no falsehood in any other part of scripture (for "it is impossible for God to lie," Hebrews 6 [verse 18]), truth cannot deny itself, 2 Timothy 2 [cf. 2 Tim. 2.13]; from which it is clear that scripture is of the highest authority, with regard to its principal author and its instrumental author, because the instrumental author is in complete agreement with the principal author; not only does he not lie, but he cannot lie. "For God is true, but every man is a liar." Romans 3 [verse 4].[182]

Ideas that we will immediately associate with the tradition of mystical reading dominate this passage: we learn from a secret place, the souls of expert individuals who tell us the mysteries God has told them. But Fournier is writing about biblical authors, not mystical interpreters, whose literal text is the communication of those secrets. The agreement of principal and instrumental authors, of God and prophets, apostles, and angels (such as the angel of the Apocalypse), emphasizes the supernatural

---

[182] *Postilla super Mattheum*, f. 4ra–rb: "Ideo oportuit quod per Deum omnia scientem uel per creaturam ipsum Deum cognoscentem, diuina scriptura traderetur, ne humana natura uarie esset constituta. Unde Augustinus libro xi. *De ciuitate Dei* dicit capitulo iii., 'Christus prius per prophetas, deinde per seipsum, postea per apostolos quantum satis esse indicauit loqutus. Etiam scripturam condidit, que canonica nominatur, eminentissime auctoritatis, cui fidem habemus de hijs rebus quas ignorare non expedit nec per nos ipsos nosse ydonei sumus.' 'Sicut ergo de uisibilibus que non uidimus, eis credimus qui uiderunt, ita de hijs que animo ac mente sentiuntur, hoc est de inuisibilibus, que nostro sensu ratiocinare remota sunt, hijs oportet nos credere, qui hoc in illo incorporeo humano disposita didiscerunt uel manentia contuentur.' Hij autem fuerunt sancti prophete et apostoli ac etiam angeli per quos sacra scriptura ministerialiter est a Deo hominibus alijs tradita. Ut enim dicit Petrus in secunda epistola capitulo i. [ii. Pe. i.20–1], 'hoc primum intelligentes quod omnis prophetia scripture propria interpretacione non fit. Non enim uoluntate humana allata est aliquando prophetia, sed spiritu sancto inspirati loquti sunt sancti Dei homines,' ubi dicit glossa, nullus sanctorum et prophetarum propria sua interpretatione populis uite dogmata predicauit, sed que a Deo didiscerant in secreto, hec plebi Dei observuanda tradebant. Sed diuini gentium de corde suo fingebant, quod patet, quia prophetia non est talibus uerbis, et tali modo loqutionis scripta, quali utuntur homines seculares in locutione sua et quali seculares scripture sunt composite et interpretate. Sic ergo auctor sacre scripture principalis est Deus, et noui testamenti immediate Christus est auctor, quia 'multiphariam multisque modis olim Deus loqutus est patribus in prophetis, sed nouissime diebus istis loqutus est nobis in filio, quem constituit heredem uniuersorum per quem fecit et secula,' Ad Hebreos i. [He. i.1–2], quia etiam si ipse nouum testamentum non scripsit, tamen uerbo et opere ipsum docuit, et opere compleuit, et quia ipse Deus est cui etiam sapientia et ueritas appropriuntur, ideo in nouo testamento, sicut nec in aliqua alia parte scripture falsitas potest esse, 'Deum enim impossibile est mentiri,' Ad Hebreos vi. [He. vi.18], ueritas negare seipsam non potest, ii. Ad Thimotheum ii. [cf. ii. Ti. ii.13]; ex quo patet, quod est auctoritatis eminentissime, quantum eius auctor principalis nam eius instrumentalis, eo quod ei est totaliter consentaneus; non solum non mentitur sed nec mentiri potest. 'Est enim Deus uerax, omnis autem homo mendax.' Ad Romanos iii. [Ro. iii.4] de quo auctore in themate dicitur 'precepit rex.'" The last phrase, "concerning which authority it is spoken in the theme, 'the king commanded,'" refers to a previously mentioned biblical text, the source of which I have not been able to locate: I have omitted it from my translation. The passage quoted on page 155, above, follows immediately upon this one.

content and purpose of biblical doctrine among readers. The readers in view were theologians, and theology colored textual judgments. For example, Fournier openly sacrificed philology to the established orthodoxy of the virgin birth when he treated Isaiah 7.14, *Ecce virgo concipiet, et pariet filium*, "behold a virgin will conceive and give birth to a son." He noted the discrepancy between Jerome's "virgin" and Isaiah's עלמה, *'alma*, maiden, but he nevertheless chose Jerome's *virgo* as the more accurate term, more accurate than Isaiah's chosen Hebrew.[183] Jerome was a holy man. Strengthened by the faith of the church, he knew Isaiah's intention better than the average Hebrew reader.

This would seem a weak explanation to sixteenth-century interpreters, who in defense of the authority of the Hebrew text would insist (against the strict meaning of the term) on the virginal עלמה.[184] Still, late medieval interpreters moved closer to the literal text, and like the sixteenth-century defenders of the virginal "maiden," they believed that the text spoke Christian dogma unambiguously enough. The consensus of holy readers determined the literal sense. The literal sense is an eternal truth.

How far could this drive them to the rhetoric of the letter? It is true that Hermann of Schildesche discovered a kind of primitively rhetorical approach to biblical language, as we saw in the last chapter; yet he had very restrained confidence in it. A half-century later, the chancellor of the university of Paris, Jean Gerson, appealed to the peculiar logic of the Bible in rhetorical terms. It is ironic that he chose language reminiscent of Wyclif, whom Gerson helped to condemn as a heretic posthumously at the Council of Constance, but Gerson meant something quite different. Like Wyclif and, it seems, all interpreters, he believed in the need to convert language, but to make the point he appealed to rhetoric, in order to distinguish philosophical uses of logic from biblical reasoning:[185]

The literal sense of sacred scripture is not to be taken according to the sense of logic and dialectics, but rather according to the expressions used in rhetorical speech and according to tropes and figured expressions which common use conveys, with consideration of the circumstances of the letter from what precedes

---

[183] Ibid., tractate 6, chapter 9, ff. 78va–82ra. The Hebrew term for "virgin" is בתולה.

[184] For example, John Calvin, *A Harmony of the Gospels*, 3 vols. (Grand Rapids: Eerdmans, 1972), 1:67–68.

[185] *De sensu litterali sanctae scripturae*, Gerson, *Oeuvres* 3:334 (p. xiv for the date). The reference to the "circumstances of the letter" may be a historical circumstance, but I suspect what Gerson means is a textual circumstance – its place within the ideally conceived structure of a book within the overall thematic structure of the Bible. The passage refers us to the seven *claves* of Lyra's prologue (*Glossa cum Lyra*, 1:3vb–4rb, mistakenly equated with the seven rules of Tyconius; they actually are an adaptation of Tyconius' rules by Isidore of Seville, *De summo bono*, i.20).

and what follows. For sacred scripture has, like moral and historical science, its own proper logic, which we call rhetoric.

Gerson went well beyond Wyclif. He singled out rhetoric as the principal vehicle for overcoming obstacles of irregular, ordinary speech, a position that arose from Gerson's 1402 *Against the Curiosity of Scholars* and that he repeated several times during the Council of Constance.[186] A failure to distinguish between forms of demonstration in logic and in rhetoric was even cited by bishop Jacob Balardi of Lodi, in the sermon he preached at the execution of the Hussite Jerome of Prague in 1416, as a basis of heretical reasoning.[187] It marks a new scepticism about the use of logic in theology which Michael Shank has also discovered in Heinrich of Langenstein, who at Vienna in the years preceding his death in 1397 abandoned the conviction he earlier formed as a student at Paris, that Aristotelian rules of dialectic applied directly and without adjustment to the most mysterious Christian doctrine, the doctrine of the Trinity.[188] Although rhetoric was conceived by Gerson and Balardi in a minimal sense, as a method of disentangling meaning from figurative nouns (which was what they thought tropes to be), their argument had a purpose very similar to that of theologians of the sixteenth century. Rhetoric was supposed to help one translate problematic speech into theological discourse.[189]

Gerson's tiny work on biblical interpretation displayed the exegetical associations of his conservative mind. His insistence on literal interpretation, as Karlfried Froehlich pointed out, was an element of his controversy with the Parisian theologian Jean Petit. Petit stood opposite Jean Gerson in the conflict between the dukes of Orléans and Burgundy, the latter convinced that Louis d'Orléans, heir apparent, inappropriately dominated the royal court, taking advantage of king Charles VI's mental illness and corrupting the traditional fabric of royal government, balanced as it was between king, counsel, administrators and judges, and the three estates.[190] After the duke of Burgundy accomplished the assassination of Louis d'Orléans in November 1407, the Dominican theologian Jean Petit soon formulated a justification of it, which helped pave the way to

---

[186] Michael H. Shank, "University and Church in Late Medieval Vienna: *Modi Dicendi et Operandi*, 1388–1421," Hoenen, Schneider, and Wieland, *Universities in the Middle Ages*, pp. 43–59, here 51–3; idem, *Unless You Believe*, pp. 178–85.
[187] Shank, "University and Church," p. 53. [188] Shank, *Unless You Believe*, pp. 122–38.
[189] Consider also propositions 4, 5, 6, and the reasons for erroneous interpretation: Gerson, *De sensu litterali, Œuvres*, 3:335, 338–40.
[190] Bertrand Schnerb, *L'Etat bourguignon, 1363–1477* (Paris: Perrin, 1999), pp. 141–71.

a royal pardon for the duke of Burgundy and his ceremonious reconciliation with the wife and son of his victim in March of 1409.[191] This won Burgundy new influence at the royal court, and that provoked a princely coalition, formed in April 1410, to oppose him in support of the young Charles d'Orléans, a fifteen-year-old boy when he succeeded his father three years before. Gerson, who had earlier served the father of the duke of Burgundy, sided with the supporters of Orléans and soon began to register suspicions of Burgundy, by complaining of the evils of tyrannicide. In 1413, two years after Petit died, when the new duke of Orléans reentered Paris, Gerson openly condemned the dead Dominican and carried through a campaign against his case for Burgundy into the Council of Constance. During the Council, in 1415, the tide again turned in favor of the duke of Burgundy, now just after Agincourt supported by the English. Gerson found himself, if confirmed in his loyalties, prevented for the rest of his life from returning to Paris.[192]

The duke of Burgundy was a murderer only to the extent that the assassination of the duke of Orléans contradicted the biblical commandment, "Thou shalt not kill." Petit insisted that it was justified killing, consistent with the spirit, if not the letter, of the law.[193] By diminishing the significance of the grammatical meaning of the words and by interpreting them in the light of the biblical message overall, the valence of the biblical text, in this case the commandment against killing, could rise above its most restricted meaning (never kill anyone). It was sometimes good to kill. The argument was a little conniving, but in its main points no different from the usual theologian's distinction between condemnable murder and killing in a just war.[194] Is the meaning of the Bible grammatical and exterior or spiritual and interior, Petit asked? And is not the spiritual and interior meaning more intrinsic to the letter than its grammatical meaning? Petit and his supporters were trying to work their text into a compatible theological framework; he was not trying to wave off the ten commandments with mystical exegesis. The Burgundian party of theologians who later supported his case tried to distinguish between a grammatical-literal sense that hurts the soul and a theological-literal sense that is true. Gerson had an easier time of it.

---

[191] Froehlich, "Always to Keep," pp. 27–43. For the reconciliation, Marie-Thérèse Berthier and John-Thomas Sweeney, *Le Chancelier Rolin, 1376–1462* (Précy-sous-Thil: Editions de l'Armançon, 1998), p. 43.

[192] Connolly, *John Gerson*, pp. 164–7, remains a useful overview.

[193] The following depends upon Froehlich's exposition of the extensive documents of the controversy, "Always to Keep," pp. 27–43.

[194] Consider, for example, Thomas Aquinas, *ST* 1 a2ae, q. 100 a. 8 ad 3.

He simply argued that grammatical and spiritual meaning must always agree. Understanding biblical language rhetorically, one could identify a theological-literal sense with the grammatical-literal sense. Or in other words, there was no real difference between theological and grammatical meanings – a point that expresses well the general convictions of late medieval intellectuals but differs significantly from classic, twelfth-century views of sacred interpretation.

In both the Burgundian and the Orléanist cases, the theologians hoped to bring the letter into harmony with thought. What they lacked was an agreed concept of rhetoric that could help them move consistently from poetic narrative to dialectic, with Gerson leaning toward the literalist side of the spectrum. He had come little distance since his campaign against the *Roman de la Rose* (the poem he repeatedly condemned a decade before this controversy, in 1402), in whose "garden" he found no sublime purpose and certainly no Christian allegory. It was rather a literal succession of lascivious images that enflamed the passions of youth and, accordingly, eroded their Christian moral fabric, encouraging the climate of corruption at the troubled court of Charles VI.[195] Extracting ideas from texts was exactly what was happening in the vast majority of late medieval Bible commentaries, judging from the texts that I have studied. Gerson explicitly associates the common exegetical technique with rhetoric, which is worth noting, and names it the peculiar logic of the Bible (was he goading the logicians?). Although earlier theologians, like Hermann of Schildesche, explored the rhetorical analysis of biblical texts and others associated meaning with biblical literature as such, Gerson may have been the first, and until the end of the Middle Ages the only, theologian to associate the common textual attitude with rhetoric as a discipline. Instead of a shared notion of rhetoric, theologians possessed a shared assumption about the importance of logic and the consistency of biblical literature with true knowledge. Gerson's association of textual study with rhetoric could not overcome this prevailing assumption.

An exposition of the Bible as an intellectual and moral document had been given far away at the university of Vienna, by Heinrich of Langenstein about two decades before the controversy over Jean Petit. Its detailed argument merits close attention, for it reflects well the absence of rhetoric as a field of study and the prevalence of logical methods and assumptions. In his commentary on Jerome's prologue to the Bible (this was written before he developed critical views of the applicability

---

[195] Gerson, *Œuvres complètes*, 2:65–70, 10:25–8.

of Aristotle to theology), Langenstein, like Wyclif, considered the relationship of biblical language to thought. The heretical Wyclif enjoyed little influence among scholastic theologians after his day. Langenstein's influence must have been great, given the fact that he enjoyed a platform as professor of theology and rector of Vienna to rival, in Central Europe, the Parisian one of his younger contemporary, Jean Gerson – although no one has of yet tried to measure that influence beyond Vienna.[196] His ability to develop criteria for reasoning from biblical literature, in the lectures he began as professor in 1385, may have contributed to his declining confidence in the universality of logic, which Michael Shank traced to the early 1390s. A method of biblical argument could replace logical certainty.[197] But his desire to conceptualize the rational quality and content of biblical language matched a broader trend to associate the literal meaning of the Bible with theological abstractions.

Langenstein argued, like a rector, that philosophy and theology must be equally committed to the pursuit of truth, and their relationship was intimate and complementary. "Everything right about human cognition is ordered to the righteousness of correct moral action" ('ad iusticiam recte operacionis'); philosophy is about right thinking, and scripture is about doing and teaching.[198] The philosopher sticks to reason, seeks the truth empirically ('per experienciam et discursum ex creaturis') from the histories and writings of diverse peoples and from the observation of diverse peoples, always ready to change his mind when proven wrong and never quick to embrace an opinion. Nevertheless, nothing he discovers will contradict any article of faith.[199]

A theologian interpreting the Bible will therefore be answerable in some way to the canons of philosophy, but how? The answer is in the nature of language. Langenstein began with a common view, that the spoken word is the most natural form of human expression.[200] A living

---

[196] Shank, *Unless You Believe*, pp. 122–23, 191–4. For Parisian influence (it was shrinking outside of France), see Hilde de Ridder-Symoens, "Mobility," *Universities in the Middle Ages*, p. 291.

[197] In his commentaries on Jerome's prologues to the Bible and the Pentateuch, Langenstein's view of biblical language is related to his view of translation (as will be seen shortly) and Christian apologetics with Jews, which Michael Shank has also placed in the context of Langenstein's changing attitude toward logic, drawing on his commentary on Ge. 1.26, lectured and written after the texts examined here. Shank, *Unless You Believe*, pp. 152–6.

[198] Stadtbibliothek Mainz, Hs. I 449, f. 71va: "Circa quod uerus philosophus precipue studiosus esse debet, quia tota rectitudo humane [*del* condicionis *!*] cognicionis ordinatur ad iusticiam recte operacionis, sicud ergo in sacra scriptura ille dicitur uerus et magnus doctor theologus qui facit et docet, sic inter phylosophos ille est uerus et magnus phylosophus qui et recte intelligit. Et ea que intelligit, ad finem debitum ordinat. Et [qui] rectificat finem pro sequendo, recte et uere moraliter uiuere reperitur."

[199] Ibid., ff. 71vb–72ra.   [200] Spade, "Semantics," in *CHLMP*, p. 189.

170 *Divine speech*

voice has, he said, "spiritual energy." This conviction could lead to a prejudice for oral speech over the written text of holy scripture:

It seems to me that spiritual energy proceeds from the living voice according to five main causes, namely from two intrinsic and three extrinsic ones. The first of the intrinsic causes is that the spoken words of people are more natural than figures or characters and are naturally ordered to the expression of mental concepts; to that extent many words of human beings and beasts signify naturally. The reason for this can be because a spoken word admonishes more effectively and tenaciously. The second reason or cause is that a person more naturally delights in a good and consonant proportion of words and sounds than in the beauty of figures, by witness and by experience. The delight of the spirit provokes, expands, and strengthens spirits, and this encourages one to attend more diligently and comprehend more perfectly, but a disproportion of spoken words can grow contrary and bore those who hear.

The first extrinsic cause by which a living but not a written voice may acquire energy is the bodily gestures which rhetoricians use while speaking, who indeed display with gestures what is expressed in speech, and so this is as though they express it twice, wherefore what they say is more memorably retained and more perfectly understood. The second extrinsic cause is that while examining a book, sight is scattered and distracted by the variety and number of objects that confront sight, on account of which less of what a person reads makes an impression; while one person reads and the others listen, the hearing is fixed only on the voice of the speaker in the manner of the distraction of the moon.[201] It is otherwise for the one who reads in a book, just as for the one who hears someone who speaks perfectly, while many other people around him mumble slurred words, because the one who reads cannot see one utterance without seeing many others confusedly. The third extrinsic cause is from the manner of order and quality of the representation of circumstances of the fact or affair about which is spoken.[202]

---

[201] The light that rules the night, Ge. 1.16, and so dominates one's attention. Or, as Rosemary Williams suggests, the moon drags their attention as it drags water to make tides.

[202] From his commentary on the prologue to the Bible, Stadtbibliothek Mainz, Hs. I 449, ff. 81vb–82rb: "Uidetur michi quod spiritualis energia uiua uoce oriatur ex quinque causis precipue scilicet ex duabus intrinsecis et tribus extrinsecis. Intrinsecarum prima est quod uoces sunt hominum magis connaturaliter quam figure uel karacteres et sunt naturaliter ordinate ad expressionem conceptuum mentalium, in tantum quod eciam multe uoces hominum et brutorum naturaliter significant. Huius racio potest esse quia efficacior et tenacior monet una uox. Secunda racio uel causa est quod homo magis naturaliter delectatur in bona et consonanti uocum proporcione et sonorum quam pulchritudine figurarum teste et experiencia. Delectatio autem spiritus excitat et dilatat et confortat, et hoc facit ad diligencius attendendum et per consequens ad perfeccius intelligendum et e conuerso, quia disproporcio uocum concrescat condra [*supersc* et] efficit in audientibus tedium inducendo. Prima causa extrinseca qua energiam acquerit uox uiua et non scriptura sunt gestus corporales quibus utuntur rethores in pronunciando, qui quidem gestibus effigiant illud quod sermone exprimitur, et ita idem quasi bis exprimunt quare et memoracius tenetur quod dicunt et perfeccius intelligitur. Secunda causa extrinseca est quod inspiciendo librum uisus dispergitur et distrahitur propter diuersitatem et multitudinem obiectorum uisui

There is no limit to the priority of spoken to written words here – a point that could, perhaps, more easily have been made in the terms of the rhetorical art of *actio*, delivery, about which Langenstein seems completely unaware. He was therefore forced to make what is in fact a rhetorical point in terms of the nature of words. Reading is like trying to listen to just one speaker in a murmuring crowd. Spoken language, to the contrary, accompanied as it is by gestures and inflections, imminently conveys mental speech. If one listens to a text read, it is like looking at the night sky and being distracted from the clutter of stars by the overwhelming visual impression of the moon. Hearing words focuses attention.

Langenstein was most interested in the *extrinsic* causes, which have to do with the conditions in which speech occurs. After a brief discussion of how the "energy" and "style" or "manner of speaking" of an orator creates the "spiritual energy" of an oration, he elaborated, in five propositions, the mechanisms by which spoken language acquires power:

The first proposition is that every spiritual operation that each vowel is said to perform proceeds entirely apart from the ways treated [that is, apart from oratorical energy, style, and manner of speech], from a concurrence of a certain extrinsic cause, which it accomplishes at the intonation of such and such words about a fact or at some sort of performance. And in that way the verbal forms of the sacraments are said to have energy and operation, not through their intrinsic power, but from divine action and precept (*dictum*). And similarly the words of incantation and the symbols of a witch are also said to have power, because while demons work at their utterance, they become, as God permits, such like performances, to the deception of good people, when their sins demand it, who have made time for superstitions.

The second proposition is that one of two equally disposed people gets further by hearing the given utterance than the other by carefully reading it for the same amount of time. It is demonstrated from the previously submitted causes of vocal energy.

The third proposition is that a living voice instructs more easily and conveniently than written letters. It is easily demonstrated, because a thousand hear the reading or utterance of one person at the same time, and they understand all at once, for which people it would be difficult and tedious to benefit to such an extent through the same amount of time by reading.

occerencium [*leg* occurencium]. Propter quod minus inprimitur quod homo legit [*del* auditus solum figitur] uno autem legente et alijs audientibus, auditus solum figitur ad uocem loquentis per modum lune detrahentis. Est contra de legente in libro, sicud de audiente unum loquentem perfecte, multis alijs circa se murmurantibus inperfectis uocibus, quia legens non potest unam diccionem uidere non uidendo multas alias confuse. Tercia causa [*del* est]extrinseca est ex modo ordine et qualitate representationis circumstanciarum facti uel negotii, de quo dictatur."

The fourth proposition is that a word uttered rhetorically would have greater energy than a piece of writing, no matter how beautifully figurative the writing. It is demonstrated similarly from the previously submitted causes, with which causes nevertheless it stands that vocal eloquence of any person is always of less energy than a written saying. With the aforementioned causes it also stands that if one of two equally disposed people endeavors to learn by reading alone and another by hearing, by reason of the ordinary run of things, the first person could make more progress, and this on account of the greater quantity of books than of teachers and those who read vocally [namely, lecturers], therefore, etc.

Another [the fifth] proposition is that the oracle of the Holy Spirit in scripture is of greater energy than the eloquence of Demosthenes or the living voice of any other rhetorician, and this with regard to the effect and progress of denotation, although not with regard to the advantage of the excellence by which human and artistic rhetoric often tickles ears uselessly: as it may force contrition or another produced feeling upon those who hear, so rhetoric knew to fortify falsehood and iniquity, so that often while that rhetoric persuaded and overshadowed matters, equity collapsed and the truth was ruled out. And therefore Cicero spoke well in the beginning of the old *Rhetoric*, "Often I've wondered whether bad men contributed more to people and cities than good men by copious talk and the greatest devotion to eloquence. I see not the least part of evil and troublesome things introduced by the most eloquent people."[203]

---

[203] The third extrinsic cause of the spiritual energy of the spoken word is, Heinrich explained, how a doctor's or rhetor's style has its "energia" and "stilus" or "modus loquendi," which excite passions or desires in those who hear or read. To this he adds the propositions (f. 82rb–82vb): "Prima proposicio est quod omnis spiritualis operacio quam facere dicitur queque uocalis omnino preter tactos modos oritur, ex concursu alicuius extrinsece cause que ad prolacionem talium uel talium uerborum facit ex facto, uel ad talem uel talem effectum. Et illo modo forme uerbales sacramentorum energiam uel operacionem habere dicuntur, non per intrinsecam eorum uirtutem, sed ex diuino capto et dicto. Et similiter uerba incantatoria seu karacteres operatricis seu uirtutem habere dicuntur, eo quod operantibus demonibus ad eorum prolacionem fiunt Deo permittente similes uel tales effectus ad deceptionem exigentibus peccatis bonorum hominum qui supersticionibus uacant. Secunda proposicio est quod unus duorum equaliter dispositorum datum sermonem audiendo plus proficit, quam alter eundem per idem tempus perlegendo. Patet ex causis uocalis energie premissis. Tercia proposicio est quod facilius et commodius erudit uox uiua quam littera scriptura. Patet faciliter, quia unius leccionem uel sermonem perpetuo tempore mille audiunt et simul intelligunt quos difficile et tediosum esset per idem tempus tantum proficere legendo. Quarta proposicio est quod maiorem energiam haberet uox rethorice prolata, quam [*del* uox] scriptura quantumlibet figurata pulchre. Patet similiter ex causis premissis, cum quibus tamen stat quod semper cuiuscumque uocale [*del* obsequium] eloquium est minoris energie, quam dictamen scriptum. Cum predictis eciam stat quod si unus duorum equaliter dispositorum conaretur discere legendo solum et alter solum audiendo, de communi cursu primus magis proficeret. Et hoc propter maiorem copiam librorum quam doctorum uel uocaliter docencium lectorum, igitur et cetera. Alia proposicio est quod maioris energie est spiritus sancti in scripturis eloquio Demostinis uel cuiuscumque rethoris uiue uocis oraculum, et hoc quantum ad denotacionis effectum et profectum, licet non ad bonitatis priuilegium quo humana et artificialis rethorica sepius aures inutiliter detillat [*leg* titillat]: quam conpunccionem uel aliam factam affeccionem audientibus ingerat, que eciam falsitatem et iniquitatem sic armare nouit, quod sepe ipsa persuadente et adumbrante equitas subcubuit, et ueritas dissepuit. Et ergo bene dixit Tulius in principio ueteris *Rethorice*, sepe et multum hoc mecum cogitaui an mali plus attuluerunt

I should begin by pointing out the recontextualization of Cicero's remarks on the abuse of the abundant style in a philosophical context that depends upon supposition, concurring powers, and the disposition of the soul. The absence of argumentative structures and strategies of persuasion would be, to a sixteenth-century reader of Cicero, remarkable, perhaps shocking. According to the first proposition, energy occurs when vowels are uttered, because one of the three extrinsic causes (gestures, the concentration of attention, and the quality of representation of a fact or an affair) occurs with the utterance. Thus the words spoken at the performance of sacraments are effective because of a concurrence of fact – the fact of divine power and precept. So too, the words and symbols of a sorceress are effective because of a concurrence of fact – the fact of demonic power. The second proposition draws a conclusion from the causes of verbal energy. Of two people equally eager to learn, the one who hears the spoken word will understand more than the one who spends the same time reading. The third proposition appeals to convenience somewhat tautologically. Since Langenstein believed that comprehension occurs spontaneously when language is heard, one thousand people can learn at once by listening to a single person, whereas by reading, the same text would have to be read one thousand times. The argument seems to presuppose the difficulty of acquiring one thousand copies of a text at the turn of the fifteenth century. The fourth proposition adds the denial, that literary adornment can compensate for the unnatural context of written speech. To this he now adds a contradictory opinion. He bluntly states that "vocal eloquence of any kind is always of *less* energy than a written saying." It seems that his intention is to claim that such an assertion is possible given the extrinsic causes previously outlined. There is no reason why, for example, two extrinsic causes, the concentration of attention and the quality of representation of a fact or an affair, could not also occur in written language, and in fact, the application of rhetoric could enhance the concentration of a reader's attention and the quality of the representation of fact or event. Langenstein, however, simply acknowledged a possible conclusion from this premise, which goes against his previous statements, with an appeal to circumstance. If two people decide to try to learn, one by reading and one by hearing, the first *could* make greater progress because of the greater availability of books than of teachers. His fifth proposition finally approaches the question of biblical language. The eloquence of the Holy Spirit may seem inferior to

hominibus et ciuitatibus, an boni copia dicendi ac summum elloquencie studium. Video non minimam per disertissimos homines partem malorum et incommodorum invectam."

the art of classical rhetoric, but it is superior in its energy because of the effect of its meaning. Langenstein is referring again to the patristic idea of the redemptive purpose of scriptural speech. In short, an argument for the superiority of written language in general, and more specifically holy scripture, will need to take three extrinsic causes into account. Those three causes each emphasize the dynamic context of speech: its performance (gestures), auditory experience (the concentration of attention), and its immediate representation of a subject to the mind (the quality of representation of a fact or an affair). Written language in general can be called superior to spoken language on the grounds of convenience (the proportion of books to teachers) or on the grounds of spiritual effects (the eloquence of the Holy Spirit).

The dynamic context of speech extends to its most rudimentary elements, namely the process by which meaning is attached to terms. In his commentary on the prologue to the Pentateuch, Heinrich applied this conviction to the work of translation. Here he described the difficulty in guaranteeing a link between a proper noun and a thing signified, by examining the case of naming children:

> The imposition of names depends upon the free choice of human beings, which free choice God grants with regard to this most of all: in the common run and custom of human affairs, by which custom people at some time used to impose names on their sons according to the saints, sometimes according to progenitors or godfathers, ignoring the interpretation of the names but regarding the honesty and famousness of the people to be remembered. This is clear.[204]

The names have an original "imposition," a historical meaning if you will, but this is not the usage that determines the significance of the name, since it was given with an eye to a more immediate context, namely the regard of one's contemporaries. The same difference between original imposition (a past ascribed meaning) and a contemporary imposition (a current ascribed meaning) applies to non-verbal utterances that assume particular meanings, like some sighs:

> ...Nor are you to believe the apparent truth which every proper noun may have according to its original imposition in a certain language, signification,

---

[204] Stadtbibliothek Mainz, Hs. I 449, from the commentary on the prologue to the Pentateuch, f. 221ra–221rb, on the semantics of categorematic terms. Heinrich offers three propositions, the first of which explains that "inposicio nominum dependet a libero arbitrio hominum quod dimittit Deus quantum ad hoc plurimum communi cursui et consuetudini humane, qua homines consueuerunt quandoque inponere filijs suis nomina secundum sanctos quandoque secundum progenitores uel patrinos non attendendo interpretacionem nominum sed probitatem uel famositatem recolendorum hominum. Clarum est hoc."

or interpretation. This is clear because it is apparent that often certain false vocalizations, which signified neither parts nor a whole in any idiom, have been imposed on certain things as though proper nouns, like "bu" and "ba."[205]

Finally, the difference between original imposition also applies to translation from one language to another: "if the interpretation of a noun should have assonance with a property or event, this is either from a causal imposition or from human intention or from divine arrangement, but never from a [stellar] constellation."[206] This last point may seem slightly gratuitous to us, but since Langenstein has emphasized the importance of human volition and concurrent powers, he found himself compelled to reaffirm its freedom here from cosmic power. The meaningfulness of a noun depended upon the agreement of a thing and an interpretation, but nouns could receive their meaning by special divine revelation. If this happened by the influence of the stars, "then people with similar fortunes would have similar names, the falsehood of which is obvious, because many people are called by the same name who are yet different in physical constitution, manners, and fortunes."[207] This last point, a solution unlikely to occur to a student of rhetoric, serves to remind us that his theory of language, like late medieval definitions of biblical literature, assumed the close association of physical with cosmic and metaphysical circumstances, while it also assumed the priority of oral over written denotation.

Langenstein therefore emphasized the experience of cognition at a moment of reading over against the personal or historical conditions of writing; or in other words, he emphasized the purpose of the text in the experience of salvation. The Holy Spirit was much involved in the work of translation itself, he argued in connection with the traditional distinction

---

[205] Ibid.: "Secunda proposicio est non estis credere nec uerisimile quod omne proprium nomen habeat secundum originalem eius inposicionem in aliqua lingwa significacionem et interpretacionem. Apparens quia est uerisimile quod multociens uoces ficte alique quas nec partes nec tote in aliquo ydeomate significabant inposite fuerint quibusdam tamquam propria nomina, sicud bu uel ba."

[206] Ibid.: "Tercia proposicio est si interpretacio nominis quandoque proprietati uel euentui consonet, hoc est uel ex causali inposicione uel ex hominum intencione uel ex diuina disposicione, nunquam autem ex constellacione."

[207] Ibid., f. 221va: "causalis est plurimum nominum imposicio quoad concordiam interpretacionis cum re"; "de diuina predisposicione patet de multis [del de] quibus nomina ex speciali diuina reuelacione fuerunt inposita"; fourth, "si concordia uel consonancia interpretacionis nominum cum re esset secundum constellaciones, tunc semper homines similiter fortunati et fataliter dispositi haberent similia propria nomina, cuius tamen falsitas manifesta est, quia plurimi uocantur eodem nomine qui tamen sunt diuersi in conplexionibus et moribus et fortunis."

between literal and mystical senses: "every sense of divine scripture, literal and spiritual (allegorical, tropological, and anagogical), which is most of all taken from the property of things and a transference of dictions, is found in Latin translation just as it appears in the Hebrew, because that [property or transference] from which the senses in this manner intended by the Holy Spirit are taken was not allowed to fluctuate in the translation of the scriptures from Hebrew into Latin, but the senses could be served [by the translation]."[208] Langenstein assumed the connection between the semantics of things and metaphor, as interpreters commonly did, and argued that semantic transference was intended by the Holy Spirit in the composition of the Bible and gets carried over from one language to another. Translation, too, was a cognitive reading experience, and the purpose of the text would be as real there as in any act of reading. Moreover, the spiritual meaningfulness of biblical texts, in spite of the role of divine agency in its composition, was not predetermined:

> not everything that can be understood can be noted or represented in the given words of scripture, [which] are from the intention of the Holy Spirit. This is clear, because many senses irrelevant to salvation and to Christian faith often can be elicited by human industry from a different property or condition of the Hebrew or Latin language. From which I say against some people that when a recommended theme (*thema recommendacionis*) is taken from holy scripture, it ought not to be said, in the analysis (*divisio*) of it, that the Holy Spirit there may signal these or those things which someone by his own ingenuity upon a trifling opportunity imagines appears to be represented or denoted there, because it is to work against the Holy Spirit to describe as nourishment the meanings or significations at some time or another [discovered] by human curiosity or triviality, which is not to be done.[209]

The meaningfulness of texts was not predetermined; it rested upon its contemporary religious purpose, which pointed again to the dangers

---

[208] Ibid., f. 232vb: "omnis sensus diuine scripture litteralis et spiritualis allegoricus, tropoloycus et anagogicus maxime qui ex proprietate rerum et transsumpcione diccionum sumitur ita inueruntur in translacione latina sicud hebraica apparet, quia illa ex quibus huiusmodi sensus a spiritu sancto principaliter intendi sumuntur non oportuit in translacione scripturarum de hebreo in latinum uariari sed poterant seruari."

[209] Ibid., f. 233ra: "non omnia que intelligi possunt possunt notari uel significari in datis uerbis scripture, [que] sunt de spiritus sancti intencione. Clarum est hoc, quia multi sensus inpertinentes saluti et fidei christiane sepe ex humana industria elici et [*del* fingi] possunt ex uaria proprietate et condicione sermonis hebraici uel latini, et ergo ad hoc est de diuinis scripturis sicud de alijs igitur propositum. Ex quo infero contra aliquos, quod, quando ex sacra scriptura thema sumitur recommendacionis, non debet dici in diuisione quod ibi spiritus sanctus innuat hec uel illa que aliquis suo ingenio ex leui occasione fingit ibi significari uel denotari apparet, quia contrarium facere est spiritui sancto sensus uel significaciones humana quandoque curiositate uel leuitate uictus attribuere, quod non est faciendum."

of curiosity and ingenuity. Therefore genuine translation was supernatural:

> The suppliant interpretation of divine language is a gift of the Holy Spirit. It is otherwise in the translation of human writings, because in the divine scriptures words not only signify in the common and regular manner, but they represent in various ways by way of similitude or by way of figurative transference. Similarly things and the circumstances of things and the order of words and the manners of speaking in the divine scriptures introduce diverse mysteries. And consequently the work of living scripture, when a transposition has been completed, is a special grace of God. Nevertheless it is to be recognized that the translation of one language into another can be done three ways, because a word can be translated from a word, a meaning from a meaning, or a combination of the two. In the first way, the substance of words (*corpora uerborum*) had by human ingenuity cannot be made a translation of divine scripture from Hebrew into Latin, insofar as in this manner various equivocations of the Hebrew words cannot be preserved nor can equivocations which are not in the Hebrew be avoided in the Latin words. In the second and third ways of transferring, namely sense from sense completely or combined [that is, both sense for sense and word for word together], a translation cannot be done by human industry alone, in such a way that all the senses of divine scripture intended in scripture by the Holy Spirit and in various ways are intelligibly discharged, since they were otherwise designated to be handled secretly and subtly. It is true that with regard to the superficial and grammatical sense of divine scripture, nothing prevents translation in the second and third manner by human ingenuity when there is an abundance of words and the skill of languages has been perfected.[210]

Like most if not all theologians of his day, Langenstein believed that the transfer of meaning in metaphor evaded grammatical explanation and

[210] Ibid., ff. 240va–241ra: "Interpretacio sermonum supplex diuinorum est donum spiritus sancti. Secus autem est in translacione scripturarum humanarum, quia in scripturis diuinis non solum uerba communi et regulari modo significant, sed uarijs modis similitudinarie et transsumptiue representant. Similiter et res et circumstancie rerum et ordo uerborum et modi loquendi in huiusmodi in diuinis scripturis uaria important misteria. Et per consequens opus est uitalis scripture perfecta transgressione Dei gracia specialis. Est tamen aduertendum quod tripliciter potest fieri translacio unius lingwe in aliam, quia potest transferri uerbum ex uerbo uel sensus ex sensu uel mixtum ex utroque. Primo modo nihil humano ingenio habita corpora uerborum posse fieri translaccionem diuine scripture, de hebreo in latinum, quantum hoc modo diuerse equiuocaciones diccionum hebraicarum seruari non possent nec caueri equiuocaciones in diccionibus latinis, ubi non sunt in hebraicis. Secundo autem et tercio modis transferrendi scilicet sensum ex sensu ex toto uel mixtum fieri non potest translacio sola humana industria, ut salutentur intelligibiliter omnes sensus diuine scripture a spiritu sancto in ipsa intenti et uarijs modis ut alias tetigi latenter et subtiliter designati. Uerum est quod quantum ad sensum superficialem et grammaticalem diuine scripture nihil prohibet ipsam eciam secundo et tercio modo humano ingenio habita uerborum copia et lingwarum pericia perfecta." He then refers the reader to Jerome's letter to Pammachius for more on the subject. There follows a defense of the superiority of Christian scripture to the texts of the Jews, a point made in answer to Nicholas of Lyra's identification of discrepancies between the Hebrew and the Vulgate (ff. 241rb–244rb).

was therefore divine. It was also divine when the transfer of meaning in metaphor was transferred yet again from one language to another. This implied, to him as to others, the privileged authority of Jerome's Vulgate. The idea of divine influence over the transfer of meaning was intrinsic to traditional assumptions about allegory. The fact that scripture portrayed mysteries indirectly, that is in non-dogmatic narratives, pointed to divine agency. Translation, like the composition of scripture in the first place, involved divine action.

Langenstein treated the rhetorical foundation of mystical reading – the divine denotations of biblical metaphor – as a problem of language. Again, Langenstein's students would be impressed by traditional hermeneutical themes discussed as language philosophy. They may have been less aware of the rather untraditional textual attitude suggested by his method. The coherence of scriptural writing is determined, at once textually and supernaturally, in the text's transmission and human reception.

Remembering that Langenstein argues from problems of the imposition of meaning on terms in the sentence, it is clear that he never assumed that writing just says what authors mean. There was no self-evident correspondence between authorial intention and reading comprehension. The text as a text could be separate from meaning, as Langenstein so openly explained. This separability of writing, language, and thought on the one hand restated the widespread conviction that thought, or I should say true thoughts, stood above both writers and what was written. In Langenstein we find this conviction reshaped. The distinction between letter and meaning has diminished. The correspondence of writing, text, and reading is emphasized instead. Writing and reading are bound subjectively, by the Spirit's inspiration of writers, readers, and even translators. The meaningfulness of a text becomes definite within a kind of fraternity of God, authors, translators, and readers. This was precisely the kind of fraternity that monastic readers once ascribed to mystical reading. Langenstein has given it a linguistic-theological explanation.

Insofar as biblical language is concerned, this assumes that scripture's ordinary speech must and can easily be converted into theological discourse, an assumption we have also seen in Wyclif, Fournier, and Gerson. The logical culture of late medieval scholasticism required this assumption. Whether one were a modalist, a terminist, or, like Wyclif, a realist with a hybrid view of the logic of biblical words, one applied a technique of converting the casual language of the Bible into a dialectical form. Neal Ward Gilbert showed over twenty-five years ago that Wyclif's conviction of the truthfulness of biblical speech as such, *de virtute sermonis*, was also shared by thinkers as diverse as Robert Holcot and Jean Gerson,[211] and to that I would add that Wyclif displayed not merely a shared commitment to the constructive rather than speculative use of logic, but also a common sense of biblical textuality.

6. HISTORY

The logical context of scripture was, according to Wyclif, atemporal. Given the tendency to intellectualize the content of the Bible, his seems to have been a generally shared conviction. It may therefore be misleading to claim that since Andrew of St. Victor, and especially since the mid-thirteenth century, commentators had possessed "a driving desire to understand exactly how things happened."[212] Late medieval interpreters had some such desire, but did it really drive them? Historical curiosity seems to have been subordinate to theological goals, surely by the time of Thomas Aquinas, whose literal sense was ultimately concerned not with the way things were but with the way things are and always must be, according to God.[213] The true legacy of thirteenth-century interpretation was represented in late thirteenth-century authors like Nicholas Gorran and in many, perhaps all, interpreters after him, whose sense of the past was subordinate to the common experiences shared between biblical actors and writers and later saints.

What happened to Nicholas of Lyra? It was the study of Hebrew, scholars have said, that moved biblical interpreters to discover history. "The Jew, however despised and persecuted, could put [the exegete] in touch with the patriarchs, the prophets and the psalmist."[214] Nicholas of Lyra, as the highpoint of the medieval recovery of Hebrew exegesis, has seemed to many to represent the fruition of medieval historical interpretation.[215] There can be no denying that Lyra, in his way, wanted

---

[211] Gilbert, "Ockham, Wyclif, and the 'via moderna.'"
[212] Especially in their commentaries on the Hebrew Bible. Smalley, *Study*, pp. 371, 362–63. Problems with these assumptions in the early fifteenth century were suggested to Karlfried Froehlich in his study of the controversy over the assassination of the duke of Orleans: "Always to Keep," pp. 24–9, 44–8.
[213] *ST* 1a, q. 1, a. 10 read with *ST* 1a, q. 1, a. 2.
[214] Smalley, *Study*, pp. 362–3.
[215] Ibid., p. 355; *Le Moyen Age et la Bible*, p. 146; Herman Hailperin, *Rashi and the Christian Scholars* (Pitsburg: University of Pittsburgh Press, 1963), pp. 251–52, and for the extent of his use of rabbinical exegesis, 137ff. For the more prevalent interest of scholars in Hebrew exegesis in the late twelfth and early thirteenth centuries, see David J. Wasserstein, "Grosseteste, the Jews, and Medieval Christian Hebraism," *Robert Grosseteste: New Perspectives on His Thought and Scholarship*, ed. J. McEvoy (Turnhout: Brepols, 1995), pp. 357–76, here 362–3 and the literature noted there.

to understand the things of the Old Testament as they really were, down to the very furniture and cultic devices of Israel's temple.[216] His digressions into theological topics were few and brief.[217] But he himself published abridgments of the *Postilla* for the use of preachers, and his successors assumed that his aim was pious and clerical.[218] Incited by the accusations of Pablo of Burgos, who raised the accusation of judaizing against Lyra, the fifteenth-century German Franciscan, Matthias Döring, published a widely known defense. There he let Pablo's allegation of Lyra's inferior Hebrew stand. Lyra's intention, he said, was to defend Catholic orthodoxy, not Judaism.[219] It seems a fair point. Lyra believed that the Hebrew patriarchs understood and proclaimed the Christian covenant, and that the prophets of Israel often spoke of Jesus. The Psalms contain "all of scripture [that is, both testaments] in the manner of praise"; in them, prophecy is especially clear.[220] He also used Hebrew exegesis polemically to argue for the truth of Christianity.[221] The point was not forgotten among those who used him, like Heinrich Egher of Kalkar, Carthusian prior in the Rhineland. In a letter to another Carthusian written in 1406, Egher recalled Lyra's intentions. Lyra noticed, he said, the great neglect given to the literal sense of scripture, so he concentrated on it, confounding the Jews with citations from their own books. But then, Heinrich observed, he gave "most beautifully,"

---

[216] *Le Moyen Age et la Bible*, p. 418.
[217] Langlois, "Nicolas de Lyre," p. 369, noted two such modest digressions. One at 1 Kings 17.8 treats dueling (whether it is permissible), and another at Ex. 7.12 asks whether a magician, by demonic power, can change sticks into snakes.
[218] Ibid., p. 225.
[219] Pablo of Burgos's criticisms are found in *Glossa cum Lyra*, ff. 4vb–7ra. See also Reinhardt, "Werk," pp. 347–49. Matthäus Döring, Franciscan, student at Oxford, professor of Erfurt, and (since 1427) thirty-four years provincial minister of Saxony, wrote the rebuttal of Pablo printed with Lyra's *Postilla*, ibid., ff. 8vb–9rb, esp. 9ra–9rb. He reasserted the priority of the literal sense and defended the use of non-Christian sources on the principle that anything that does not contradict the faith is a legitimate tool. Only at the conclusion does he make brief mention of Pablo's accusation that Lyra's Hebrew was bad. To Pablo, this contributed to what he regarded as a misuse of Jewish interpretation (cf. an early biographer who praised Lyra's Hebrew and its effectiveness in refuting Jewish arguments; Heinrich Rüthing, "Kritische Bemerkungen zu einer mittelalterlichen Biographie des Nikolaus von Lyra," *Archivum Franciscanum Historicum* 60 (1967): 42–54, here pp. 52–3). Döring pointedly mentions that Lyra's aim was the exaltation of the Catholic faith, so that his inferior knowledge of Hebrew was inconsequential. A more recent Franciscan defense of Lyra's Hebrew exegesis, which points out his rebuttals of Jewish interpretations for the sake of Christian ones, is Schwendinger, "Vaticiniis." Consider also Marco Adinolfi, "Due strane nelle postille di Nicola de Lyre," *Rivista Biblica* 6 (1958): 255–62.
[220] *Glossa cum Lyra*, 3:83ra–84vb, esp. 83vb (finalis causa). Also Minnis, "Authorial Intention," pp. 19–20.
[221] See the contributions by Patton, Smith, and Van Liere in Krey and Smith, *Nicholas of Lyra*, pp. 19–81. Schwendinger, "Vaticiniis," pp. 130–3, made a similar point long ago, although apologetically.

pulcherrime, a moral exposition.[222] Lyra's accomplishment was to do this from the Hebrew Bible itself, in complete agreement with the apologetic and missionary strategy promoted by the mendicant orders.[223]

What exactly was Lyra's influence? Klaus Reinhardt addressed this question systematically some time ago, and his findings have more recently been confirmed in a narrower, more exegetical way by Philip Krey. Reinhardt reviewed copies and translations of Lyra's commentaries in one broad region, the Iberian peninsula. He confirmed Pablo of Burgos's claim that Lyra was, next to the Ordinary Gloss, the most widely disseminated commentary on the Iberian peninsula, and the copies show that interest was greatest in the *Postilla litteralis*.[224] But how was he read? Three of the five interpreters examined, all active in the fifteenth century, were sharply critical of Lyra (Pablo of Burgos, Jaime Pérez, Alfonso Fernández), and one of them may not have actually used Lyra's commentaries at all (Nicolau Eimeric).[225] Another Catalan Franciscan, Poncio Carbonell (d. 1350), revised Lyra's moral commentary on Job by adding Lyra's literal interpretation to it.[226] This fusion of literal and moral exegesis seems foreign to Lyra's historicizing, and no interpreter imitated Lyra's refined literalism. Philip Krey studied the influence of Lyra's interpretation of the Apocalypse. After examining the Apocalypse commentary by Poncio Carbonell, John Wyclif's commentary on the Apocalypse, some Wyclif sermons, the Apocalypse gloss of the Lübecker Bible, and the Low German Bible published at Lübeck in 1494, Krey concluded, "Lyra's Apocalypse commentary had many readers but few followers."[227] Pierre Auriol exercised at least as strong an influence on late medieval interpretation, and there is nothing to suggest that Lyra changed the way commentators worked.

When Lyra was appreciated, it was as a tool and not as a model. Gustav Benrath's study of Wyclif's biblical interpretation, which surveyed all his Bible commentaries, provides a convenient opportunity to see in depth the nature of Lyra's influence on the entire work of one interpreter. Wyclif relied on Lyra's *Postilla* more than any other late medieval

---

[222] Rüthing, "Bemerkungen," pp. 51–2. The letter is better known for its claim that Lyra studied Hebrew as a boy with Jewish teachers.

[223] Jeremy Cohen, *The Friars and the Jews* (Ithaca: Cornell, 1982), p. 171. See also Deeana Copeland Klepper, "Nicholas of Lyra's *Questio de adventu Christi* and the Franciscan Encounter with Jewish Tradition in the Middle Ages," Ph.D. Dissertation, Northwestern University, 1995, chapter 6.

[224] Reinhardt, "Werk," p. 339.   [225] Ibid., pp. 342–58.   [226] Ibid., pp. 342–3.

[227] Philip Krey, "Many Readers but Few Followers: The Fate of Nicholas of Lyra's Apocalypse Commentary in the Hands of His Late-Medieval Admirers," *Church History* 64 (1995): 185–201.

commentary, but how? Although in the interpretation of the Psalms and the Song of Songs Lyra's opinion carried much weight, Wyclif frequently distanced himself from interpretations taken from Rashi.[228] In the Prophets and in the books of the New Testament, Wyclif routinely used Lyra for his account of the literal sense, the division of books, and historical information.[229] In some instances Wyclif challenged Lyra's views.[230] But these borrowings comprise a scant portion of Wyclif's own interpretations, which were elaborate and theologically discursive, which is to say that he refused to follow Lyra's exegetical style. Lyra provided a good tool. The same could be seen in the commentaries of Denys the Carthusian, who used Lyra as a source of Hebrew and rabbinical explanation.[231] Other interpreters, like Johannes Klenkok, even used Lyra for allegories, and Denys the Carthusian criticized Lyra for allegorizing: both cases show that Lyra could be and was seen in radically diverse ways (which is why it may be pointless to seek a trajectory of literal exegesis from Lyra to Luther).[232] On at least one occasion, Denys the Carthusian goes so far as to accept Pablo of Burgos over Nicholas, precisely because Burgos (who boasted in his preface that his Hebrew was better than Lyra's) had, Denys alleged, a better grasp of biblical metaphor.[233] Lyra provided little help with rhetoric, and it was rhetoric that could answer the growing textual orientation of exegesis, with its intellectual and doctrinal, rather than historical, preoccupations.

Does Lyra represent the culmination of medieval exegesis? It would seem safe to assume even on this limited evidence that the *Postilla* was an exegetical sourcebook serving the distinct interests of other late medieval interpreters, which interests are also reflected in Lyra's prologues. The *Postilla* did not change the way commentaries were written. Like other late medieval interpreters, Lyra believed that biblical literature and its literal interpretation belonged to a life of the soul that reached well beyond historical investigation, as we have seen. He lacked theological or

---

[228] Benrath, *Wyclif*, pp. 24, 25–32, 38, 42–3, 44–5.
[229] Ibid., pp. 69–71, 93, 98–103, 117, 127–31, 134, 137, 139, 157, 163, 168, 172, 180 n. 364, 244–6, 251, 301, 303–5, 307.
[230] Ibid., pp. 120, 141, 187, 255, 325.
[231] See Denys the Carthusian's commentaries on Genesis and Exodus, *Opera*, vol. 1.
[232] For Klenkok, Ocker, *Johannes Klenkok and the Interpretation of the Bible*, forthcoming.
[233] *Ennaratio in Genesim*, xlix., art. c., *Opera* 1: 444–5. See also his commentary on Pseudo-Dionysius the Aereopagite, *De ecclesiastica hierarchia*, art. xli., *Opera* 15:501. The opposition of a rhetorically metaphorical letter and mystical meaning in this passage did not prevent Denys from distinguishing historical and mystical meanings consistently in other places: for example, his commentary on Exodus, where chapter by chapter he provides first a literal interpretation and then a spiritual one.

historical scepticism. The ability to abstract ideas was crucial. According to Lyra, scripture contains the science of *vox*, which issues from the voice to signify a word, and the science of *propria*, "proper things" in the writings that express the divine word.[234] These are the sciences that Lyra's care for the letter and his Hebraic excursuses hoped to grasp. Both constitute knowledge of God. Although nothing here nullifies the historical circumstances in which the words were spoken or written, the past does not confine textual meaning: only its theological content is absolute. It is known by the study of words *and* ideas. The faith of the patriarchs and prophets in the things revealed to them (which were beliefs about events and divine actions that had not yet occurred) compromises any conviction of temporal and cultural distance; the Bible is the knowledge of God, which is given to the church and in which all truth is the same in principle.

That is, late medieval theologians saw Lyra within the context of their own intellectualizing approach to the Bible. The causal definitions we studied earlier summarized well the late medieval sense of the text as once-divine speech still being heard, especially when those definitions are seen in the contexts of verbal interpretation, personal regeneration, prophecy, and translation. That sense of the text allowed readers to do what monastic writers had done in the tradition of contemplative reading: to see reading as a way of thinking with prophets, apostles, and saints. Interpreters felt they preserved the great repository of Christian learning. But they did it by literal rather than mystical reading.

---

[234] *Glossa cum Lyra*, f. 3rb. Was this related to a theory of illumination? Consider Pelster, "Quodlibeta und Quaestiones des Nikolaus von Lyra," pp. 964–5.

CHAPTER 5

Reformation

The characteristics of divine speech studied in the previous chapter form a distinct picture of the late medieval Bible. Scholars shared an attitude toward the text. It had these essential components: an association of spiritual or ultimate meaning with the literal sense; the communion of divine and human writers with past and present readers; and a presupposition of continuity between all genuinely religious writers and readers. In the case of John Wyclif, continuity was argued in extreme terms: the text is atemporal. It seems that most interpreters preferred to see continuity in more historical terms: writers and readers agreed over time. But in each case, the effect of continuity was the same, namely to nullify, at the level of meaning, the differences of the past from the present. The sense of continuity did not require a denial of historical contingency. It simply assumed that the literal truths of the Bible were not historically contingent. The letter always made for true theology, even if poorly understood at some historical moments. The ancient Jews may not have known the coming of Christ, but their patriarchs and prophets did. The Christological allegories of the Old Testament could, and often did, slip into the literal realm of human authorial intention because of a prophetic divine–human synergy that anticipated the divine and human synergies of sacramental grace. Biblical writers knew what we know. What is ultimately meaningful about what they said is the thoughts we share in common and our similar experiences.

This chapter considers the question whether the late medieval attitude toward the text was fundamentally distinct from that of the Reformation.[1] A good deal of authoritative opinion has pointed to Bible

---

[1] The educational contexts of Reformation exegesis and the early modern development of commentary literature are not treated in this book. I feel this is justified because the Reformation appears here only to help clarify what was and was not distinct about late medieval exegesis. For an introduction to the academic contexts of theology during and after the Reformation, consider *Universities in Early Modern Europe (1500–1800)*, ed. Hilde De Ridder-Symoens

study and biblical hermeneutics as the source of Martin Luther's theological discovery, making his scriptural exegesis the intellectual origin of Protestantism and the source of whatever turning point in European history and culture Protestantism is supposed to have produced.² This always assumes that what Luther and the early Protestants did as interpreters belonged to a frame of mind at odds with medieval Bible scholarship, or (in its most extreme statement) with medieval culture overall. This chapter considers three areas of Reformation scholarship – dialectic, rhetoric, and the concept of divine speech – in order to argue that, although Protestant theology developed new and distinct methods, those methods reinforced the textual attitude studied in the previous three chapters. I make no pretense of treating this topic comprehensively, and I am very reliant on the work of experts in this field. But it seems to me that even a partial and preliminary treatment will help underscore the importance of a late medieval textual attitude in the history of European religion and culture.

I. DIALECTIC

In chapter 2 I argued that a specific view of biblical signification can explain the preoccupation of late medieval Bible study with ideas, that it signals a dramatic alternative to Victorine reading practice, and that it points to the fact that theologians portrayed the Bible in their commentaries as intrinsically related to theological science. Verbal signification and the reading practice that I have associated with it owed no particular philosophical debt. It is best to think of verbal signification as a viewpoint on the text that emerged in the practice of Bible reading, consistent with but not dependent upon other aspects of scholasticism. I now want briefly to give evidence that late medieval assumptions about textual meaning (verbal signification and the nearness of a present religious world of thought to the text) were reinforced by Protestant biblicism.

(Cambridge: Cambridge University Press, 1996), pp. 419–31, 474–87, 500–9, 593–99, and *Le temps des Réformes et la Bible*, ed. G. Bedouelle and B. Roussel (Paris: Beauchesne, 1989), pp. 201–12 (an excellent summary of Luther's university career as a Bible scholar) and 219–20 (educational contexts at Zürich, Basel, and Strasbourg, important centers of exegesis at the height of the Reformation, from about 1525 to 1540). For a survey of the development of commentary literature see Richard Muller, "Biblical Interpretation in the Sixteenth and Seventeenth Centuries," *Historical Handbook of Major Biblical Interpreters*, ed. D. K. McKim (Downers Grove: Intervarsity, 1998), pp. 123–52. For the study of Hebrew, Stephen G. Burnett, *From Christian Hebraism to Jewish Studies. Johannes Buxtorf (1564–1629) and Hebrew Learning in the Seventeenth Century* (Leiden: Brill, 1996), pp. 103–33 and for Hebrew and Greek, *Le temps des Réformes*, pp. 125–56.

² See Ebeling, Herman, Hirsch, and Holl in the bibliography.

The Reformation attack on scholasticism did not include an attack on all aspects of late medieval Bible reading. It left standing what I suggest was the unique verbal and intellectual orientation of late medieval Bible scholarship, even while rejecting the particular religious doctrines that gave flesh to that orientation. To get a glimpse of how this occurred, it is necessary to consider a particular criticism of scholastic culture that was very influential among Protestants. That criticism of scholastic culture undermined the logical preoccupations of earlier theologians, but it reinforced and expanded that aspect of late medieval exegesis most clearly reflected in the theory of verbal signification, namely the association of literal meaning with a religious world of thought.

Between 1490 and the 1520s, scholars began to abandon the logical techniques of "speculative grammar" and other established methods that had become popular in the schools from the second half of the thirteenth century to the end of the fifteenth century. In the 1530s the new dialectics of the humanists Lorenzo Valla and Rudolf Agricola were adapted and widely propagated in northern Europe by Philip Melanchthon, Bartholomaeus Latomus, and Jean Sturm, and later in an accessible if debased form by Peter Ramus. The new dialectics replaced the old techniques.[3]

One of the main characteristics of this change is the humanist rediscovery of a distinction between logical and grammatical uses of language.[4]

---

[3] E. J. Ashworth, "The Defeat, Neglect, and Revival of Scholasticism," *The Cambridge History of Later Medieval Philosophy*, ed. Norman Kretzmann, Anthony Kenny, and Jan Pinborg (Cambridge University Press, 1982), pp. 787–96, here 789–91, 795–6 (*CHLMP*). Idem, "Traditional Logic," *The Cambridge History of Renaissance Philosophy*, ed. C. B. Schmitt, Quentin Skinner, and Eckhard Kessler (Cambridge University Press, 1988), pp. 151–53, 161–2 (*CHRP*). For the rediscovery of Agricola in the second decade of the sixteenth century and the dissemination of editions of the *De inventione dialectica*, especially from Louvain, Cologne, and Paris, see Mack, *Renaissance Argument*, pp. 257–79, and for Latomus, pp. 286–9. Mack has, however, demonstrated how selective the use of Agricola was, although commentaries and epitomes of Agricola do stress his application of dialectic to everyday speech and to literature (ibid., pp. 280–302). For Peter Ramus' equally selective use of Agricola, ibid., pp. 34–55. Mack's detailed study confirms, however, Agricola's general influence in terms of reinforcing the close and complementary relationship of dialectic and rhetoric, the application of dialectic to ordinary speech and literature, the importance of dialectical invention and disposition, the connection of argumentative "topics" with discursive style, and the connection of these "topics" with the real world. See especially ibid., p. 363. A decline of medieval logic was once thought to be signaled by the criticisms of modalism in the work of Lorenzo Valla in the middle of the fifteenth century and in the work of Alexander Hegius and Johannes Synthen in the late fifteenth century, but widespread change in the teaching of logic did not take place until the 1530s. Cf. Terence Heath, "Logical Grammar, Grammatical Logic, and Humanism in Three German Universities," *Studies in the Renaissance* 18 (1971): 9–64; J. Ijsewijn, "Alexander Hegius (d. 1498): *Invectiva in modos significandi*," *Forum for Modern Language Studies* 7 (1971): 299–318.

[4] Heath, "Logical Grammar," p. 49. G. A. Padley, *Grammatical Theory in Western Europe, 1500–1700* (Cambridge University Press, 1976), p. 38, for Melanchthon's distinction between grammar and logic.

Medieval scholars, assuming that an utterance represents to the mind some thing – and this act of representation constitutes its meaningfulness – assumed that logical demonstration provided the best tool for the acquisition of knowledge through Latin speech.[5] Theories of supposition were basic to this approach. They accounted for the ways particular meanings are attached to particular terms within a logical proposition.[6] But these theories of meaning had formal propositions in view rather than ordinary speech. The proposition was a declarative sentence unsullied by alluring imagery and the argumentative structure of discourse that captivate and encourage assent, or in other words, it was a sentence unsullied by rhetoric. Medieval logic would not address meaningfulness at the level of discourse, certainly not at the level of narratives as complex and diverse as those of the Bible. This must be why the transition from Bible narrative to theology sometimes seems so clumsy, for example, when Klenkok moves from the word "chosen" in Acts to a discussion of future contingents that does not seem to have any relation to the narrative context, or when Eimeric defends the orthodoxy of ancient Christology in conjunction with the geneology of Christ, or when Langenstein focuses on the imposition of meaning upon terms. The theological context of the word sometimes seemed more real to the scholar than the narrative context.

The humanist Lorenzo Valla in the middle of the fifteenth century showed that logic could not set general linguistic standards – that ordinary language was meaningful by different rules, namely the rules of rhetoric.[7] There is evidence that about the same time there was a trend to shift attention away from the analysis of the signification of terms and propositions to the broader structure of discourse. It may be that soon after Valla logicians shifted their interest from the so-called *vetus ars*[8] and its focus on terms and propositions to the *nova ars*[9] and its study of the *use* of propositions in arguments.[10] At the end of the century, Rudolf Agricola made logical demonstration subordinate to the study of

---

[5] See Jan Pinborg, "Speculative Grammar," *CHLMP*, pp. 254–69.
[6] E. J. Ashworth, "Chimeras and Imaginary Objects: A Study in the Post-Medieval Theory of Signification," *Vivarium* 15 (1977): 57–79, reprinted idem, *Studies in Post-Medieval Semantics*, (London: Variorum, 1985), no. 3, here pp. 59–60. This was especially true in speculative grammars, for which see pp. 68–70, above.
[7] Lisa Jardine, "Humanistic Logic," *CHRP*, p. 179.
[8] The treatment of Aristotle's *Categories* and *De interpretatione* and Porphyry's *Isagoge* in the first three tracts of Peter of Spain's influential *Summulae logicales*.
[9] The treatment of Aristotle's *Prior* and *Posterior Analytics*, the *Topics*, and the *Sophistici elenchi* in tracts four through six of Peter of Spain.
[10] Heath, "Logic and Grammar," pp. 41–54. But see also Ashworth's criticism of Heath's suggestion that this shift reflected the influence of speculative grammar: Ashworth, "Traditional Logic," *CHRP*, pp. 154–5.

persuasive arguments, as it was in classical rhetoric. Through Agricola's influence, scholars became increasingly interested in the anaylsis of specific forms of argument known from Cicero as "topics."[11] It was here that the distinction between ordinary speech and the formal language of dialectic mattered most, for rather than isolate the disciplines of logic and rhetoric, it seemed to sharpen the complementarity of rhetoric and dialectic, as one can readily see in the adaptation and popularization of Agricola's method by Philip Melanchthon.[12]

In his most frequently printed textbook of dialectic, *Questions of Dialectic* (*Erotemata dialectices*),[13] Melanchthon stressed the practical. Dialectic, he said, is a discursive skill, "the skill and the method of teaching rightly, in order, and plainly, which is done by defining correctly, dividing, connecting true arguments, correcting false connections between them, and refuting errors."[14] The sum of Melanchthon's dialectic is the definition and arrangement of arguments and the techniques of refutation. He distinguished this teaching practice from rhetoric by appeal to the distinct forms of language in each. Dialectic studies any subject matter with an unadorned description of things; "but rhetoric adds decoration in these matters, which can be brightened up with an abundance and brilliance of language and variously painted."[15] The point is supported by a somewhat rhetoricized Plato.[16]

---

[11] Jardine, "Humanistic Logic," *CHRP*, p. 182. "Topics" refers to dialectical "topics," as in Cicero's *Topics*, which studied the analysis of propositions and their arrangement into syllogisms and entire discourses, or in other words, the structure of arguments. A particularly clear account may be found in Wilbur Samuel Howell, *Logic and Rhetoric in England, 1500–1700* (New York: Russell and Russell, 1961), p. 15. For Melanchthon's adaptation of Agricola's emphasis on dialectical topics, which he thinks of as something like a "commonplace" in rhetoric, see Mack, *Renaissance Argument*, pp. 327–33, esp. 328.

[12] For the complex relationship of Melanchthon to Agricola see ibid., pp. 356–74.

[13] A Latinization of the Greek, ἐρώτημα διαλεκτικῆς:

[14] W. Risse, *Bibliographica Logica*, vol. 1, *1472–1800* (Hildesheim: E. Olms, 1965); Mack, *Renaissance Argument*, p. 320; Philip Melanchthon, *Erotemata dialectices* (1547), book i, *Opera omnia*, ed. Gottlieb Bretschneider Karl (Halle: C. A. Schwetschke et Filius, 1846), 13:514. This final version of Melanchthon's dialectic improved the discussion of the *locus causarum*, but it is otherwise substantially the same as the predecessors of 1520 and 1528. Ibid., cols. 509–10.

[15] *Erotemata dialectices*, i, p. 515: "Dialectica circa omnes materias versatur, et rerum summas propriis verbis nude proponit, nec unam sententiam pluribus verbis aut adhibitis luminibus figurarum pingit, sed Rhetorica addit ornatum in his materiis, quae orationis copia et splendore illustrari et varie pingi possunt."

[16] *Erotemata dialectices* i, cols. 516–17. Melanchthon's Plato contrasts with Platonist interest in naturally significant spoken languages. (Melanchthon here assumes, as did most of his contemporaries, with their medieval predecessors, that spoken language is meaningful by convention.) See E. J. Ashworth, "'Do Words Signify Ideas or Things?' The Scholastic Sources of Locke's Theory of Language," *Journal of the History of Philosophy* 19 (1981): 299–326, reprinted idem, *Studies*

Dialectic

As in medieval logic, the new dialectic assumed that language represents things directly, or at least that it should. But unlike medieval logic, it was especially sensitive to the need to convert ordinary speech into direct language. Meaning occurs in the connections established by the mind between words that variously represent diverse objects of knowledge. So for example in Melanchthon's elementary discussion of the basic types of attribution, the so-called "predicables" (species, genus, difference, property, accident), he observed that attribution is built upon a natural order connecting names with things in variable ways. The most specific attribution involves species, while the other predicables connect the noun with various more universal features of the thing (at the level of genus, difference, property, or accident).[17] Neither universal names, which are merely more general predicates of universals that actually exist in nature, nor the names of particular species exist outside of the mind, but meaning is established by the connection of the things represented by each. "It is really an act of understanding when one paints an image in the mind, which is therefore called common because it can be applied to many individuals, so that while one carries about an image of a stag in the mind, one knows stags wherever they are presented, when one brings together the figure with the image in the mind."[18] Language facilitates the mind's creation of such connections in diverse ways, partly because of the variety of objects of knowledge,[19] and partly because the language

---

in *Post-Medieval Semantics* (London: Variorum, 1985), no. 7, pp. 306–7; Margreta de Grazia, "The Secularization of Language in the Seventeenth Century," *Journal of the History of Ideas* 41 (1980): 323–4.

[17] *Erotemata dialectices*, i, cols. 518–23. Species is a common noun nearest to particular things, as in the answer to the question, "What is Plato?" "Plato is a human being." Human being is the species. The attribution of the species to a particular instance of it, for example human being to Plato, is necessary, Melanchthon explains, because the mind must carry about a general image in order to recognize particular instances of it. Genus is a common noun for many species, as in the answer to the question, "What is a horse?" "Horse is an animal." Animal is the genus. Difference is that which constitutes a certain species with the genus, as in the answer to the question, how may it be that the rational constitutes the species human being with the animal? Difference shows how it is the species human being. Property is a tendency (*inclinatio*) or something adjoining always at least potentially inherent in all the particular instances of a species, as the tendency toward an erect body is a property of the species human being. Accident is what is mutably present in something, not as a part of its substance or subsisting through itself, as in the heat of warm water. Heat is an accident.

[18] *Erotemata dialectices*, i, col. 520. He takes this "common image" to be the same as Plato's "ideas," "Haec forma non est res extra intellectionem, sed ipse actus intelligendi, pingens hanc imaginem."

[19] For example, "absolute" things that, according to Melanchthon, can be understood without connecting them to other abstract things, for example, the absolute thing "warmth," in contrast with "making warm," which involves the transfer of heat into something else, which is therefore a "relative" thing. *Erotemata dialectices*, i, cols. 544–5.

used may not correlate directly with a particular thing or with the goal of a discourse. Melanchthon's ideal is philosophical language that refers very directly and transparently to abstract things like an object's essence, causes, parts, or accidents. But ordinary speech is not so uniform; it requires "definition," which is to say that it requires some account of how it indirectly refers to things like essence, causes, parts, or accidents.[20] Dialectic therefore relies on grammar to provide itself a translation of spoken and figurative language into "pure speech." Melanchthon illustrated this point with the example of biblical language: "it is necessary to understand the diction"; even literal speech cannot be taken at face value.[21] His point is not that *all* religious language is metaphorical, as some theologians would say today, but rather that even literal language is only meaningful within specific discursive contexts, such as the context of a particular book of the Bible or of the teaching of the Bible as a whole. The meaning of language is associated with the broader argument of a discourse, even if the language is transparent. So for example, in the Gospel of John, chapter 1, the meaning of the noun "God" is conditioned by other elements of the text, namely its assertion that the Son is co-creator. Melanchthon must have had Michael Servetus in mind (who defined the Son of God as a being born of God's substance at a point in time):

> The Son of God is called God. And lest there should be ambiguity in the name, it adds that all things were created through the Son. Therefore John affirms the Son to be truly God, omnipotent and creator with the Father. The conclusion is valid, because it is not ours to paint opinions about God from our imaginations, but concerning Him one is to understand as He Himself has revealed, and divine speech is to be heard and from it the meaning is to be taken up, which meaning produces a clear and uncorrupted property.[22]

The text is the theological argument. The association of the noun "God" with a theological point depends upon this argument, as it is clarified by another phrase in the text. To think otherwise is to entertain

---

[20] Definition is introduced in book one, ibid., cols. 563–4, and again as a *locus* in book four, cols. 663–9. The latter treatment lists definition as the first of twenty-eight *loci rerum* (a *locus* is a nodal point of an argument), and accordingly definition is preoccupied with the place of particular sayings within the main structure of an argument, its relation to the matters to be confirmed or refuted. *Erotemata dialectices*, iv, cols. 663–4.

[21] *Erotemata dialectices*, i, cols. 563–4.

[22] "... ut Iohan. 1. Filius Dei vocatur Deus. Et ne sit ambiguitas in nomine, addit, omnia per Filium condita esse. Ergo Iohannes affirmat Filium vere Deum esse, omnipotentem et conditorem cum Patre. Valet consequentia, quia non est nostrum fingere de Deo opiniones ex nostris imaginationibus, sed de eo sentiendum est, sicut se patefecit, et sermo divinus audiendus est, et ex eo sumenda sententia, quam perspicua et incorrupta proprietas gignit." *Erotemata dialectices*, iv, col. 668.

a groundless fabrication of one's imagination. Only when words understood literally produce absurdities must one take recourse to a figurative explanation, absurdity here meaning not merely something offensive to plain reason (as in philosophy) but something offensive to the unambiguous commands of God and the articles of faith. The task of translating figurative language into direct speech is facilitated by grammar and rhetoric, a point Melanchthon derived from Augustine but explained in terms of the coordination of figurative speech with philosophical truth.[23] The discovery of meaning progresses from figurative language through pure speech to its context in discourse.

Melanchthon outlined, in short, a process of abstraction that is more deliberately associated with narrative, the product of which is generally the same as the product of late medieval Bible reading. The new logic showed just how close the logical demonstration and the rhetorical presentation of a point could be, in part because logical and grammatical uses of language now more clearly overlapped. The proximity of logic and rhetoric occurred not merely because they aimed at the same goal of persuasion. It was because now each discipline had a contextual approach that overlapped that of the other, insofar as both saw discourse rather than propositions as the context of meaning – discourse teaching doctrine. The knowledge of things may be more important, as Erasmus once said alluding to the beginning of Augustine's *On Christian Doctrine* (students of theology found it at the start of Peter Lombard's *Sentences*); yet the knowledge of words comes first:

But some, the 'uninitiated' as the saying goes, while they hurry on to learn about things, neglect a concern for language and, striving after a false economy, incur a very heavy loss. For since things are learnt only by the sounds we attach to them, a person who is not skilled in the force of language is, of necessity, short-sighted, deluded, and unbalanced in his judgment of things as well. Finally you may observe that none are more given to constant quibbling over the minutiae of language than those who boast that they pass over mere words and concentrate on the matter itself.[24]

---

[23] Ibid., cols. 668–9. Augustine, *On Christian Doctrine*, book 3, chapters 30–7, trans. Robertson, pp. 104–17. Tyconius' rules were well known throughout the Middle Ages through Augustine and, in altered and abbreviated form, through Isidore, *Sententiarum libri tres*, i.19, *PL* 83:581–6. Isidore's version is reproduced by Hugh of St. Victor, *Didascalicon*, vol. 4, *PL* 176:791–3, and it was also adapted by Nicholas of Lyra (for which, see p. 142, n. 102, above. In addition, see Margaret Deansley, *The Lollard Bible and Other Medieval Biblical Versions* (Cambridge University Press, 1966), p. 167.

[24] Erasmus, *On the Method of Study*, p. 666. Augustine, *On Christian Doctrine* i.2. Peter Lombard, *I Sent.* d. 1, Peter Lombard, *Sententiarum Libri Quatuor* (Paris: Louis Vivès, 1892), pp. 9–10. Evans, *Language and Logic*, 1:51.

It was therefore necessary to complement logic with rhetoric, without confusing the two.

The fruit of these convictions in theology is best known in John Calvin's biblical commentaries, sermons, and *Institutes of the Christian Religion*, where the analysis of scriptural texts in terms of precisely this kind of rhetoric and dialectic yields coherent doctrine without recourse to propositions of the traditional, medieval variety.[25] The textual orientation of Agricolan dialectic in Protestant exegesis and theology contrasts sharply with the medieval doctrine of the four-fold meaning of the Bible, which presupposed a strong difference between literal and mystical signification, based upon the difference between superficial appearances and authentic meaning. The Reformation, by contrast, assumed that the literal text stood close to the supernatural meaning about which it speaks, and that the framework of biblical truth was its narrative structure. This seems to confirm an earlier exegetical trend: the signification of words and the expectation that theological reflection was the purpose and substance of interpretation. It would seem safe to conclude that Reformation Bible study built on a gradual abandonment of Victorine assumptions and interpretive techniques in the late Middle Ages.

2. RHETORIC

In chapter three, I argued that Bible scholars attempted to analyze biblical texts verbally, but they were hindered by the lack of rhetoric as a discipline. Lacking rhetoric, late medieval scholars had to rely all the more on theology to conceptualize the text as an artifact that produces religious knowledge. In the early sixteenth century, Agricolan dialectic furnished a way to conceive of rhetoric and theology as partners, something that medieval theologians could scarcely imagine, as I pointed out in the Introduction. In addition, the application of the new humanist classicism to Bible study strengthened the Protestant conviction that their own religious writing was entirely textual, insofar as the Bible is concerned, and theologically comprehensive (whatever they did had to pose a convincing alternative to an extremely well-developed system of knowledge, namely scholasticism). The prerequisite of a new, discourse-oriented approach to biblical imagery was Rudolf Agricola's demonstration of the compatibility of discursive reason and rhetorical analysis.

---

[25] Millet, *La dynamique de la parole, passim*, and for the use of propositional argumentation in the rhetorical context of the presentation of evidence, ibid., pp. 627–55, esp. 645–55.

Agricola had as one of his goals the restoration of the complementarity of dialectic and rhetoric, as it was taught at the beginning of Aristotle's *Rhetoric* and elaborated by Cicero, Quintilian, and more recently Valla.[26] The logical syllogism and its preoccupation with the resolution of opposing points of view sank from its central function in medieval argument to a role subsidiary to persuasion, which is discussed in book two of Agricola's *On Dialectical Invention*. This change of place elevated the subjects of book three – the art of influence, persuasive strategy, and delivery – to a new importance. Agricola's concession of the human context of argumentation, of the centrality of structure and style, affected the interpretation of texts in the Reformation by suggesting how rhetoric taught not only an orator's methods of expression but also a method of criticism. He made it possible for intellectuals of the early sixteenth century to apply rhetoric to exegesis and theology, by reconciling rhetoric to logic.

The reconciliation of rhetoric to logic was clear enough in Agricola's long and difficult *On Dialectical Invention*, but Bartholomaeus Latomus' popular epitome of the book brought it to a wide audience.[27] By the 1530s there existed a movement among theologians to use rhetoric to construct and analyze the convergence of biblical language, divine revelation, and present-day speech. By the middle of the sixteenth century, Protestant theology had taken a decisive rhetorical turn: Melanchthon's rhetoric and theology (especially influential in Germany), Peter Ramus' dialectic and rhetoric (influential first in France, then in Germany, England, and the Low Countries), and Calvin's *Institutes of the Christian Religion* (influential among Protestants almost everywhere, outside a few Lutheran territories and their universities, after the 1560s).[28] Melanchthon's rigid opponent, Matthias Flacius Illyricus, a leader of the so-called "gnesio

---

[26] Erasmus also played an important role in the application of classical rhetoric to Christian sources and in the development of a textual hermeneutic, as Kathy Eden and Manfred Hoffmann have shown (see their works in the bibliography). See also John W. O'Malley, "Grammar and Rhetoric in the *pietas* of Erasmus," *The Journal of Medieval and Renaissance Studies* 1 (1988): 81–98, who emphasizes the role of grammar over rhetoric in Erasmus' "philosophy of Christ." I focus here on Agricola because the handbooks based upon his dialectics seem to have done the most to accomplish and propagate among early sixteenth-century intellectuals a reconciliation of dialectic and rhetoric. Given the degree to which theology was a logical discourse, this reconciliation seems to me to have been an important prerequisite for the widescale adaptation of rhetoric to Protestant theology. Reformers needed to formulate doctrine in comprehensive terms whose certainty was not merely rhetorical.

[27] Mack, *Renaissance Argument*, p. 286.

[28] Walter J. Ong, *Ramus, Method, and the Decay of Dialogue* (Cambridge, Mass.: Harvard University Press, 1958), pp. 295–318; Robert Kolb, "Melanchthon's Influence on the Exegesis of His Students," *Philip Melanchthon and the Commentary*, ed. T. J. Wengert and M. P. Graham (Sheffield: Academic Press, 1997), pp. 20–47.

Lutherans" in the middle of the century, also adapted rhetorical methods in his treatments of exegesis and doctrine, in his massive *Clavis sacrae scripturae*, the *Key to Sacred Scripture*.[29] Flacius is well known as an opponent of Melanchthon's theological influence in Germany. His work shows that the new methods glanced over the deep lines dividing Lutherans in the third quarter of the century into two camps, one more sympathetic to the Melanchthonian and Calvinian strains of international Protestantism and one resisting it. The exegetical needs of Protestant scholastic theology absorbed rhetoric – just as Catholic preaching had earlier absorbed humanism.[30]

The new rhetorical theology often associated with John Calvin owed a great deal to Melanchthon the rhetorician.[31] It was Melanchthon who expanded the three classical genres of eloquence – judicial, deliberative, and panegyric or epideictic – to include a fourth, the "didactic genre," the *genus* διδασκαλικὸν, as he called it.[32] Within didactic writing, as in the other genres, one might observe a variety of "commonplaces," *loci communes*. According to Cicero, such general ideas could be philosophical or moral, and they could be employed by an orator in many different cases, wherefore they are "common."[33] To Melanchthon and the many Protestant theologians influenced by him, the commonplaces of the didactic genre were doctrinal focal points.[34] They were ideas shared by

---

[29] See Eden, *Hermeneutics and the Rhetorical Tradition*, pp. 90–100; Muller, *Post-Reformation Reformed Dogmatics*, 2:97–108, who notes the elaboration of the *loci* or "common-place" method in the second half of the sixteenth century and the expanding use of philology.

[30] For rhetoric in Catholic preaching and theology: John W. O'Malley, *Praise and Blame in Renaissance Rome: Rhetoric, Doctrine, and Reform in the Sacred Orators of the Papal Court, c. 1450–1521* (Durham: Duke University Press, 1979), pp. 36–76, 123–94; Frederick J. McGinness, *Right Thinking and Sacred Oratory in Counter-Reformation Rome* (Princeton University Press, 1995), pp. 9–61; John W. O'Malley, *The First Jesuits* (Cambridge, Mass.: Harvard University Press, 1993), pp. 253–64; and most especially Marc Fumaroli, *L'Age de l'éloquence* (Geneva: Droz, 1980), pp. 116–391.

[31] William J. Bouwsma, *John Calvin. A Sixteenth Century Portrait* (Oxford University Press, 1988), pp. 113–27; idem, *Calvin's Theology as* Theologia Rhetorica (Berkeley: Center for Hermeneutical Studies, 1987). For a summary of scholarship on Calvin's relation to humanism and his use of rhetoric see Millet, *Calvin et la dynamique de la parole*, pp. 11–24. For rhetoric and Melanchthon's theology see John R. Schneider, "The Hermeneutics of Commentary: Origins of Melanchthon's Integration of Dialectic and Rhetoric," *Philip Melanchthon (1497–1560) and the Commentary*, ed. Timothy J. Wengert and M. Patrick Graham (Sheffield Academic Press, 1997), pp. 20–47.

[32] Philip Melanchthon, *Elementa rhetorices*, in *Phillipis Melanthonis opera quae supersunt omnia*, 13:421. For the development of the didactic genre in Melanchthon's rhetorical writings, see Millet, *Le dynamique de la parole*, pp. 138–141.

[33] Cicero, *De inventione* II, 15, 48; Quintilian, *Institutiones oratoriae*, II, 4, 22; Millet, *Le dynamique de la parole*, p. 97.

[34] Timothy J. Wengert, "The Lutheran Origins of Rhetorical Criticism," *Biblical Interpretation in the Era of the Reformation*, pp. 118–140, here 135. Laplanche, *L'Ecriture, le sacré et l'histoire: Erudits et politiques Protestants devant la Bible en France au xviie siècle* (Amsterdam: Holland University

very diverse passages of scripture, which, insofar as these diverse passages betray the common themes and aims of texts and their authors, could be studied together – and they were, in repeatedly revised compendia like Melanchthon's *Loci communes* and John Calvin's *Institutes of the Christian Religion*, to name only the two most famous.³⁵ The technique presumed the coordination of commentary and theological compendium. It also encouraged dialectic within a rhetorical frame, which is what gave the compendia a systematic structure that followed Cicero's definition of the parts of a speech, as we find it employed, for example, in Calvin's *Institutes*: a presentation of problems and answers (*exordium* and *narratio*), evidence from authoritative, biblical sources (*argumentatio*), and the rebuttal of contrasting points of view (*refutatio*).³⁶ In other words, humanist

Press, 1986), pp. 63–72, 82; Robert Kolb, "Teaching the Text: The Commonplace Method in Sixteenth Century Lutheran Biblical Commentary," *Beiträge zur historischen Theologie* 49 (1987): 571–85; Richard A. Muller, "William Perkins and the Protestant Exegetical Tradition: Interpretation, Style and Method," in William Perkins, *A Commentary on Hebrews 11 (1609 Edition)*, ed. John H. Augustine (New York: Pilgrim Press, 1991), pp. 71–94, here 74–6; idem, "'Scimus enim quod lex spiritualis est': Melanchthon and Calvin on the Interpretation of Romans 7.14–23," *Melanchthon and the Commentary* (Sheffield Academic Press, 1997), pp. 216–37, here 219–20. Muller points out how Calvin used his *Institutes* to explore the structure of biblical arguments from the standpoint of the entire Bible rather than the rhetorical structure of particular books, which suggests a deployment of rhetorical notions of argumentative structure slightly distinct, in its results, from Melanchthon's deployment of rhetoric (which allows more elaborate digressions into doctrine within the commentary). Muller, in *Post-Reformation Reformed Dogmatics*, (Grand Rapids: Baker Book House, 1987), 2: 97–108, notes the elaboration of the *loci* method in the second half of the sixteenth century and continued philological interest. The method was also established among Remonstrants, for example, in the lectures of Conrad Vorstius given at Steinfurt (before he succeeded Jacob Arminius in the theology faculty at Leiden): *Commentarius in omnes epistolas apostolicas exceptis secunda Timotheum, ad Titum, ad Philemon, et ad Hebraeos* (Amsterdam: Guilielmus Blaeus, 1631). In it, the exegesis of each letter begins with an *argumentum et partitio epistolae* (a division of chapters into parts and a description of each), a *paraphrasis* (translation of the text from Greek into Latin), *scholia* (notes on the Greek text), and *loci communes* (the doctrinal contents of each chapter with copious cross references). For the minimal use of the commonplace method in Catholic theology, consider Melquiades Andrés Martín, *La teología española en el siglo XVI*, 2 vols. (Madrid: Editorial Católica, 1976–77), 2:386–424; Jared Wicks, "Doctrine and Theology," *Catholicism in Early Modern History: A Guide to Research*, ed. John O'Malley (St. Louis: Center for Reformation Research, 1988), pp. 227–51, here 235. Some Protestants, however, preferred the method of annotation above the method of common places in biblical interpretation, for example, Matthias Flacius Illyricus and Theodore Beza: *Le temps des Réformes et la Bible*, p. 259.

35 This also provided a strong impetus toward the building of comprehensive "systems" of theology among Protestants. See Richard Muller, *The Unaccommodated Calvin* (Oxford University Press, 2000), pp. 177–81.

36 A rhetorical structure was quite evident to early modern readers, if for no other reason, because it was also reflected in the apparatuses created soon after publication of the 1559 edition that circulated in early editions, for example, the *argumenta* and *marginalia* of William Lawn and the *marginalia* of Nicholaus Colladon and Edmund Bunney. I have examined these in the edition of the *Institutes* published in Calvin's *Opera omnia* (Amsterdam: J. J. Schipper, 1671). See Muller, *Unaccommodated Calvin*, pp. 62–78. Consider also the very detailed study of structure in Millet, *La dynamique de la parole*, pp. 554–656.

adaptations of the classical system of rhetorical invention – the process by which arguments were identified and then fashioned, unfolded, and defended by an author systematically – encouraged the synergy of rhetoric and dialectic in Protestant theology, which was for many the basis of the dependence of theology on biblical narrative.

The didactic genre, through the collection of commonplaces, helped Protestant theologians move beyond ethical preoccupations emphasized by humanism and summarized in a compendium, an *Enchiridion*, as Erasmus had done. The didactic genre allowed Melanchthon and Protestant theologians after him to refine textual, philological, and rhetorical techniques learned from Erasmus and focus on religious doctrines. Early Protestant interpreters, for example Martin Bucer, were from the beginning clearly inclined to do this.[37] There was no need to abandon the humanist conviction that theological discourse equaled admonition. It was just no longer exclusively Erasmus' admonition to a Christianity of virtue, even given how pregnant a notion virtue could be. It was also admonition to adore, to believe, and to obey, which things were provoked, for example, by specific knowledge of God's attributes.[38] Protestant collections of "commonplaces" provided an alternative to traditional textbooks of theology. The alternative seemed a strong one because it rested on biblical language, where within the traits of particular writers there lurked not only common ideas, upon which Protestant confessions were based, but also singular ideas and even a style peculiar to divine speech, God's expressiveness toward human beings. The rhetorical quality of scripture implied, to Protestant scholars, the contact of God in heaven, an ancient text, and an interpreter in the present all speaking the same things, as Olivier Millet has shown in his exhaustive study of Calvin's rhetoric.[39] It was a notion of prophecy, and it coordinated Bible, commentary, and

---

[37] Millet, *Le dynamique de la parole*, p. 141. Bucer did so independent of the new dialectic. His language philosophy was a form of modalism: Irena Backus, "La théorie logique de Martin Bucer: quelques remarques sur les conditions de vérité et sur la prédication chez Pierre Crockaert, Georges de Trébizonde, Ralph Lever et Martin Bucer," *Logique et théologie au xvie siecle: aux sources de l'argumentation de Martin Bucer*, ed. I. Backus, P. Fraenkel, *et al.* (Geneva: Revue de Théologie et de Philosophie, 1980), pp. 27–39 (what Backus describes as "realism" could better be seen as a form of modalism).

[38] In both nature and holy scripture, as in Calvin's *Institutes*, I.i.3, I.x.2. See also Millet, *Le dynamique de la parole*, p. 567, for the strong assertion of the importance of divine attributes made in the first chapter of the French *Institutes* of 1541. Protestant interpreters could thus associate the moral content of the medieval anagogical sense and the doctrinal content of the medieval allegorical sense with the letter of scripture.

[39] See Millet, *La dynamique*, pp. 515–54. Or in the words of Wolfgang Musculus, in the early Elizabethan translation of his *Loci communes*, "as touching their [Christ, the apostles, the prophets, and the patriarchs] doctrin, thei be not dead, thei be not departed from us, thei have not bereaft

religious language, be it in a sermon, a catechism, or a piece of academic writing.

To Protestants, therefore, the context of biblical meaning could be purely literary and predominantly doctrinal at the same time. At its widest dimension, the context of scripture, or of a particular book within scripture, was defined as *scopus* or *status*, which was simply the argumentative goal or question of a piece of writing, "the principal question or a sentence that contains the sum of the matter to which all arguments are to be referred, as to the principal conclusion."[40] Protestants could see these goals within the Bible as rather uniform, doctrinal, and encouraging piety, as Heinrich Bullinger, the Zürich reformer, did when he reduced the entire *scopus* of scripture to the "testament of the Lord."[41] Others more sophisticated, like John Calvin, would rather limit their description of *scopus* in commentaries to the contextual aims of particular books within the Bible; but Calvin would still criticize his peers for not rising above philology by heeding the *scopus* of a book.[42] As Calvin already explained in his "Preface to the Reader" of 1539, in words that remained in all subsequent editions of his *Institutes*, the four books of the *Institutes* were no more than "the sum of religion (*religionis summam*) in all its parts, that if anyone rightly grasps it, it will not be difficult for him to determine what he ought especially to seek in Scripture, and to what *scopus* (*quem in scopum*) he ought to relate its contents."[43] He believed the *Institutes* described the *scopus* of scripture purely in terms relevant to faith, under his famous four rubrics: the knowledge of the Creator, the

---

us of the doctrine of the truth, but by a nere way of scripture thei do talk with us as truly, as sufficiently, and as holsomly, as thei spake with them amongst whom thei were bodily conuersant. So by the benefit of scriptures we have also the Patriarkes, the Prophets, Christ, and the Apostles, no lesse than thei among whom thei lived." Wolfgang Musculus, *Common Places of Christian Religion* (London: Reginald Wolfe, 1563), f. 160r.

[40] Melanchthon, *Elementa rhetorices*, book one, "De statibus," *Opera* 13:429–431. See also Marjorie O'Rourke Boyle, *Erasmus on Language and Method in Theology* (University of Toronto Press, 1977), pp. 75–83.

[41] Bullinger, *Ratio studiorum*, f. 30r. The book was written in 1527 but published posthumously. Similarly, chapter 5 of the First Helvetic Confession alleged: "The *status* of all this canonical Scripture is God clearly wanting to be a man, declaring his benevolence through his son Christ. This benevolence comes to and is received by us by faith alone; it is expressed in true charity towards friends": Philip Schaff, *Creeds of Christendom*, 3 vols. (New York: Harper and Brothers, 1877), 3:211–12. For additional examples, see Muller, *Post-Reformation Reformed Dogmatics*, 2: 211–30.

[42] Such criticism was made in a letter of May 1540 to Pierre Viret, where he directed it at the Basel reformer Johannes Oecolampadius: D. Schellong, *Calvins Auslegung der synoptischen Evangelien* (Munich: Christian Kaiser, 1969), p. 14.

[43] Trans. McNeill, 1:4–5. *Joannis Calvini Opera selecta*, ed. Peter Barth and Wilhelm Niesel, 5 vols. (Munich: Christian Kaiser, 1926–62), 3:6. See also Muller, *Unaccommodated Calvin*, pp. 28–9 and *passim*.

knowledge of God the Redeemer, the way Christ's benefits are received, and the means by which God holds people in Christ's fellowship.

The rhetorical construction of such broad sites of textual meaning also allowed Protestant interpreters to reconsider context microscopically at the level of words; they reassessed the biblical image. The image could no longer render meaning by reference beyond the text. Meaning had to reside in the writing as a whole and in the language of particular passages. For it was, as Heinrich Bullinger explained, context that determined how figurative language was used. Was the image built on an analogy between two things, as in "Christ the lamb," where the meekness of a lamb and the humility of Christ can be compared in the act of sacrifice? Or was the reader confronted by a standard trope, such as those enumerated by Fulgentius (the late fifth-century monk and bishop who unravelled Virgilian myths), Erasmus, and Quintilian: *aenigma, paroemia, ironia, sarcasmus, hyperbole, synechdoche, metaphora, allegoria*, etc.?[44] Either through analogy or trope, the figures in a sentence are understood as meaningful within the "proper meaning" of the sentence, that is, within mundane mechanisms of literary expression. Theological allegory succumbed to redefinition as poetic ornamentation.[45] Martin Luther's early appeal to tropes before his conflict with the papacy, once taken as evidence, however slight, of his debt to humanism, suggests that recourse to rhetorical explanation of imagery accelerated before the Reformation.[46]

Imagery could be defined in a purely textual, non-metaphysical way, without undermining a theologian's ability to make metaphysical assertions. That was a *sine qua non*: one had to make assertions – for example, God exists and Christ is both divine and human – even if one were a Protestant and refused to defend those assertions by formal logic. Without a method of rhetorical invention it was difficult to link a literary approach at the level of a passage with a literary approach at the level of complete books or the Bible as a whole. Late medieval interpreters experimented with literary explanations at the level of passages and relied on theological and dialectical arguments to explain the meaning of complete narratives and the Bible as a whole. In the absence of rhetoric, late medieval scholars were somewhat restricted to words and sentences as contexts of meaning apart from narrative structures. Rhetoric allowed Protestants to do better what late medieval interpreters had begun to do

---

[44] Bullinger, *Ratio studiorum*, ff. 32r–33r.
[45] Millet, *Le dynamique de la parole*, p. 291.
[46] Helmar Junghans, *Der junge Luther und die Humanisten* (Göttingen: Vandenhoeck und Ruprecht, 1985), pp. 241–56.

in their literal exegesis, namely wed textual to theologically discursive knowledge.

3. DIVINE SPEECH

Around the year 1500, Desiderius Erasmus followed the example of the Italian humanist Lorenzo Valla and turned from the study of classical literature to the New Testament. Since his youth he had admired Valla's grammar, *On the Elegance of the Latin Language* (*De linguae latinae elegantia*, which is, as its title proclaims, a treatise on good taste in Latin). He would soon discover Valla's *Collation of the New Testament* in an abbey near Louvain and publish it, in 1505, under a title foreshadowing his own future *Annotations on the New Testament*. Erasmus saw his efforts to restore good Latin and approach afresh the text of the New Testament in Greek as a continuation of Valla's combined grammatical and textual enterprises. His efforts (like Petrarch's long before) were also inspired by St. Jerome, to whose scholarly example Erasmus appealed again and again in self-defense against the critics of his project.[47]

The conjunction of Latin erudition and textual study was a key element of Erasmus' theology, as he explained it in the three prefaces to his Greek New Testament of 1516, the *Paraclesis*, the *Ratio verae theologiae*, and the *Apologia*. Recently, the *Paraclesis* and the *Ratio* (more than the famous treatise of 1503, *The Handbook of the Militant Christian*) have been shown to express systematically the orientation, method, and content of his theology for the remainder of his life.[48] Fundamental to that theology was the conviction that the text of scripture portrays the doctrine of Christ through a peculiar language, in its own way enigmatic.[49] In scripture, Christ spoke without syllogisms and oratorical devices. In the Bible, truth "is the more powerful, the simpler it is."[50] Indeed, "Christ frequently accommodated himself to the weakness of the disciples."[51]

---

[47] Erika Rummel, *Erasmus' Annotations on the New Testament. From Philologist to Theologian* (Toronto: University of Toronto Press, 1986), pp. 5, 15–17. The seeds of "biblical humanism" and the correlation of biblical and secular poetics can also be traced to Petrarch's *De otio religioso*, Coluccio Salutati's *De seculo et religione*, Giannozzo Manetti's translations from Hebrew and Greek into Latin, and Aurelio Brandolini's preface to his *In sacram Hebreorum historiam*: Charles Trinkaus, *"In Our Image and Likeness": Humanity and Divinity in Italian Humanist Thought* (London: Constable, 1970), pp. 563–614; consider also pp. 689–712.

[48] Hofmann, *Rhetoric and Theology, passim.*   [49] Ibid., p. 35.

[50] *Paraclesis*, trans. J. C. Olin, *Christian Humanism and the Reformation* (New York: Fordham University Press, 1965), p. 94.

[51] *Ratio seu methodus compendio perveniendi ad veram Theologiam*, Desiderius Erasmus, *Ausgewählte Werke*, ed. A. Holborn and H. Holborn (Munich: C. H. Beck, 1933, reprinted 1964), p. 203.

The simple language of the Bible was an idiom in its own right, which Erasmus tried to replicate in the "paraphrases" that he composed after the publication of his Greek New Testament, but this idiom also presented special challenges.[52] The simplicity and clarity of scripture could not be taken for granted. Some of its tropes and allegories had to be unraveled with the help of classical learning. In addition, one must enhance biblical language rhetorically by paraphrase, making the Bible more transparent – not improving upon it as Erasmus' opponents alleged.[53] Textual criticism, grammar, and rhetoric sufficed to the task, when employed by a soul genuinely seeking to follow Christ. The idea that biblical language was simple and that this simplicity was a literary feature of it was a common patristic teaching, as we have seen.[54] It was widely available in the Middle Ages in the first prologue to the Bible, which was Jerome's letter to Paulinus.

When Erasmus edited and annotated that letter in his 1516 edition of Jerome, he revealed in a passing anecdote his awareness of medieval commentary on it, but he ignored the passage treating the unlearned wisdom of the apostles.[55] Perhaps he hoped to disassociate his source from scholastic commentary, since his own prefaces to the New Testament stood in the place of the traditional New Testament prologue and, in content at least, were very comparable to Jerome's letter to Paulinus: one could say that his prefaces replaced the traditional prologue.[56] Jerome's letter was mentioned neither in the *Paraclesis* nor in the *Ratio verae theologiae*, perhaps again because that letter was associated with traditional scholastic commentary. Erasmus nevertheless embraced Jerome's sense of humble speech in scripture as the basis of Christian culture. In those works, he repeatedly contrasted the simplicity of Christ's teaching and

---

[52] Rummel, *Erasmus' Annotations*, pp. 103–5.
[53] A point Erasmus made in response to Noel Beda's accusation that it was wrong to alter biblical style: Rummel, *Erasmus' Annotations*, pp. 98–9. His method was to resolve obscure passages in the Greek text of the New Testament in several ways: "in some cases it was a matter of correcting a grammatical error or replacing an unidiomatic expression with a proper Latin phrase; in other instances a polysemous and therefore ambiguous word had to be replaced with an unequivocal term; sometimes the meaning of a sentence could be clarified by restructuring it, at other times a fuller translation was required to convey the meaing of a succinct Greek phrase. It is obvious from the corrective measures listed that the aim of achieving clarity overlapped with another goal: correct Latin usage. The two objectives are closely linked by the tenet that a grammatically and idiomatically correct translation is at the same time also a lucid version" (ibid., pp. 90–1). Erasmus did also admit that the apostles' style was sometimes bad and mistaken: ibid., pp. 140–2.
[54] Page 112, above.
[55] *Collected Works of Erasmus*, 61:207–27, esp. 209–10, 218–19.
[56] Valla, by contrast, began his *Collatio Novi Testamenti* with Jerome's letter to pope Damasus, which served as preface to the New Testament in the medieval Vulgate: Lorenzo Valla, *Collatio Novi Testamenti*, ed. A. Perosa (Florence: Sansoni, 1970), pp. 3–10.

the rhetorical methods appropriate to handle it with the work of theologians and their complicated syllogisms and obscure ideas.

Protestant theologians adapted the Erasmian and patristic notion of biblical simplicity as a foundation of religious reason. Martin Luther and all those influenced by him insisted on the simplicity of scripture as one of its foremost characteristics, whether they learned this from Jerome (in Erasmus' edition), Augustine, John Chrysostom (an author that Erasmus also promoted again and again), or in the prefaces to Erasmus' New Testament. In Luther and his early followers the simplicity of the Gospel and the sincerity of a textual, biblical approach to theology stood in stark contrast to scholastic resistance to vernacular biblical translation, scholastic dialectics, and the necessity of ecclesiastical authority as arbiter of interpretations. That is, the context of their notion of biblical simplicity was polemical, and it was created not by Luther but first by the satirical literature that burgeoned around the year 1510, to which Erasmus (along with Thomas Murner, Sebastian Brant, and others) contributed a substantial part. It intensified during that decade in the controversies over Johannes Reuchlin and indulgences. Thus, the polemic came to be preoccupied with questions of translation, and especially among the first Protestants it set the clarity of scripture against the teaching authority of bishops, popes, and theologians. Questions of translation briefly eclipsed the patristic and Erasmian biblical literary ideal as a basis of culture.[57]

It did not take long for Protestants to broaden their idea of biblical language, by emphasizing the congruence of rhetorical and what we might call fideistic approaches to interpretation. In Luther's first series of biblical lectures, the *Dictata super Psalterium* of 1512 to 1515, he had a notion of scripture's particular elegance.[58] To this he added the idea that God communicates in biblical language both externally and internally, so that there is subjective confirmation and a kind of interaction of divine self-expression and human attentiveness in the act of reading.[59] Subjective confirmation was, in turn, related to other emerging aspects of Luther's theology already before the outbreak of the indulgence controversy in the autumn of 1517, most importantly his sense of the difference between

---

[57] So for example, Andreas Osiander, in his 1522 preface to the Bible, emphasized the importance of studying biblical languages, as the recent work of Erasmus had shown, but he treats rhetoric not at all: Andreas Osiander, *Gesamtausgabe*, 1:64–66.

[58] Brian Gerrish, *Grace and Reason. A Study in the Theology of Luther* (Oxford: Clarendon Press, 1962), pp. 28–42; B. Hägglund, "Evidentia sacrae scripturae. Bemerkungen zum 'Schriftprinzip' bei Luther," *Vierhundertfünfzig Jahre lutherische Reformation, 1517–1967. Festschrift für Franz Lau zum 60. Geburtstag* (Göttingen: Vandenhoeck und Ruprecht, 1967), pp. 122–3. See also Martin Brecht, *Martin Luther*, trans. J. Schaaf, 3 vols. (Philadelphia: Fortress, 1985–1993), pp. 128–37.

[59] Junghans, *Der junge Luther*, pp. 275–86. Consider also Brecht, *Martin Luther*, pp. 130–44.

letter and Spirit and the need for readers of the Bible to experience the text internally through faith.[60] It was this emphasis on faith that distinguished his work most from the exegesis of his predecessor as professor of the Bible at Wittenberg, Johannes Staupitz.[61] By 1525, Luther's subjective emphasis was complemented by a strong statement of the clarity of scripture that drew on Erasmus: obscurity in the Bible is due to human ignorance of its vocabulary and grammar, Luther said, but its clarity exists both externally and internally, in the external word preached and the internal word known through the Spirit of God in the heart.[62]

The first Protestants emphasized this subjective aspect of biblical interpretation, the internal clarity of the word in the heart, which interpreters of Luther have often observed and associated with mysticism.[63] We find it at the beginning of the Swiss Reformation, in the writings of Huldrich Zwingli: for example, in the sermons he delivered to the Dominican nuns of Oetenbach in the summer of 1522 and then published under the title *On the Clarity and Certainty of the Word of God*.[64] The sermons begin with an

---

[60] The idea of faith as a form of certainty in the word of Christ already appears in Luther's marginal notes to Peter Lombard's *Sentences* of 1509/10: Berndt Hamm, "Warum wurde für Luther der Glaube zum Zentralbegriff des christlichen Lebens?" *Die frühe Reformation in Deutschland als Umbruch*, ed. B. Moeller (Gütersloh: Gütersloher Verlagshaus, 1998), pp. 103–27, here 113–14. See also Gerhard Ebeling, *Evangelische Evangelienauslegung. Eine Untersuchung zu Luthers Hermeneutik* (Munich: Christian Kaiser, 1942; reprinted Darmstadt: Wissenschaftliche Buchgesellschaft, 1962), pp. 274ff and idem, "Die Anfänge von Luthers Hermeneutik," *Zeitschrift für Theologie und Kirche* 48 (1951): 172–230, reprinted in idem, *Lutherstudien*, 3 vols. (Tübingen: J. C. B. Mohr, 1971–89), 1:1–68, dating a preliminary hermeneutical breakthrough between 1513 and 1515. Preus argued that Luther departed from "medieval" interpretation by perceiving people in the Old Testament as Christians under the promise of future salvation, and he presented this as a correction of Ebeling. But Ebeling pointed out that the terms of an evangelical, Lutheran dichotomy applied to both Old and New Testaments as a dichotomy of testaments (i.e. covenants) ("Anfänge," p. 45). The same was found in Luther's 1517/18 lectures on Hebrews: Kenneth Hagen, *A Theology of Testament in the Young Luther. The Lectures on Hebrews* (Leiden: Brill, 1974), esp. pp. 68–70. Cf. Preus, *Shadow*, pp. 171–3, 200–11, esp. 200 n. 1; consider also pp. 148, 181 n. 12). David Steinmetz has noted how, in Luther's *Dictata super Psalterium*, the word of God is experienced by the saints in this life in the mode of the Spirit. Moreover, in the external words of God given to prophets and patriarchs (i.e. the text of the Bible), Christians receive by faith the future rewards signified by those words: "in certain circumstances the possession of the signs is the possession of the things signified": David C. Steinmetz, *Luther and Staupitz. An Essay in the Intellectual Origins of the Protestant Reformation* (Durham, NC: Duke University Press, 1980), p. 59.

[61] Ibid., p. 66.

[62] *De servo arbitrio*, WA 18:699–703; Rudolf Hermann, "Von der Klarheit der heiligen Schrift: Untersuchungen und Erörterungen über Luthers Lehre von der Schrift in 'De servo arbitrio,'" *Studien zur Theologie Luthers und des Luthertums* (Göttingen: Vandenhoeck und Ruprecht, 1981), pp. 170–255, pp. 233–8.

[63] See Brecht, *Martin Luther*, pp. 137–44.

[64] *Von Klarheit und Gewissheit des Wortes Gottes, Huldreich Zwinglis sämtliche Werke*, ed. E. Egli and G. Finsler, vol. 1 (also *Corpus Reformatorum*, vol. 88) (Berlin: C. A. Schwetschke und Sohn, 1905), pp. 328–84. An English translation may be found in *Zwingli and Bullinger*, trans. and ed. Geoffrey W. Bromiley, vol. 24 of *The Library of Christian Classics* (Philadelphia: Westminster, 1953), pp. 59–95.

anthropology. Human beings, Zwingli said, are a picture (*bildnus*) of God, insofar as they are capable of desiring blessedness, a desire that springs from the spiritual image made at the creation of Adam and renewed, according to the apostle Paul, through Christ. This relationship between divine maker and human image implied to Zwingli the dependence of human beings on the divine word: since a person is a picture of God, only the word of the creator and painter can give joy and certainty.[65] "So strong, certain, and alive was the word of God," "so powerful," "so starck, gwüß und lebendig war das wort gottes, so krefftig," he says repeatedly, that God can accomplish his will by the mere utterance of it, as is evident from many passages of Genesis and the New Testament.[66] Having proved on biblical evidence the fact of this power, one would expect the meaning of scripture to be transparent. "How clear is it, then? Why does God speak through parables and riddles; does he want his word to be understood?"[67] Zwingli regarded this as an insolent question, since God need not give account of divine choices and actions to human beings. But he answered it nonetheless. God used parables and riddles to provoke human interest: the wise person will try to uncover the mystery, and once having done so, will treasure the meaning all the more.[68] There is, then, a reciprocity between the divine word and those who hear it, and this reciprocity has as its prerequisite the anthropology with which Zwingli began. Human beings are naturally dependent upon the divine word that gives joy and certainty. Likewise, understanding can only occur within God's favor. When the Word of God is not believed, God's judgment is at hand.[69] In the background of reading and comprehension is communion between God and a believing soul, but this mutual exchange takes place with the word itself. Scripture, Zwingli explained, offers its own light. Such is the power of the divine word that comprehension occurs simply as the words are spoken, whenever they are heard in faith, as Zwingli shows from numerous passages of the Old and New Testaments.[70] From the New Testament passages, he expands the argument to include a rejection of the human traditions that obscure the message directly conveyed to believing souls by the Holy Spirit in the Bible and the need for total resignation to the divine will before

---

[65] Zwingli, *Von Klarheit*, pp. 342–53.
[66] He also briefly discusses passages from the prophet Ezekiel: ibid., pp. 353–8.
[67] Ibid., p. 358: "Ee wir anhebind von der clarheit des gotsworts reden, wellent wir fürkummen, das nit die fyend siner clarheit harnach widerredind, sprechende: Wie klar ist es dann? Warumb redt er durch glychnussen und räterschen, wil er, das sin wort verstanden werde?"
[68] Ibid., pp. 358–60. [69] Ibid., p. 361. [70] Ibid., pp. 361–70.

the Gospel can be understood.[71] The Gospel is more than the writings of Matthew, Mark, Luke, and John. It comprises the whole will of God proclaimed to human beings, so that there is no truly divine message apart from the message of the Gospel.

In 1522 the program of reform at Zürich, as at other cities, was modest, if its message was robust, and these convictions fit the day. Zwingli broke the Lenten fast, took a wife, debated with friars, and preached. Like him, many civic preachers with a humanistic education claimed to preach purely from scripture. In reality, they mostly complained from scripture – against materialistic religion, the papacy, and scholastic theology.[72] This attracted the interest of the more and less learned laity who already enjoyed the religious satires of people like Murner and Erasmus; but now the familiar complaints were reinforced by scriptural discourse, by preaching. With it came homiletical criticism, that is, the ability to distinguish between biblical teaching and the rest. This depended upon the cultivation of a particular kind of subjectivity, as Zwingli pointed out in his own appropriation of the Lutheran theme. His treatise on scriptural clarity ended with a list of twelve brief rules of interpretation, by which one might also test preachers, and which promote a listener-oriented, soul-oriented criticism of sermons. Seek regeneration from God, give preference to the humble and resist the proud, identify the work of God through the word in personal renewal, the diminishing of self, and the feeling of joy.[73] Zwingli's rules of interpretation address the will of the reader. These are the conditions of textual meaning. It was a preacher's conceit – that sermons will reform people, then society, from inside out – and it was widespread. This peculiar form of reading, as a kind of religious subjectivity, seemed just as relevant to the urban and territorial impositions of reform of the 1530s and to semi-clandestine Calvinist churches "under the cross" in the 1550s as it was to Luther and Zwingli in the early 1520s. From it came the distinctive Protestant doctrines of the clarity and authority of the Bible.

Early Protestants agreed on the importance of subjective apprehension of the divine word in scripture. Reformation pamphlets alleged that the

---

[71] This also involves polemic against religious orders and pilgrimages. Ibid., pp. 370–82.
[72] Nicely summarized by Euan Cameron, *The European Reformation* (Oxford University Press, 1991), pp. 106–10. However, the fact that scriptural citations, for example in Reformation pamphlets, now implied the juxtaposition of ecclesiastical authority and biblical teaching could grant the citations a greater, more exclusive, authority than they would earlier have enjoyed: Bernd Moeller and Karl Stackmann, *Städtische Predigt in der Frühzeit der Reformation* (Göttingen: Vandenhoeck und Ruprecht, 1996), pp. 298–9.
[73] Zwingli, *Von Klarheit*, pp. 383–4.

message of scripture, the Gospel, was personally addressed to the reader who read with faith, for the sake of overcoming the corruption of the human will and effecting salvation.[74] Luther's associate at Wittenberg, Philip Melanchthon, relied on both the law and the Gospel to give testimony to their own truthfulness in the hearts of believers. The Bible is not, he once said in an interesting statement of scripture's symbolic character, composed of Egyptian hieroglyphs but stands as a kind of effigy of Christ, who took on flesh in order to be known by human beings.[75] Martin Bucer, architect of the Reformation in Strasbourg, insisted that no comprehension of scripture is possible apart from faith, which to Protestants of the 1530s must have seemed a truism. The authority of scripture comes from Christ and cannot be recognized except by the action of Christ's Spirit in a person.[76] Faith is the prerequisite of reading.

The fideistic approach of the early Protestants was supported by rhetoric. In the early 1520s Melanchthon suggested that scripture possessed thematic unity[77] and rhetorical embellishment together: "The other sacred writers [in the Old Testament] also have been mindful of this grace, but not clearly enough to be understood unless Paul had illuminated the whole argument by so many epistles and disputations.

[74] Moeller and Stackmann, *Städtische Predigt*, pp. 312–19.
[75] Letter of Melanchthon to Johannes Hess, February, 1520, *Melanchthons Briefwechsel*, 10 vols., ed. Hans Scheible (Sttutgart: Foman-Holzboog, 1997–2000), 1:7; Melanchthon, *Selected Writings*, trans. C. L. Hill (Minneapolis: Augsburg, 1962), p. 51. But he added late in life external testimonies, which encouraged a more objective approach to biblical authority in subsequent Lutheranism: Werner Elert, *The Structure of Lutheranism*, trans. W. A. Hansen (St. Louis: Concordia, 1962), p. 197. The first Lutheran collection of proofs for scriptural authority was produced in lectures by Georg Major in Wittenberg and published in German translation by a former student in 1544: Timothy J. Wengert, "Georg Major (1502–1574). Defender of Wittenberg's Faith and Melanchthonian Exegete," *Melanchthon in seinen Schülern*, ed. H. Scheible (Wiesbaden: Harrassowitz, 1997), pp. 129–55, here 132. See also Otto Ritschl, *Dogmengeschichte des Protestantismus*, 4 vols. (Leipzig: J. C. Hinrichs, and Göttingen: Vandenhoeck und Ruprecht, 1908–27), 1:108–21. Ritschl associated the emerging Protestant scholastic approach to biblical authority with a doctrine of inspiration which he found first formulated by Heinrich Bullinger and especially John Calvin: ibid., pp. 62–68, 174–5. Edward Dowey tried to limit the significance of this doctrine and its objective approach to authority to Calvin's view of God as creator, dissociating it from the experience of revelation of the redeeming God in Christ: E. Dowey, *The Knowledge of God in Calvin's Theology* (New York: Columbia, 1952), pp. 86–147. Richard Muller has recently emphasized the need to develop objective definitions of biblical authority in the context of confessional polemics in the second half of the sixteenth century, which presumes a more natural development of the Protestant "scholastic" approach: *Post-Reformation Reformed Dogmatics*, 2:86–96.
[76] From section 9 of Bucer's preface to his *Commentary on Romans* published at Strasbourg, 1536: *Common Places of Martin Bucer*, trans. D. F. Wright (Appleford: Sutton Courtenay Press, 1972), pp. 185–6.
[77] Grace, insofar as "peace of conscience and absolute virtue" are concerned, was known before the time of Christ by both Jews and Gentiles. Melanchthon, *Declamatiuncula divi Pauli doctrinam*, in *Melanchthons Briefwechsel*, no. 76, 1:166–76, and *Selected Writings*, pp. 31–46, here 37–8.

With what rhetorical figures, what flowers and ornaments of speech he captivates the reader in his works I can by no means express in words."[78] Those who seek "the beauty and structure of virtue" need look no further. The "clever thoughts of philosophers" have become obsolete.[79] The idea that faith in Christ provides subjective confirmation of the truth and authority of the Bible presupposes a theological conviction shared by Luther, Zwingli, and all Protestants, namely, that scripture is all about that experience, and this message is obvious to those who believe. The tautology – that belief indicates the thematic unity of the Bible and perception of that unity confirms faith – was ignored.[80] Rhetoric helped Protestants ignore it because rhetoric taught them to see the main argument of the Bible as an objective literary feature, and as such it provided the starting point for all discussions of argumentative structure in particular books and the commonplaces treated there. As Stephen Burnett has recently pointed out, Martin Luther criticized the Hebraist Sebastian Münster and Erasmus alike for preoccupation with philology and a failure to subject the meaning of words to the *res*, the subject matter, of the entire Bible.[81]

Scholars could now redefine this theological conviction in literary terms as "scope." The "scope" of the Bible was, foremost, the grand theme of salvation, articulated in various ways, for example, as "grace" according to Melanchthon, or "the testament of the Lord" according to Heinrich Bullinger, Zwingli's successor in Zürich.[82] All of scripture, Wolfgang Musculus argued, consists of four parts: the knowledge of God, faith, godly love, and justice, and these themes are set out and examined systematically in his treatment of commonplaces.[83] Exegesis is only

---

[78] Ibid.   [79] Ibid.

[80] There was a similar tautology in the late medieval idea that papal authority confirmed true scriptural interpretations, which authority itself was biblically proven: Ocker, "Fusion," pp. 140–1, n. 34.

[81] Stephen G. Burnett, "Reformation-Era Christian Hebraism at a Crossroads: Martin Luther, Sebastian Münster, and the Proper Use of Jewish Biblical Commentaries," unpublished paper presented to the Sixteenth Century Studies Conference, Toronto, Canada, October 1998. I am grateful to Prof. Burnett for providing me with a copy of his paper.

[82] For Bullinger see p. 197, above. Consider also Johannes Brenz, *Die rechte und warhafftige Außlegung des gantzen Gesatz Gottes allen menschen hoch von noetten zu wissen*, first published in German and Latin (*Argumenta et sacrae scripturae summa, librorum veteris uidelicet et novi testamenti*) in 1544 and reprinted at least fourteen times in the sixteenth century. W. Köhler, *Bibliographia Brentiana* (Berlin: C. A. Schwetschke und Sohn, 1904), p. 57 no. 135, p. 58 no. 137.

[83] Musculus, *Common Places of Christian Religion*, f. 160r–160v, where he also insists that the doctrine of faith in question includes both a general faith in God as creator and a special faith in Christ as redeemer. Calvin viewed his *Institutes of the Christian Religion* as a collection of commonplaces (as his prefatory letter to the reader of 1539 and later editions makes clear) centered around similar dual themes (knowledge of God the creator and of Christ the redeemer, as the opening

complete when it has established articles of faith or exhortation.[84] Scripture is a labyrinth, said Matthias Flacius Illyricus, through which *scopus* leads the way.[85] Scope could be attributed to human authorship, for example in the commentary on the Epistle to the Romans by Johannes Brenz, architect of the Reformation in Würtemberg, where he introduced the author, the apostle Paul, as a minister of the Gospel whose authority stems from Christ. He then summarized, in typical Protestant fashion, Paul's argument in the Epistle. John Calvin approached the scope of a book in a similarly particular way, emphasizing the intentions of individual biblical authors.[86] Any such concession to the authorial role of individual writers betrays sensitivity to the historical circumstances of writing and the historical conditions that color the meaning of the text, but nevertheless, the interpreters' interest was less historicized and more preoccupied with the coordination of divine and human minds. Whether handled on the grand scale of central ideas in the Bible or on the limited scale of the themes of a particular book or author, doctrine, as the sum total of divine discourse, circumscribed biblical literature and served as the conclusion of methodical analysis.

Rhetoric helped interpreters unite diverse interests: the doctrinal coherence of the Bible that I just considered, the polemical need to overcome hierarchical church authority (the need continued well beyond the beginning of the Reformation), and the conviction of a subjective experience of the divine word accomplished by faith.[87] Rhetoric helped them unite these diverse interests in what they understood to be objective terms. Quintilian's *Institutiones Oratoriae* was rediscovered by Poggio Bracciolini, a Roman papal secretary attending the Council of Constance, at the Monastery of St. Gall in the early fifteenth century,

---

chapters of book 1 make clear), taking a Ciceronian approach of repeating a few strong ideas (as is very apparent to anyone who has read the *Institutes* from beginning to end). See also Muller, *Unaccommodated Calvin*.

[84] A common conviction among Protestant interpreters of south Germany and Switzerland in the fourth decade of the sixteenth century: *Le temps des Réformes et la Bible*, p. 247.

[85] Ibid., pp. 260–1.

[86] J. Brenz, *Explicatio Epistolae Pauli ad Romanos*, ed. S. Strohm (Tübingen: J. C. B. Mohr, 1986), 1:3–6. His exposition of Ephesians, by contrast, began with brief observations about the city of Ephesus, Paul, and the "loci insigniores in hac epistola." J. Brenz, *Kommentar zum Briefe des Apostels Paulus an die Epheser nach der Handschrift der Vaticana Cod. Pal. lat. 1836*, ed. W. Köhler (Heidelberg: Carl Winter, 1935), p. 8. In both cases, his prefatory remarks happen also to resemble the kind of prefatory remarks made in early medieval commentaries: Minnis, *Medieval Theory*, pp. 16–17. For Calvin, see p. 197, above.

[87] A vivid example is provided by Lambert Daneau, analyzed by Olivier Fatio, *Méthode et théologie* (Geneva: Droz, 1976), pp. 63–87. See also Richard Muller, *Ad Fontes Argumentorum. The Sources of Reformed Theology in the Seventeenth Century*, vol. 40 of Utrechtse theologische reeks (Utrecht: Faculteit der Godgeleerdheid, 1999).

and it transformed the study of rhetoric in the fifteenth and early sixteenth centuries.[88] Whereas the Middle Ages knew the classical sources of rhetoric in the partial form of technique (taught by Cicero's *De inventione* and *Rhetorica ad Herennium*) and divided it into discrete poetic, epistolary, and preaching disciplines, Quintilian for the first time provided a rationale for its use. "Poggio made it possible...for a reader to view rhetoric as part of an integrated social system built around a respect for civic life."[89] It was in the region of the mind where style passes over to attitudes that rhetoric took hold of religion. The idea of biblical simplicity taught by Erasmus, Jerome, Augustine, Gregory of Nazianzus, and others seemed consistent with Quintilian's insistence that direct, clear speech, *perspicuitas*, is a crucial feature of eloquence, and this encouraged the fusion of classical rhetoric and faith.[90] The simplicity and clarity of scriptural rhetoric was, after all, the Gospel – a particular message that was embraced by souls. This indicated the usefulness of the Bible, but that purpose stood against ecclesiastical tradition. As Wolfgang Musculus, the Augsburg reformer, complained in a typical argument that recalls the polemics of the early Reformation (he argues the connection of biblical simplicity and faith), the church is corrupt; how can anyone rely on it? He demurred (I quote the early Elizabethan translation):

The adversaries crie out, that the holy scriptures be to darke, to gather any certaine iudgement out of them. Let them make answer unto Augustine,[91] who beying of contrary opinion noteth this: The holy spirite hath so nobly and holsamely tempered the holye scriptures, that he might with the easy places of it serue the gredy honger of menne, and with the darker places take away our loathesomnes. For there is no point almost found of the darkest of it, which is not moste playnely spoken in some other place.... But they whiche be euill affected towards the doctrine of the truth, have their mindes so blinded, that they can not abide the light of the holy scriptures. Wherefore the same which is to godly men cleerer than the sunne, is unto them darker than any cloude. Yf the gospel of God bee darke, it is darke unto them that do peryshe, sayth

---

[88] *Contemporaries of Erasmus*, s.v. Bracciolini, Poggio.
[89] Murphy, *Rhetoric in the Middle Ages*, p. 360.
[90] Consider Heinrich Bullinger, *De scripturae sanctae auctoritate* (Zürich: Froschauer, 1538), f. 33v; John Calvin, *Commentarius in Epistolam Pauli ad Romanos*, ed. T. H. L. Parker (Leiden: Brill, 1981), p. 1; Girardin, *Rhétorique et théologie. Calvin, le commentaire de l'Epitre aux Romains* (Paris: Editions Beauchesne, 1979) pp. 228–30; Matthias Flacius Illyricus, *Clavis scripturae sanctae* (Basel: Sebastian Henricpetri, 1567), 2:176, 450ff. esp. 463–6 ("De simplicitate sermonis sacri"). For Erasmus see Hoffmann, *Rhetoric and Theology*, p. 174.
[91] The margin provides the reference: *De doctrina christiana* ii.6.

the Apostle, whose myndes the god of this worlde, the bellye, glorye, selfe loue, hatered, etc. hath blynded, so that the light of the gospell of the glorye of Christ dothe not syne unto them.[92]

Rhetorical method allowed early Protestants to assume the literal clarity of texts and to insist on a convergence of voices, if you will, an extremely peculiar conversation between biblical saints and apostles, God, and human beings here and now. It also allowed them to advocate a double opinion about rhetoric not unlike that of Jerome: pagan rhetoric is vain and limited in its usefulness; nevertheless it is useful, even important, when it is made subject to a living voice. Christ, the apostles, the prophets, and the patriarchs of ancient Israel are alive, "As touching their doctrin, thei be not dead, thei be not departed from us," Musculus said.[93] For scripture is a place far better than the "garden of pleasure, out of which Adam was thruste out for his disobedience." For those who believe, it is another garden,

wherein they doo heare the uoyces and oracles of God, they doo see the appearynges of the Angels, they be conuersant with the holy Patriarches, Prophetes, with Christ him self, and the Apostles, they haue the most pleasaunt ayer of the holy spirite breadeth upon them, they doo feed of the tree of lyfe, not onely taking no hurte, but excedying profite, ye they do eate of the tree of lyfe, and bee made partakers of it for euer, they doo walke betwixt the most bewtifull and fertile trees, and they bee so cherished with the delites of this garden, that they wote not whether thei by in body or out of the bodie, and doo utterly forget all wordly matters, ye and all trouble, care and afflictions also.[94]

To this the "writinge of the Oratours and Philosophers" compares badly: it is "a drye and thurstie desert... full of the barren sande of hungrye talk, wherin is nothyng but uile shardes of uayne knowledge." One may read from "this deserte of Ethnike wrytynge," but it must not be "the principall studie"; it must be "the seruant" of faith, "so that it deceaue not the mindes of the readers with the allurementes of painted speach, but do dispatch from it the huyngry and emptie soules, to the aboundance of the holy Scriptures."[95] The holy conversation that God undertook with prophets, apostles, and souls in Musculus' day created a concert of voices that granted Protestant theologians tremendous self-confidence,

---

[92] Musculus, *Common Places of Christian Religion*, f. 151r. For an excellent overview of Musculus' exegesis see *Le temps des Réformes et la Bible*, pp. 246–9.
[93] Musculus, *Common Places*, f. 160r.
[94] Ibid., f. 162v. [95] Ibid., f. 162v–163r.

as has recently been observed in the writings of John Calvin.[96] The Bible becomes a place, a garden of pleasure, where one converses with spiritual (and supernatural) friends. It is a school, a "school of the Holy Spirit," wrote Calvin in 1539,[97] where everything taught is important. That was an anthropological claim. The Spirit, after all, did its work in people, not in books – creating and confirming faith, performing the good in passively justified sinners, and granting them confidence in God's good will and salvation.

By the middle of the sixteenth century, Catholic, Lutheran, and Calvinist confessions became entrenched, and biblical exegesis, using the methods developed by the previous generation, helped establish them.[98] Entrenchment was further served by a new interest among Protestants in Aristotelian forms of argument.[99] In the second half of the sixteenth century, Protestants heightened the objective appearance of the holy conversation, by arguing and listing evidence for the supernatural quality of divine speech, by explaining the mechanism (inspiration) that put God's words in the writings that were made long ago, and by listing rules for correct interpretation that combined rhetorical, theological, and spiritual criteria.[100] They could find a precedent for resting biblical authority on inspiration in the thought of the late thirteenth-century theologian John Duns Scotus.[101] But it would be wrong to conclude that mechanical views of inspiration dominated late medieval views of the

[96] Millet, *Dynamique de la parole*, pp. 525–46. Consider also Engammare, "Calvin: A Prophet without a Prophecy," *Church History* 67 (1998), 643–61, *passim*.

[97] *Institutio religionis Christianae*, III.xxi.3, ed. P. Barth and W. Niesel, *Opera selecta*, 5 vols. (Munich: C. Kaiser, 1959), 4:372.

[98] *Le temps des Réformes et la Bible*, pp. 252–53.

[99] In the exegesis of Theodore Beza, for example, who juxtaposed Aristotle with Ramus' logic: *Le temps des Réformes et la Bible*, p. 439. The return to dialectical argumentation in Protestant theology could also be facilitated by Melanchthon's Aristotelianism, as in the case of Beza's colleague Lambert Daneau: Fatio, *Méthode et théologie*, pp. 35–62.

[100] For evidence of biblical authority and inspiration, see note 75, above. For rules of interpretation, consider Zacharius Ursinus, *Doctrinae christianae compendium seu commentarii catechetici* (Geneva: Eustathius Vignon, 1589): facing p. 1 immediately following the index, he lists "causae cur homines non intelligunt scripturas sacras" (1. caecitas naturalis, 2. sapientia carnis, 3. sine amore eas legunt, 4. praeiudicium hominum, 5. impoenitentia, 6. non emendandi studio eas legunt), "regulae ad intelligendas scripturas necessariae" (1. preces ut spiritus sanctus tollat caecitatem, 2. lecturi scripturas abnegent seipsos, 3. adsit animus discendi cupidus, 4. cor conversum, 5. animus plenus amore Dei, 6. finis est gloria Dei, vitae, doctrinae et morum emendatio in nobis), and "causae cur parum proficiamus in scripturis" (1. intermissio, 2. ignorantia vocabulorum, 3. ignorantia scopi, 4. ignorantia praecipuarum partium, 5. ignorantia summae tum legis tum evangelii, 6. non sequi analogiam fidei et consensum scripturarum, 7. excursus extra limites scripturae, 8. contemptus interpretum, 9. neglectus principalis argumenti, 10. nimia insolentia ἐν τῷ ῥητῷ).

[101] For Scotus see Seybold, *Die Offenbarung*, p. 142.

Bible or the concerns of later sixteenth-century Protestants, a conclusion easily reached if inspiration is understood purely in the context of text-making rather than in a broader anthropological context, such as we know it, for example, in the writings of Martin Luther.[102] Behind the emerging "scholastic" Protestant definitions of biblical authority stood an early Protestant conviction of the convergence of voices in scriptural study that (1) was partly facilitated by rhetoric, (2) remained consistent with specific views of religious experience, (3) made a sharp contrast with speculative theology, and (4) stood as a foundation for what they regarded as a restored church free of corrupt power and erroneous traditions. Scripture alone, they said, can serve as a norm for faith, and this "principle," as it came to be known, was tied to assumptions about the nature of biblical literature. The Bible's divine speech possesses a rhetoric that aims to create an experience of God.

Both the late medieval reliance on inspiration and the Protestant reliance on faith subordinated the reader to divine action and put him or her in the context of an experience of redemption shared by prophets, apostles, and saints. Wolfgang Musculus' "garden of pleasure," paradise in a book, described late medieval exegesis as well as his own. The hermeneutical difference between Musculus and his Catholic predecessors was the fact that his predecessors approached the text at the level of sentences, while Musculus and his Protestant contemporaries approached it at the level of discourse. This does not mean that late medieval interpreters looked at biblical meaning in piecemeal fashion. They connected a biblical sentence to broad regions of meaning, to comprehensive religious and philosophical truth. But their best tool was logic. They lacked a literary method for handling the narrative construction of the Bible as a whole.[103] In other words, before the rise of humanism in theology, the place where discrete biblical meanings congealed in a coherent body of knowledge was the science of theology. The adaptation of classical rhetoric in the Reformation facilitated another way of connecting discrete biblical meanings in a coherent body of knowledge. Protestant interpreters argued that it was the Bible as a whole text, as a book, the aggregate of all the narrative parts. The difference from

---

[102] Cf. Otto Ritschl, tracing the seventeenth-century's views of verbal dictation back through Flacius to Zwingli, Bullinger, Bucer, and Calvin: *Dogmengeschichte des Protestantismus*, 1:62–68, 142–52, 166–73.

[103] The only late medieval interpreter that I know who relied systematically on the structure of biblical arguments in the entire Bible and in a single book (the textual structure of divine covenants) was John Baconthorpe in his commentary on Matthew. See Ocker, "Fusion."

late medieval textuality was slight, but significant. Like late medieval interpreters, the Protestants believed that biblical knowledge was theology. But Protestants could believe that their theology was nothing more than a summary of biblical teachings put in order.

Matthias Flacius Illyricus, the Lutheran theologian of the mid-sixteenth century applauded by Wilhelm Dilthey as the author of the first treatise on hermeneutics, divided medieval interpretation into two epochs, one governed by authorities and another governed by monks and theologians stirring "various superstitions and the ignorant thorniness of corrupt philosophy" into their expositions. He was correct insofar as he identified the fusion of external ideas with exegesis as a dominant characteristic of medieval commentaries.[104] But how did the new theologians differ? "At last in our time, by God's enormous kindness, the sacred scriptures began to be greatly prized and diligently studied by many, and their meaning began to be preached to the people of God, and their mysteries to be profitably expounded."[105] Flacius attributed the inferiority of previous interpreters to the inferiority of their auxiliary sciences, to bad translations and a bad understanding of Aristotle, which led interpreters to screw up the words and the things of the mystical books: they could not understand what was meant by "sin," "justice," "faith," "justification," "law," "Gospel," "good work," "flesh," "free will," or even "custom"; nor could they understand what pertains to "reason," or what "intellect" can know, and what volition can will of the good.[106] This crime, for it obscured the voice of salvation, was very useful to Flacius because it undermined the legitimacy of Catholic authority; it relegated its practices to useless superstitions and rendered Catholic arguments against Protestants, in his mind, flaccid. Having taken great pains to ensure that his readers had the equipment to overcome the old debilities in over two thousand columns of his *Clavis sacrae scripturae (The Key to Sacred Scripture)*, he associated the work of exegesis with preaching, with the function of the Bible among Protestants. Embedded in his polemic are the convictions that scholars are now beginning to recognize as predominant features of sixteenth-century humanism, as it was used in Protestant thought: a new philology, a "correction" of Aristotelian logic, and "true" preaching. If Flacius and his contemporaries succeeded in eliminating the exegetical

---

[104] It was of course very pejoratively said. From the preface to *Clavis scripturae sanctae*, 1:a5 verso. See also G. Moldaenke, *Schriftverständnis und Schriftdeutung in Zeitalter der Reformation*, vol. 1, *Matthias Flacius Illyricus* (Stuttgart: W. Kohlhammer, 1936), p. 124.
[105] Matthias Flacius, *Clavis scripturae sacrae*, 1:a5 verso.
[106] Ibid., f. a4 recto.

role of some institutionally defined, non-exegetical sources (for example, the papal court and canon law), it was not to compromise the existence of an abstract universe in which prophets, apostles, professors, and preachers all said the same things. The conviction that the letter of the Bible should communicate spiritual truth that was retold in theological discourse and that informed the belief and practice of a community – its intertextuality – was a late medieval legacy.

Conclusion

At one time, the ambivalence of metaphor proved the need for supernatural explanations of textual meaning. Allegory was the "machine" that lifted souls across the chasm separating the world from God.[1] In late medieval theology, the extra-textual, metaphysical qualities of metaphor began to diminish, preparing the way for verbal imagery to recover its privileged place as the greatest instrument of style, even in the Bible.

The status of verbal figures was changing. The difference between human speech and spiritual knowledge diminished. Human speech came to be seen as more like divine speech, and divine speech – a language accommodated to feeble human minds – became transparent to faith, expressing plainly matters that were infinitely good. On the diverse evidence we have examined – Gorran, Holcot, Baconthorpe, Schildesche, Klenkok, Langenstein, and others – it seems safe to conclude that late medieval biblical interpreters were most accustomed to see this transfigured letter as a foundational element of theological discourse, in which the Bible conditioned and was conditioned by the strings of comments, quotations, syllogisms, and devout affirmations and longings with which clergy were taught to fill their minds and which they adapted to their publics. In commentaries, the letter "communicated" with a variety of other influential works: Peter Lombard's *Sentences,* the canon law, the Ordinary Gloss, the *Historia scholastica,* patristic and other sacred literature (variously codified in the previous works), and pagan, usually philosophical, writings. By thinking of the literal meaning of the Bible in the context of theological problems, theologians created interactions between these diverse texts, which their definitions of the Bible and their confidence in the coordinated wills of prophets, apostles, saints, and good readers reinforced. If there was something odd about the ancient past,

---

[1] "Machine" is Gregory the Great's term for allegory. Matter, *Voice of My Beloved,* p. 55.

something remote and exotic in the rites of Israel (which some but not all theologians believed), Jewish difference nevertheless reinforced the validity of the text for a Christian present, and this was manifest in the covenantal conditions of biblical literature. Dialectical adaptations of rhetoric by early Protestants reinforced the biblical quality of the present moment. They offered textual frameworks for creating the same kind of intellectual context, in which a godly communion of ancient and modern people participated in sacred deeds and events. Protestants may have expressed more deliberately than their predecessors the coherence of scripture and theological *literature*, and the immediacy that before was known in sanctity, they invested in faith. But both before and after the Reformation, the wonder of contemplative reading was being transposed into the literal sense.

There was a huge difference between late medieval and Protestant interpretation. The difference was the field of rhetoric. Yet the rhetorical methods of exegesis that became common in European schools after the 1530s seem to have grown naturally from late medieval exegetical trends. Like late medieval theology, sixteenth-century rhetoric led the reader not only to meaning but to meaning in the context of experience, of oneself and others.[2] I say rhetorical methods *seem* to have grown from late medieval trends because I am not prepared to prove such a linear evolution from late medieval commentaries to sixteenth-century exegesis. Proof would require evidence, I suppose, of self-conscious recognition of continuity, for example, a scholar using the new rhetoric to revise a late medieval commentary; and that is not how it happened, at least not among Protestants. Instead, they saw humanistic scholarship, clothed for theology in the *Novum Instrumentum* (1516) of Desiderius Erasmus – the first published critical edition of the Greek New Testament – as replacing the inferior tools and commentaries of their predecessors, as Flacius said in his contentious way. Having said that, I can only wonder if the comparative commentaries of some early Protestant humanists, such as Jean Mercier, which juxtapose select Christian and Jewish commentaries of the Middle Ages with contemporary Protestant ones, had, in part, the effect of demonstrating continuity with the recent past.[3] It would be hard to extrapolate from Mercier's technique more than his consuming

---

[2] Eden, *Hermeneutics and the Rhetorical Tradition*, pp. 101–4.
[3] Johannes Mercerus, *Commentarii locupletissimi in Prophetas quinque priores inter eos qui minores vocantur, quibus adiuncti sunt aliorum etiam et veterum (in quibus sunt Hebraei) et recentium commentarii, ab eodem excerpti* (Paris: Robert Estienne, 1573). Mercier gave excerpts from Jerome, Lyra, Oecolampadius, and various rabbis. See also *Le temps des Réformes et la Bible*, p. 271.

intellectual hunger. My claim in this book is therefore modest: only that *mutatis mutandis*, at the foundational level of the conceptualization of the biblical text Protestants were not so innovative after all. At the level of their sense of *why* texts are meaningful, they continued late medieval trends.

Protestants continued what I have inexactly called a textual attitude. The textual attitude that developed in late medieval Europe consisted of an association of spiritual or ultimate meaning with the literal sense, the communion of (divine and human) writers with (past and present) readers, and a sense of continuity between all religious writers and readers. This attitude assumed a continuity of meaning that extended subjectively and inter-subjectively outside the Bible. The correspondence of literatures, exegetical and doctrinal/dogmatic/philosophical, was based on a conviction of profound similarity, an aesthetic similarity of literatures, a shared biblical poetic. According to that poetic, the external world, and the literal text with it, was seamlessly joined to internal and divine truths in a late medieval reader's experience. The late medieval biblical poetic made a sharp contrast with its monastic predecessor, according to which internal and divine truths cast their shadows on the reader's world, allowing the reader to move from shadow to image and from image to divine source. The late medieval biblical poetic located divine truth in the text and in the world. According to it, truth – this study must conclude – was more directly present in the image of language.[4]

Missing from both late medieval and Reformation exegesis was historicism. By historicism I mean the pervasive "modern" conviction of the historically conditioned quality of all human thought and action and a focus on particular individual and social experiences as conditions and

---

[4] My conclusion is identical with Jeffrey Hamburger's conclusion about the role of religious art in his study of the convent of St. Walburg: "we should not think of each drawing as a rebus, a visual puzzle whose symbolic correspondences we are to decode – the language of 'this stands for that' or of 'signifier and signified.' If anything, the drawings, like much devotional imagery, are designed to collapse such distinctions, to the point of closing the gap between the self and their subject. Unlike signs, the drawings seek to establish a reciprocal presence, of Christ to the viewer and of the viewer to Christ, a mutual regard enacted by the imagery itself." Jeffrey F. Hamburger, *Nuns as Artists. The Visual Culture of a Medieval Convent* (Berkeley: University of California Press, 1997), p. 215. If such a view is absent from devotional literature, where, as Hamburger goes on to argue, "pleasure lies beyond, rather than in, the text," I hope I have shown that a similar reciprocity of presence and the collapse of self and subject matter was characteristic of late medieval biblical textuality. I also believe it played a role in Christian anti-semitism. Ocker, "Ritual Murder and the Subjectivity of Christ: A Choice in Medieval Christianity," *Harvard Theological Review* 91 (1998): 153–92, here, 176–92.

qualifiers of the universal.⁵ I am not talking about historical curiosity *per se*, which is present in medieval commentaries, but about a frame of mind that subordinates knowledge to historical contingency. It may seem obvious to us that a growing conviction of the externality of knowledge in words and texts should suggest the importance of historical circumstances, but as I've tried to show, theologians were not really motivated by an interest in the past. For that matter, they did not see the words and texts of the Bible as products of historical contingency as we would. The historical contingency of the biblical text was subordinate to divine cooperation, the text's theological content, and its redemptive purpose. Theologians were motivated by an interest in doctrines, textually and dialectically handled.

The late medieval biblical poetic must have had something to do with changing religious and social expectations. Was divine knowledge in the Bible the exclusive possession of the few in the monastic estate of prayer, sheltered from the bellicose *saeculum*, as it had been in the tenth and eleventh centuries, or was it available to the many in all their stations in life? Verbal signification suggested that it was available to the many. Any well-intending reader could insert himself into the conversation of God, prophets, apostles, and saintly commentators, inserting himself into a textual scene that encompassed sacred literature broadly conceived (the Bible and commentaries together), inserting himself like a patron figure at the foot of a painted cross or before a painted *pietà*. It seems to me that reading was an experience very much like passional devotion, in which the reader hoped to take a place in the scene and experience its very emotions. The difference between Victorine and later perspectives had to do with the power of representation, with a growing dissatisfaction over an old conviction that absolute truth was hidden in nature, behind and beyond complex symbols, and that it was available only to those

---

⁵ See Otto-Gerhard Oexle, *Geschichtswissenschaft im Zeichen des Historismus. Studien zu Problemgeschichten der Moderne* (Göttingen: Vandenhoeck und Ruprecht, 1996), pp. 18–72. Ernst Cassirer once pointed out that the tension between history and philosophy (or rationally derived truth) in the Enlightenment was finally overcome by Herder's philosophy of history, which embraced historical particularity and change within a framework of human progress: *The Philosophy of the Enlightenment* (Princeton University Press, 1951), pp. 197–233. It was the assumption of positive development and progress that was deeply contested in the debate over historicism at the beginning of the twentieth century. It is therefore necessary to distinguish historicism as a problematic of modernity from historical positivism as it developed after Herder. See Oexle, *Geschichtswissenschaft*, pp. 95–133. As Donald Kelley pointed out thirty years ago, Karl Popper's attack, *The Poverty of Historicism*, is not relevant to this problematic of historicism: Donald R. Kelley, *Foundations of Modern Historical Scholarship. Language, Law, and History in the French Renaissance* (New York: Columbia, 1970), p. 4 n. 4.

who approached it by transforming their natures, by a kind of soul-travel away from the detritus of paradise in ordinary human life and toward internal spaces where creation had been restored just enough to serve as a kind of gateway to heavenly perfection. Late medieval signs – in words, imagery, and nature – still pointed imposingly to the truth about the universe, but their meaning became more widely accessible to sincere minds. Gradually God, the angels, and the saints seemed much closer to the world, and the science of metaphor easily unveiled their presence. Such transfigured perceptions affected the connotations of revelation (as an attitude and as a theological doctrine), the connotations of history, and the connotations of language. Revelation became at once textual and subjective. Biblical history became a landscape of present experience. Language could be beautiful in its ambiguities and eventually cease to be regarded as a spiritual obstacle. The fables of the poets were not without philosophy, nor was theology without poetry. This change did not make revelation, history, and language more secular, in the sense of strictly mundane, but rather elevated history and language, along with the mundane world, toward revelation. The change helped refashion Christianity as a religion less exclusively clerical, as a popular religion in the early modern sense.[6]

The theoretical basis for the new attitude toward the text was Thomas Aquinas' theory of verbal signification, but the most vivid expression of it comes from the Protestant reformer Wolfgang Musculus, who described the Bible as a "garden of pleasure." Musculus alleged, in what has become for me the best trope for late medieval interpretation, that the text returns to the garden of Eden, the world as God first made it, where the holy converse among each other and with God. The text is a new Eden.

The time of this biblical poetic extended from the thirteenth into the sixteenth century. The Reformation appears as a moment within this

---

[6] For the encouragement of popular Bible reading see *Le temps des Réformes et la Bible*, p. 219; Ole Peter Grell, *Dutch Calvinists in Early Stuart London* (Leiden: E. J. Brill, 1989), pp. 34–5, 37; idem, *Calvinist Exiles in Tudor and Stuart England* (Aldershot: Scolar Press, 1996), pp. 62–63; Patrick Collinson, *The English Puritan Movement* (London: Jonathan Cape, 1967), pp. 168–76; William Hunt, *The Puritan Moment. The Coming of Revolution in an English County* (Cambridge, Mass.: Harvard University Press, 1983), pp. 94–5; J. C. van Slee, *De Rijnsburger Collegianten* (Utrecht: HES Publishers, 1980), pp. 30–4. It was to be controlled by an educated clergy who bore the main responsibility of Bible study: Schellong, *Calvins Auslegung der synoptischen Evangelien*, p. 10. Susi Hausamann, *Römerbriefauslegung zwischen Humanismus und Reformation* (Zürich: Zwingli Verlag, 1970), pp. 15–16; Girardin, *Rhétorique et théologue* pp. 87–8. See also Max Engammare, "De la chaire au bûcher: La Bible dans l'Europe de la Renaissance," *Bibliothèque d'Humanisme et Renaissance* 61 (1999), 737–61, here 753–61 and the literature cited there.

broad time, but not a turning point. This means that Luther's breakthrough was much less "hermeneutical" than scholars have alleged.[7] When Luther rejected the four-fold sense, his purpose was to affirm the spirituality of the letter.[8] Verbal signification and theological exegesis had indicated as much for two hundred years.

[7] Consider Heinz Schilling's response to Thomas A. Brady, *The Protestant Reformation in German History*, vol. 22 of Occasional Papers of the German Historical Institute (Washington, DC: German Historical Institute, 1998), p. 44. Karl Holl, "Luthers Bedeutung für den Fortschritt der Auslegungskunst," in his *Gesammelte Aufsätze zur Kirchengeschichte*, 3 vols. (Tubingen: J. C. B. Mohr, 1932), pp. 544–82, putting the breakthrough between 1516 and 1519, and Ebeling, *Evangelische Evangelienauslegung*, pp. 274ff.; idem, "Die Anfänge von Luthers Hermeneutik," dating a preliminary hermeneutical breakthrough between 1513 and 1515; Hirsch, note 8, below. More recently, Peter Harrison, *Bible, Protestantism and the Rise of Natural Science*, pp. 93–4.

[8] Immanuel Hirsch, "Initium theologiae Lutheri," in his *Lutherstudien*, 2 vols. (Gütersloh: C. Bertelsmann, 1954; article written in 1918 and first published in 1920), pp. 9–35, esp. 29–35, traces Luther's discovery of passive justification to his first lectures on the Psalms (1513–15), where the discovery is facilitated by an adaptation of medieval tropology. Ebeling had to concede that Luther's distinction between law and Gospel coexisted with the four-fold sense in the *Dictata* (Ebeling, "Anfänge," pp. 51, 53), but insisted that his use of allegory was innovative, in that it was measured by a theology of the cross (ibid., p. 46) – which is an exaggerated claim, given the fact that christological interpretations (including those focused on the passion of Christ) were commonly taken as both literal and allegorical meanings of scriptural texts. Preus believed that a change of viewpoint can be observed at Luther's expositions of Pss. 129 and 142, where there is an equivalence of Old Testament Jews and Christians (*Shadow*, pp. 171–3). For the relation of Ebeling's understanding of the dichotomy to his own adaptation of Heideggar see Miikka Ruokanen, *Hermeneutics as an Ecumenical Method in the Theology of Gerhard Ebeling* (Helsinki: Luther-Agricola Society, 1982), pp. 64ff.

Appendix: Selections from commentaries

The orthography varies tremendously within and between the manuscripts used in this study. As is common in the editing of late medieval texts and because it provides a glimpse of differences of pronunciation (and therefore also represents the regional diversity of the originals), I have generally followed the originals. The reader will therefore encounter *w* for *v*, *y* for *u*, *j* for *i* (especially as *ij*) and an occasional inverted dipthong, for example, *eu* for *e*.[1] I've broken this rule by making the irregular use of *v* uniform, always rendering *v* as *u*. I tried to follow the arrangement of the manuscripts as much as possible, but this has frequently proved impossible. So for example, when *paragraphus* marks indicate something like paragraph divisions in Latin sources, I separate paragraphs according to them. But in some manuscripts they are sometimes used to indicate the ends of sentences. The punctuation of the texts, as is true for most late medieval scholastic manuscripts, is grossly inconsistent, sometimes heavy and sometimes scant, and so although I have tried to punctuate consistently with or analogously to the originals, in the interest of clarity I have also modified the punctuation freely to suit syntax. When I quote commentary, the quotations of the source that serves as the basis of the exposition within that quote are italicized, while other quotations within the quote remain in quotation marks, as I mentioned in the Preface.

1. Nicholas Gorran, on Ex. 3.2, Würzburg, Universitätsbibliothek, M.p.th. fol. 155, ff. 7rb–7vb.

Apparuitque ei dominus in flamma, quod factum est ut dicit Andree[2] ne possent ei sculpturam effingere. Flamma autem est in continuo motu,

---
[1] See p. 233, l. 58, below.
[2] Andrea de Sancto Victore, *Expositio super Heptateuchum*, Ex. 3.2, CCCM 53:98.

et sic non potest effingi. Quia autem effingeretur, habet esse sub certis terminis *ignis*, quod factum est propter maximam eius potestatem actiuam, ut sic se ostenderet esse super egyptios, sicut ignis est super omnia elementa. Deuteronomium iv.,[1] "Deus noster ignis consumens est." *De medio rubi*, ad signandum quod apparebat ad minandum populum humilem et afflictum. Rubus enim humilis est uilis rubus, et signat populum hebreorum rubum humilitatem et uilem. Unde flamma in rubo est potencia Dei in populo, pro auxilio conferendo. Uel scilicet hebreis in hoc ostendit se dominus liberaturorum populorum de urente captiuitate egyptiorum. Deuteronomium iv.,[2] "uos tulit dominus, et eduxit de fornace Egypti."

Et nota quod quamuis Deus appareat in omni creatura per effectum potencie sapiencie et bonitatis, tamen spiritualiter dicitur alicubi apparere ad ostensionem alicuius effectus notabilis sicut hic, *et uidebat quod rubus arderet et non conbureretur*, in quo signabatur quod per flammam afflictionis populus non consumebatur, sed magnus fouebatur. Supra i.,[3] "quanto opprimebant eos, tanto multiplicabantur et crescebant." Uel in hoc signabatur quod Deus existens in medio populi hebrei in rubo non consummebat in eis aculeos peccatorum, quamuis affligeret eos ut flamma ignis per oppressionem egyptiorum. Uel in hoc signabatur quod lex erat danda populo que ad cognicionem peccati illuminaret, ut flamma, et tamen peccatorum spinas consummeret per ardorem caritatis. *Dixit ergo Moyses*, id est apud se deliberauit, *vadam*, scilicet ad inquirendum, *et uidebo uisionem*, mirabile signum, *hanc magnam*, id est alicuius magni ostensum, *quare non conburatur rubus*. Nota quod hec uisio magna dicitur propter magnitudinem misterii.

Nam ignis in rubo est diuinitas in humanitate. Johannes i.,[4] "uerbum caro factum est." *Ardet et non conbureretur*, quia humanitas a diuinitate non consumitur. Item, *ignis in rubo*, partus in uirgine, *ardet* caritate interius *sed non conbureretur*, id est non uiolatur in partu ecclesie rubus quam uiderat Moyses, et cetera. Item, *ignis in rubo*: tribulacio in ecclesia *ardet*, quia cruciatur exterius, *sed non conburitur*, quia non consumit interius.

Et si queritur utrum Moyses ista misteria intellexerit, respondeo: creditur probabiliter quod sic, sicut dicitur de Abraham, Johannes viij.,[5] "Abraham exultauerit ut uideret diem meum," et cetera.

Uel sic, *ignis in rubo*: tribulacio in uiro iusto qui *ardet caritate sed non conbureretur* tribulacione uel caritate.

[1] Deut. 4.24.   [2] Deut. 4.20.   [3] Ex. 1.12.   [4] Jn. 1.14.   [5] Jn. 8.56.

Cernens autem dominus, id est angelus in persona domini, *quod pergeret ad uidendum*, scilicet mirabile signum, *uocauit eum de medio rubi*, scilicet uolens loqui de communi utilitate, *et ait, Moyses, Moyses*.

Et nota quod bis eum nominat, quia ad duplicem intellectum spir-
45 itualem scilicet et litteralem uocabat, uel quia duo conpleturus erat in populo per eum, scilicet educcionem populi de Egypto et deduccionem in deserto. Psalmus,[1] "deduxisti sicut oues populum tuum in manu Moysis et Aaron."

2. Jacques Fournier, Chapter 24 and the Beginning of Chapter 25 of His Exposition of the Prologue to the Gospel according to Matthew, Barcelona, Biblioteca Nacional de Catalunya, Ms. 550, ff. 11vb–12ra.

[xxiv. capitulum]

Quare euangeliste mense quadrate dicuntur, capitulum xxiv. Ubi considerandum quod modus quo euangelia sunt scripta est planus, quoad hystoriam et precepta est deuotus, quoad promissa et Christi facta pro nobis est etiam multiplex et obscurus, quoad mistica et diuina, que omnia
5 signantur in auctoritate: premissa sententia eius planicies exprimitur in *mensa*, sed deuotio in *holocausto*, sed eius multiplicitas in *lapidibus quadris*.[2] Dicit ergo quadrate mense. Per mensam enim scriptura planicies intelligitur, sicut enim mensa est plana et habundans dapibus, sic quod quibus in illa exsistens potest accipere cibum sibi congruentem, ita et scriptura
10 est in aliquibus locis plana et aperta, ac pro captu cuius quasi cibos spirituales ministrans. Unde Augustinus in epistola ad Uolusianum dicit,[3] "modus ipse dicendi quo euangelium contexitur omnibus accessibile" est. "Ea que aperte continet, quasi amicus familiaris sine fuco ad cor loquitur indoctorum atque doctorum, ea uero que misterijs occultat nec
15 ipse eloquiam superbam erigit, quo non audeat accedere mens tardiuscula et inerudita quasi pauper ad diuitem, sed inuitat omnes humili sermone, quos non solum manifeste pascit, sed etiam secreta exerceat ueritate." "Hijs salubriter et praui corriguntur et parui nutriuntur et magna oblectantur ingenia," de qua mensa in Psalmo dicitur,[4] "parasti
20 in conspectu meo mensam, aduersus eos qui tribulant me," huius autem mense uel dicitur quod est quadrata uel dicitur quod quatuor angulos habet, secundum illud Exodi xxv.,[5] "quatuor circulos aureos preparabis, et pones eos in quatuor angulis mense per singulos pedes." Ubi dicit

---

[1] Ps. 77.20.   [2] In prologo *Glossae* non inuenitur.
[3] Ep. cxxxvii.18, CSEL 44:122–3.   [4] Ps. 23.5.   [5] Ex. 25.26.

interlinearis,¹ "euangelii libros," quatuor dicit, "per quorum fidem omnis scriptura sacra per totum mundum legitur et intelligitur." Et ibi, "per singulos pedes," dicit glossa, "mensa tabernaculi quatuor pedes habet, quia uerba celestis oraculi uel hystorice uel allegorice uel tropologice, id est moraliter, uel anagogice accipiuntur." Unde et quadrata mensa signat quatuor modos, quoad moralia, quos continet scriptura, secundum enim Jeronimum super Mattheum,² "quatuor sunt qualitates, de quibus sacra euangelia texuntur, precepta, mandata, testimonia, exempla, id est preceptis iusticia, in mandatis caritas, in testimonijs fides, in exemplis perfectio." Quantum etiam ad hystoricum sensum, quatuor sunt modi loquendi in euangelio, scilicet hystorice, prophetice, prouerbialiter, doctrinaliter. Tria autem ultima istorum per modum hystorie ab euangelistis proponuntur, licet in suo loco prophetice, prouerbialiter uel ut simplex doctrina sint dicta, secundum quod patet de prophetia quando narratur Elyzabet dixisse,³ "unde hoc michi ut ueniat mater domini mei ad me," et de prouerbia quando multe parabole dicte a domino narrantur ab eis et eodem modo de simplici doctrina, quam dixerunt dominum dixisse. Ex quo patet quod bene quadrangula est uel quadruplex est mensa, quia cum ipsi omnia narrent hystorice, tamen illa que narrant uel sunt hystorica simpliciter uel prohetica uel prouerbia uel simplex doctrina. Et quia tam multiplex habet, est huius narratio hystorica, et tamen in omnibus est plana, manifestum est quod bene quadrata mensa dici possunt. In hiis enim mensis quidem quilibet querit inuenire potest, dicente Crisostomo in expositione super Mattheum exponendo illud,⁴ "misit seruos suos uocare inuitatos ad nuptias." Sicut regale prandium multis ciborum speciebus ornatum, ita et conuiuium scripturarum diuersis iusticiarum speciebus est decoratum. Et super illud "prandium meum paraui." Ex omni lege et ex omnibus prophetis scripturarum mensas ornaui. Et super illud,⁵ "omnia parata sunt," quod queritur ad salutem, totum iam adimpletum est in scripturis, qui ignorans est inuenit ibi quod discat, qui contumax est et peccator inuenit ibi futura iudicii flagella que timeat, qui laborat inuenit ibi gloriosas promissiones uite perpetue, quas manducando amplius excitetur ad opus, qui pusillanimus est et infirmus inuenit ibi mediocres iusticie cibos, qui et si pinguem naturam non faciant tamen mori non permittunt, qui magnanimus est et fidelis inuenit ibi spirituales escas continentiores uite, que perducant eum proprie [ad]

---

¹ *Glossa ordinaria* ad loc.; *Glossa cum Lyra*, 1:178 interlinearis et marginalis. interlinearis] *leg* interlinearis glossa.
² Cf. Hieronymus, *In Matheum*, praef., CCL 77:3–4; *Glossa cum Lyra*, 5:3r–3v.
³ Lk. 1.43.   ⁴ Mt. 22.3.   ⁵ Mt. 22.4.

60 angelorum naturam, qui percussus est a dyabolo et inebriatus est in peccatis inuenit ibi medicinales cibos, qui eum per penitenciam preparent ad salutem. Nichil ergo minus est in hac mensa quam necessarium habet salus humana. Unde et euangeliste hiis mensis sunt administratores appositi, ut unusquisque sumat de hac mensa, quod uoluerit, secundum
65 illud Hester i.,[1] "rex statuerat preponens mensis singulos de principibus suis, ut sumeret unusquisque quod uellet."

[xxv. capitulum]
Quare omnia dicta et facta domini in euangelijs posita sunt exitatiua deuotionis, et faciunt quantum in se hominem esse dei holocaustum,
70 capitulum xxv.
Sequitur *ad holocaustum*. Ubi ostenditur quod hec scriptura excitat ad devotionem, quoad illa que fecit pro nobis dominus ac etiam eius promissa. In ueteri enim testamento multe erant hystorie, que ad deuotionem animum non excitabant, ymo magis quedam ad lasciuiam sicut
75 patet in multis hystoriis, quedam etiam ad cruditatem sicut patet in multis hystoriis, quedam etiam ad crudelitatem, sicut etiam patet in multis locis. Hystoria autem noui testamenti omnis excitat homines, si diligenter attendant, ad deuotionem, et maxime domini facta pro nobis, ac eciam promissa. Unde Bernhardus in secundo sermone de dominica in octauas
80 Epiphanie dicit, sicut in Christo ostensum est quod totus est suauis, totus salubris, totus desiderabilis, totus delectabilis, sic et in operibus eius reperies [*leg.* repraesentes], nam et superficies ipsa tamquam a foris considerata, decora est ualde, et siquis fregerit nucem, intus inueniet, quod iocundius sit, et multo amplius delectabile. Non sic apud patres ueteris
85 testamenti reperies, nam et in operibus eorum decora et delectabilis est significatio mistica, ipsa tamen si per se considerentur, inuenientur aliquando minus digna, ut sunt facta Jacob, adulterium Dauid, et multa similia; preciosa quidem sunt fercula sed uasa non adeo preciosa....

3. Hermann of Schildesche, *Compendium de Quatuor Sensibus Sacre Scripture*, from the Second Chapter. The text survives in five manuscripts, all from the fifteenth century and written on paper. They are listed here with the sigla used in my edition of selections:

B   Basel, Universitätsbibliothek, A VII 45 ff. 133r–145v (the selection edited here, ff. 135v–136r)

---

[1] Esther i.3. Barcelona, Biblioteca Central Ms 550, f. 12ra.

M Munich, Bayerische Stadtbibliothek, Clm 26821, ff. 71r–84r (the selection edited here, f. 73r)
L Lüneburg, Ratsbibliothek, Theol. Fol. 73, ff. 106ra–114ra (here f. 108rb–108vb)
W Vienna, Dominikanerkloster, 46/268, ff. 131v–141v (here ff. 132v–133v)
S Stuttgart, Landesbibliothek, Theol. Quart. 55, ff. 37r–50r (here ff. 38r–39r)

M shortens Hermann's prologue, which is dedicated to the Würzburg protonotary Michael of Lyon, and explains how Michael asked Hermann to write up his cathedral lectures on the subject of the Bible.[1] The scribe of M either worked from a damaged manuscript or was sloppy: in the selection edited here he skips, mid-sentence, an entire page and continues writing within the following chapter. S omits the prologue altogether. W contains a damaged conclusion. Four manuscripts closely share readings and thus form a group: B, M, L, and W. In this group, L is the most independent, both in orthography (in this selection, for example, *historiacus* for *hystoricus*) and in errors, while W also makes egregious mistakes (e.g. *uocatur* for *uetatur*). Of only cosmetic significance is the fact that the spaces for the rubrics in L and S remain unfilled. In this group, B seems closest to the common source, preserving for example a correct case ending (*multos boues et multas oues*) where W and L (this is part of the section omitted by M) incorrectly repeat a case ending from a following noun (*multas boues et multas oues*). S is, as the notes below will reveal, more sharply independent of these four manuscripts, such that it must belong to a separate group stemming from a much less influential archetype. A tradition-critical edition[2] would therefore follow B, as representing the most influential tradition, for its primary readings, taking when necessary more correct readings from other members of the group B, M, L, W, which is how I proceed below in this and the following selections. I also follow the orthography of B, only in cases of extreme difference (e.g. the spelling of names) noting variants. I begin at the top of the chapter.

---

[1] Zumkeller, *Schriften*, p. 23.
[2] For tradition-critical editing, see Kurt Ruh, "Votum für eine überlieferungskritische Editionspraxis," in *Probleme der Edition mittel- und neulateinischer Texte*, ed. Ludwig Hödl and Dieter Wuttke (Boppard: Harald Boldt, 1978), pp. 35–40. For related problems with text archetypes as the basis of textual reconstruction, see Horst Fuhrmann, "Überlegungen eines Editors," ibid., pp. 1–34, here 14–15 n. 26 and the literature noted there.

Sensus ergo[1] litteralis est quando uel[2] narratur aliquid gestum uel non[3] gestum uel precipitur aliquid seu uetatur[4] gerendum, secundum quod Augustinus dicit[5] circa principium libri *De utilitate credendi*,[6] et secundum hoc prima facie sensus litteralis diuiditur in sensum[7] hystoricum,[8] in quo[9] narrantur gesta aliquorum, sicut in libro Genesi gesta narrantur Adam,[10] Noe, Abraham, Ysaac, Jacob et aliorum patriarcharum, et in alijs libris Moysi narrantur[11] gesta filiorum Israel, in libris[12] Josue et Judicum ipsius gesta et[13] judicum Israel, in libris Regum et Paralipomenon[14] gesta regum Israel et Juda et sic de aliis libris qui hystorici[15] nominantur.[16] Secundo[17] sensus litteralis diuiditur in non hystoricum,[18] et sicut in omnes illos libros ubi[19] ad litteram aliquid uetatur uel precipitur gerendum, ut in libris sapientialibus et in multis libris prophetalibus et[20] in epistolis Pauli. Nichil tamen prohibet quandoque quin[21] in eodem libro[22] occurant[23] et sensus litteralis hystoricus et eciam[24] non hystoricus,[25] cum aliquid narratur gestum et ad litteram[26] aliquid precipitur uel uetatur gerendum,[27] sicut in libro Exodi,[28] ubi narrantur gesta filiorum Israel in Egypto et eorum[29] exitus de Egypto, et tamen eis ibi plura precipiuntur[30] gerenda, ut decem precepta legis, et multa uetantur[31] ibidem, et istud est tamen[32] in multis alijs libris[33] Moysi quam[34] prophetarum. Istud eciam fit in quatuor ewangelijs, ubi et[35] narrantur Christi et apostolorum gesta, et multa precipiuntur[36] uel[37] uetantur gerenda. Ista est ergo[38] prima sensus litteralis diuisio, quod quidam est hystoricus, quidam non[39] hystoricus. Secunda diuisio eius[40] est[41] quod utrumque istorum

---

[1] ergo] *om* S   [2] uel] *om* S   [3] non] litterales sensus quid est *add* W   [4] uetatur] uocatur W
[5] Augustinus dicit] Apostolis (!) dicitur L   [6] Augustinus, *De utilitate credendi*, iii.5.
[7] sensum] litteralem *add* M, S   [8] hystoricum] historiacum L   [9] in quo] secundum quem S
[10] narrantur gesta] *trans* W. Adam] Ade M, L, W, S   [11] Noe ... narrantur] *om* W
[12] libris] libro W, M   [13] ipsius gesta] *trans* L. et] *om* L
[14] Paralipomenon] Paralipomenum W   [15] hystorici] historiaci L   [16] L, f. 108va
[17] Secundo] sic eciam S   [18] hystoricum] historiacum L
[19] sicut ... ubi] sicut in omnes alios libros ubi L et adhunc reducuntur omnes libri in quibus S
[20] et] *om* B, W, L, M
[21] quandoque quin] quin quandoque M, W, L quia quandoque S
[22] libro] *del* con   [23] occurant] occurat W, L   [24] eciam] *om* L
[25] historicus] historiacus L   [26] ad litteram] *om* S   [27] et ad litteram ... gerendum] *om* L
[28] Exodi] Exodo L   [29] W, f. 133r.
[30] ibi plura precipiuntur] plura precipiuntur ibi S, W
[31] uetantur] *del* ibidem B. ut patet *add* M, L, W   [32] tamen] tam M
[33] libris] *marg add* tam W   [34] quam] *add* eciam S   [35] ubi et] ut et M. ubi eciam S
[36] multa precipiuntur ...] multa ad non propriam ... M (*scriba transit ad medium iii. capituli praetermittitque probabiliter unam paginam in fonte eius*)
[37] uel] et S   [38] est ergo] *trans* W, L, S. igitur S
[39] non] *add* est W. quod quidam est hystoricus ... hystoricus] *om* S. hystoricus] historiacus L
[40] diuisio eius] *om* S   [41] est] istorum membrorum subdiuisio *add* S

membrorum subdiuiditur per proprium et figuratum. Est enim[1] sensus litteralis hystoricus proprius[2] quando sub proprijs uerbis narrantur gesta alicuius, ut in libro Iudicum capitulo ix.[3] narrantur gesta Abimelech sub proprijs uerbis, ubi narratur quomodo interfecit septuaginta duo filios Jeroboal[4] fratres suos. Ipse qui spurius fuit uoluit regnare in Sychem.[5] Sed sensus hystoricus[6] non proprius est quando gesta alicuius narrantur figuratiue puta parabolice uel enigmatice, ut ibidem ix. capitulo,[7] ubi sub figura enigmatis quasi poetice de eo narrantur quod "ligna[8] siluarum iuerunt[9] ut ungerent sibi regem et tandem dixerunt rampno,"[10] per quam arborem[11] ipse significabatur,[12] "impera[13] nobis." Huius eciam exemplum habemus ii. Reg. xi. capitulo,[14] ubi narrantur proprie ea que Dauid gessit cum Bersabee[15] et cum Uria marito eius et[16] quomodo[17] illa concubuit et maritum eius[18] per Joab in excidio[19] mortis poni mandauit. Sed eadem eius[20] gesta ibidem narrantur figuratiue sub parabolam quam[21] xii. capitulo[22] Nathan propheta[23] ipsi Dauid proposuit de quodam[24] diuite qui habebat multos boues et multas oues[25] et de paupere qui non habuit nisi unam[26] ouiculam quam eciam[27] nutriuerat in sinu suo, et quomodo diues illo pauperi accepit[28] unicam ouiculam suam[29] et comedit eam cum quodam suo hospite qui aduenerat peregrino.[30] Iste ergo[31] sensus est quidam[32] sensus litteralis eciam[33] hystoricus non[34] tamen proprius, quia uerbis proprijs non narrantur ea que gesta sunt,[35] sed translatis et figuratiuis. Sensus eciam litteralis non historicus proprius est cum uerbis proprijs aliquid[36] precipitur uel uetatur. Precipitur,[37] ut Deuteronomii vi.,[38] "diliges dominum Deum tuum ex toto corde," et cetera,[39] uetatur, ut in Psalmo,[40] "Israel, si me audieris, non erit in te

---

[1] enim] *om* L
[2] hystoricus proprius] *trans* S. hystoricus] historiacum L
[3] Ju. 9.1–5.   [4] Jeroboal] Jerobabel L   [5] Sychem] Sechem L Sichem S
[6] hystoricus] historiacus L figuratiuus siue *add* S
[7] ix. capitulo] *trans* S. Ju. 9.8.   [8] ligna] lingua (!) W   [9] iuerant] *del et* S
[10] rampno] oliue S per quid arborem *add* L (= *rhamno, Ju. 9.14, 15,* = *rubo*)
[11] per quam arborem] *rep* L   [12] significabatur] figurabatur W   [13] B, f. 135r.
[14] xi. capitulo] *trans* S. 2 Sam. 11.1–17.   [15] Bersabee] Barsabee W Bersabe S
[16] et] ut L *om* S   [17] quomodo] quando L quem S
[18] illa concubuit et maritum eius] cum illa concubuit et maritum eius W, L, *om* S
[19] excidio] exilio L   [20] Sed] et S. eadem eius] *trans* S. S, f. 39r.
[21] quam] *om* L quando S   [22] 2 Sam. 12.1–4.
[23] xii. capitulo Nathan propheta] *trans* S   [24] L, f. 108vb.
[25] multos boues et multas oues] multas boues et multas oues W, L multas et multas boues S
[26] unam] unicam W   [27] eciam] *om* W, L, S   [28] accepit] cepit L
[29] ouiculam suam] *trans* S   [30] qui aduenerat peregrino] *trans* S
[31] Iste ergo] Est ergo iste L Iste igitur S   [32] quidam] quidem W
[33] eciam] et W, L, S   [34] non] *del* proprius W   [35] gesta sunt] *trans* L
[36] aliquid] aliud L   [37] uel ueteratur. Precipitur] *om* W   [38] Deut. 6.5.
[39] et cetera] *om* S *del* uocatur B   [40] Ps. 81.8–9.

Deus recens, neque adorabis deum alienum."[1] Figuratiuus autem est quando in proprijs[2] et translatis uerbis aliquid precipitur uel[3] uetatur[4]; ut[5] Apoc.[6] iii. collirio iniunge, "oculos,"[7] id est leni fomento principue[8] interiores oculos mentis tue[9] sanes. Duo enim oculi mentis sunt[10] intellectus et affectus. Primo autem intellectum illuminat et affectum inflammat, ut dicit ibi[11] quedam glossa. Uetatur autem[12] aliquid translatis uerbis, ut Mattheus vii.,[13] "Nolite sanctum dare canibus," id est peccatoribus, uel "margaritas proicere ante porcos," id est preciosam doctrinam docere inter porcinos et carnales homines, qui non sunt capaces ipsius. In quibus[14] libris sacre scripture sint[15] sensus litterales hystorici[16] proprij et eciam non hystorici,[17] satis potest patere ex iam dictis.[18] Figuratiui autem maxime sunt in libro Canticorum, ubi amor Christi ad ecclesiam uel ad deuotam animam introducitur sub figura sponsi et sponse.

4. Hermann of Schildesche, *Compendium de Quatuor Sensibus Sacre Scripture*, from the Third Chapter, the Beginning of the Chapter. B, 136v–137v. M, ff. 73r–74r. W, ff. 133v–134v L, ff. 109ra–109va S, ff. 39v–40v.

Tercium capitulum in quo subdiuiduntur sensus litterales figuratiui et ostenditur quod sunt quatuor scilicet tropicus, parabolicus, symbolicus, et poeticus et ponitur eorum sufficiencia.[19]

De figuratiuis ergo[20] sensibus utile est uidere quomodo reducantur ad sensum litteralem et quomodo differant[21] a sensibus mysticis, quod michi fateor non esse facile declarare, quia in hijs que ego legi doctorum dictis tam[22] antiquorum quam modernorum[23] admodum[24] pauca uel pene nulla de premissis[25] me fateor inuenisse. Non est tamen impossibile esse[26] plura que ego non uidi. Primo ergo uidendum est qui et quot sunt hij sensus. Secundo quomodo reducuntur ad sensum litteralem. Tercio quomodo differunt a sensibus misticis. Sunt autem quatuor prout michi uidetur,[27] et sunt sensus tropicus communiter dictus,

---

[1] adorabis deum alienum] et cetera W *add* Et W, S
[2] in proprijs] sub inproprijs S   [3] uel] aliud L   [4] uetatur] *add* precipitur W, L
[5] ut] in S   [6] Apoc. 3.18.   [7] oculos] *add* tuos S   [8] W, f. 133v.
[9] mentis tue] *trans* L   [10] oculi mentis sunt] *trans* S *add* ut S   [11] ibi] ibidem S
[12] autem] eciam aliquando S   [13] Mt. 7.6.   [14] quibus] *del* quidem uerbis W
[15] sint] sunt L   [16] hystorici] historiaci L   [17] hystorici] historiaci L   [18] dictis.] *add* Et S
[19] Tercium capitulum . . . sufficiencia] *om* L, S
[20] ergo] autem L   [21] differant] *del* diff di W   [22] tam] *om* S
[23] tam antiquorum quam modernorum] quam modernorum tam antiquorum L
[24] admodum] *om* S   [25] de premissis] *om* L   [26] esse] fore S   [27] michi uidetur] *trans* W

sensus parabolicus,[1] sensus[2] symbolicus et sensus enigmaticus qui et poeticus a quibusdam dicitur, quorum suffi[3]ciencia sic accipitur. Sensus enim figuratiuus est quando aliquid narratur gestum uel precipitur aut uetatur uerbis impropijs et translatis, ut supra patuit in ii.[4] capitulo. Uel[5] ergo locucio qua hunc facit scriptura retinet plura uerba propria et assumit alique translata, tamen illa omnino sensum[6] proprium non obtegunt aut obscurant, et sic[7] est sensus[8] tropicus a figura tropi dictus sub qua omnes locuciones translate et methaphorice continentur, ut patet in[9] primo Etimologiarum per Ysidorum et[10] in *Doctrinali* et[11] *Grecissimo*.[12] Dicit enim[13] Ysidorus capitulo xxii. quod in tropo modi locucionum fiunt a propria significacione ad non propriam[14] similitudinem, quarum omnia nomina difficile est[15] annotare. Sed ex omnibus Donatus xiii. uti[16] tradenda, conscripsit hec Ysidorus et[17] extra[18] de hoc infra[19] patebit. Uel[20] locucio scripture assumit tot uerba translata quod obscurant et obtegint sensum et faciunt sermonem obscurum. Et hoc[21] potest contingere duobus[22] modis.[23] Uel enim in illa[24] translacione uerborum cum omnes transferentes secundum aliquam similitudinem transferant, ut dicit Aristoteles, assumuntur similitudines in natura rerum[25] possibiles, et[26] sic[27] est sensus parabolicus, sicut patet in parabola Cristi. Luce viii. "Exijt[28] qui seminat seminare[29] semen suum,"[30] et in multis alijs parabolis suis[31] quas possibile fuit sic[32] euenisse eciam si in ueritate non euenerunt. Uel assumuntur similitudines in natura rerum impossibiles, ut cum per[33] similitudinem assumitur quod ligna siluarum uel animalia bruta loquantur uel aliud[34] talium faciant quod secundum naturam est impossibile. Hoc tamen adhuc potest esse duobus modis quia uel[35] ea que propria sunt rerum corporalium attribuuntur rebus pure spiritualibus, ut cum Deus dicitur habere alas ut[37] in Psalmo, "sub umbra alarum tuarum protege nos"[37] uel aliquid similem, uel[38] angeli dicuntur

---

[1] parabolicus] et *add* W   [2] sensus] *del* sy B   [3] W, f. 134r.
[4] ii. capitulo] capitulo iii. W   [5] Uel] *om* S   [6] sensum] secundum L   [7] sic] *om* W
[8] sensus] *om* L   [9] in] *om* L   [10] et] *om* S   [11] et] in *add* S
[12] Eberhardus Bethuniensis, *Graecissimus*, i, lines 95–8, ed. Wrobel, p. 8.
[13] enim] ibi *add* L   [14] ad non propriam] *hic resumit* M   [15] est] propria *add* L
[16] uti] usui B, M, L, W; parte sui S
[17] hec Ysidorus et] et de hoc Ysidorus S exemplum *del* S
[18] extra] exemplum plura S   [19] infra] *marg add* L   [20] Uel] fit quando *add* S
[21] hoc] *om* M   [22] M, f. 73v.   [23] L, f. 109 rb.   [24] in illa] ulla L
[25] in natura rerum] *trans* S. S, f. 40r.   [26] et] *supersc add* M ut L *om* S   [27] sic] uerum S
[28] B, f. 137r.   [29] seminare] *om* M   [30] seminare semen suum] *om* L
[31] suis] *om* M, W, L   [32] sic] sicut W   [33] per] in L *om* S   [34] aliud] aliquid M, W, L
[35] uel] iam M *om* L   [36] ut] ut patet S
[37] nos] me S   [38] uel] ut L

uolare, ut[1] Ysaias vi.,[2] et sic est[3] sensus symbolicus, qui maxime panditus est per Dyonisium qui quoad ea quibus[4] Deo talia attribuuntur plura de ipso[5] tangit ix. capitulo[6] *De diuinis nominibus*,[7] et quantum ad ea quibus angelis talia attribuuntur de ipso tractat[8] xv. capitulo liber *De angelica Ierarchia* quasi per totum. Uel ea que sunt propria spiritualium seu[9] racionabilium attribuuntur irracionabilibus, ut[10] lignis[11] ungere regem uel animalibus[12] loqui, et sic est sensus poeticus, id est[13] fictus. Poesis enim fictio interpretatur, ut Judicum ix. legitur "yerunt[14] ligna[15] siluarum ut[16] ungerent sibi regem, dixeruntque oliue impera nobis."[17]

Tropicus ergo sensus committere dictus est, quando ponuntur alique uerba translata, non tamen tot quod omnino obscurent sensum, ut cum narratur aliquid gestum figuratiue, tamen aliquo modo[18] apertis uerbis, ut xxii. capitulo secundi libri Regum, legitur de Dauid, "Ipse tanquam tenuis ligni[19] uermiculus residens inter ligna[20] saltus." Et per hoc innuitur quod ipse sit[21] paruus et delicatus quasi tenerrimus ligni[23] uermiculus inter omnes suos[23] uiros robustos sui exercitus[24] fortissimi residebat. Istud[25] eciam contingit cum[26] aliquid figuratiue precipit.[27] Ut Romanos xii.[28] dicitur de inimico "si esurierit ciba illum,[29] si sitit, potum da illi."[30] Et subditur quod est ad propositum hoc enim "faciens carbones ignis[31] ingeres[32] super caput eius." Istud est tropicum,[33] "carbones ignis,"[34] id est urentes penitencie gemitus. Secundum ergo Augustinum[35] iii. *De doctrina christiana* capitulis xii. et xvi. ista uidetur tropica locucio non tamen enigmatica, que sensum obtegat[36] omnino. Uel aliquid[37] figuratiue uetatur[38] cum mixtione propriorum uerborum, ut in Psalmo ciiii. "Nolite tangere Cristos meos," id est sacerdotes. Uel "nolite obturare[39] corda uestra,"[40] id est non [in] sinibus[41] nimis pertinaces. Et ista locucio uariatur multis modis et forte septem modis qui secundum regulas Tyconii[40] declarantur, de quibus plenius in illo[41] alio

---

[1] ut] *om* L
[2] vi. Ysaias] vi. Ysidorus M. vii. Ysaias W Ysaias vi. L. Is. 6.2.
[3] est] *om* W   [4] quibus] *spat* S   [5] de ipso] *om* L   [6] ix. capitulo] *trans* L
[7] nominibus] et De simbolica theolica *add* S   [8] tractat] tractatur S   [9] seu] uel S
[10] ut] *del* linguis W. W, f. 134v   [11] lignis] lingnis W   [12] animalibus] irracionabilis *add* S
[13] id est] *om* S   [14] yerunt] inherunt S   [15] ligna] lingna W   [16] ut] ua *del* W
[17] nobis] De sensu tropyce *add* M   [18] tamen aliquo modo] *trans* S   [19] ligni] lingni W
[20] ligna] lingna W   [21] sit] sicud L   [22] ligni] lingni W *om* S   [23] suos] *om* M, W, L, S
[24] exercitus] et *add* S   [25] M, f. 74r.   [26] cum] quando S
[27] precipit] precipitur M, W, L, S   [28] Ro. 12.20.   [29] illum] *add* et L. L, f. 109va.
[30] potum da illi] da illi potum L   [31] ignis] ingnis W   [32] ingeres] congeres L, S
[33] S, f. 40v.   [34] ignis] ingnis W   [35] ergo Augustinum] *trans* M, W, L
[36] obtegat] obtigat S   [37] aliquid] ad W   [38] uetatur] uocatur W
[39] obturare] obdurare M, L   [40] uestra] *om* L   [41] sinibus] modis et forte *del* S
[40] Tyconii] Tyntonij B Dithoni S   [41] illo] *om* S

tractatu¹ plura reperientur, de quo² supra dixi³; qui uelit ea uidere⁴
70 uideat. Augustinus autem has regulas tangit iii. libro *De doctrina christiana*
capitulo xxxviii.,⁵ ubi ipse subiungit omnes⁶ hec⁷ regulas excepta una,
que est de promissis et lege uel spiritu et littera, aliud ex alio faciunt
intelligi, quod est proprium tropice⁸ locucionis.⁹ Hec Augustinus.¹⁰ Ego
tamen omnino non¹¹ excludo quoniam alique istarum vii. regularum
75 in alijs plerisque sensibus uendicent sibi locum. Sed credo quod huic
magis proprie applicentur sensui. Nec tamen secundum Augustinum
per has vii. regulas¹² licet quam plurime declarentur omnes tropici locuciones possunt modi¹³ expediri, sicut et secundum Ysidorum omnium¹⁴
troporum¹⁵ nomina difficile est¹⁶ annotare.

[The chapter continues with the explanation of parabolic, symbolic, and poetic senses, where, as in his elaboration of tropical meaning, Hermann offers biblical examples of the definitions already given.]

5. Hermann of Schildesche, *Compendium de Quatuor Sensibus Sacre Scripture*, Chapters 4 and 5 (complete). B, f. 139r; M, f. 76r– v; W, f. 136r; L, f. 110vb; S, f. 42v.

Quartum capitulum in quo ostenditur quomodo quatuor sensus figuratiui sensui litterali adherent et ad ipsum reducuntur.¹⁷

Restat ergo¹⁸ uidere quomodo¹⁹ hij quatuor²⁰ figuratiui sensus²¹ ad-
hereant sensui litterali et qualiter ad ipsum reducuntur.²² Quod eciam
5 magis inquisitiue quam determinatiue prosecuturus. Credo satis faciliter
posse declarari de sensu tropico communiter dicto quomodo litterali
sensui²³ adhereat, cum ut supra²⁴ dictum est proprietatem usitate locucionis pro maiori²⁵ parte in tali sensu uerba propria seruent licet alique

---

¹ tractatu] super huius nominatura *add* S   ² B, 137v.   ³ de quo supra dixi] *om* S
⁴ uidere] ibidem *add* S   ⁵ capitulo xxxviii.] *trans* S   ⁶ omnes] ueteres B
⁷ hec] istas S   ⁸ tropice] passionis *add* S   ⁹ locuucionis] *del* hoc B *om* W
¹⁰ hec Augustinus] Augustini B   ¹¹ omnino non] *trans* L
¹² regulas] applicentur sensui *add* S   ¹³ modi] om M, L, S
¹⁴ omnium] *del* cor{porum} M. sicut et secundum Ysidorum omnium] sicut primum Ysidori probatur quod omnium S
¹⁵ troporum] tropicorum L   ¹⁶ est] *del* a W
¹⁷ et ad ipsum reducuntur] *om* M. W, f. 136v. Quartum . . . reducuntur] *om* L, S
¹⁸ ergo] *supersc add* W   ¹⁹ quomodo] quorum S   ²⁰ quatuor] modi *add* L
²¹ figuratiui sensus] *trans, rep* sensus S
²² reducuntur] Uero ii. Rethorice Aristoteles quodlibet agit de exemplo potest una sufficiencia colligi de qua pluribus sensibus littere adherentibus quia eciam species exempli de quibus persuadet aliquos ut illo dicit, "sunt historia parabola et fabula que dicuntur in Ysopio et Libiana." Qui uelit hanc sufficienciam prosequi uideat ea que scripsi in maiore tractatu de hiis sensibus *add* L
²³ litterali sensui] *trans* L, S   ²⁴ litterali sensui . . . supra] *om* M   ²⁵ maiori] sensui *add* L

translata et methaphorica misceantur.¹ Quapropter estimo quod iste sensus circat² tam hystoricum quam eciam³ non hystoricum⁴ litteralem⁵ ubicumque eo modo quo dictum est⁶ aliqua uerba methaphorica uel trop⁷ica intercurrunt in sacra scriptura, et tamen sensus et⁸ proprietas uerborum non omnino obtegitur nec totaliter obscuratur.

Quomodo⁹ sensus parabolicus reducitur ad litteralem.

De sensu tamen parabolico credo¹⁰ quod proprie magis¹¹ ad sensum litteralem¹² hystoricum reducitur¹³ quod¹⁴ satis planum estimo¹⁵ in quibusdam parabolis¹⁶ Cristi quia ut plurimum illa figuratiua¹⁷ et parabolica¹⁸ eius locucio loquitur de aliquibus gestis judeorum ad litteram, sicut patet de parabola [de] uinee¹⁹ locatis agricolis et de occisione seruorum patrisfamilias²⁰ per quos prophete intelliguntur et tandem de occisione filij sui per quem Cristi intelligitur²¹ et eius mors a iudeis inflicta. Et in pluribus alijs parabolis eius hoc est facile uidere. Et in aliquibus parabolis ueteris testamenti, sicut de parabola quam proposuit Nathan propheta regi Dauid ii. Regum xii.²² de qua²³ supra habitum est in ii. capitulo. Non nego tamen²⁴ quin alique Cristi²⁵ parabole²⁶ magis accomodate ad sensum litteralem non hystoricum reducantur, sicut est parabola de x. uirginibus²⁷ in qua figuratiue nobis insinuantur pocius in re²⁸ agenda quam²⁹ narrentur³⁰ gesta, scilicet ne per hoc quod a nobis rectum foris³¹ geritur.³² Fauor aut³³ humana³⁴ gracia requiratur secundum Gregorium uel secundum Augustinum, ut gaudium de bono opere non in opinione hominum sed in³⁵ interiori desiderio consciencie teneamus. Nec propter hoc omnino hec³⁶ de hijs que per nos sunt gerenda,³⁷ ita³⁸ per Cristum esse dicta existimo, quoniam³⁹ eciam de gestis per judeos⁴⁰ illorum temporum qui omnia propter homines faciebant, ut

---

¹ S, f. 42v. ² circat] teneat W ³ eciam] om W ⁴ L, f. 111ra.
⁵ litteralem] in litterale W ⁶ est] et add S ⁷ M, f. 76v.
⁸ et tamen sensus] om L; et] semper add S
⁹ Quomodo] rubrica Quomodo W. Quomodo...litteralem] om L
¹⁰ credo] om S ¹¹ proprie magis] trans S ¹² litteralem] om S
¹³ reducitur] reducatur W, L, S ¹⁴ quod] om S ¹⁵ satis planum estimo] trans S
¹⁶ parabolis] parabolica S. B, f. 139v. ¹⁷ figuratiua] figuratura M
¹⁸ Cristi quia ut plurimum illa figuratiua et parabolica] om S
¹⁹ uinee] uien del W. Mt. 20.1–16. ²⁰ Mt. 21.33–41, Mk. 12.1–9, Lk. 20.9–16.
²¹ et tandem...Cristi intelligitur] om L ²² xii.] prout S ²³ qua] hoc S
²⁴ tamen] om M ²⁵ Cristi] sup add M ²⁶ Cristi parabole] trans L ²⁷ Mt. 25.1–13.
²⁸ in re] uite S ²⁹ quam] add quod S ³⁰ narrentur] recte add S
³¹ rectum foris] trans L ³² foris geritur] trans S
³³ aut] corr autem B autem M. fauor aut] om S et humana del S
³⁴ humana] et humana S ³⁵ in] om L, S
³⁶ Nec propter hoc omnino hec] nec hec solum S
³⁷ gerenda] corr agenda M ³⁸ ita] om S ³⁹ quoniam] quod S ⁴⁰ per iudeos] iudeorum L

35 dominus dicit Luca¹ xi.², accomodata³ per Cristum⁴ possunt intelligi fore dicta. Similiter omnino potest dici de parabola suorum illorum quibus ille homo⁵ peregre proficiscens⁶ "tradidit"⁷; "alij uero duo, alij autem unum." Mattheum xxv.⁸ Quedam igitur⁹ sunt parabole eius que sensu litterali hystorico, quedam uero quam¹⁰ sensui litterali non hystorico¹¹
40 accomodacius applicantur, quod eciam¹² breuitatem relinquo discretis lectoribus huius operis subtilius indagandum.¹³

Quomodo symbolicus reducitur¹⁴ ad litteralem.¹⁵

Sensus autem symbolicus hoc modo litterali adheret quia quasdam proprietates ueras que in re sunt in Deo et ex natura rei et in ipsis
45 angelis¹⁶ spiritualibus nititur exprimere licet per remotas et ualde alienas similitudines, quia enim diuinas et angelicas proprietates inuisibiles non bene intelligere possumus nisi per¹⁷ corporales et uisibiles¹⁸ creaturas. Ideo eas non proprie sed in propriis nominibus rerum nobis notarum cogimur circumloqui. Intendimus tamen per¹⁹ has similitudines licet re-
50 motas aliquid rem²⁰ ipsam²¹ Dei et angelorum nature ueraciter et ad litteram²² designare,²³ propter quod iste sensus reducitur ad litteralem et ei deseruit et²⁴ ipsi adheret. Tamen ita uarie²⁵ et multiformiter hic sensus in diuinis libris uariatur. Quod an²⁶ magis litterali²⁷ hystorico uel non hystorico adhereat non uidetur michi posse faciliter assignare.

55 De poetico tamen in aliquibus locis planum est quod deseruit sensui hystorico ut de illo poemate²⁸ Iudicum ix. quod²⁹ ad litteram dicitur de hystoria³⁰ Abimelech quomodo ligna³¹ siluarum unxerunt sibi³² regem. Et de probleumate³³ Sampsonis ibidem capitulo xiv.³⁴ ubi dicitur "de comedente exiuit cibus, et de forti egressa est dulcedo," quidem³⁵
60 ad litteram intelligitur de leone quem interfecit Sampson in cuius ore post mortem eius indicauerat examen apum. Unde postea Sampson³⁶

---

¹ ut dominus dicit Luca] ut dicit beatus Lucas S
² xi.] ut *add* L   ³ accomodata] ergo *add* S   ⁴ Cristum] ipsum W
⁵ homo] posergre {?} *del* S   ⁶ proficiscens] proficissens W
⁷ tradidit] bona sua et uni quidem dedit quinque talenta *add* W, S bona sua et uni uerodedit quinque talenta *add* L. W, f. 137r.
⁸ Mt. 25.14–15. S, f. 43v.   ⁹ igitur] ergo L   ¹⁰ L, f. 111rb.
¹¹ quedam...non hystorico] *om* W, S   ¹² eciam] p *del* M propter *add* L   ¹³ M, f. 77r.
¹⁴ reducitur] deducitur M   ¹⁵ Quomodo...ad litteralem] *om* L
¹⁶ angelis] seu subtancijs S   ¹⁷ per] principales et S   ¹⁸ et uisibiles] *om* S   ¹⁹ per] *om* S
²⁰ aliquid rem] ad et in S   ²¹ rem ipsam] in ipsa M, W   ²² et ad litteram] *om* S
²³ designare] nature *add* S   ²⁴ et] seu M, W, L, S   ²⁵ uarie] *corr* farie M
²⁶ an] autem W   ²⁷ B, f. 140r.   ²⁸ poemate] poete S
²⁹ Iudicum ix. quod] iuda circa x. S   ³⁰ hystoria] historico S   ³¹ ligna] lingna W
³² sibi] *om* M, L, S
³³ probleumate] problemate S. The term is adapted from the Greek noun πρόβλημα.
³⁴ Ju. 14.8, 14.   ³⁵ quidem] quod W, L, S   ³⁶ postea Sampson] *trans* M, S

transiens assumpsit de faucibus et mandibula mortui[1] leonis cibum. Ita ut uere[2] de parte leonis prius cum uiueret comedente exiuit cibus et de ipso leone prius forti egressa est dulcedo mellis.

Sed de poemate[3] quorumdam psalmorum et canticorum ubi nix et grando, nox et dies, lux et tenebre poetice inducuntur[4] ad laudandum domini satis patet quod ibi sensus poeticus[5] deseruit sensui[6] litterali non hystorico. Plura alia de ista materia in tractatu alio requirantur.[7]

Quintum capitulum quomodo quatuor sensus[8] figuratiui litterales a sensibus figuratiuis mysticis distinguantur.[9]

Post hec[10] utile est inquirere quomodo hij sensus quatuor figuratiui littere adherentes et litterali sensui subseruientes[11] a sensibus misticis distinguantur, qui[12] et ipsi sunt figuratiui.[13] De quo difficultas oriri uidetur exinde quod allegoria est quidam tropus[14] et species tropi secundum Ysidorum et *Grecissimum*, quare ergo sensus tropicus pertinet ad litteralem et allegoricus ad sensos mysticos.[15] Item enigma est species allegorie ut dicit Ysidorus i. *Ethymologiarum* capitulo xxii. Quare ergo duo sensus enigmatici scilicet symbolicus et poeticus pertineant ad sensum litteralem? Sensus autem allegoricus ad mysticos reducatur huius.[16] Oportet inquirere racionem. Primo ergo uidenda est differencia[17] inter figuratiuos litterales et figuratiuos mysticos.[18] Secundo dissolui possunt ea[19] que circa hanc materiam dubium ingerere uidentur et que iam pretacta sunt. Uidetur autem michi quod inter istos[20] sensus[21] hinc et inde possit quintuplex differencia[22] assignari. Prima est quod ea[23] ex quibus assumitur[24] significacio in sensibus mysticis habent fundamentum[25] in rebus. Quoniam[26] Iherusalem, que potest fundare sensus mysticos, ut supra patuit secundo capitulo, fuit uera res, et uera ciuitas et agnus paschalis et lapis quem Jacob capiti suo subposuit[27] dormiendo fuerunt uere res per[28] que[29] Cristus allegorice significatur. Sed ea ex quibus assumitur[30] significacio in sensibus figuratiuis litteralibus, non[31] oportet

---

[1] mortui] *om* L [2] Ita ut] *trans* S. uere] *om* S [3] poemate] poete S
[4] inducuntur] inducantur W [5] poeticus] poticus B [6] L, f. 111va. [7] S, f. 44r.
[8] sensus] *om* W [9] B, f. 77v. Quintum ... distinguantur *om* L, S [10] Post hec] Est hoc S
[11] sensui] *del* serui W. subseruientes] *del* de B [12] qui] ut *add* S
[13] sunt figuratiui] *trans* L. W, f. 137v. [14] tropus] tropicus S
[15] Eberhardus Bethuniensis, *Graecismus*, i, line 120, ed. Wrobel, p. 9.
[16] huius] autem *add* S [17] est differencia] *trans* S [18] mysticos] sac *del* S
[19] ea] per *add* S [20] istos] hos S [21] sensus] *del* mysticos B *rep* W [22] differencia] *om* L
[23] ea] *del* q M [24] assumitur] sumitur L [25] fundamentum] fundamenta W
[26] Quoniam] *om* S Unde L
[27] subposuit] supposuit M. capiti suo supposuit] supposuit capiti suo L. B, f. 140v.
[28] per] *om* L [29] que] *del siglum* xpos W [30] assumitur] sumitur M, S, L [31] non] *om* W

quod habeant fundamentum in rebus,[1] unde ille uitulus[2] saginatus, qui dicitur occisus in parabola de filio prodigo, Luce xiv.,[3] ad litteram non oportet quod fuit uerus[4] uitulus, nec ille arbores que[5] in libro Judicum[6] dicuntur iuisse ad ungendum sibi regem uere arbores fuerunt, nec um-
95 bra alarum Dei[7] est aliquid in rebus, uel nares uel manus uel oculi qui Deo et[8] angelis per sensum symbolicum ascribuntur oportet mirari[9] in rebus esse uel fuisse.[10] Et istam differenciam tangit Augustinus viii. libro *Super Genesim ad litteram* capitulo vi. dicens "neque enim ouis illa scilicet que in paschate[11] ymolabatur non erat ouis plane erat ouis[12] occidebatur
100 et[13] manducabatur, et tamen eo uero facto quoddam aliud figurabatur, non sicut ille uitulus saginatus qui redeunti[14] minori filio in epulis cesus[15] est. Ibi quippe[16] ipsa narracio[17] figuratum est[18] non rerum significacio[19] gestarum." Et paruum infra subdit, "ipsius autem domini narracio, scilicet de filio prodigo parabola, fuit de qua nunquam exigitur, ut eciam
105 ad litteram facta monstrentur que sermone proferuntur. Cristus[20] autem lapis est unctus a Jacob et lapis reprobatus ab edificantibus[21] sed illud scilicet[22] de lapide uncto et reprobato eciam in rebus gestis factum est." Hec Augustinus.

Secunda differencia inter istos sensus hinc et inde est quod eadem
110 uerba sacre scripture multipliciter possunt exponi in sensibus mysticis ab alio sic et[23] aliter et[24] omnes sani intellectus qui de sensu litterali quicumque possunt eruere et in mysticos transferre. Ipsi littere[25] sunt[26] inditi[27] a Deo et a[28] spiritu sancto secundum quod Augustinus dicit xii. libro *Confessionum* capitulo xxxi.[29] Ita quod sensus mystici respiciunt[30]
115 in sensu litterali omnia fundamenta que ueritati et sane[31] fidei consona sunt.

Sensus tamen figuratiui litterales non oportet quod tot in littera propria respiciant fundamenta, sed uerificantur plerumque in determinatis materijs et non in alijs sicut parabola de uinee locacione solum uerificata[32]
120 est ad litteram in judeis Cristum crucifigentibus. Et parabola Nathan

---

[1] L, f. 111vb.   [2] uitulus] *del* sagina W   [3] xiv.] xv. W xx. S. Lk. 15.23.
[4] uerus] ueterus W *om* S   [5] que] qui W   [6] Ju. 9.10.   [7] Ps. 17.8.   [8] et] uel S
[9] mirari] mouere L *add* usque M, W, S, L   [10] S, f. 44v.   [11] M, f. 78r.
[12] plane erat ouis] *trans* S   [13] et] *del* mandantur W   [14] redeunti] reuerenti L sensus S
[15] cesus] casus S   [16] Ibi quippe] *trans* S
[17] ipsa narracio] per huiusmodum narracionem aliquid S
[18] est] tamen L   [19] significacio] signo S   [20] W, f. 138r.
[21] ab edificantibus] ad edificandum S   [22] scilicet] *om* L
[23] ab alio sic] *rep* B, S, *rep et add* et M, L, W   [24] aliter et] *om* S   [25] littere] *supersc* S
[26] sunt] *om* M possunt S. sunt inditi] *trans* L   [27] inditi] induci S   [28] a] *om* L, S
[29] capitulo xxxi.] *trans*. L   [30] respiciunt] *om* M   [31] L, f. 112ra.   [32] uerificata] locata L

de Dauid ii. Regum xii. Et sensus poeticus Judicum ix.[1] de lignis[2] siluarum uerificatus fuit de Abimelech,[3] quod eciam in nonnullis[4] sensibus symbolicis non est difficile demonstrare.[5]

Tercia ergo differencia sequens ex ista uidetur esse quod exposicio[6] sensuum mysticorum sacre scripture ex diuina prouidencia et per se uidetur esse inserta quia sicut Apostolus dicit i. [Ad] Corinthios xii.[7] Omnia[8] que contingebant judeis[9] contingebant eis in figura, et tota lex uetus non fuit nisi quedam umbra futurorum bonorum, Hebreos x.[10] Et Augustinus dicit in libro *De uera religione* quod totum[11] uetus tes[12]tamentum non fuit nisi ymago noui testamenti. Hoc tamen non oportet ita sentire de figuratiuis sensibus litteralibus, qui magis uidentur per accidens inserti uel propter indisposicionem[13] intellectus nostri, ut patet de sensu symbolico, quia secundum Dyonysium[14] uero est[15] possibile aliter nobis lucere[16] diuinum radium nisi methaphoris sacris[17] circumuelatum,[18] uel[19] propter maiorem intencionem adhibendam, ut patet de alijs sensibus qui lectores uel auditores in ammiracionem per sua enigmata[20] erigendo ipsos[21] magis reddunt attentos.

Quarta differencia sequitur ex premissis quod isti[22] figuratiui litterales [sensus], excepto forte symbolico, quantum ita proprie uel magis inueniuntur in scripturis[23] poetarum et gentilium. Unde dicit Augustinus[24] ii.[25] libro *De doctrina christiana* capitulo xvii. ex[26] Varrone[27] narrante mussas[28] nouem a tribus[29] fabris fabricatas quolibet eorum[30] trinas[31] fabricantes. Quidam intellexerunt non quidem diuinas[32] a Joue[33] et Minerua creatas, sed pocius omne modum musice artis, quia constat ad[34] omnem sonum qui materies cantilenarum est[35] triformate[36] esse nature, aut enim uoce editur, sicuti[37] est eorum[38] qui proprijs faucibus sine aliquo organo cantant, aut flatu, sicut[39] tubarum aut tybiarum,[40] aut pulsu, sicut in cytharis[41] aut tympanis. Et libro iii.[42] capitulo vii.[43] ostendit per Neptunum, qui a gentilibus deus omnium aquarum dicebatur, quosdam

---

[1] ix.] *om* S   [2] lignis] lingnis W   [3] Abimelech] *in parte supersc* {lech} S
[4] in nonnullis] in non in illis S   [5] demonstrare] monstrare W   [6] B, f. 141r.
[7] 1 Cor. 10.11.   [8] S, f. 45r.   [9] judeis] eis W   [10] He. 10.1.   [11] totum] tota M *om* S
[12] M, f. 78v.   [13] indisposicionem] disposicionem L   [14] Dyonysium] Augustinum L
[15] uero est] non W   [16] lucere] circa *del* L   [17] sacris] circa *del* L
[18] circumuelatum] cognoscere *add* S   [19] uel] eciam *add* S   [20] enigmata] enigma W
[21] ipsos] *om* S   [22] isti] sensus *add* S   [23] scripturis] scriptura S prophetarum *add* L
[24] Augustinus] *om* L   [25] ii. libro] in libro ii. S   [26] ex] quod M, W, L de S
[27] Varrone] nararne {!} S   [28] mussas] musas M, W, L
[29] tribus] *add* cibus W. narrante mussas nonem atribus] attentando musas nonem et octibus S
[30] L, f. 112 rb.   [31] trinas] trinos S. W, f. 138v.   [32] diuinas] diuinos S
[33] a Joue] *om* L   [34] ad] *om* M   [35] est] tfo *del siglum* L   [36] triformate] *leg* triformiter
[37] sicuti] sic S   [38] est eorum] *trans* W   [39] sicut] *del* ty B   [40] aut tybiarum] *om* L
[41] cytharis] eciam *add* S   [42] iii.] in S   [43] capitulo vii.] *trans* S

150 poetarum intellexisse non quidem deum aliquem[1] sed uniuersum mare et[2] omnia flumina aut[3] aquas ceteras que fontibus prorumpunt. Ex[4] quibus omnibus patet figmenta poetica esse[5] sensum parabolicum et poeticum et eciam tropicum communiter dictum[6] eciam quoad aliquos ueros sensus plerumque in scripturis gentilium magis[7] exquisite et pro-
155 prie quam in scripturis sacris[8] reperiri, sed non ut cibum sanctorum hominum sed pocius porcorum, ut Augustinus ibidem dicit. Sensus tamen mystici eo[9] modo quo per spiritum sanctum sacre scripture sunt inditi non fuerunt[10] unquam proprie in scripturis gentilium usitati, quia[11] non inueniuntur scripture gentilium que de Cristo et[12] ecclesia[13] alle-
160 gorice exponantur, uel de sancta anima tropoloyce uel de uita eterna[14] anagogice. Sed isti sensus et modi exponendi sacram scripturam per Cristum et apostolos sunt inuenti[15] et per alios sanctos diuina inspiracione inspiratos quamuis aliqui gentiles de Cristo dicantur uaticinia cecinisse sicut Augustinus in libro *De symbola contra judeos* Sybillam[16] dicit
165 de Cristo apertissime[17] prophetasse. Et in sacra scriptura scilicet Numeri xxiii.[18] hoc idem legitur de Balaam, qui fuit gentilis. Et quidam dicunt quod Ouidius in libro[19] *De uetula* uideatur Cristi et cristianorum tempora descripsisse.

Quinta differencia est quod et ipsi figuratiui sensus litterales
170 quantum[20] fiunt fundamenta exposicionis mystice et sensuum mysticorum, sicut parabola Mattheum xxii. de rege qui fecit nupcias filio suo, secundum exposicionem Gregorii, fundat sensum allegoricum de copulacione Cristi et ecclesie et est[21] sensum tropologicum quoad peccatorem sine ueste nupciali ingredientem ad conuiuium sacramentorum Cristi,
175 et propter hoc proicitur[22] in tenebras exteriores, et eciam quandoque[23] talis parabola[24] fundat[25] sensum anagogicum, sicut Gregorius ostendit de illa cena que signat cenam ultimam uite eterne, de qua in parabolis dixit Cristus Luce xiv., "Homo quidam fecit cenam magnam." Sed[26] sensus mystici non fiunt ulterius fundamenta sensuum maiorum, et iste
180 dicere pronunc sifficiant licet[27] plures posent assignari.

[1] aliquem] illum S   [2] et] aut L   [3] aut] et S   [4] Ex] et L   [5] esse] et W, L, S
[6] dictum] dictos S   [7] S, f. 45v.   [8] sacris] id potitur *add* S   [9] eo] eodem S
[10] M, f. 79r.
[11] usitate quia] quo de ipso ut ecclesia allegorice *corr* L
[12] et] ut L   [13] ecclesia] est W *supersc add* L   [14] B, f. 141v.   [15] inuenti] adinuenti S
[16] Sybillam] sibilla M   [17] apertissime] predicasse *del* W   [18] xxiii.] xiii. S. Nr. 23.1–30.
[19] L, f. 112va.   [20] quantum] quantumque M   [21] est] eciam S   [22] proicitur] eicitur S
[23] quandoque] *om* S
[24] quandoque talis parabola] *trans* L. parabola] quantum *add* S
[25] fundat] *om* M, L
[26] Sed] non B, M, W, S
[27] licet] licent M

Ad illud ergo quod inducitur, quod allegoria est quidam[1] tropus et species tropi, dicendum est quod[2] cum[3] differentie quodammodo sint extra racionem generis, ut Aristoteles dicit, non est[4] irracionabile[5] quod quantum alique species secundum aliquid suo generi condiuidatur, sicut patet cum absolute dicitur[6] animalis magis uidetur intelligi[7] de animali irracionabili quam de homine, et cum dicitur absolute corpus magus intelligitur secundum usum de inanimato quam de animato,[8] et sic non est inconueniens quod quamuis[9] figuratiua esposicio generaliter[10] tropi nomine censeatur[11] et dicatur tropica, et tamen[12] quedam tropica non[13] sibi uendicet[14] specialiter sicut quoddam animal specialiter uendicat sibi[15] non homines[16] propter oppositam[17] differenciam impliciti ingenere[18] inclusam animali secundum aliud[19] in genere condiuisum. Uel potest aliter dici,[20] quod Ysidorus ibi magis[21] loquitur gramatice quam theologice, et[22] allegoria,[23] prout eam theologus considerat,[24] in multis differt ab allegoria prout eam gramaticus considerat, ut[25] statim patebit.

Ad secundum, quod dicitur quod[26] enicma est species allegorie, potest dici uno modo hoc[27] uerum esse secundum consideracionem gramatici.[28] Non tamen hoc oportet[29] esse verum secundum consideracionem theologi uel potest aliter[30] dici, sicut prius dictum est,[31] quod species quandoque[32] gemina[33] condiuiditur. Unde eciam Ysidorus ibidem dicit quod inter allegoriam et enigma differencia[34] est quod allegoria est quedam uis[35] gemina sub re alia[36] aliud figuraliter indicans. Enigma uero est sensus tantummodo obscurus per quasdam ymagines obumbratus. Hec ergo prununc sufficiant de differencia sensuum litteralium et[37] misticorum.

[1] quidam] quidem S [2] W, f. 139r. [3] cum] tamen W, L [4] S, f. 46r.
[5] irracionabile] racionale S [6] absolute dicitur] trans S [7] intelligi] intellige W
[8] quam de animato] om L [9] quamuis] queuis M, W
[10] generaliter] generali S [11] M, f. 79v. [12] tamen] cum M
[13] Et tamen quedam tropica] om W. tamen quedam tropica] om. S non] nomen M, W, L, S
[14] sibi uendicet] trans S. Uendicet = uindicet [15] uendicat sibi] trans M, S. sibi] om L
[16] non homines] nomen hominis M, W, L, S [17] oppositam] appositam S
[18] ingenere] om S [19] aliud] aliquid M, W, L [20] Uel potest aliter dici] rep S
[21] ibi magis] trans L [22] et] de S [23] L, f. 112vb. [24] considerat] et add W
[25] in multis differt...considerat] om S. ut] et S [26] quod] species al del L
[27] hoc] dici add L [28] consideracionem gramatici] trans S [29] hoc oportet] trans L, S
[30] B, f. 142r. [31] est] om W [32] species quandoque] trans L [33] gemina] generi M, S
[34] differencia] dictum W [35] uis] om L [36] alia] animali B, M, W
[37] et] est S sensuum add M, W, S

Bibliography

UNPUBLISHED SOURCES

Anonymous (Nicholas de Lyra). *Claues sacre scripture.* Stadtbibliothek Mainz, Hs 177, ff. 274r–275v.

Anonymous. *De quatuor sensibus sacre scripture.* Stadt- und Universitätsbibliothek Frankfurt am Main, Ms. Praed. 124, f. 17r–17v.

Anonymous. *Über die vernünftige Bildung des Menschen aus der Schrift.* Stadtbibliothek Mainz, Hs. 165, ff. 311ra–311va.

Henricus de Hassia. *Commentaria in prologis Biblie et Genesin,* Stadtbibliothek Mainz, Hs. I 449, ff. 51ra–244rb.

Hermannus de Schildesche. *Compendium de sensibus sacrae scripturae.* Basel, Universitätsbibliothek, A VII 45 ff. 133r–145v; Munich, Bayerische Stadtbibliothek, Clm 26821, ff. 71r–84r; Lüneburg Ratsbibliothek Theol. Fol. 73, ff. 106ra–114ra; Vienna, Dominikanerkloster, 46/268, ff. 131v–141v; Stuttgart, Landesbibliothek, Theol. Quart. 55, ff. 37r–50r.

Jacques Fournier. *Postilla super Mattheum,* Barcelona, Biblioteca Nacional de Catalunya, Ms 550, ff. 1ra–364va.

Jan Milíč of Kroměříž. *Quot modis sacra scriptura potest exponi.* Munich, Bayerische Staatsbibliothek, Clm 3097, ff. 241ra–249vb.

Johannes Baconthorpe. *Postilla super Mattheum.* Cambridge, Trinity College, James Ms 348, ff. 99ra–191ra.

Johannes Klenkok. *Exposicio litteralis in quattuor libris Sentenciarum.* Erfurt, Wissenschaftliche Allgemeinbibliothek, Amplon. F. 117, ff. 1–166; Amplon. Q. 118, ff. 86r–107v, 119r–135v (books I, II); Klosterneuburg, Stiftsbibliothek, Ms. 304, ff. 68r–195r; Siena, Biblioteca Comunale, G.V.16., ff. 1r–105v (books I, III, IV, and the *redactio lectoris* of book II).

Postilla super Actus Apostolorum, Eichstätt, Bayerische Staatsbibliothek, Ms. 204, ff. 117ra–192rb.

Questiones super II. Sententiarum. Eichstätt, Bayerische Staatsbibliothek, Ms. 471, ff. 157v–186r. Incorrectly attributed to Facinus de Ast.

Questiones super totam materiam canonice Johannis. Oxford, Bodleian Library, Hamilton Ms. 33, ff. 247ra–258v.

Johann Michael. *Lectura super Bibliam.* Munich, Bayerische Staatsbibliothek, Clm 9411, ff. 7r–288v.

Johannes Wyclif. *Postilla super Actus apostolorum*. Vienna, Österreichische Nationalbibliothek, Ms. 1342, ff. 294vb–323ra.
Johann Müntzinger. *Liber leccionum epistolarum sancti*. Basel, Universitätsbibliothek, A V 28, ff. 146r–226v.
Expositio super oratione dominica. Würzburg, Universitätsbibliothek, M.ch.f. 109, ff. 316r–328r. Middle High German, in spite of the Latin title.
Nicolaus Eimericus. *Postilla super epistolam Pauli ad Galatos*. Barcelona, Biblioteca Nacional de Catalunya, Ms. 1280. This appears to be an autograph, on comparison with Barcelona, Ms. 1278.
Postilla super Lucam. Barcelona, Biblioteca Nacional de Catalunya, Ms. 1287, ff. 1r–139r.
Postilla super Mattheum. 3 vols. Barcelona, Biblioteca Nacional de Catalunya, Ms. 1278. The autograph.
Nicholas de Gorran. *Euangelia et epistolae cum diuisionibus cum sermonibus*. Stadtbibliothek Mainz, Hs. I. 153, ff. 4–65.
Postilla super Exodum. Würzburg, Universitätsbibliothek, M.p.th. fol. 155, ff. 2ra–113vb.
Postilla super Genesim. Würzburg, Universitätsbibliothek, M.p.th. fol. 151, ff. 9v–36rb, 58vb–169vb.
Postilla super Lucam. Würzburg, Universitätsbibliothek, M.ch. fol. 277, ff. 3ra–297vb.
Petrus Aureolus. *Compendium literalis sensus totius divine scripture*. Biblioteca de la Universida de Barcelona, Ms. 121, ff. 1ra–109va.
Robertus Holcot. *Postilla super librum Sapientie*. Stadtbibliothek Mainz, Hs. II 480, ff. 1ra–380va; Hs. I 26, 1ra–355vb.
Tabula in postillam super librum Sapientie. Stadtbibliothek Mainz, Hs. I 208, ff. 105r–130v.

PUBLISHED SOURCES AND COLLECTIONS

Acta capitulorum generalium ordinis praedicatorum, ed. B. M. Reichert, 3 vols. Rome: Typographia polyglotta s.c. de propaganda fidei, 1898–1900.
Anonymous. *Praefatio* (to Rabanus Maurus' *Allegoria*). In *Spicilegium Solesmense*, vol. 3, pp. 436–45, ed. Jean Baptista Pitra. Paris: Didot, 1855; reprinted Graz: Akademische Druck- und Verlagsanstalt, 1963.
Aristotle. *Works*, trans. W. D. Ross. 12 vols. Oxford: Clarendon, 1908–52.
Augustine. *On Christian Doctrine*, trans. D. W. Robertson. Indianapolis: Bobbs-Merrill, 1958.
Letters, trans. W. Parsons and R. B. Eno. Washington, DC: Catholic University of America Press, 1951–89.
The Literal Meaning of Genesis, trans. J. H. Taylor, 2 vols. New York: Newman Press, 1982.
Augustinus de Ancona. *Summa de potestate ecclesiastica*. Augsburg: Johannes Schüssler, 1473.

Auriol, Pierre. *Scriptum super primum Sententiarum*. Edited by E. M. Buytaert. St. Bonaventure, New York: The Franciscan Institute, 1952–56.
Bacon, Francis. *Works*, ed. Basic Montagu. London: William Pickering, 1825–34.
Bacon, Johannes. *Questiones in quatuor libros Sententiarum et Quodlibetales*, 2 vols. Cremona: Marcus Antonius Balpierus, 1618.
Biblia Latina cum glossa ordinaria: Facsimile Reprint of the Editio Princeps, Adolph Rusch of Strassburg 1480/81. 4 vols., Brepols: Turnhout, 1992.
Biblia. Quid in hac editione praestitum sit, vide in ea quam operi praeposuimus, ad lectorem epistola. Paris: Robertus Stephanus, 1545.
Biblia sacra cum glossis, interlineari et ordinaria, Nicolai Lyrani postilla et moralitatibus, Burgensis additionibus et Thoringi replicis. Lyon: Anthoine Vincent, 1545.
Bonaventura. *Opera omnia*, 10 vols. Quaracchi: Collegium S. Bonaventure, 1882–1902.
Brenz, J. *Explicatio Epistolae Pauli ad Romanos*, ed. S. Strohm. Tübingen: J. C. B. Mohr, 1986.
Kommentar zum Briefe des Apostels Paulus an die Epheser nach der Handschrift der Vaticana Cod. Pal. lat. 1836, ed. W. Köhler. Heidelberg: Carl Winter, 1935.
Breviarium Romanum. Pars Autumnalis. Torino: Typographia Pontificia, 1900.
Bucer, Martin. *Common Places of Martin Bucer*, trans. D. F. Wright. Appleford: Sutton Courtenay Press, 1972.
Bullinger, Heinrich. *In omnes apostolicas epistolas*. Zürich: Froschauer, 1537.
Ratio studiorum. Zürich: Johann Wolf, 1594.
De scripturae sanctae auctoritate. Zürich: Froschauer, 1538.
Calov, Abraham. *Biblia Novi Testamenti illustrata*. Dresden and Leipzig, 1719.
Calvin, John. *Commentarius in Epistolam Pauli ad Romanos*, ed. T. H. L. Parker. Leiden: E. J. Brill, 1981.
A Harmony of the Gospels, ed. D. W. Torrance and T. F. Torrance, 3 vols. Grand Rapids: Eerdmans, 1972.
Opera selecta, ed. Peter Barth and Wilhelm Niesel, 5 vols. Munich: Christian Kaiser, 1926–62.
Cassiodorus. *Institutiones*, ed. R. A. B. Mynors, Oxford University Press, 1937.
Corpus Christianorum Series Latina. 176 vols. Turnholt: Brepols, 1954–
Corpus Iuris Canonici, 2 vols., ed. Emil Friedberg. Leipzig: Bernhardt Tauchnitz, 1879, 1891.
Corpus Iuris Civilis, 3 vols., ed. Theodor Mommsen. Berlin: Weidmann, 1877, 1880, 1883.
Corpus Reformatorum, 101 vols., ed. C. G. Bretschneider. Brunswick: A. Schwetschke et Filius, 1863+.
Corpus Scriptorum Ecclesiasticorum, 89 vols.+. Vienna: Hoelder-Pichler-Tempsky, 1866–1986+.
Dionysius Carthusiensis. *Opera omnia*. 42 vols., Montreuil: Typis Cartusiae S. M. de Pratis, 1896–1913.
Opera selecta, ed. Kurt Emery, vol. 1, *Bibliotheca manuscripta*. Turnholt: Brepols, 1991.

Durand, Guillaume. *Speculum Guilhelmi Durantis cum additionibus Johannis Andree.* Cologne: Antonius Koberg, 1486.
Eberhardus Bethuniensis. *Graecismus*, ed. J. Wrobel. Breslace: Wilhelm Koebner, 1887.
Erasmus, Desiderius. *On the Method of Study*, trans. Brian McGregor, vol. 24 of *Collected Works of Erasmus*. Toronto: University of Toronto Press, 1978.
  Paraclesis, trans. J. C. Olin, *Christian Humanism and the Reformation*. New York: Fordham University Press, 1965.
  Ratio seu methodus compendio perveniendi ad veram Theologiam, Ausgewählte Werke, ed. A. Holborn and H. Holborn. Munich: C. H. Beck, 1933; reprinted 1964.
  Paraphrasis in tertium Psalmum Domine quid multiplicati, in vol. 5/2 of *Opera omnia Desiderii Erasmi Roterdami*. Amsterdam/New York/Oxford: North-Holland, 1985.
Flacius Illyricus, Matthias. *Clavis scripturae sanctae*. Basel: Sebastian Henricpetri, 1567.
Gerardus Magnus. *Epistolae*, ed. Wilhelm Mulder, vol. 3 of *Tekstuitgaven van Ons Geestelijk Erf*, Antwerp: Uitgever Neerlandia, 1993.
Gerson, Johannes. *Oeuvres complètes*, 10 vols., ed. P. Glorieux. New York: Desclée et Cie, 1962.
Gilbert de la Porrée. *The Commentaries on Boethius*, ed. N. Häring. Toronto: Pontifical Institute of Mediaeval Studies, 1966.
Gregorius Ariminensis. *Lectura super primum et secundum Sententiarum*, ed. D. Trapp and V. Marcolino, 6 vols., vols. 6–12 of Spätmittelalter und Reformation, Texte und Untersuchungen. Berlin: Walter de Gruyter, 1981–7.
Guillelmus de Ockham. *Scriptum in librum primum Sententiarum ordinatio*, ed. Gedeon Gál, vol. 1 of *Opera theologica*. St. Bonaventura, NY: Franciscan Institute, 1967.
  Summa logicae, ed. P. Boehner. St. Bonaventure, NY: Franciscan Institute, 1951.
  Opera plurima, Lyon, 1494–6; réimpression en facsimilé avec un tableau des abréviations, London: Gregg Press, 1962.
Henricus de Frimaria (falsely attributed to Nicholas of Lyra). *Praeceptorium divinae legis*. Cologne: n. p., 1477 or 1497.
  Tractatus de quatuor instinctibus, ed. Robert G. Warnock and Adolar Zumkeller. *Der Traktat Heinrichs von Friemar über die Unterscheidung der Geister. Lateinisch-mittelhochdeutsche Textausgabe mit Untersuchungen*. Würzburg: Augustinus-Verlag, 1977.
Henricus Gandavensis. *Lectura ordinaria super sacram scripturam Henrico de Gandavo adscripta*, ed. R. Macken. Vol. 36 of Henricus de Gandavo, *Opera omnia*. Leuven: University Press and Leiden: E. J. Brill, 1980.
Hugh of St. Victor. *On the Sacraments of the Christian Faith*, trans. Roy J. Deferrari. Cambridge, Mass.: Mediaeval Academy of America, 1951.
Hugo de Sancto Caro. *Postilla super Bibliam*. 6 volumes. Basel: Johannes Amerbach, 1502.
Jan Milíč z Kroměříže. *Tři řeči synodní* [Jan Milíč of Kroměříže. Three Synodal Sermons], ed. Vilém Herold and Milan Mráz. Prague: Academia, 1974.

Jean Gerson. *L'Oeuvre polémique*, vol. 10 of *Oeuvres complètes*. Paris: Desclée et Cie, 1973.
Johannes Andreae. *Summa de sponsalibus et matrimonio*. Cologne: n.p., 1505.
Johannes Duns Scotus. *De primo principio. A Treatise on God as First Principle*, trans. A. J. Wolter. Chicago: Franciscan Herald, 1966.
  Quaestiones quodlibetales, ed. and trans. Felix Alluntis. Madrid: Biblioteca de Autores Cristianos, 1968.
Johannes of Erfurt. *Die Summa Confessorum des Johannes von Erfurt*, ed. Norbert Brieskorn. Frankfurt am Main: Peter Lang, 1980.
Joannes Hus. *Opera omnia*. Prague: Academia Scientiarum Bohemoslovacae, 1988.
Johannes Wyclif. *De civili dominio*, ed. J. Loserth. London: Trübner and Co., 1904.
  Latin Works, 33 vols. London: Published for the Wyclif Society by Trübner and Co., 1883–1992.
  De ueritate sacrae scripturae, ed. Rudolf Buddensieg, 2 vols. Leipzig: Dieterich, 1904.
Leibniz, Gottfried Wilhelm. *Discourse on Metaphysics. Correspondence with Arnauld. Monadology*, trans. G. R. Montgomery. La Salle, Ill.: Open Court, 1950.
Luther, Martin. *De servo arbitrio*. In WA 18:551–787. Weimar: Hermann Böhlaus Nachfolger, 1908.
  First Lectures on the Psalms. 2 vols., ed. Hilton C. Oswal, vols. 10, 11 of *Luther's Works*. St. Louis: Concordia, 1974.
Malebranche, Nicolas. *Oeuvres*, ed. Jules Simon, 2 vols. Paris: Charpentier, 1995, first published 1674.
Matthias de Janov. *Regulae Veteris et Novi Testamenti*, ed. Vlastimil Kybal, 4 vols. Innsbruck: Libraria Universitatis Wagnerianae, 1908–1913.
Matthias Flacius Illyricus. *Clavis scripturae sanctae*. Basel: Sebastian Henricpetri, 1567.
Melanchthon, Philip. *Briefwechsel: kritische und kommentierte Gesamtausgabe*, ed. Heinz Scheible, 10 vols.+ 3 supplementary. Stuttgart: Fromann-Holzboog, 1977–2000.
  Elementa rhetorices. In vol. 13 of *Phillipis Melanthonis opera quae supersunt omnia*, ed. Karl Gottlieb Bretschneider. Halle: C. A. Schwetschke et Filius, 1846.
  Erotemata dialectices (1547). Ibid.
  Selected Writings, trans. C. L. Hill. Minneapolis: Augsburg, 1962.
Mercerus, Johannes. *Commentarii locupletissimi in Prophetas quinque priores inter eos qui minores vocantur, quibus adiuncti sunt aliorum etiam et veterum (in quibus sunt Hebraei) et recentium commentarii, ab eodem excerpti*. Paris: Robert Estienne, 1573; first published Geneva, 1565.
Musculus, Wolfgang. *Common Places of Christian Religion*. London: Reginald Wolfe, 1563.
Patrologia Cursus Completus Series Latina. 221 vols., 5 supplementary vols. Paris: Garnier Frères, 1879–1974.

Newton, Issac. *Opticks*. New York: Dover, 1952.
Osiander, Andreas. *Gesamtausgabe*, 10 vols., ed. Geshard Müller. Eütersloh: Mohn, 1975–88.
Peter Lombard. *Sententiarum libri quatuor*. Paris: Louis Vivès, 1892.
Peter of Spain. *The Summulae logicales of Peter of Spain*, ed. Joseph Mullaley. Notre Dame: University of Notre Dame Press, 1945.
Petrus Aureoli. *Compendium literalis sensus totius divine scripture*. Edited by Philibert Seeboeck. Quarracchi: Collegia S. Bonaventurae, 1896.
  Scriptum super primum Sententiarum, ed. E. M. Buytaert, 2 vols. St. Bonaventure, NY: The Franciscan Institute, 1952–6.
Petrus d'Alliaco. *Tractatus et Sermones*. Strasbourg, 1490. Reprinted Frankfurt am Main: Minerva, 1971.
Petrus Comestor. *Historia scholastica*. PL 198:1645.
Pitra, Jean Baptista. *Spicilegium Solesmense*, vol. 3, Paris: Didot, 1855; reprinted Graz: Akademische Druck- und Verlagsanstalt, 1963.
Plutarch. *Complete Works*, trans. John Langhorne and William Langhorne. New York: Wheeler Publishing Company, 1909.
Tauler, Johann. *Die Predigten Taulers*, ed. Ferdinand Vetter, vol. 11 of Deutsche Texte des Mittelalters. Zürich: Weidmann, 1968.
Thomas Aquinas. *Opera omnia*. 34 vols. Paris: Vivès, 1839–95.
  The Doctrine of Scripture. Translated by John W. Beardslee. Grand Rapids: Baker Book House, 1981.
  On the Power of God, trans. L. Shapcote. Westminster, Md.: Newman Press, 1952.
Thomas de Chobham. *Summa de arte praedicandi*, ed. F. Morenzoni, CCM 82.
Ursinus, Zacharius. *Doctrinae christianae compendium seu commentarii catechetici*. Geneva: Eustathius Vignon, 1589.
Valla, Lorenzo. *Collatio Novi Testamenti*, ed. A. Perosa. Florence: Sansoni, 1970.
Vorstius, Conrad. *Commentarius in omnes epistolas apostolicas exceptis secunda Timotheum, ad Titum, at Philemon, et ad Hebraeos*. Amsterdam: Guilielmus Blaeus, 1631.
Wendelin Steinbach. *Opera exegetica*, ed. H. Feld, 3 vols. Wiesbaden: Franz Steiner, 1976–87.
William of Sherwood. *Introduction to Logic*, trans. N. Kretzmann. Minneapolis: University of Minnesota Press, 1966.
Zwingli, Huldrich. *Von Klarheit und Gewissheit des Wortes Gottes, Huldreich Zwinglis sämtliche Werke*, ed. E. Egli and G. Finsler, vol. 1 (also *Corpus Reformatorum*, vol. 88). Berlin: C. A. Schwetschke und Sohn, 1905.

SECONDARY SOURCES

Adams, Marilyn McCord. *William Ockham*, vol. 26/1–2 of Publications in Medieval Studies. Notre Dame: University of Notre Dame Press, 1987.
Ad Litteram, ed. M. D. Jordan and K. Emery. Notre Dame: University of Notre Dame Press, 1992.

Aikema, Bernard. *De heilige Hieronymus in het Studeervestrek, of: Hoe Vlaams in Antonello da Messina?* Nijmegen University Press, 2000.
Aillet, Marc. *Lire la Bible avec S. Thomas. Le passage de la* littera *à la* res *dans la Somme théologique.* Fribourg: Editions Universitaires, 1993.
Aland, Kurt and Aland, Barbara. *The Text of the New Testament.* Leiden: E. J. Brill, 1987.
Allen, Judson Boyce. *The Ethical Poetic of the Later Middle Ages.* Toronto: University of Toronto Press, 1982.
Andrés Martín, Melquiades. *La teología española en el siglo XVI*, 2 vols. Madrid: Editorial Católica, 1976–7.
Arts libéraux et philosophie au Moyen âge. Paris: J. Vrin, 1969.
Ashworth, E. J. "The Defeat, Neglect, and Revival of Scholasticism," *The Cambridge History of Later Medieval Philosophy*, ed. Norman Kretzmann, Anthony Kenny, and Jan Pinborg. Cambridge University Press, 1982, pp. 787–96.
  "Traditional Logic," *The Cambridge History of Renaissance Philosophy*, ed. C. B. Schmitt, Quentin Skinner, and Eckhard Kessler. Cambridge University Press, 1988.
  "Chimeras and Imaginary Objects: A Study in the Post-Medieval Theory of Signification." *Vivarium* 15 (1977): 57–79; reprinted idem, *Studies in Post-Medieval Semantics.* London: Variorum, 1985.
Auer, Johann. *Die Entwicklung der Gnadenlehre in der Hochscholastik.* Freiburg: Herder, 1951.
Auerbach, E. *Literary Language and Its Public in Late Latin Antiquity and in the Middle Ages*, trans. R. Manheim. New York: Pantheon Books, 1965.
  "Sacrae scripturae sermo humilis," *Neuphilologische Mitteilungen* (1941): 57–67; reprinted idem, *Neue Dantestudien*, vol. 5 of İstanbul Yazilari (Istanbuler Schriften). Istanbul: Ibrahim Horoz Basimevi, 1944.
Backus, Irena. "La théorie logique de Martin Bucer: quelques remarques sur les conditions de vérité et sur la prédication chez Pierre Crockaert, Georges de Trébizonde, Ralph Lever et Martin Bucer," *Logique et théologie au xvie siecle: aux sources de l'argumentation de Martin Bucer*, ed. I. Backus, P. Fraenkel, *et al.* Geneva: Revue de Théologie et de Philosophie, 1980.
Bartelink, G. J. M. "Sermo piscatorius. De 'vissertaal' van de apostelen," *Studia Catholica* 35 (1960): 267–73.
Benrath, Gustav Adolf. "Traditionsbewußtsein, Schriftverständnis und Schriftprinzip bei Wyclif," *Antiqui und Moderni*, ed. A. Zimmermann. Vol. 9 of Miscellanea Mediaevalia. Berlin: Walter De Gruyter, 1974.
  Wyclifs Bibelkommentar, vol. 36 of Arbeiten zur Kirchengeschichte. Berlin: Walter de Gruyter, 1966.
Berthier, Marie-Thérèse and John-Thomas Sweeney. *Le Chancelier Rolin, 1376–1462.* Précy-sous-Thil: Editions de L'Armançon, 1998.
The Bible in the Medieval World: Essays in Memory of Beryl Smalley, ed. Katherine Walsh and Diana Wood. Oxford: Blackwell, 1985.
Biblical Hermeneutics in Historical Perspective, ed. Mark S. Burrows and Paul Rorem. Grand Rapids: Eerdmans, 1991.

Biblical Interpretation in the Era of the Reformation, ed. Richard A. Muller and John L. Thompson. Grand Rapids: Eerdmans, 1996.

Bolyard, Charles. "Knowing *naturaliter*. Auriol's Propositional Foundations," *Vivarium* 38 (2000): 162–76.

Bouwsma, William J. *John Calvin. A Sixteenth Century Portrait*. Oxford University Press, 1988.

——— *Calvin's Theology as* Theologia Rhetorica. Berkeley: Center for Hermeneutical Studies, 1987.

Boyle, Marjorie O'Rourke. *Erasmus on Language and Method in Theology*. Toronto: University of Toronto Press, 1977.

Brady, Thomas A. *The Protestant Reformation in German History*. Vol. 22 of Occasional Papers of the German Historical Institute. Washington, DC: German Historical Institute, 1998.

Brecht, Martin. *Martin Luther*, trans. J. Schaaf, 3 vols. Philadelphia: Fortress, 1985–1993.

Breen, Quirinus. *Christianity and Humanism*. Grand Rapids: Eerdmans, 1968.

Brinkmann, Hennig. "Die Zeichenhaftigkeit der Sprache, des Schriftums und der Welt im Mittelalter." *Zeitschrift für deutsche Philologie* 3 (1974): 1–11.

——— *Mittelalterliche Hermeneutik*. Tübingen: Max Niemeyer, 1980.

Brown, Peter. *Religion and Society in the Age of St. Augustine*. New York: Harper and Row, 1972.

——— "St. Augustine's Attitude to Religious Coercion," *Journal of Roman Studies* 54 (1964): 107–16.

Bruns, Gerald. *Hermeneutics Ancient and Modern*. New Haven: Yale University Press, 1992.

Buc, Philippe. *L'Ambiguïté du livre. Prince, pouvoir, et peuple dans les commentaires de la Bible au Moyen Age*, vol. 95 of Théologie Historique. Paris: Beauchesne, 1994.

Burnett, Stephen G. *From Christian Hebraism to Jewish Studies: Johannes Buxtorf (1564–1629) and Hebrew Learning in the Seventeenth Century*. Leiden: Brill, 1996.

——— "Reformation-Era Christian Hebraism at a Crossroads: Martin Luther, Sebastian Münster, and the Proper Use of Jewish Biblical Commentaries," unpublished paper presented to the Sixteenth Century Studies Conference, Toronto, Canada, October 1998.

Cambridge History of the Bible, ed. G. W. H. Lampe, S. L. Greenslade, P. R. Ackroyd, and C. F. Evans, 3 vols. Cambridge University Press, 1963–70.

Cambridge History of Later Medieval Philosophy, ed. Norman Kretzmann, Anthony Kenny and Jan Pinborg. Cambridge University Press, 1982.

Cameron, Euan. *The European Reformation*. Oxford University Press, 1991.

Camporesi, Piero. *Rustici e buffoni*. Turin: Einaudi, 1991.

Cassirer, Ernst. *The Philosophy of the Enlightenment*. Princeton University Press, 1951.

Chenu, Marie-Dominique. "Histoire et allégorie au douzième siècle," *Glaube und Geschichte. Festgabe Joseph Lortz*, 2 vols. Baden-Baden: Bruno Grimm, 1958, 2:59–71.

La théologie comme science au xiiie siècle, no. 33 of Bibliothèque Thomiste. 3rd enlarged edition. Paris: J. Vrin, 1969.
La théologie au douzième siècle, vol. 45 of Etudes de philosophie médiévale. Paris: J. Vrin, 1957.
"Lecture de la Bible et philosophie," *Mélanges offerts à Etienne Gilson*. Paris: J. Vrin, 1959.
"Les deux âges de l'allégorisme scripturaire au moyen âge," *Recherches de Théologie Ancienne et Médiévale* 18 (1951): 19–28.
Clanchy, M. T. *Abelard: A Medieval Life*. Oxford: Blackwell, 1997.
Cohen, Jeremy. *The Friars and the Jews*. Ithaca: Cornell, 1982.
Collinson, Patrick. *The English Puritan Movement*. London: Jonathan Cape, 1967.
Connolly, James L. *John Gerson: Reformer and Mystic*. Louvain: Libraire Universitaire, 1928.
Copeland, Rita. *Rhetoric, Hermeneutics, and Translation in the Middle Ages*. Cambridge University Press, 1991.
Courtenay, William J. *Adam Wodeham: An Introduction to His Life and Writings*, vol. 21 of Studies in Medieval and Reformation Thought. Leiden: E. J. Brill, 1978.
"The Articles Condemned at Oxford Austin Friars in 1315," *Via Augustini. Augustine in the Later Middle Ages, Renaissance and Reformation*, ed. H. A. Oberman and F. A. James. Leiden: Brill, 1991, pp. 5–18.
Covenant and Causality in Medieval Thought. London: Variorum, 1984.
"Erfurt CA 2 127 and the Censured Articles of Mirecourt and Autrecourt," *Die Bibliotheca Amploniana. Ihre Bedeubung im Spannungsfeld von Aristotelismus, Nominalismus und Humanismus*, ed. A. Speer. Berlin: Walter de Gruyter, 1995, pp. 341–62.
"The Bible in the Fourteenth Century: Some Observations," *Church History* 54 (1985): 176–87.
"The Lost Matthew Commentary of Robert Holcot, O.P.," *Archivum Fratrum Praedicatorum* 50 (1980): 103–12.
"Nominalism and Late Medieval Religion," *The Pursuit of Holiness in Late Medieval and Renaissance Religion*, vol. 10 of Studies in Medieval and Reformation Thought. Leiden: E. J. Brill, 1974.
Schools and Scholars in Fourteenth-Century England. Princeton University Press, 1987.
"Was there an Ockhamist School?" *Philosophy and Learning. Universities in the Middle, Ages*, ed. M. J. F. M. Hoenen, J. H. J. Schneider, and G. Wieland. Leiden: E. J. Brill, 1995, pp. 276–91.
Crombie, A. C. *Augustine to Galileo*, 2nd revised edn., 2 vols. London: Heinemann, 1952.
Cultural Context of Medieval Learning, ed. J. E. Murdoch and Edith Dudley Sylla. Baston: D. Reidel Company, 1975.
Curtius, Ernst Robert. *European Literature and the Latin Middle Ages*, trans. W. R. Trask. Princeton University Press, 1953.

De Angelis, Enrico. *La critica del finalismo nella cultura cartesiana. Contributi per una ricerca.* Florence: Le Monnier, 1967.
Deansley, Margaret. *The Lollard Bible and Other Medieval Biblical Versions.* Cambridge University Press, 1966.
De Hamel, Christopher. *Glossed Books of the Bible and the Origins of the Paris Booktrade.* Woodbridge, Suffolk: D. S. Brewer, 1984.
Delègue, Yves. *Les machines du sens. Fragments d'une Sémiologie Médiévale.* Paris: Editions des Cendres, 1987.
De Lubac, Henri. *Exègése médiévale: Les quatre sens de l'Ecriture,* 4 vols. Paris: Aubier, 1954–1964.
Denifle, Heinrich. *Die abendländischen Schriftausleger bis Luther über Justitia Dei (Rom 1,17) und Justificatio.* Mainz: Franz Kirchheim, 1905.
De Rijk, Lambert Marie. *Die mittelalterlichen Traktate De modo opponendi et respondendi. Einleitung und Ausgabe der einschlägigen Texte.* Münster im Westfalen: Aschendorff, 1980.
De Vooght, Paul. *Les sources de la doctrine chrétienne d'après les théologiens du quatorzième siècle et du début du quinzième siècle.* Bruges: Desclée de Brouwer, 1954.
Dilthey, Wilhelm, *Gesammelte Schriften,* 23 vols. Leipzig and Stuttgart: B. G. Teubner, 1914–58.
Domanyi, Thomas. *Der Römerbriefkommentar des Thomas von Aquin.* Frankfurt am Main: Peter Lang, 1979.
Douglass, Jane Dempsey. *Justification in Late Medieval Preaching: A Study of John Geiler of Keisersberg,* vol. 1 of Studies in Medieval and Reformation Thought. Leiden: E. J. Brill, 1966.
Dowey, E. *The Knowledge of God in Calvin's Theology.* New York: Columbia, 1952.
Duba, William. "The Immaculate Conception in the Works of Peter Auriol," *Vivarium* 38 (2000): 5–34.
Duclow, Donald F. "Meister Eckhart on the Book of Wisdom: Commentary and Sermons." *Traditio* 43 (1987): 215–35.
Ebeling, Gerhard. "Die Anfänge von Luthers Hermeneutik," *Zeithschrift für Theologie und Kirche* 48 (1951): 172–230. Reprinted in *Lutherstudien,* 3 vols., Tübingen. J. C. B. Mohr, 1971–89.
    Evangelische Evangelienauslegung. Eine Untersuchung zu Luthers Hermeneutik. Munich: Christian Kaiser, 1942; reprinted Darmstadt: Wissenschaftliche Buchgesellschaft, 1962.
Eckermann, Willigis. *Wort und Wirklichkeit. Das Sprachverständnis in der Theologie Gregors von Rimini und sein Weiterwirken in der Augustinerschule,* vol. 33 of Cassiciacum. Würzburg: Augustinus-Verlag, 1978.
Eckermann, Willigis (ed.). *Schwerpunkte und Wirkungen des Sentenzenkommentars Hugolins von Orvieto O.E.S.A.* Würzburg: Augustinus-Verlag, 1990.
Eden, Kathy. *Hermeneutics and the Rhetorical Tradition.* New Haven: Yale University Press, 1997.
Ehrle, Franz. *Der Sentenzenkommentar Peters von Candia.* Münster: Aschendorf, 1925.

Eissfeldt, Otto. *The Old Testament. An Introduction*, trans. P. R. Ackroyd. San Francisco: Harper and Row, 1965.
Elert, Werner, *The Structure of Lutheranism*, trans. W. A. Hansen. St. Louis: Concordia, 1962.
Engammare, Max. "Calvin: A Prophet without a Prophecy," *Church History* 67 (1998): 643–61.
"De la chaire au bûcher: La Bible dans l'Europe de la Renaissance," *Bibliothèque d'Humanisme et Renaissance* 61 (1999): 737–61.
"Qu'il me baise des baisiers de sa bouche." Le Cantique des cantiques à la Renaissance. Geneva: Droz, 1993.
Evans, Gillian. *The Language and Logic of the Bible*, 2 vols. Cambridge University Press, 1984–5.
Fatio, Olivier. *Méthode et théologie*. Geneva: Droz, 1976.
Feld, Helmut. *Die Anfänge der modernen biblischen Hermeneutik in der spätmittelalterlichen Theologie*. Number 66 of Vorträge des Instituts für Europäische Geschichte. Wiesbaden: Franz Steiner, 1977.
Fischer, M. "Des Nicholaus von Lyra Postillae perpetuae in vetus et novum testamentum in ihrem eigenthumlichen Unterschied von der gleichzeitigen Schriftauslegung," *Jahrbücher für Protestantische Theologie* 15/3 (1889): 452.
Frank, Isnard. *Hausstudium und Universitätsstudium der Wiener Dominikaner bis 1500*. Vienna: Böhlau, 1988.
Frede, Michael, "The Original Notion of Cause," *Doubt and Dogmatism*, ed. M. Schonfield *et al*. Oxford: Clarendon, 1980.
Froehlich, Karlfried. " 'Always to Keep to the Literal Sense Means to Kill One's Soul': The State of Biblical Hermeneutics at the Beginning of the Fifteenth Century," *Literary Uses of Typology from the Late Middle Ages to the Present*, ed. E. Miner. Princeton University Press, 1977.
"Bibelkommentare–zur Krise einer Gattung," *Zeitschrift für Theologie und Kirche* 84 (1987): 465–92.
"Christian Interpretation of the Old Testament in the High Middle Ages," *Hebrew Bible/Old Testament. The History of its Interpretation*, ed. Magne Saebo, 3 vols. Göttingen: Vandenhoeck and Ruprecht, 2000, I/2.
"Formen der Auslegung von Matthäus 16,13–18 im lateinischen Mittelalter." Diss., Basel, 1960. Published in part Tübingen, 1963.
"Johannes Trithemius on the Fourfold Sense of Scripture," *Biblical Interpretation in the Era of the Reformation*.
"Saint Peter, Papal Primacy, and the Exegetical Tradition, 1150–1300," *The Religious Roles of the Papacy: Ideals and Realities, 1150–1300*, ed. Christopher Ryan, vol. 8 of Papers in Mediaeval Studies. Toronto: Pontifical Institute of Mediaeval Studies, 1989, pp. 3–44.
Fumaroli, Marc. *L'Age de L'éloquence*. Geneva: Droz, 1980.
Funkenstein, Amos. *Theology and the Scientific Imagination from the Middle Ages to the Seventeenth Century*. Princeton University Press, 1986.
Gadamer, Hans-Georg. *Truth and Method*. New York: Continuum, 1975.

Ganoczy, Alexander. "Jean Major, exégète gallican," *Recherches de Science Religieuse* 56 (1968): 457–95.
The Young Calvin. Grand Rapids: Eerdmans, 1987.
Genres littéraires dans les sources théologiques et philosophiques médiévales. Définition, critique et exploitation. Louvain-la-Neuve: Institut d'Etudes Médiévales de l'Université Catholique de Louvain, 1982.
Gerrish, Brian. *Grace and Reason. A Study in the Theology of Luther.* Oxford: Clarendon Press, 1962.
Gertz, Sunhee Kim. *Poetic Prologues.* Frankfurt am Main: Vittorio Klostermann, 1996.
Ghellinck, J. de. *Le mouvement théologique du douzième siècle.* No. 10 of Museum Lessianum, section historique. Paris: Desclée-De Brouwer, 1948.
Le mouvement théologique du xiie siècle. Bruges: Editions de Tempel, 1948.
"'Pagina' et 'sacra pagina.' Histoire d'un mot et transformation de l'objet primitivement désigné," *Etudes d'histoire littéraire et doctrinale de la scolastique médiévale offertes à Auguste Pelzer.* Louvain: Université de Louvain, 1947, pp. 23–59.
Gibson, Margaret. "The *De doctrina christiana* in the School of St. Victor," *Reading and Wisdom. The* De doctrina christiana *in the Middle Ages*, ed. E. D. English. Notre Dame: University of Notre Dame Press, 1995, pp. 41–7.
"The Study of the Bible in the Middle Ages." *Journal of Ecclesiastical History* 39 (1988): 230–2.
Gilbert, Neal Ward. "Ockham, Wyclif, and the 'via moderna,'" *Antiqui und Moderni*, ed. A. Zimmermann. Berlin: Walter De Gruyter, 1974, pp. 85–125.
Grell, Ole Peter. *Calvinist Exiles in Tudor and Stuart England.* Aldershot: Scolar Press, 1996.
Dutch Calvinists in Early Stuart London. Leiden: E. J. Brill, 1989.
Girardin, Benoît. *Rhétorique et théologie, Calvin, le commentaire de l'Epitre aux Romains.* Paris: Editions Beauchesne, 1979.
Gössmann, Elisabeth. *Glaube und Gotteserkenntnis im Mittelalter*, vol. 1/2b of *Handbuch der Dogmengeschichte*, 4 vols. and numerous parts, ed. Michael Schmaus *et al.* Freiburg: Herder, 1971–1990.
Antiqui und Moderni im Mittelalter. Munich: Ferdinand Schöningh, 1974.
Grabmann, Martin. *Die Sophismataliteratur des 12. und 13. Jahrhunderts mit Textausgabe eines Sophisma des Boetius von Dacien.* Münster: Aschendorf, 1940.
Geschichte der scholastischen Methode, 2 vols. Freiburg im Breisgau: Herder, 1909–11.
Gruber, Hans-Günter. *Christliches Eheverständnis im 15. Jahrhundert. Eine moralgeschichtliche Untersuchung zur Ehelehre Dionysius' des Kartäusers*, vol. 29 of Studien zur Geschichte der katholischen Moraltheologie. Regensburg: Friedrich Pustet, 1989.
Guisberti, Franco. *Materials for a Study on Twelfth-Century Scholasticism.* Naples: Bibliopolis, 1982.

Hagen, Kenneth. *A Theology of Testament in the Young Luther. The Lectures on Hebrews.* Vol. 12 of Studies in Medieval and Reformation Thought. Leiden: E. J. Brill, 1974.

Hägglund, B. "Evidentia sacrae scripturae. Bemerkungen zum 'Schriftprinzip' bei Luther." *Vierhundertfünfzig Jahre lutherische Reformation, 1517–1967. Festschrift für Franz Lau zum 60. Geburtstag.* Göttingen: Vandenhoeck und Ruprecht, 1967.

Hailperin, Herman. *Rashi and the Christian Scholars.* Pittsburgh: University of Pittsburgh Press, 1963.

Hamburger, Jeffrey F. *Nuns as Artists. The Visual Culture of a Medieval Convent.* Berkeley: University of California Press, 1997.

Hamm, Berndt. *Frömmigkeitstheologie am Anfang des 16. Jahrhunderts.* Tübingen: J. C. B. Mohr, 1982.

Promissio, Pactum, Ordinatio. Freiheit und Selbstbindung Gottes in der scholastischen Gnadenlehre. Tübingen: J. C. B. Mohr, 1977.

"Warum wurde für Luther der Glaube zum Zentralbegriff des christlichen Lebens?" *Die frühe Reformation in Deutschland als Umbruch,* ed. B. Moeller. Gütersloh: Gütersloher Verlagshaus, 1998, pp. 103–27.

Häring, Nikolaus, "Commentary and Hermeneutics," *Renaissance and Renewal in the Twelfth Century,* ed. R. L. Benson and G. Constable. Cambridge, Mass.: Harvard University Press, 1982.

Harrison, Peter. *The Bible, Protestantism and the Rise of Natural Science.* Cambridge University Press, 1998.

Hausamann, Susi. *Römerbriefauslegung zwischen Humanismus und Reformation: eine Studie zu Heinrich Bullingers Römerbriefvorlesung von 1525.* Zürich: Zwingli-Verlag, 1970.

Heath, Terence. "Logical Grammar, Grammatical Logic, and Humanism in Three German Universities," *Studies in the Renaissance* 18 (1971): 9–64.

Herman, Rudolf. *Studien zur Theologie Luthers und des Luthertums,* vol. 2 of *Gesammelte und nachgelassene Werk.* Göttingen: Vandenhoeck und Ruprecht, 1981.

Hermann, Ulrich. "Dilthey, Wilhelm (1833–1891)." TRE: 752–61.

Herold, Vilém, and Milan Mráz. *Jana Milíče z Kroměříže. Tři řeči synodní* (Jan Milič of Kroměříže. Three Synodal Sermons). Prague: Academia, 1974.

Hirsch, Immanuel. "Initium theologiae Lutheri," *Lutherstudien,* 2 vols. Gütersloh: C. Bertelsmann, 1954.

Hoenen, Maarten J. F. M. "Late Medieval Schools of Thought in the Mirror of University Textbooks. The *Promptuarium argumentorum* (Cologne 1492)," *Philosophy and Learning. Universities in the Middle Ages,* ed. M. J. F. M. Hoenen, J. H. J. Schneider, and G. Wieland. Leiden: Brill, 1995, pp. 329–69.

Hoffman. F. *Crathorn, Quästionen zum ersten Sentenzenbuch. Einführung und Text.* Münster: Aschendorff, 1988.

Die theologische Methode des Oxforder Dominikanerlehrers Robert Holcot. Münster: Aschendorff, 1972.

"Der Satz als Zeichen der theologischen Aussage bei Holcot, Crathorn und Gregor von Rimini," *Der Begriff der Repraesentatio im Mittelalter. Stellvertretung, Symbol, Zeichen, Bild.* Berlin: Walter de Gruyter, 1971, pp. 296–313.

Hoffmann, Manfred. *Rhetoric and Theology. The Hermeneutic of Erasmus* Toronto: University of Toronto Press, 1994.

Hohmann, Thomas. *Heinrich von Langenstein: Unterscheidung der Geister, lateinisch und deutsch.* Munich: Artemis, 1977.

Holl, Karl. *Gesammelte Aufsätze zur Kirchengeschichte,* 3 vols. Tübingen: J. C. B. Mohr, 1932.

Howell, Wilbur Samuel. *Logic and Rhetoric in England, 1500–1700.* New York: Russell and Russell, 1961.

Hudson, Anne. *The Premature Reformation. Wycliffite Texts and Lollard History.* Oxford: Clarendon, 1988.

Hurt, William. *The Puritan Moment. The Coming of Revolution in an English County.* Cambridge, Mass.: Harvard University Press, 1983.

Ijsewijn, J. "Alexander Hegius (d. 1498): *Invectiva in modos significandi*," *Forum for Modern Language Studies* 7 (1971): 299–318.

Interpretation and Allegory. Antiquity to the Modern Period, ed. Jon Whitman. Leiden: E. J. Brill, 2000.

Izbicki, T. M. *Protector of the Faith: Cardinal Johannes de Turrecremata and the Defense of the Institutional Church.* Washington, DC: Catholic University of America, 1981.

Jackson, B. Darrell. "The Theory of Signs in *De doctrina christiana*," *Augustine. A Collection of Critical Essays,* ed. R. A. Markus. New York: Anchor Books, 1972, pp. 92–147.

Jaeger, C. Stephen. *The Envy of Angels. Cathedral Schools and Social Ideals in Medieval Europe, 950–1200.* Princeton University Press, 1994.

Jolly, Penny Howell. "Antonello da Messina's *Saint Jerome in His Study*: An Iconographic Analysis," *The Art Bulletin* 65 (1983): 238–53.

Junghans, Helmar. *Der junge Luther und die Humanisten.* Göttingen: Vandenhoeck und Ruprecht, 1985.

Jussen, Bernhard and Craig, Koslofsky, ed. *Kulturelle Reformation. Sinnformationen im Umbruch.* Göttingen: Vandenhoeck und Ruprecht, 1999.

Kaluza, Zénon. "La crise des années 1474–1482: l'interdiction du nominalisme par Louis XI," *Philosophy and Learning. Universities in the Middle Ages,* ed. M. J. F. M. Hoenen, J. H. J. Schneider, and G. Wieland. Leiden: Brill, 1995, pp. 293–327.

Nicolas d'Autrecourt. Ami de la vérité, vol. 42/1 of *Histoire littéraire de la France.* Paris, 1995.

"Le problème du 'Deum non esse' chez Etienne de Chaumont, Nicolas Aston et Thomas Bradwardine," *Mediaevalia Philosophica Polonorum* 24 (1979): 3–19.

Les querelles doctrinales à Paris. Nominalistes et realistes aux confins du xive et du xve siècles. Bergamo: Pierluigi Lubrina, 1988.

Kelley, Donald R. *Foundations of Modern Historical Scholarship. Language, Law, and History in the French Renaissance.* New York: Columbia, 1970.

Klepper, Deeana Copeland. "Nicholas of Lyra's *Questio de adventu Christi* and the Franciscan Encounter with Jewish Tradition in the Middle Ages," Ph.D. Dissertation, Northwestern University, 1995.
Köhler, W. *Bibliographia Brentiana*. Berlin: C. A. Schwetschke und Sohn, 1904.
Kolb, Robert. "Melanchthon's Influence on the Exegesis of his Students," *Philip Melanchthon and the Commentary*, ed. T. J. Wengert and M. P. Graham. Sheffield: Academic Press, 1997.
"Teaching the Text: The Commonplace Method in Sixteenth Century Lutheran Biblical Commentary," *Beiträge zur historischen Theologie* 49 (1987): 571–85.
Kretzmann, Norman. "Aristotle on Spoken Sound," *Ancient Logic and Its Modern Interpretations*, ed. J. Corcoran. Dordrecht: Reidel, 1974, pp. 3–21.
Kreuzer, Georg. *Heinrich von Langenstein unter besonderer Berücksichtigung der Epistola pacis und der Epistola concilii pacis*. Paderborn: Ferdinand Schöningh, 1987.
Krey, Philip D. W. "Many Leaders but Few Followers: The Fate of Nicholas of Lyra's Apocalypse Commentary in the Hands of his Late-Medieval Admirers," *Church History* 64 (1995): 185–201.
Nicholas of Lyra's Apocalypse Commentary. Kalamazoo: Medieval Institute Publications, 1997.
Krey, Philip D. W. and Lesley Smith, eds. *Nicholas of Lyra: The Senses of Scripture*. Leiden: E. J. Brill, 2000.
Kurtscheid, Bertrand. "Die Tabula utriusque iuris des Johannes von Erfurt," *Franziskanische Studien* 1 (1914): 269–90.
Lafleur, Claude. "Les 'Guides d l'étudiant' de la faculté des arts de l'Université de Paris au xiiie siècle," *Philosophy and Learning. Universities in the Middle Ages*, ed. M. J. F. M. Hoenen, J. H. J. Schneider, and G. Wieland. Leiden: E. J. Brill, 1995, pp. 137–99.
Landgraf, Artur Michael. *Einführung in die Geschichte der theologischen Literatur der Frühscholastik*. Regensburg: Gregorius-Verlag, 1948.
Lang, Albert. "Johann Müntzinger, ein schwäbischer Theologe und Schulmeister am Ende des 14. Jahrhunderts, *Aus der Geisteswelt des Mittelalters*, ed. A. Lang. 3 vols. Münster: Aschendorf, 1935, 2: 1200–30.
Die theologische Prinzipienlehre der mittelalterlichen Scholastik. Frieburg im Briesgau, 1964.
Die Wege der Glaubensbegründung bei den Scholastikern des 14. Jahrhunderts. Volume 30/1–3 of Beiträge zur Geschichte der Philosophie und Theologie de Mittelalters. Münster: Aschendorf, 1930.
Langlois, Charles-Victor. "Nicolas de Lyre, Frère Mineur." *Histoire Littéraire de la France* 36 (1924): 355–400.
Laplanche, François. *La Bible en France entre mythe et critique xvie-xixe siècle*. Paris: Albin Michael, 1994.
L'Ecriture, le sacré et l'histoire. Erudits et politiques Protestants devant la Bible en France au xviie siècle. Amsterdam: Holland University Press, 1986.
Lauwers, Michel. " 'Religion populaire', culture folklorique, mentalités," *Revue d'Histoire Ecclésiastique* 82 (1987): 221–58.

Leader, Damian Riehl. *The University to 1546*, vol. 1 of *A History of the University of Cambridge*. Cambridge University Press, 1988.
Leclercq, Jean. *The Love of Learning and the Desire for God*, trans. C. Misrahi. New York: Fordham University Press, 1982.
Le Moyen Age et La Bible, ed. Pierre Riché and Guy Lobrichon. Paris: Beauchesne, 1984.
Lerner, Robert E., ed. *Neue Richtungen in der hoch- und spätmittelalterlichen Bibelexegese*. Munich: Oldenbourg, 1996.
Lewis, C. S. *The Discarded Image: An Introduction to Medieval and Renaissance Literature*. Cambridge University Press, 1964.
List, Gerhard, and Gerhardt Powitz. *Die Handschriften der Stadtbibliothek Mainz*, vol. 1. Wiesbaden: Otto Harrossowitz, 1990.
Lübke, Anton. *Nikolaus von Kues. Kirchenfürst zwischen Mittelalter und Neuzeit*. Munich: Georg D. W. Callwey, 1968.
Luoghi e metodi di insegnamento nell'Italia medioevale (Secoli xii–xiv), ed. L. Gargan and O. Limone. Galatina: Congedo, 1989.
McGinness, Frederick J. *Right Thinking and Sacred Oratory in Counter-Reformation Rome*. Princeton University Press, 1995.
McGrath, Alister. *The Intellectual Origins of the European Reformation*. Oxford: Blackwell, 1987.
McKim, Donald K. *Historical Handbook of Major Biblical Interpreters*. Downers Grove, Ill.: Intervarsity, 1998.
Macmullen, R. "A Note on Sermo humilis," *Journal of Theological Studies* ns 17 (1966): 108–12.
McNeil, Mary Germaine. *Simone Fidati and His De gestis domini salvatoris*, vol. 21 of Studies in Medieval and Renaissance Latin Language and Literature. Washington, DC: Catholic University of America, 1950.
Mack, Peter. *Renaissance Argument: Valla and Agricola in the Traditions of Rhetoric and Dialectic*. Leiden: Brill, 1993.
Maier, Anneliese. "Der Kommentar Benedikts XII. zum Matthaeus-Evangelium," *Archivum Pontificum Historicum* 6 (1968): 398–405.
Die Vorläufer Galileis im 14. Jahrhundert. Rome: Edizioni di storia e letteratura, 1949.
Maieru, Alfonso. *Terminologia logica della tarde scolastica*. Rome: Edizioni dell' Ateneo, 1972.
Mailhiot, M.-D. "La pensée de saint Thomas sur le sens spirituel." *Revue Thomiste* 59 (1959): 613–63.
Manthey, Franz. *Die Sprachphilosophie des heiligen Thomas von Aquin und ihre Anwendung auf Probleme der Theologie*. Paderborn: Ferdinand Schöningh, 1937.
Markus, R. A. "St. Augustine on Signs," *Augustine. A Collection of Critical Essays*, ed. R. A. Markus. New York: Anchor Books, 1972, pp. 61–91.
Masai, François, and Martin Wittek. *Manuscrits datés conservés en Belgique*. 3 vols. Bruxelles: Editions Scientifiques E. Story-Scientia, 1968.
Matter, E. Ann. *The Voice of My Beloved. The Song of Songs in Western Medieval Christianity*. Philadelphia: University of Pennsylvania Press, 1990.

Meier, Christel. "Argumentationsformen kritischer Reflexion zwischen Naturwissenschaft und Allegorese," *Frühmittelalterliche Studien* 12 (1978): 116–59.
Gemma spiritalis. Methode und Gebrauch der Edelsteinallegorese vom frühen Christentum bis ins 18. Jahrhundert, vol. 34/1 of Münstersche Mittelalter-Schriften. Munich: Wilhelm Fink, 1977.
"Überlegungen zum gegenwärtigen Stand der Allegorie-Forschung mit besonderer Berücksichtigung der Mischformen," *Frühmittelalterliche Studien* 10 (1976): 1–69.
Mercker, Hans. *Schriftauslegung als Weltauslegung. Untersuchungen zur Stellung der Schrift in der Theologie Bonaventuras*. Munich: Ferdinand Schöningh, 1971.
Metzger, Bruce M. *The Canon of the New Testament*. Oxford: Clarendon, 1987.
Meuthen, Erich. *Die alte Universität*, vol. 1 of *Kölner Universitätsgeschichte*. Vienna: Böhlau, 1988.
Meyer, Heinz. *Die Zahlenallegorese im Mittelalter, Methode und Gebrauch*, vol. 25 of Münstersche Mittelalter-Schriften. Munich: Wilhelm Fink, 1975.
Meyer, Heinz, and Rudolf Suntrup. *Lexikon der mittelalterlichen Zahlenbedeutungen*, vol. 56 of Münstersche Mittelalter-Schriften. Munich: Wilhelm Fink, 1987.
Michaud-Quentin, Pierre. *Universitas. Expressions du mouvement communautaire dans le moyen-âge*, vol. 13 of L'Eglise et l'état au moyen âge. Paris: J. Vrin, 1970.
Michalski, Konstanty. "Les courants critiques et sceptiques dans la philosophie du quatorzième siècle," *Bulletin International de l'Académie Polonaise des Sciences et des Lettres, classe d'histoire et de philosophie* (1925), 192–244.
Miethke, Jürgen. *Okhams Weg zur Sozialphilosophie*. Berlin: Walter De Gruyter, 1969.
Millet, Olivier. *Calvin et la dynamique de la parole: étude de rhétorique réformée*. Geneva: Editions Slatkine, 1992.
Minnis, Alistair. "'Authorial Intention' and 'Literal Sense' in the Exegetical Theories of Richard FitzRalph and John Wyclif." *Proceedings of the Royal Irish Academy*, 75 C(1975):1–30.
Medieval Theory of Authorship: Scholastic Literary Attitudes in the Later Middle Ages, 2nd edition. Philadelphia: University of Pennsylvania Press, 1988.
Minnis A. J., and A. B. Scott. *Medieval Literary Theory and Criticism, c. 1100–1375: The Commentary Tradition*. Oxford: Clarendon, 1988.
Moeller, Bernd. "Die Rezeption Luthers in der frühen Reformation," *Reformationstheorien. Ein kirchenhistorischer Disput über Einheit und Vielfalt der Reformation*, ed. B. Hamm, B. Moeller, and D. Wendebourg. Göttingen: Vandenhoeck und Ruprecht, 1995.
Moeller, Bernd and Karl Stackmann. *Städtische Predigt in der Frühzeit der Reformation*. Göttingen: Vandenhoeck und Ruprecht, 1996.
Moldaenke, G. *Schriftverständnis und Schriftdeutung im Zeitalter der Reformation*, vol. 1, *Matthias Flacius Illyricus*. Stuttgart: W. Kohlhammer, 1936.
Morey, James H. "Peter Comestor, Biblical Paraphrase, and the Medieval Popular Bible," *Speculum* 68 (1993): 10.

Mulchahey, M. Michèle. *"First the Bow is Bent in Study." Dominican Education before 1350*. Toronto: Pontifical Institute of Mediaeval Studies, 1998.
Müller, Johannes. *Martin Bucers Hermeneutik*. Gütersloh: Gerd Mohn, 1965.
Muller, Richard. *Ad Fontes Argumentorum. The Sources of Reformed Theology in the Seventeenth Century*, vol. 40 of Utrechtse theologische Reeks. Utrecht: Faculteit der Godgeleerdheid, 1999.
— *Post-Reformation Reformed Dogmatics*. 2 vols.+. Grand Rapids: Baker Book House, 1987.
— "'Scimus enim quod lex spiritualis est': Melanchthon and Calvin on the Interpretation of Romans 7.14–23," *Philip Melanchthon and the Commentary*, ed. T. J. Wengert and M. Patrick Graham. Sheffield Academic Press, 1997, pp. 216–37.
— *The Unaccommodated Calvin*. Oxford University Press, 2000.
— "William Perkins and the Protestant Exegetical Tradition: Interpretation, Style and Method," in William Perkins, *A Commentary on Hebrews 11 (1609 Edition)*, ed. John H. Augustine. New York: Pilgrim Press, 1991.
— "*Vera Philosophia cum sacra Theologia nusquam pugnat*: Keckermann on Philosophy, Theology, and the Problem of Double Truth," *Sixteeth Century Journal* 15 (1984): 341–65.
Muralt, André de. "La causalité divine et le primat de l'efficience chez Guillaume d'Occam," *Historia Philosophiae Medii Aevi. Studien zur Geschichte des Philosophie des Mittelalters*, ed. B. Mojsisch and O. Pluta, 2 vols. Amsterdam: B. R. Grüner, 1991, 2: 745–69.
Murdoch, John E. "From Social into Intellectual Factors: An Aspect of the Unitary Character of Late Medieval Learning," *The Cultural Context of Medieval Learning*, ed. J. E. Murdoch and Edith Dudley Sylla. Volume 26 of Boston Studies in the Philosophy of Science. Boston: D. Reidel Company, 1975.
— "*Mathesis in philosophiam scholasticam introducta*. The Rise and Development of the Application of Mathematics in Fourteenth Century Philosophy and Theology," *Arts libéraux et philosophie au moyen âge* (Paris and Montreal, 1969).
Murphy, James J. *Rhetoric in the Middle Ages*. Berkeley: University of California Press, 1974.
Nielsen, Lauge Olaf. "The Critical Edition of Peter Aureoli's Scholastic Works," *Editori di Quaracchi 100 anni dopo, bilancio e prospettive*. Rome: Edizioni Antonianum, 1997, pp. 217–25.
Nuchelmans, Gabriel. *Theories of the Proposition*. No. 8 of North-Holland Linguistic Series. Amsterdam and London: North-Holland Publishing Company, 1973.
Oberman, Heiko Augustinus. *Contra vanam curiositatem*, vol. 113 of Theologische Studien. Zürich: Theologischer Verlag, 1974.
— *Forerunners of the Reformation*. New York: Holt, Rinehart, and Winston, 1966.
— *The Harvest of Medieval Theology. Gabriel Biel and Late Medieval Nominalism* Cambridge, Mass.: Harvard University Press, 1963.

Ocker, Christopher. "Augustinianism in Fourteenth-Century Theology," *Augustinian Studies* 18 (1987): 81–106.
"The Fusion of Exegesis and Papal Ideology in Fourteenth-Century Theology," *Biblical Hermeneutics in Historical Perspective*, ed. M. Burrows and P. Rorem. Grand Rapids: Eerdmans, 1991, pp. 131–51.
Johannes Klenkok: A Friar's Life, c. 1310 to 1374, volume 83/5 of the Transactions of the American Philosophical Society. Philadelphia: American Philosophical Society, 1993.
"Ritual Murder and the Subjectivity of Christ: A Choice in Medieval Christianity," *Harvard Theological Review* 91 (1998): 153–92.
Oexle, Otto-Gerhard. *Geschichtswissenschaft im Zeichen des Historismus. Studien zu Problemgeschichten der Moderne*. Göttingen: Vandenhoeck und Ruprecht, 1996.
Ohly, Friedrich "Vom geistigen Sinn des Wortes im Mittelalter," *Schriften zur mittelalterlichen Bedeutungsforschung*. Darmstadt: Wissenschaftliche Buchgesellschaft, 1977, pp. 1–31.
Olin, John C. *Christian Humanism and the Reformation*. 3rd edn. New York: Fordham University Press, 1987.
O'Malley, John W. *The First Jesuits*. Cambridge, Mass.: Harvard University Press, 1993.
O'Malley, John W. "Grammar and Rhetoric in the *Pietas* of Erasmus," *The Journal of Medieval and Renaissance Studies* 1 (1998): 81–98.
"A Note on Gregory of Rimini: Church, Scripture, Tradition," *Augustinianum* 5 (1965): 378.
Praise and Blame in Renaissance Rome: Rhetoric, Doctrine, and Reform in the Sacred Orators of the Papal Court, c. 1450–1521. Durham: Duke University Press, 1979.
Ong, Walter J. *Ramus, Method, and the Decay of Dialogue*. Cambridge, Mass.: Harvard University Press, 1958.
Osler, Margaret J. "From Immanent Natures to Nature as Artifice: The Reinterpretation of Final Causes in Seventeenth-Century Natural Philosophy," *The Monist* 79 (1966): 388–403.
Padley, G. A. *Grammatical Theory in Western Europe, 1500–1700*. Cambridge University Press, 1976.
Pagden, Anthony "Rethinking the Linguistic Turn: Current Anxieties in Intellectual History," *Journal of the History of Ideas* 49 (1989): 519–29.
Paqué, R. *Das Pariser Nominalistenstatut. Zur Entstehung des Realitätsbegriffs der neuzeitlichen Naturwissenschaft*. Berlin: Walter de Gruyter, 1970.
Parker, T. H. L. *Calvin's New Testament Commentaries*. London: SCM Press, 1971.
Pasnau, Robert. *Theories of Cognition in the Later Middle Ages*. Cambridge University Press, 1997.
Pelster, Franz. "Die quaestio Heinrichs von Harclay über die zweite Ankunft Christi und die Erwartung des baldigen Weltendes zu Anfang des xiv. Jahrhunderts," *Archivo Italiano per la storia della pietà* 1 (1951): 25–82.
"Quodlibeta und Quaestiones des Nikolaus von Lyra, O.F.M. (†1349)," *Mélanges de Ghellinck*. Gembloux, 1951, pp. 951–73.
Pépin, Jean. *Dante et la tradition de l'allégorie*. Paris: J. Vrin, 1970.

Pinborg, Jan. "Die Entwicklung der Sprachtheorie im Mittelalter," vol. 42/2 of BGPTM. Münster: Aschendorf, 1967.
Pluta, Olaf, ed. *Die Philosophie im 14. und 15. Jahrhundert: In Memoriam Konstanty Michalski (1879–1947)*, vol. 10 of Bochumer Studien zur Philosophie. Amsterdam: B. R. Grüner, 1988.
Post, R. R. *The Modern Devotion. Confrontation with Reformation and Humanism.* Leiden: E. J. Brill, 1968.
Powitz, G. *Die Handschriften des Dominikanerklosters und des Leonhardstifts in Frankfurt am Main*, vol. 2/1 of *Kataloge der Stadt- und Universitätsbibliothek Frankfurt am Main*. Frankfurt am Main: Vittorio Klostermann, 1968.
Preus, James Samuel. *From Shadow to Promise: Old Testament Interpretation from Augustine to the Young Luther.* Cambridge, Mass.: Harvard University Press, 1969.
Probleme der Edition Mittel- und neulateinischer Texte, ed. Ludwig Hödl and Dieter Wuttke. Boppard: Harold Boldt, 1978.
Quétif, J., and J. Echard. *Scriptores ordinis praedicatorum*, 4 vols. New York: Burt Franklin; 1959 reprint of the edition of Paris, 1719–23.
Rahner, Karl. "La doctrine des 'sens spirituels' au moyen âge en particulier chez saint Bonaventure," *Revue d'Ascétique et de Mystique* 14 (1933): 263–99.
Reeves, Marjorie. *The Influence of Prophecy in the Later Middle Ages.* Notre Dame: University of Notre Dame Press, 1969.
Reinhard, Wolfgang. "Was ist katholische Konfessionalisierung?" *Die katholische Konfessionalisierung*, ed. W. Reinhard and H. Schilling. Münster: Aschendorf, 1995.
Reinhardt, Klaus. "Das Werk des Nicolaus von Lyra im mittelalterlichen Spanien," *Traditio* 48 (1987): 344–6.
Reventlow, Henning Graf. *The Authority of the Bible and the Rise of the Modern World.* Philadelphia: Fortress, 1985.
Reynolds, Suzanne. *Medieval Reading: Grammar, Rhetoric and the Classical Text.* Cambridge University Press, 1996.
Rice, Eugene F. *Saint Jerome in the Renaissance.* Baltimore: Johns Hopkins, 1985.
Ridderbos, Bernhard. *Saint and Symbol. Images of Saint Jerome in Early Italian Art.* Groningen: Bouma, 1984.
Ringbom, Sixton. *Icon to Narrative. The Rise of the Dramatic Close-Up in Sixteenth-Century Painting.* Åbo Akademi, 1965.
Risse, W. *Bibliographica Logica*, vol. 1, *1472–1800*. Hildesheim: G. Olms, 1965.
Ritschl, Otto. *Dogmengeschichte des Protestantismus*, 4 vols. Leipzig: J. C. Hinrichs, and Göttingen: Vandenhoeck und Ruprecht, 1908–27.
Robertson, D. W. *Essays in Medieval Culture.* Princeton University Press, 1980.
Robinson, James M. "Hermeneutic since Barth," *The New Hermeneutic*, ed. James M. Robinson and John B. Cobb. New York: Harper and Son, 1964.
Rotta, Paolo. *Il cardinale Nicolò di Cusa. La vita ed il pensiero.* Milan: Vita e Pensiero, 1928.

Rummel, Erika. *Erasmus' Annotations on the New Testament. From Philologist to Theologian*. Toronto: University of Toronto Press, 1986.
Ruokanen, Miikka. "Hermeneutics as an Ecumenical Method in the Theology of Gerhard Ebeling," volume 13 of Publications of the Luther-Agricola Society. Helsinki: Luther-Agricola Society, 1982.
Rüthing, Heinrich. "Kritische Bemerkungen zu einer Mittelalterlichen Biographie des Nikolaus von Lyra," *Archivum Franciscanum Historicum* 60 (1967): 42–54.
Schaff, Philip. *Creeds of Christendom*, 3 vols. New York: Harper and Brothers, 1877.
Schellong, D. *Calvins Auslegung der synoptischen Evangelien*. Munich: Christian Kaiser, 1969.
Schepers, H. "Holcot contra dicta Crathorn," *Philosophisches Jahrbuch* 77 (1970): 320–54; 79 (1972): 106–36.
Schild, Maurice. *Abendländische Bibelvorreden bis zur Lutherbibel*. Gütersloh: Gerd Mohn, 1970.
Schilling, Heinz. "Confessional Europe," *Handbook of European History, 1400–1600*, ed. T. A. Brady, H. A. Oberman, and J. D. Tracy, 2 vols. Leiden: E. J. Brill, 1995 2: 641–75.
"Die Konfessionalisierung von Kirche, Staat und Gesellschaft–Profil, Leistung, Defizite und Perspektiven eines Geschichtswissenschaftlichen Paradigmas," *Die katholische Konfessionalisierung*, ed. W. Reinhard and H. Schilling. Münster: Aschendorf, 1995, pp. 1–49.
Schneider, John R., "The Hermeneutics of Commentary: Origins of Melanchthon's Integration of Dialectic and Rhetoric," *Philip Melanchthon (1447–1560) and the Commentary*, ed. Timothy J. Wengert and M. Patrick Graham. Shelfield Academic Press, 1997, pp. 20–47.
Schneyer, Johannes Baptist. *Repertorium der lateinischen Sermones des Mittelalters*, 9 vols. Münster: Aschendorf, 1969–80.
Schnerb, Bertrand. *L'Etat bourgignon, 1363–1477*. Paris: Perrin, 1999.
Schulte, Johann Friedrich von. Die Geschichte der Quellen und Literatur des canonischen Rechts. Graz: Akademische Druck- und Verlagsanstalt, 1956.
Schum, Wilhelm. *Beschreibendes Verzeichnis der Amplonianischen Handschriftensammlung zu Erfurt*. Erfurt, 1887.
Schüssler, Hermann. *Der Primat der Heiligen Schrift als theologisches und kanonistisches Problem in Spätmittelalter*, Vol. 86 of Veröffentlichungen des Instituts für Europäische Geschichte Mainz. Wiesbaden: Franz Steiner, 1977.
Schütz, Christian. *Deus absconditus, Deus manifestus: Die Lehre Hugos von St. Viktor über die Offenbarung Gottes*, vol. 56 of Studia Anselmiana. Rome: Pontificium Institutum S. Anselmi, 1967.
Schwendinger, Fidelis. "De Vaticiniis Messianicis Pentateuchi apud Nicolaum de Lyra, O.F.M.," *Antonianum* 4 (1929): 3–44, 129–66.
Seybold, Michael. *Die Offenbarung. Von der Schrift bis zum Ausgang der Scholastik*. Freiburg: Herder, 1971.
Shank, Michael H. "University and Church in Late Medieval Vienna: *Modi Dicendi et Operandi*, 1388–1421," *Philosophy and Learning. Universities in the*

Middle Ages, ed. M. J. F. M. Hoenen, J. H. J. Schneider, and G. Wieland. Leiden: Brill, 1995, pp. 43–59.

"Unless You Believe You Shall Not Understand." Logic, University, and Society in Late Medieval Vienna. Princeton University Press, 1988.

Simonin, H.-D. "Les écrits de Pierre de Tarentaise," *Beatus Innocentius V (Petrus de Tarantasia O. P.) Studia et Documenta.* Rome: S. Sabina, 1943, pp. 163–335.

Smalley, Beryl. "The Bible and Eternity: John Wyclif's Dilemma," *Journal of the Warburg and Courtauld Institutes* 27 (1964): 73–89. Reprinted eadem, *Studies in Medieval Thought and Learning.*

English Friars and Antiquity in the Early Fourteenth Century. Oxford: Basil Blackwell, 1960.

"John Baconthorpe's Postill on St. Matthew," *Medieval and Renaissance Studies* 4 (1958): 91–115. Reprinted in eadem, *Studies in Medieval Thought and Learning.* London: The Hambleton Press, 1981.

"Problems of Exegesis in the Fourteenth Century," *Antike und Orient im Mittelalter*, ed. Paul Wilpert. Vol. 1 of Miscellanea Mediaevalia. Berlin: Walter de Gruyter, 1962, pp. 26–74.

"Robert Holcot, O. P.," *Archivum Fratrum Praedicatorum* 26 (1956): 5–97.

"Some Latin Commentaries on the Sapiential Books in the Late Thirteenth and Early Fourteenth Centuries," *Archives d'Histoire Doctrinale et Littéraire du Moyen Age* 18 (1950–51): 103–28.

The Study of the Bible in the Middle Ages. Oxford: Basil Blackwell, 1942, 1952.

"Use of the 'Spiritual' Sense of Scripture in Persuasion and Argument by Scholars in the Middle Ages," *Recherches de Théologie Ancienne et Médiévale* 52 (1985): 44–63.

Spicq, Ceslas. *Esquisse d'une histoire de l'exégèse latine au moyen âge.* Paris: J. Vrin, 1944.

Spinka, Matthew. *John Hus' Concept of the Church.* Princeton University Press, 1966.

Stegmüller, Friedrich. *Repertorium Biblicum Medii Aevi*, 11 vols. Madrid: Conseio Superior de Investigaciones Científicas, 1940–80.

Steinmetz, David. "Calvin among the Thomists, *Biblical Hermeneutics in Historical Perspective.* Grand Rapids: Eerdmans, 1991.

"Luther and the Ascent of Jacob's Ladder," *Church History* 55 (1986): 179–92.

Luther and Staupitz. An Essay in the Intellectual Origins of the Protestant Reformation. Durham, NC: Duke University Press, 1980.

Steneck, Nicholas H. *Science and Creation in the Middle Ages: Henry of Langenstein (d. 1397) on Genesis.* Notre Dame: University of Notre Dame Press, 1976.

Steveler, Paul A. and Katherine H. Tachau. *Seeing the Future Clearly. Questions on Future Contingents by Robert Holcot.* Toronto: Pontifical Institute of Mediaeval Studies, 1995.

Stoelen, A. "De Chronologie van de Werken van Dionysius de Karthuizer: De eerste Werken en de Schriftuurkommentaren," *Sacris Erudiri* 5(1953): 361–401.

Stroick, Clemens. *Heinrich von Friemar. Leben, Werke, philosophisch-theologische Stellung in der Scholastik.* Freiburg: Herder, 1954.

Sylla, Edith. "Autonomous and Handmaiden Science: St. Thomas Aquinas and William of Ockham on the Physics of the Eucharist," *The Cultural Context of Medieval Learning*, ed. J. E. Murdoch and E. D. Sylla. Boston: D. Reidel Company, 1975, pp. 349–91.
Tachau, Katherine. "The Preparation of a Critical Edition of Pierre Auriol's Sentences Lectures." *Editori de Quaracchi 100 anni dopo, bilancio e prospettive*, ed. A. Cacciotti and B. Faes de Mottoni. Rome: Edizioni Antonianum, 1997, pp. 205–26.
   Vision and Certitude in the Age of Ockham. Optics, Epistemology and the Foundations of Semantics, 1250–1345. Leiden: E.J. Brill, 1988.
Tavard, George. *Holy Writ or Holy Church: The Crisis of the Protestant Reformation*. New York: Harper and Brothers, 1959.
Thijssen, J. M. M. H. *Censure and Heresy at the University of Paris, 1200–1400*. Philadelphia: University of Pennsylvania Press, 1998.
Die Handschriften der Universitätsbibliothek Würzburg, 5 vols. Wiesbaden: Otto Harrassowitz, 1973–94.
Torrell, Jean-Pierre. *Théorie de la prophétie et philosophie de la connaissance aux environs de 1230* Louvain: Spicilegium Sacrum Lovaniense, 1977.
Tov, Emanuel. *Textual Criticism of the Hebrew Bible*. Minneapolis: Fortress, 1992.
Trinkaus, Charles. "The Religious Thought of the Italian Humanists, and the Reformers: Anticipation or Autonomy?" in C. Trinkaus (ed.), *The Pursuit of Holiness in Late Medieval and Renaissance Religion*. Leiden: E. J. Brill, 1972, pp. 339–66.
   "In our Image and Likeness": Humanity and Divinity in Italian Humanist Thought. London: Constable, 1970.
Turner, Denys. *Eros and Allegory: Medieval Exegesis of the Song of Songs*. Kalamazoo: Cistercian Publications, 1995.
Tuve, Elizabeth. *Elizabethan and Metaphysical Imagery. Renaissance Poetic and Twentieth-Century Critics*. Chicago: University of Chicago Press, 1947.
Ullmann, Walter. "John Baconthorpe as Canonist," *Church and Government in the Middle Ages: Essays Presented to C. R. Cheney on His Seventieth Birthday*. Cambridge University Press, 1976. Reprinted in Ullmann, *Scholarship in the Middle Ages*. London: Variorum Reprints, 1978.
Universities in the Middle Ages. Edited by Hilde De Ridder-Symoens. Volume 1 of *A History of the University in Europe*. Cambridge University Press, 1992.
van Slee, J. C. *De Rijnsburger Collegianten*. Utrecht: HES Publishers, 1980.
Verger, Jacques. "*Studia* et universités," *Le scuole degli ordini mendicanti (secoli xiii–xiv)*, vol. 17 of *Convegni del Centro di Studi sulla spiritualità medievale*. Rimini: Maggioli Editore, 1978.
Via Augustini: Augustinianism in the Later Middle Ages, Renaissance, and Reformation, ed. Heiko A. Oberman and Frank A. James. Leiden: E. J. Brill, 1991.
Vidal, J. M. "Les oeuvres du pape Benoît xii." *Revue d'Histoire Ecclésiastique* 6 (1905): 557–65, 785–810.

Vosté, I.-M. "Beatus Petrus de Tarentasia Epistularum S. Pauli interpres," *Beatus Innocentius V (Petrus de Tarentasia O. P.). Studia et Documenta*. Rome S. Sabina, 1943, pp. 337–412.

Walsh, Katherine. *Richard Fitzralph in Oxford, Avignon and Armagh*. Oxford University Press, 1981.

Warnock, Robert G. and Adolar Zumkeller. *Der Traktat Heinrichs von Friemar über die Unterscheidung der Geister. Lateinisch-mittelhochdeutsche Textausgabe mit Untersuchungen*, vol. 32 of Cassiciacum. Würzburg: Augustinus-Verlag, 1977.

Wasserstein, David J. "Grosseteste, the Jews, and Medieval Christian Hebraism," *Robert Grosseteste: New Perspectives on His Thought and Scholarship*, ed. J. McEvoy. Turnhout: Brepols, 1995, pp. 357–76.

Waxman, Meyer. *A History of Jewish Literature*, 4 vols. New York: Thomas Yoseloff, 1960.

Wengert, Timothy J. "Georg Major (1502–74). Defender of Wittenberg's Faith and Melanchthonian Exegete," *Melanchthon in seinen Schülern*, ed. H. Scheible. Wiesbaden: Harrassowitz, 1997, pp. 129–55.

Werbeck, W. *Jacobus Perez von Valencia. Untersuchungen zu seinem Psalmenkommentar*. V. 28 of Beiträge zur historischen Theologie. Tübingen: J. C. B. Mohr, 1959.

White, Graham. "Ockham and Wittgenstein." *Die Gegenwart Ockhams*, ed. Wilhelm Vossenkuhl, Rolf Schönberger. Weinheim: VCH, Acta Humaniora, 1990.

Wicks, Jared. "Doctrine and Theology," *Catholicism in Early Modern History: A Guide to Research*, ed. John O'Malley. St. Louis: Center for Reformation Research, 1988, pp. 227–51.

Wilks, Michael. *The Problem of Sovereignty in the Later Middle Ages*, Cambridge University Press, 1963.

Winkler, Eberhard. *Exegetische Methoden bei Meister Eckhart*, vol. 6 of Beiträge zur Geschichte der biblischen Hermeneutik. Tübingen: J. C. B. Mohr, 1965.

Witt, Ronald G. *'In the Footsteps of the Ancients.' The Origins of Humanism from Lovato to Bruni*. Leiden: E. J. Brill, 2000.

Wood, Rega and Robert Andrews. "Causality and Demonstration: An Early Scholastic Posterior Analytics Commentary," *The Monist* 79 (1996): 325–56.

Wriedt, Markus. *Gnade und Erwählung. Eine Untersuchung zu Johann von Staupitz und Martin Luther*. Mainz: Philipp von Zabern, 1991.

Xiberta, B. *De Scriptoribus Scholasticis Saeculi XVI. ex Ordine Carmelitanorum*. Louvain: Revue d'Histoire Ecclésiastique, 1931.

Zier, Mark A. "The Manuscript Tradition of the Glossa Ordinaria for Daniel, and Hints at a Method for a Critical Edition," *Scriptorium*, 47 (1993): 3–25.

Zumkeller, Adolar. *Erbsünde, Gnade, Rechtfertigung und Verdienst nach der Lehre der Erfurter Augustinertheologen der Spätmittelalters*. Würzburg: Augustinus-Verlag, 1984.

Schriftum und Lehre des Hermann von Schildesche O. E. S. A. (g. 1357). Würzburg: Augustinus-Verlag, 1959.

Index

Abraham, 46–7, 79, 82, 84, 94, 221
Agostino of Ancona, 122
Agricola, Rudolf, 186, 187–8, 192–3
Albertino Musato, 2
Alexander of Hales, 25
Alexander of Villa Dei, 60, 98
allegory, 3, 17, 18, 21, 22, 34, 38, 48, 50, 58, 74–7, 83, 91, 101–3, 104, 110, 145, 147, 149, 198
Allen, Judson, 18, 56, 138
Andrew of St. Victor, 20, 179, 220
Anselm of Laon, 10, 11, 20
Aristotle, 2, 4, 26, 29, 32, 38, 41, 73, 119, 124–7, 129, 133–4, 154, 210, 229, 238
Augustine, 2, 4, 16, 32, 36–7, 40, 54, 61, 73, 87, 89, 94, 102, 103, 105, 108, 119, 123, 143, 148, 163, 191, 201, 230–1, 235–7
authority, 26, 76–7, 160

Bede, 10, 51
Benedict XII, Pope, *see* Jacques Fournier
Benrath, Gustav, 181–2
Boethius, 38, 74
Bonaventure, 1, 13, 21, 25, 41–2, 93, 144
Brenz, Johannes, 207
Bucer, Martin, 196, 205
Bullinger, Heinrich, 198

Calvin, John, 192, 195, 197–8, 207, 210
Cambridge, 57, 115, 121
canon law, 9, 51, 59, 148
causes, 29, 45, 53, 92, 123–42, 170
Cicero, 1, 73–4, 114, 173, 193, 195, 208
circumstances (*circumstantiae*), 16, 33, 98, 148
concordance of the Bible, 14
Copeland, Rita, 5, 73–4
Courtenay, William J., 5, 70, 117, 120
creation, 19

Dante, 2
Delègue, Yves, 6, 7, 38–9

Denys the Carthusian (Denys van Leeuwen), 13, 23, 80, 85–6, 154, 182
Descartes, René, 127
didactic genre, 194–6
Dionysius the Carthusian, *see* Denys the Carthusian
discernment of spirits, 159–60
divisions of the Bible, 26–9, 94–5, 140
Donatus, 60, 98, 128, 229
double-literal sense, 83, 142–9

Eckhart, 14, 29, 64, 93, 107, 144
eloquence, 139, 173
Erasmus, Desiderius, 198, 199–201, 208, 215
Erfurt, 59, 78, 94
Evans, G. R., 76, 162
Evrard of Bethune, 60, 98, 102, 229

Flacius Illyricus, Matthias, 193–4, 207, 212
fourfold sense, 20–1
Froehlich, Karlfried, 18, 112
Funkenstein, Amos, 127, 128

Gerhard Groote, 119, 122
Gilbert de la Porrée, 144–5
Glossa Ordinaria, *see* Ordinary Gloss
grammar, 68–70, 73–5, 107, 110, 191, 200
Gregory the Great, Pope, 103–4, 237
Gregory of Rimini, 59

Häring, Niklaus, 5, 145
Hebrew language, 176–7, 179–80
Hebrew patriarchs, 47
Heinrich of Friemar, 14, 78–9, 156
Heinrich of Langenstein, 28, 52, 80, 84, 107–8, 114, 146–9, 149–61, 169–78
Henry of Ghent, 42, 111
Hermann of Schildesche, 38, 94–106, 224–38
Historia scholastica, *see* Peter Comestor
history, 22–3, 34, 38, 74, 109–10, 137, 138, 179–83, 216–17, 226

263

Holy Spirit, 17, 108, 130, 140, 146, 150–2, 155, 172, 175–7, 201–4, 210
Hugh of St. Cher, 43, 51
Hugh of St. Victor, 9, 15, 19, 22, 26, 28, 34–5, 38, 49, 74
humble speech, 107, 112–23

intention, 147, 156
interlinear glosses, 9, 66–8
inspiration, 155–6, 210–11
invention (*inventio*), 73
Isidore of Seville, 2, 93, 98, 102, 229, 234, 238

Jacques Fournier, 22, 25, 29, 56–7, 87–93, 113–14, 116, 122, 154–5, 163–4, 222–4
Jan Hus, 25, 145–6
Jean Gerson, 22, 119, 122, 150
Jean of Mirecourt, 117–18
Jean of Nivelle, 14
Jerome, 62, 84, 88–90, 105, 112–13, 123, 149, 200, 208
Jerome of Prague, 118
Johann Michael, 25, 79
Johann Müntzinger, 13, 29, 65–8, 137–8
Johannes Andreae, 121
Johannes Calderinus, 14, 122
Johannes Klenkok, 59–63, 70, 107, 182
Johannes Staupitz, 202
John Baconthorpe, 24, 29, 57–9, 115
John Duns Scotus, 70, 78, 160, 210
John Ruysbroek, 119
John Wyclif, 13, 29, 64, 118, 122, 145–6, 154, 162–3, 179, 181–2

Kaluza, Zénon, 120
Krey, Philip, 181

Lactantius, 2
Lang, Albert, 51
Latomus, Bartholomaeus, 186, 193
liberal arts, 15, 19, 20, 69, 108, 153
literal sense, divisions of 94–9
loci communes, 194–5
logic, 5, 69, 115, 117–18, 147, 162, 185–92, 198
Luther, Martin, 13, 121, 182, 198, 201–2, 206, 211, 219

Maier, Anneliese, 125, 127
marginal glosses, 9, 10, 66–8
Markus, R. A., 32–3
Matthew Döring, 22, 180
Matthew of Janow, 118, 144, 154
Melanchthon, Philip, 186, 187–92, 193–6, 205–6

Mercier, Jean, 215
metaphor, *see* proper and improper uses of words
Millet, Olivier, 196
Minnis, Alastair, 29, 42, 93, 129–31
modism, 69
Mosaic law, 27, 79, 149, 156–7, 211
Moses, 46–7, 78–9, 80–4, 221–2, 226
Murdoch, John, 77
Musculus, Wolfgang, 6, 208–9, 211, 218
myth, 1, 3, 147

natural signification, 31–7, 75–6
Nicholas Gorran, 13, 25, 27, 43–8, 80–4, 114, 122, 130, 179, 220–2
Nicholas of Autrecourt, 117
Nicholas of Lyra, 6, 13, 20, 21, 23, 26, 42, 52, 64–5, 78, 83n, 85, 109, 114, 130, 131–8, 142–4, 179–83
Nicolau Eimeric, 28, 63–4, 139–41
nominalism, 70, 119–20

obscure speech, 3
Ohly, Friedrich, 4
Ordinary Gloss, 10, 11, 14, 16–17, 51, 75, 83–4, 89, 113, 181
Oxford, 57, 59, 115, 121, 162

parabolic sense, 21, 41, 93, 95, 97, 99–100, 142–9, 228, 232
paraphrase, 200
Paris, 3, 10, 43, 59, 68–9, 78, 94, 116, 119–21
parts of speech, 195
Peter Abelard, 31
Peter Comestor, 13, 14, 62, 75, 85
Peter Lombard, 14, 59, 62, 64, 116, 119, 121, 191, 214
Peter of Tarantasia, 137
Petrarch, 2
philosophy, 15, 32, 59, 68–70, 112–23, 169, 199, 206, 209
Pierre Auriol (Aureol), 13, 24, 28, 49–51, 93
plain sense, 89, 92
Plutarch, 1
poetry, 1, 4, 56, 93, 97–9, 101, 103, 147, 217
postilla, 11
Prague, 65, 145
Prologues, biblical, 8, 128–30
proper and improper uses of words, 35, 38, 93–4, 94–9, 161–2, 177–8, 231–2
prophecy, 56, 141, 153

questions, 11, 60
Quintilian, 207–8

Ramus, Peter, 186, 193
Reformation, 26
Reuchlin, Johannes, 201
revelation, 36, 41, 60, 150–1, 160–1, 218
rhetoric, 5, 73–5, 86, 107, 171, 172, 191, 192–9, 207, 215
Richard FitzRalph, 59–60, 118, 141–2
Richard of St. Victor, 16, 31
Robert Holcot, 13, 52–5, 70, 79–80, 154

Schüssler, Hermann, 160
School of St. Victor, *see* Victorines
scope, 206
Scotists, 119 (*see also* John Duns Scotus)
semantics, 32–4, 100
Sentences, 11, 15 (*see also* Peter Lombard)
sermo humilis, *see* humble speech
simplicity, 112–23, 199, 203
Smalley, Beryl, 2, 154
Song of Songs, 6, 16–18
speculative grammar, 68–70
Stephen Langton, 14
Sturm, Jean, 186
subject of the Bible, 25
supposition, 104

Talmud, 9
terminism, 70, 119
theology, Bible and, 1, 26, 41, 44, 48–9, 51–71, 116, 148
Thijssen, J. M. M. H., 117

Thomas Aquinas, 1, 6, 13, 21, 29, 30, 38–42, 43, 59, 85, 93, 116, 127, 130, 144, 145–6, 179, 218
Thomas Chobham, 37
Thomas Gallus, 14
Thomas of Strasbourg, 117
tradition, 76–7
translation, 30, 159–60, 161, 174–8
trivium, *see* liberal arts
Turner, Denys, 6, 7, 23
Tyconius, 98, 142–3
typology, 6, 18

Valla, Lorenzo, 186, 187, 193, 199
Varro, 1, 236
verbal signification, 37–41, 65, 77, 78, 93, 110, 185, 218
via antiqua, via moderna, 119–20
Victorines, 3, 7, 12, 15, 22–3, 31–7, 42, 101–2, 107, 108–9 (*see also* Andrew of St. Victor, Hugh of St. Victor, Richard of St. Victor)
Vienna, 169
Vulgate, 8

Wendelin Steinbach, 109–11
William Crathorn, 52
William Ockham, 61, 70, 114, 116–18, 127, 128, 160

Zwingli, Huldrich, 202–4